Confessions, Truth, and the Law

D1563404

Confessions, Truth, and the Law

Joseph D. Grano

Ann Arbor

THE UNIVERSITY OF MICHIGAN PRESS

To My Mother and Father
and to Maura, Megan, and Daniel

First paperback edition 1996
Copyright © by the University of Michigan 1993
All rights reserved
Published in the United States of America by
The University of Michigan Press
Manufactured in the United States of America

1999   1998   1997   1996   4   3   2   1

A CIP catalogue record for this book is available from the British Library.

Library of Congress Cataloging-in-Publication Data

Grano, Joseph D.
    Confessions, truth, and the law / Joseph D. Grano.
       p.   cm.
    Includes bibliographical references and index.
    ISBN 0-472-10168-4 (alk. paper)
       1. Confession (Law)—United States. 2. Police questioning—United
States. 3. Criminal procedure—United States.   I. Title.
    KF9664.G73   1993
    345.73'06—dc20
    [347.3056]   93-30458
                                                                      CIP

ISBN 0-472-08415-1 (pbk. : alk. paper)

Preface to the Paperback Edition

More than two years have gone by since this book was first published. In the original preface, I wrote that I had "no illusions either that I immediately (or not so immediately) will persuade academic scholars who are hostile to police interrogation or that I will help in the short run to shape judicial developments." Although I still hold this view, there have been some encouraging developments. First, in his book *Guilty: The Collapse of Criminal Justice* (Random House, 1996), New York Judge Harold J. Rothwax—who, like me, was once on the other "side"—extensively relied on arguments made in this book and on his own judicial experiences in concluding that *Miranda* should be overruled. *Miranda*, Judge Rothwax noted, "is the wrong means to the end we are seeking." Second, tackling an issue I do not address in this book, Professor Paul G. Cassell of the University of Utah College of Law has, in several recent articles, skillfully employed empirical analysis to demonstrate *Miranda*'s negative effects on both law enforcement and the goal of convicting the guilty.[1] Read in conjunction with the analysis of *Miranda* and stare decisis in chapter 8 of this book, these recent publications should remove any doubts about the desirability, indeed the necessity, of overruling *Miranda*.

This book is more than a brief against *Miranda*, however. In a larger sense, the book invites readers to think about the goals that a sound and healthy system of criminal justice should seek to further. Some high visibility trials have recently raised questions in many quarters about the health of our criminal justice system, but the average citizen has long been aware that something was radically askew. One thesis of this book is that our criminal justice system for too long has denigrated the notion that a criminal trial is supposed to be a search for truth. While I do not argue that truth discovery must trump every other goal, I do maintain that discovering the truth and convicting the guilty deserve from our courts a more exalted status than they have received in the last few decades. The issue of police

1. Paul G. Cassell, *All Benefits, No Costs: The Grand Illusion of Miranda's Defenders*, 90 Nw. U. L. Rev. _____ (1996); Paul G. Cassell, *Miranda's Social Costs: An Empirical Reassessment*, 90 Nw. U. L. Rev. 387 (1996); Paul G. Cassell & Bret S. Hayman, *Police Interrogation in the 1990s: An Empirical Study of the Effects of Miranda*, 43 UCLA L. Rev. 834 (1996).

interrogation of suspects is discussed in this book within the context of a strong predilection for discovering the truth. Hence, the title *Confessions, Truth, and the Law.*

Apart from its many constitutional flaws, which are discussed at length in this book, *Miranda's* philosophical premises are pernicious precisely because they are indifferent, perhaps even hostile, to the goal of ascertaining the truth. Taken seriously, which always is a risk as long as they are not repudiated, *Miranda's* premises threaten the very institution of police interrogation. Indeed, many commentators, lawyers, and judges believe that *Miranda* did not go far enough in restraining the police. If the day ever comes when the Supreme Court decides to take *Miranda's* way of thinking seriously, we will not need to rely on Professor Cassell's work to tell us how much damage that case has done.

This year, 1996, is the thirtieth anniversary of *Miranda*. *Miranda* came down near the end of the Warren Court's criminal justice revolution, a revolution that in the span of only seven years fundamentally altered the criminal justice systems of the several states. That the Warren Court read the Constitution differently than its predecessor and successor Courts, and that it had radically different policy preferences than these other Courts, does not prove that it was wrong or misguided. Indeed, many of the Warren Court's decisions will undoubtedly withstand the test of time. Nevertheless, the thirtieth anniversary of *Miranda* seems an appropriate time to return to basics and to give some serious thought to what criminal justice is all about. I hope this book will help provoke such rethinking.

Preface

Before writing this book, I had written several articles on various aspects of the law governing police interrogation and confessions. While I did not simply want to collect and reprint these articles, I felt confident that with most of the groundwork done, the book would be a relatively quick and easy process. I was wrong. The book took me eighteen months longer than I had anticipated. Along the way, I found myself changing the planned organization and, more importantly, adding to and modifying views and arguments I had previously expressed. I believe readers familiar with my work will find evidence of this rethinking in most of the chapters that follow.

This is not to assert that readers will find evidence of a conversion. I am getting too old for conversions, and in any event one major adult conversion (I really once was on the other "side") usually is a lifetime's quota. My views remain politically incorrect, at least in academic circles, and if anything, the rethinking I have done has made them more so. I still believe the Supreme Court's confession decisions in the 1960s were profoundly unwise and constitutionally in error (these are two different claims), and I still believe *Miranda* should be overruled even if we take stare decisis seriously.

In writing this book, I have no illusions either that I immediately (or not so immediately) will persuade academic scholars who are hostile to police interrogation or that I will help in the short run to shape judicial developments. Indeed, the tide in the Supreme Court is flowing more strongly against me now than a few years ago. My hope, however, is that critics will take the arguments in this book seriously and find them meritorious of answer. This is the approach I have tried to follow in writing this book. I have reviewed and taken issue with arguments in both a substantial body of scholarly literature and a number of judicial opinions, and I trust I have not slighted these arguments. Naturally, I believe my arguments will withstand scholarly critique, and for this reason I am cautiously optimistic that someday—maybe in my children's lifetime—our legal system will come to its senses in this area. If I in any way help to facilitate that day, so much the better; for now, the pursuit (not necessarily the achievement) of intellectual rigor and integrity is its own reward.

I am indebted to many for suggestions and comments, but I will break with custom and not name them. I do want, however, to acknowledge and thank my research assistants: Michael Brady, Erinn Dougherty, Mark Fisher, Alison Rodney, and Scott Taylor. I also want to thank June Frierson for secretarial help. Finally, I would be remiss if I did not express gratitude for the substantial financial and other support that the university and law school administrations at Wayne State University have given me over the years for my work.

Contents

Part 1
Policy Considerations

CHAPTER 1 **The Basic Objectives of Criminal Procedure**

This book is about the law in the United States that governs the admissibility into evidence of confessions and other incriminating statements by persons suspected of or charged with criminal conduct. More accurately, it is about the law that governs the police interrogation practices that produce these statements. The law governing the admissibility of statements need not be determined by the law governing police interrogation practices, but in the United States it basically is. In the United States, if the police violate a rule governing the interrogation process, at least one of constitutional magnitude, any statement they thereby obtain is typically inadmissible in evidence.[1]

A primary thesis of this book is that the law governing police interrogation in the United States is overly restrictive and formalistic. The book does not challenge, however, the connection between the rules that govern interrogation practices and those that govern the admissibility of statements. Nevertheless, in beginning this study it is appropriate to ask why the procedural law should exclude any relevant statement from evidence, regardless of how such a statement is obtained. Besides having interest in its own right, consideration of this question may help to provide a philosophical background for the book's subsequent examination of the doctrines that govern the interrogation process.

With regard to the law governing admissibility, one can imagine a criminal justice system that would allow all of an accused's alleged statements into evidence, that would inform the fact finder, perhaps a jury, of the circumstances in which such statements were made, and that would trust the fact finder to decide what weight, if any, to give to such statements. In such a system, police who engage in unacceptable interrogation conduct might be punished or disciplined in another forum, but relevant evidence would not be excluded in the accused's criminal trial. The effect of the interrogation practices on the credibility of the accused's statements would simply be left for the trier of fact to decide for itself.

Consider, for example, the following case.[2] Neighbors discovered

3

the body of the deceased in a side room of his farm house. The body showed signs of a severe beating: one shoulder had a severe wound, possibly made by an axe or a club; breaks were present in the shoulder joint, the collar bone, and one arm; the skull had several fractures and was punctured behind one ear; the bones in the top of the head were crushed into small pieces; the skin was removed from the right cheek; and the area in front of the left ear had a bad cut. Blood was everywhere, as was evidence that the murderers had attempted to burn the body.

The evening of the body's discovery, a deputy sheriff, accompanied by several other men, seized a suspect, hanged him by a rope to a limb of a tree, and, when the repetition of this procedure failed to produce a confession, tied him to the tree and whipped him. Rope burns on the suspect's neck evidenced the hangings. Two days later, the deputy arrested the suspect, who had been released after the previous beatings, and severely whipped him again. When the deputy indicated that he would continue the whipping until he obtained a statement, the suspect confessed. The same deputy and others also arrested two other suspects and whipped their bare backs with a leather strap and buckle. When the deputy again indicated that the beatings would continue until the suspects provided a detailed account of the murder, these suspects also confessed. The confessions indicated that the murder was motivated by an allegedly unpaid debt.[3]

The facts depict a brutal murder and egregiously unlawful police conduct, and presumably the most appropriate societal response to both would be criminal prosecution. The issue under consideration, however, is not whether the official misconduct warrants prosecution, which it does, but whether the criminal procedure or evidentiary rules should rely on the official misconduct as justification for excluding the defendants' confessions in their trials for murder. The issue can be made more difficult by assuming, contrary to the facts in the actual case, that the confessions led to corroborating evidence, such as the murder weapon or personal items taken from the deceased, for surely it must be conceded that the exclusion of corroborated confessions (and possibly even the corroborating "fruits")[4] increases the risk of "erroneous" acquittals.[5] Even without corroborating evidence to reduce concerns of untrustworthiness, however, one might contend that the fact finder at trial should be permitted to decide what weight, if any, to give to the confessions.

In the United States, the quick response of lawyers to the question why the confessions should be excluded is that our national Constitution requires this. Perhaps it does, although one theme of this book is that almost all the constitutional requirements imposed by the courts in this area are controversial rather than obvious. Nevertheless, to achieve perspective, it helps to put aside the Constitution, if only temporarily, to consider how we might choose to structure the criminal justice system were we permitted to build our own foundation. Would we prefer a system that admits all relevant statements, including those in the case presented, or one that excludes some statements, perhaps even those likely to be trustworthy, because of the police methods used to obtain them?

This is not a question that can be satisfactorily answered in the abstract. The rules governing police interrogation and the admissibility of statements are part of the larger body of rules governing criminal procedure in all its aspects. To ask the above question therefore is really to ask more broadly what functions the rules of procedure should serve. For example, the answer regarding admissibility would presumably be different in a procedural system whose sole function is to assure accurate fact-finding than in a system with other, perhaps equally important, functions to serve. Of course, even if accurate fact-finding is the sole or primary goal, some confessions, like those in the case under consideration, may be excluded because of the risk of unreliability, a risk that would not be present, or at least be less apparent, when the confession leads to corroborating evidence.

The purpose of this first chapter therefore is to lay some groundwork for an evaluation of the law of confessions by considering the more basic issue of the goals or functions that criminal procedure should serve.

The Influence of Ideology

Commentators frequently assert that the discovery of truth should be the primary or reigning objective of the procedural system.[6] Almost as frequently, other commentators rejoin with either the descriptive claim that the criminal justice system in the United States does not have the discovery of truth as its primary objective[7] or the normative claim that other goals, such as protecting the rights of the accused or affirming moral values, are equally or perhaps more important.[8] Of course, virtually all commentators would concede that any criminal justice system must have multiple objectives, but this concession resolves little with respect to the concrete issues confronting the system. Because the multiple goals of the criminal justice system frequently "co-exist in an unstable tension,"[9] some sense of priorities among competing goals is necessary before progress can be made on such diverse questions as police interrogation, exclusionary rules, evidentiary privileges, party responsibility for developing and presenting the case, judicial questioning of witnesses, trial by jury, discovery, and the defendant's right to waive important rights. Yet, if the critics are to be believed, many commentators have considered the competing goals of the criminal justice system merely "by trotting out tired cliches like truth-discovery, crime control, and the protection of individual rights."[10]

The view defended in this chapter, and throughout this book, is that the goal of discovering the truth should play a dominant role in designing the rules that govern criminal procedure. To say that truth discovery should be a dominant goal is different from saying that it should be the exclusive or even *the* dominant goal. This cannot be said because, as will be seen, ideological constraints necessarily limit the system's ability to improve the search for truth. Totally apart from our written Constitution, which has been put temporarily aside in this chapter, these ideological constraints exert a powerful influence on the structure of criminal procedure in this country, as they do in all countries, and thus make certain reforms presumptively unlikely if not altogether unthinkable. Nevertheless, these constraints are few in number, and once they are taken into account, the area remains abundant in which we can exercise choice in structuring the system. Within this area of choice, truth discovery should emerge, if the system is rationally designed, as a primary desideratum.

At the outset, some may insist that the existing American system, which is largely adversarial in nature at least in its judicial stages, is more likely than other systems to promote the search for truth. Were this claim descriptively true, it would help support, although by no means prove, the normative argument that truth discovery should be regarded as our system's primary goal. Unfortunately, as critics have long charged, the adversary system has many rules and tolerates many practices that make this factual claim implausible.[11] Perhaps most significantly, the system depends on advocates, who want to win their respective cases, to produce and explain the evidence that the fact finder will evaluate.[12] As Judge Jerome Frank lamented decades ago, "frequently the partisanship of the opposing lawyers blocks the uncovering of vital evidence or leads to a presentation of vital testimony in a way that distorts it."[13]

The American adversary system also permits truth to be ascertained by untrained lay jurors, and it employs numerous rules, both evidentiary and constitutional, that exclude relevant information from the fact finder.[14] Professor Mirjan Damaska has claimed that these "exclusionary rules are more numerous and surely much more elaborate in America than they are in any civilian jurisdiction."[15] Perhaps the biggest compromise with truth occurs in the plea bargaining system, in which prosecutors and defense lawyers frequently induce defendants to plead guilty to offenses less serious than those they actually committed.[16] And lest it be thought that truth is sacrificed only in response to an extreme solicitude for the accused, the rules typically preclude the court from forcing a defendant to raise certain defenses, such as insanity, even though they may have factual support.[17] Moreover, the system also gives the defendant a right to waive legal representation at trial despite the likelihood that this waiver will preclude a successful defense.[18]

Reflecting a concern for truth discovery, arguments have been presented for various reforms, some more radical than others. To cite just a few examples, Professor Lloyd Weinreb, borrowing from continental practices, has called for the creation of a judicial institution that would assume the investigative functions now lodged in the police and take responsibility for preparing accusations and proving guilt at trial. Weinreb would also modify the trial itself, converting it into a proceeding in which the prosecutor and defense counsel would serve as advisers to the court.[19] Also borrowing from continental procedure, Professor Albert Alschuler, who wants to eliminate plea bargaining, has advocated that the jury be replaced by a "mixed tribunal" of judges and lay persons and that the adversary trial be replaced by a "'mixed' system of adversarial and nonadversarial procedures."[20]

Faulting both adversarial and continental systems as premised on the outdated epistemological tradition of the scientific method, John Jackson has advocated the adoption of a "dialectic" procedure, one in which all the participants, including the ultimate decision maker, would act as fact finders and be required to justify their conclusions to each other in a continuing dialogue.[21] Less radical proposals have called for "blending" the best features of continental systems "with the best of our own traditions and procedures."[22] Along these lines, some commentators have advocated reforming the rules of professional ethics to give lawyers more incentive to pursue the truth,[23] while others have called for eliminating exclusionary rules that impede the discovery of truth.[24]

Were the American criminal system dedicated above all to the discovery of truth, many of even the more radical reform proposals would have to be taken seriously rather than ignored, as they largely are. At the very least, those who defend the status quo must concede the absence of empirical evidence to support the claim that the existing adversary system, with its emphasis on a contest between rival parties, is the best method of determining truth.[25] Similarly, they must concede that few other disciplines outside of law rely on the judgment of untrained lay persons in determining truth.[26] Indeed, an objective observer of the rules and practices of the competing systems might very well conclude "that the continental non-adversary system of procedure is more committed to the search for truth than is the Anglo-American adversary system."[27]

That the suggested reforms are not taken seriously can be attributed to inertia and complacency, but the likelihood is that something more fundamental is at stake, something that is competing with, although not necessarily displacing, the goal of truth discovery. Nor can the blame for inaction be directed entirely at the Constitution. With a flexible approach to constitutional interpretation unfortunately now regarded as de rigueur, arguments are not wanting that virtually any reform proposal can be enacted without constitutional amendment.[28]

The common explanation for the rejection of the proposed reforms is that our system's goal of truth discovery must be understood in the context of an axiomatic commitment to an *adversarial* or *accusatorial* mode of procedure. Although this explanation has some validity, the terms adversarial and accusatorial have little fixed content, as will be discussed in the next chapter, and to invoke them as a basis for rejecting reform often is to beg the question. More importantly, as Professor Damaska has argued, the tendency of a system to be more or less adversarial or inquisitorial is itself related to the society's underlying political ideology.[29] Quite simply, the goal of enhancing truth discovery often competes with society's more fundamental ideological commitments.

In Professor Damaska's view, society's most important ideological influences on the structure and nature of the procedural system come from its beliefs concerning both the organization of procedural authority and the legitimate functions of government.[30] Damaska considered these two themes separately before considering their combined effect. With regard to the organization of procedural authority, Damaska constructed two polar models, or "ideals": the first, a hierarchical ideal in which decision-making is preferably lodged in professional officials who function in a rigid relationship of superior and inferior authority and who act according to technical standards or rules, and the second, a coordinate ideal in which authority is distributed horizontally among lay officials who tend to regard justice and common sense as being on a par with technical rules. With regard to the legitimate functions of government, Damaska's competing ideals were the activist state, in which government strives to achieve a comprehensive vision of the good life, and the reactive state, in which government sees its primary function as maintaining the social equilibrium and as providing the framework for citizens to pursue their own goals.[31]

Because no society enacts its ideology in pure form, the polar ideals, which Damaska elaborated in great detail, do not describe the characteristics of any existing procedural system. Moreover, although the activist state is more likely to have a hierarchical authority structure, no logical imperative requires that either view of government's role be joined with either view of how authority should be organized, the result being four possible composite models, not taking account of the variations within models.[32] Nevertheless, particularly on the civil side, but to some extent on the criminal side as well, Anglo-American procedure, and perhaps more clearly American procedure, is strongly influenced by the beliefs that authority should be shared coordinately and that government's proper function is not to make policy but to help the parties resolve their disputes.[33] Even with the rise of the modern welfare state in the United States, the tension persists between activist and laissez-faire philosophies, with the latter continuing to exert a strong hold on the procedural system.

Some important consequences concerning truth discovery are dictated by this underlying ideology. First, "[a] certain amount of disorder," and of inconsistency and uncertainty, "must be accepted as the price of the fundamental commitment to a wider distribution of power."[34] Second, "[w]here the object of adjudication is to resolve disputes, and where the judge is not supposed to advance independent policies or values, insistence on the substantive accuracy of verdicts loses much of its raison d'être."[35] In fact, because truth may sometimes engender further turmoil, there may be tension between the goal of acceptable dispute resolution and the goal of achieving accurate fact finding. As Professor Damaska succinctly stated, it cannot simply be assumed "that a legal process, no matter what its objective or political underpinnings, inevitably favors that fact-finding style which is most likely to yield accurate results."[36]

With this much recognized, care must be taken not to overstate the claim. As Professor Damaska observed, in modern states, including the United States, criminal procedure has become "a policy-implementing," not simply a reactive, process.[37] Nevertheless, the commitment to coordinate authority, perhaps best seen in the institution of the lay jury, typically results in a corresponding commitment to certain contest forms even though they are not best suited to reveal the truth. This may account for the fact, if Professor Damaska's observations are accurate, that "more contest forms can be identified in Anglo-American criminal prosecution than in any other contemporary system of criminal justice."[38] Moreover, the persistence of reactive ideology in criminal justice is evident in certain legal doctrines, such as that making it impermissible to impose a lawyer on a criminal accused even when legal representation, as almost always, is in the accused's best interests.[39]

Whether viewed from the perspective of Professor Damaska's models or from the perspective of Judge Frank's less elaborate observation some years ago that American procedure is built on a belief in "uncontrolled competition," "unbridled individualism," and "extreme laissez-faire in the economic field,"[40] the influence of political ideology on the procedural system is difficult to deny.[41] Because of the constraints of ideology, it cannot be said that the American procedural system, civil or criminal, is committed above all to the discovery of truth. Rather, the system is committed to truth only to the extent that truth may be ascertained consistently with society's underlying political ideology. This point, which would hold equally true in virtually all societies, is one that an advocate of truth discovery must concede.

The Relative Primacy of Truth

Although necessary, the above concession does not yield as much ground as it may appear to those who disparage the relative importance of truth discovery. Professor Damaska's polar ideals illuminate the different characteristics of various procedural systems, but, as Damaska himself recognized, the actual characteristics of a particular society's procedural system can be derived deductively neither from these constructs nor from the conclusion that the society more clearly resembles one construct rather than another.

Take, for example, the previously mentioned issue whether criminal defendants should have the right to represent themselves. Forcing legal representation on unwilling defendants may seem to offend the core principles of reactive ideology, but whether the state should be activist or reactive in this instance is something that people who do not live in an "ideal" may dispute. Similarly, activist arguments have increasingly been made in the United States, despite its supposedly reactive ideology, that defendants should not be permitted to waive other rights, such as trial by jury.[42]

Perceived ideological commitment may render futile some of the more radical structural reforms that academic commentators have proffered, such as modifying the makeup of the jury or permitting judicial interrogation of the accused. Nevertheless, incremental change not only is possible in any system but also has the effect, once made, of modifying ideological beliefs. This statement makes only the obvious point that the relationship between ideology and practice is dynamic and interactive, not static and unidirectional.

Nor should one overlook that commitment to truth discovery itself may be part of the underlying ideology, particularly in criminal cases.

Most clearly, despite its willingness to permit the accused to waive certain defenses and rights, the underlying American ideology, which does not differ in this regard from its European counterpart, is intolerant of factual mistakes that lead to the conviction of innocent defendants. Erroneous acquittals may be only slightly less troublesome. The more society sees itself in the criminal justice system not simply as stepping into the victim's shoes but as promoting its own important objectives, such as safety, civil rights, or environmental protection, the more it will view erroneous acquittals as a serious policy concern.[43] Even on the civil side, where it frequently is said that acceptable dispute resolution is more important than accuracy, a procedural system that generally produced inaccurate results in pursuit of other goals might not long survive.

Some may suggest that these observations about the importance of truth appear to contradict the previously made concession that many of the rules and practices that define the American procedural system are not the best devices for discovering truth. Indeed, some may insist not only that the previous concession was more accurate but that it did not go far enough. For example, citing many of the rules and practices mentioned above, Professor Gary Goodpaster has asserted that "the criminal adversary system is structurally truth-dysfunctional."[44] Because, in his view, the adversary system is "not a good way to discover truth,"[45] Goodpaster has suggested that we need to come up with other purposes to explain the existing procedures.

Professor Goodpaster's conclusions, however, are broader than the facts warrant. First, that some features of the system may be inferior to possible alternatives for discovering truth does not prove that these features are "truth-dysfunctional."[46] A procedure that accurately discovered truth 90 percent of the time would not be rendered dysfunctional by the availability of a different procedure with a 95 percent accuracy rating, especially when such comparisons in the real world must be speculative.

Second, and perhaps more responsive to the claim of inconsistency, the system's retention of arguably less than optimal truth discovery procedures need not mean that truth is not a dominant consideration. Instead, it may mean only that skepticism exists about the truth discovery virtues of the proposed reform.[47] Just as we have no empirical basis for assuming that the adversary system is best suited to truth discovery, we have no empirical basis for assuming that inquisitorial reforms would really be better. More likely, the reluctance to institute reform may indicate a belief that the interest in discovering truth is being served to a large extent, that important subsidiary goals are also served by the existing procedures, and that the reform's perceived incremental improvement in truth discovery does not justify the significant risk to these other goals. That a system pursues objectives other than truth does not prove that truth discovery is not a dominant concern.

Another objection against the attempt to claim a special role for truth discovery in the procedural system is that any emphasis on truth must be simplistic given the "plural forms and multifaceted aspects of that beguiling concept."[48] This objection comes in two forms—one epistemological, the other metaphysical. The epistemological objection states that fact finding is an uncertain process because of its dependency on the perceptions, inferences, memory, and veracity of fallible human witnesses.[49] In Professor Goodpaster's words, the relationship between judicial truth and "'real truth,' whatever that might be, is indeterminable."[50] In its most skeptical version, the epistemological objection may even deny that any institution or discipline could ever be capable of ascertaining objective truth.[51]

The metaphysical objection, suggested in the parenthetical remark in Professor Goodpaster's just quoted words, states that the concept of truth has little meaning in legal proceedings. At its most extreme, this objection may be based on a metaphysics that denies the existence of objective truth, but the objection's more modest and plausible claim is that factual guilt and legal guilt are different concepts, the latter requiring not only a determination of historical fact but also an evaluation of intent and moral blameworthiness.[52]

The significance of the objection in its epistemological form is not readily apparent. That historical facts are often difficult to ascertain fails to prove either that such facts do not exist or that the system should not do its best to determine them accurately. Even if the difficulties in ascertaining truth stem not so much from the inherent limitations of human perception and recall as from the procedural system's flawed means of seeking to ascertain truth, this suggests the need for truth-seeking reform rather than the abandonment of truth as a goal.[53]

The more extreme form of epistemological skepticism, which denies any possibility of ascertaining objective truth, is difficult to take seriously either as a reflection of reality or as a workable foundation for a legal system. Whether the defendant was at the scene of the crime, demanded money by threatening to use a weapon, and left the scene having achieved his purpose all may be contested, but for most people these questions have objective yes or no answers, and ascertaining them does not seem that elusive a task.[54] Similarly, whether the defendants in the case at the beginning of this chapter beat the victim and whether that beating caused the victim's death are questions that can be objectively answered. Such questions are no more impossible or difficult to answer correctly than the question whether the deputy sheriff in the same case beat the defendants to obtain their confessions.

The epistemological objection is no more persuasive when criminal intent is factored into the analysis. Criminal responsibility normally requires not just an act that causes harm but also an accompanying mens rea.[55] It is because the mens rea requirement in the substantive criminal law is rooted in our society's political ideology, having originated as far back as thirteenth-century England, that efforts to impose strict criminal liability, or even responsibility premised on negligence, always are controversial.[56] The problem from a procedural perspective is that questions pertaining to a defendant's intent or knowledge are more difficult to answer correctly than questions relating to external facts. Without a confession, the fact finder typically must infer the defendant's mental state from other facts. Nevertheless, whether a defendant intended X or knew Y is no less a question of objective fact than whether the defendant carried a gun, and "[t]he characterizations 'true' and 'false' retain their respective meanings."[57]

In many cases, moreover, the intent of the offender is not contested. Rather, the contested issue is whether the defendant was the offender, whether the item sold was really narcotics, whether the weapon was concealed, whether the value of the stolen or embezzled property exceeded a certain amount, and the like. For example, in the four cases that came before the Supreme Court in *Miranda v. Arizona*[58]—one involving a rape, the other three involving robberies—the crucial question in each was whether the defendant was the actual perpetrator of the crimes, not whether the defendant had the requisite intent to be guilty of these crimes.[59]

The above discussion also responds to the metaphysical form of the objection to truth discovery as a dominant goal of the procedural system. The extreme version of the metaphysical objection, which denies the existence of objective reality, can fare no better than extreme epistemological skepticism. As already suggested, one cannot readily conceive of a legal system premised on either a metaphysics that denies objective reality or an epistemology that denies our ability to ascertain that reality.

Nevertheless, the more modest version of the metaphysical objection, which denies that the concept of truth applies to legal as opposed to factual guilt, cannot be dismissed so readily. As Professor Stephen Saltzburg has asserted, "an estimate of the results attained through evaluations of the facts in light of governing substantive principles will be neither true nor false."[60] Still, even if frequently accurate as a descriptive matter, this claim fails to demonstrate that truth discovery is not, or should not be, a dominant goal of the system.

Professor H. Richard Uviller offers this example to illustrate both that factual and legal guilt are conceptually different and that truth is not an appropriate concept to apply to verdicts in many criminal cases:

> Did the victim, moments before the defendant shot him, point a six-inch blade at the defendant and say, "I'll kill you," or did he show a two-inch knife and say, "Don't come a step closer"? That is a simple issue of factual truth, and it is quite different from the question: did the defendant act in self-defense?[61]

Judge Thomas Steffen is not so sure:

> The truth to [Uviller's] hypothetical is either the defendant acted in self-defense or he didn't. The answer to that question depends on what actually occurred before the shooting. If the defendant's conduct is analyzed in the context of truth, he is justly convicted or acquitted. If truth, for whatever reason, eludes the trier of fact, a miscarriage of justice occurs in either direction.[62]

In reality, both Uviller and Steffen are correct, but Steffen, who may not have perceived the full significance of Uviller's example, has nevertheless provided the better or more complete analysis. Uviller is correct because a homicide is justified by self-defense only when the perpetrator reasonably believes that killing is necessary to protect himself from imminent death or serious bodily injury. Moreover, in many jurisdictions, a person may have an obligation to retreat, if this can be done safely, before using deadly force in self-defense.[63] Evaluating the reasonableness of the defendant's fear or the reasonableness of the defendant's decision not to retreat cannot be equated with ascertaining who brandished what weapon or said what to whom. Thus, although the second version of Uviller's facts clearly would present a serious obstacle to a successful claim of self-defense, a fact finder could conceivably uphold or reject the claim of self-defense on either factual version. Because neither verdict would be wrong in an objective sense, the labels true and false, if applicable at all, will necessarily mean something different here than in the contexts previously considered.[64] Steffen's statement that the defendant either "acted in self-defense or he didn't" therefore is misleading.

Why then is Steffen's analysis better or more complete than Uviller's? Precisely for the reasons Steffen provided: a persuasive answer to the issue of self-defense "depends on what actually occurred," so that "if the defendant's conduct is analyzed in the context of truth, he is justly convicted or acquitted." To grasp Steffen's point, assume that before deciding on the facts, the jury in Uviller's example makes a normative decision to acquit the defendant on the first version of the facts but to convict on the second. Because reasonable people may disagree over reasonableness issues, the jury's normative judgment, if within the bounds of reasonable disagreement, will define the correct and just verdict for each hypothetical version of the facts. Nevertheless, the jury's actual verdict can be correct and just, in terms of its normative conclusions, only if the jury accurately ascertains the actual facts. Given its normative conclusions, if the jury mistakenly decides that the first factual version is true, it will render an erroneous and unjust acquittal; if it mistakenly decides that the second version is true, it will render an erroneous and unjust conviction. Thus, while the jury's normative judgment as such is not subject to assessment in terms of its truth, factual truth is a necessary condition of a correct and just normative judgment.

This defense of Steffen's views also provides a satisfactory answer to an interesting hypothetical presented by Professor Damaska. Damaska asks us to imagine a system in which jury nullification is treated as a virtue and not merely as a prerogative not to be encouraged. In such a system, should we classify a verdict that disregards the trial judge's substantive instructions as correct (i.e., in accordance with nullification law) or incorrect (i.e., not in accordance with substantive law)?[65] The answer is not difficult. As in the self-defense example, the terms true and false, unless used in an extraordinary way, are inappropriate to evaluate the normative judgment in this hypothetical. Nevertheless, to perform its normative judgment correctly, the jury in the hypothetical needs to know the truth about the underlying facts and circumstances. Suppose, for example, that a jury is willing to nullify a draft card burning law as applied to a conscientious objector but not as applied to someone simply trying to evade the draft. If such a jury, perhaps because a trustworthy confession is excluded from evidence, unwittingly acquits a draft evading defendant who is not a conscientious objector, its act of nullification will be neither correct nor just.

Because the same two conflicting normative judgments (guilty or not guilty) were possible for each version of the facts in the self-defense hypothetical, the temptation may exist to say that truth is totally irrelevant to the justice of the outcome. If this were so, however, we could substitute a cheaper coin toss procedure for the costly system of jury trial, for normative judgments not tied to factual conclusions have no more validity than a coin toss. Imagine a jury saying, for example, "Without trying to ascertain who was telling the truth, we have chosen to reject (or accept) the defendant's claim that the use of deadly force was reasonable and, hence, to convict (or acquit)." Without reaching agreement on the historical facts, we cannot begin to debate intelligently the normative options.

The discussion suggests that, except with regard to certain features required by political ideology, criminal procedure should be designed primarily to achieve the discovery of factual truth. Except for what is ideologically determined, "[t]hat procedure is best which most completely realizes the substantive law in the actual administration of justice."[66] This presumes, of course, that the substantive system can make a claim to legitimacy. In a system that has legitimacy, procedure should not be used to sabotage or even to reform the substantive law. Substantive reform should be accomplished on its own terms and not by the adoption of unsound procedure.[67] The questions that the criminal justice system must answer are determined by the substantive criminal law, and "rational procedure, embodying logical principles, prescribes what steps we must take and how we shall take them to secure the necessary answers."[68] Even when the ultimate questions to be answered are normative, the penultimate questions upon which the normative judgments depend are factual.[69]

If, as is now being suggested, the discovery of truth will be a dominant concern of any rational criminal justice system, one should expect this actually to be the case in existing systems regardless of their ideological differences. From this perspective, the Anglo-American and European systems may be seen as differing more in the means they employ than in their ends. Different legal frameworks, reflecting different political ideologies, may result in one system having more of a commitment to truth than the other, and in each there may be room for truth-promoting reforms. Nevertheless, as Judge Hans-Heinrich Jescheck pointed out in a comparative study of American and German criminal procedure, both the Anglo-American and the continental systems regard truth discovery as a dominant value:

> The goal of the German proceeding, like that of the American, is the determination of the objective truth on the basis of and within the framework of the procedural forms which the law prescribes. It is error to view the Anglo-American trial merely as a sporting match between the attorneys involved without any goal of ascertaining the truth, as unfortunately continental critics all too often assume. Similarly, it is just as wrong to view the continental trial as a means of convicting the accused at any price, a tendency of which the American critic can be guilty. *Rather, the object of both trials is the same search for the truth within the permissible legal framework.*[70]

Values That Compete with Truth

Whether or not they are regarded as part of society's political ideology, values other than truth play an important role in the procedural system and sometimes conflict with the goal of truth discovery. Most familiar, of course, is the strong "activist" belief[71] that convicting an innocent person is far worse than acquitting a guilty one, a belief that apparently is not universal.[72] Of course, the ideal situation is to avoid any mistakes by convicting all the guilty defendants and acquitting all the innocent ones. Because some mistakes are inevitable, however, the goals of convicting the guilty and of acquitting the innocent are conflicting rather than complementary. The easier the system makes it to prove guilt, the greater the likelihood that innocent persons will be convicted; the more the system protects innocent persons from being convicted, or even from being ensnared in the process, the greater the likelihood that guilty persons will escape.[73]

As indicated, the criminal justice system has adopted procedural rules allocating the risk of mistake so that conviction of the innocent will be less likely than acquittal of the guilty. It sometimes is overlooked, however, that the rules allocating the risk of mistake in accordance with this value preference may increase the overall number of mistakes. For example, a system that convicts nine guilty persons, acquits eight innocent persons, and convicts one innocent person is more accurate than one that convicts seven guilty persons, acquits nine innocent persons and acquits two guilty persons.[74] Indeed, the first system's .056 inaccuracy rate might seem far superior to the .111 inaccuracy rate of the latter. Yet, despite the desire to promote truth discovery, our society's even stronger commitment to protecting the innocent makes the second, less accurate system preferable to the first.

One need not resort to such hypothetical facts to see that the concern for protecting the innocent may decrease the overall accuracy of the system. The requirement of proof beyond a reasonable doubt not only helps more guilty than innocent defendants but also probably increases the total number of mistaken decisions.[75] That is, a lower burden of proof would probably achieve more accuracy than the reasonable doubt standard. Nevertheless, even were constitutional law not an impediment,[76] our system would resist efforts to increase accuracy by lowering the burden of proof. The desire to avoid one kind of mistake, conviction of the innocent, is sufficiently strong to justify rules that achieve this goal even at the cost of somewhat decreasing the system's overall accuracy.

Because the concern about protecting the innocent has played a significant role in shaping the law that governs police interrogation, it is particularly important in this book to view this concern in proper perspective. Conviction would become virtually impossible in a system that insisted on eliminating even the slightest risk of wrongful conviction. Our system, for example, requires proof beyond a reasonable doubt but not proof to an absolute certainty. In addition, evidentiary rules permit the use of eyewitness identification testimony even though such evidence in the best of circumstances entails a risk of mistake.[77] The courts in this instance have been unwilling to do more than fashion constitutional and other rules that marginally reduce the dangers.[78] Similarly, although the voluntariness doctrine was designed in part to reduce the risk of false confessions,[79] the courts have never been willing to bar confessions altogether as a means of eliminating the risk. While courts have promulgated various safeguards, they have perceived the cost of a total ban on confessions to be too great to justify whatever additional protection such a ban would provide for the innocent.

These examples, which are typical of a much larger number, suggest that while society may be willing to have five or ten guilty persons escape to avoid the conviction of one innocent person, its willingness to accept erroneous acquittals for this purpose is not without limit. Nor could it be. As Charles Allen stated years ago:

> I dare say some sentimentalists would assent to the proposition that it is better that a thousand, or even a million, guilty persons should escape than that one innocent person should suffer; but no sensible and practical person would accept such a view. For it is obvious that if our ratio is extended indefinitely, there comes a point when the whole system of justice has broken down and society is in a state of chaos. In short, it is only when there is a reasonable and uniform probability of guilty persons being detected and convicted that we can allow humane doubt to prevail over security. But we must never forget that ideally the acquittal of ten guilty persons is exactly ten times as great a failure of *justice* as the conviction of one innocent person.[80]

While the goal of protecting the innocent may decrease overall accuracy, it still has something to do with truth discovery. This cannot be said about other values that exert an influence on the procedural system. As already indicated, the existence of these other values does not mean that truth discovery is not a dominant value. Nor is our system unique in recognizing values that compete with truth discovery. As Professor Damaska has stated, the tension between "the tendency toward efficiency and the tendency toward protecting the rights of the defendant" will be "part and parcel of the dialectics of *any* criminal process."[81] For this reason, "[a]ny design of criminal procedure, even an extreme inquisitorial one, must establish a balance between these two."[82]

This last observation suggests that the American criminal justice system cannot profitably be viewed through the prism of competing models pertaining to truth discovery and individual rights. Most familiar, of course, are the two models that Professor Herbert Packer constructed some years ago in an attempt to understand and explain American criminal procedure.[83] Packer's Due Process Model stressed the primacy of the individual, limitations on official power, procedural formality and regularity, equality, legal rather than factual guilt, and "a mood of skepticism about the morality and utility of the criminal sanction,"[84] while his Crime Control Model stressed the repression of criminal conduct, efficiency, informality, finality, a presumption of guilt, and extrajudicial fact-finding procedures, such as police interrogation.[85] While Packer warned against the danger of perceiving one model as necessarily good and the other as necessarily bad,[86] his choice of labels, his description of the underlying values, and his discussion of the respective positions each model would take with regard to various issues made it apparent that crime control and concern for factual truth were, in Packer's view, not the goals that the cognoscenti would generally pursue.

Aside from the inherent bias they reflected, however, Packer's constructs failed to constitute true models upon which real systems could be structured or evaluated. As Professor Damaska observed with regard to the "'basically negative'" Due Process Model, "it is conceptually impossible to imagine a criminal process whose dominant concern is a desire to protect the individual from public officials."[87] This is because the model "[i]n its pure form . . . would lead not to an obstacle course, but rather to mere obstacles and no course on which to place the former."[88] Stated in terms of Professor Peter Arenella's more recent criticism, Packer's constructs "[were] not procedural models because they [did] not offer a coherent vision of how to structure the American criminal process."[89] Neither model identified the functions that American criminal procedure should serve,[90] a shortcoming that was inevitable given Professor Damaska's insight that the values underlying each model necessarily exist in tension in any system.[91]

Despite his criticisms, Professor Arenella recently attempted to "reconstruct" Packer's models in a way that would give the Due Process Model positive rather than merely negative content.[92] Contending that the Due Process Model is concerned with legal and not just factual guilt, Arenella defined legal guilt as "simply substantive guilt as well as it can be determined by a fallible procedural process that strives to protect the substantively innocent while simultaneously serving other independent procedural functions."[93] The noteworthy part of this definition of legal guilt is that it included not merely the normative questions the fact finder sometimes must answer about the defendant's conduct[94] but also questions about the state's compliance with "fair process norms that place some substantive and procedural limits on the state's exercise of power."[95] As Professor Arenella had argued a few years earlier:

> Concern over the gravity of the criminal sanction, respect for individual rights, and the felt need for community participation in guilt adjudication have all fostered legal guilt requirements that limit the state's ability to detect and convict the factually guilty. For example, the state might have reliable evidence of a defendant's factual guilt that it cannot use at trial because of the rules of evidence or because police violated the defendant's constitutional rights when seizing the evidence. . . . In all of those examples, our criminal justice system has deliberately created a discrepancy between perceived factual guilt and legal guilt to promote policies other than conviction of the factually guilty. *Thus, our system should not tolerate the conviction of a defendant who is either factually or legally innocent.*[96]

The conclusion in the last sentence of this quotation is either a nonsequitur or a tautological restatement of Arenella's definition of legal guilt. That the criminal justice system enforces some government-restricting norms by limiting the fact finder's ability to make an accurate assessment of factual guilt proves neither that it should so enforce these norms nor that all such norms should be so enforced. To the extent that the "should" in the conclusion follows from Arenella's expansive definition of legal guilt, he has attempted to resolve a controversial issue by definition: if legal guilt means all the rules of the game have been followed in convicting the defendant, then a defendant is not legally guilty when one of these rules has been violated. The issue, of course, is why the defendant should be considered not guilty, in any sense of that term, when a rule promoting a policy unrelated to truth discovery has been violated, and this issue cannot be resolved by a definition.

Whether Arenella succeeded in "reconstructing" Packer's models may also be doubted. By expansively defining the concept of legal guilt, Arenella may have given the Due Process Model "positive" content, but the fact remains that the primary purpose of this reconstructed model was to enforce limits on governmental behavior. Damaska's criticism of Packer's Due Process Model would seem equally apposite: it remains "conceptually impossible to imagine a criminal process whose dominant concern is a desire to protect the individual from public officials."[97] Making the latter desire part of the definition of legal guilt does not overcome the impediment.[98] In any event, whether or not Arenella improved upon Packer's efforts, the issue that must be confronted in any system is how to resolve the "internal conflict . . . between the desire for reliable factfinding and the concern for individual rights."[99]

Although the resolution of such an issue may turn on one's premises, it is possible that some arguments, on reflection, will be seen as less persuasive than others. Professor Arenella's defense of an exclusionary remedy for Fourth Amendment violations is worth considering in this regard. It is common ground that the Fourth Amendment protection against unreasonable searches and seizures serves important societal interests; indeed, it can be stated more strongly that some such protection is inherent in the idea of a free society.[100] The controversial issue is whether the sanction for a Fourth Amendment violation should "be located within the criminal process when the violation produces reliable evidence of substantive guilt."[101] The issue, more precisely stated, is whether the sanction for an illegal search should be the exclusion of probative evidence from the defendant's trial with the concomitant risk that the fact finder will erroneously conclude that the defendant is not factually guilty. Eschewing reliance on sanctions outside the criminal justice system, Arenella deemed exclusion necessary to preserve "the criminal process' integrity as a self-regulating legal order."[102] In Arenella's view, "[o]ur criminal justice system's moral legitimacy rests to some degree on its willingness to replace brute force with legal rules that limit the means government may use to pursue laudable goals."[103] "Permitting the state to use the fruits of such misconduct to prove substantive guilt undermines the very notion of our criminal process as a self-regulating legal order."[104]

Were "brute force" or blatantly and deliberately illegal conduct the issue, Arenella's argument might be persuasive,[105] although one could still appropriately question the wisdom of an evidentiary or remedial rule that impairs the accuracy of the fact-finding process. As Jeremy Bentham observed, "[e]vidence is the basis of justice; to exclude evidence, is to exclude justice."[106] This objection notwithstanding, consider Arenella's argument in the context of the typical Fourth Amendment case that appears in the law reports. The typical case involves either legal doctrine that is uncertain (e.g., can a station house detention for a lineup be made on less than traditional probable cause?) or the uncertain application of legal doctrine (e.g., did the police have sufficient cause for a station house detention? were the circumstances sufficiently exigent to excuse the warrant requirement?). In the typical Fourth Amendment case, the answer to the legality question is not known, and cannot be known, until the last tribunal to engage in Monday morning quarterbacking has had its say. Even then, when reasonable people can and do differ, the answer of the last tribunal is right only because no further review is possible. Given that the vast majority of Fourth Amendment cases are contestable, Arenella's claim that the use of illegally seized evidence would undermine the moral legitimacy of the criminal justice system is difficult to understand. Such a claim, if valid, would deny the moral legitimacy of the criminal justice systems in the vast majority of civilized countries that refuse to exclude evidence, especially when it results from technical or good-faith search and seizure infractions.[107]

It is unconvincing at this point to fall back on the Fourth Amendment itself as requiring an exclusionary remedy. If our Constitution actually required exclusion, or was interpreted to require exclusion, the argument just considered would be irrelevant and unnecessary. Arenella's defense of exclusion was neither based on constitutional text nor dependent on the limitation on unreasonable searches and seizures being part of a written Constitution. Instead, Arenella's "legitimation" argument was an attempt to provide a reasoned justification for the exclusionary rule, and as such, his argument would apply equally to criminal justice systems in any society taking seriously the civil or human right of persons to be free from arbitrary police conduct. One should not lightly ignore, therefore, that most other free societies have not been persuaded of the need to encumber their criminal justice systems with anything close to the American exclusionary rule.

Arenella was aware that his critics, pointing to other systems, would accuse him of "cultural myopia."[108] His response was that even inquisitorial systems protect social values unrelated to truth discovery. He also denied the existence of a *"pure* 'guilt or innocence' model of American criminal procedure."[109] Both responses were correct, although not supportive of his broad thesis. As already discussed, every system, including the American one, must reconcile the tension between the goal of truth discovery and goals that serve other purposes. This virtual truism, however, is considerably narrower than the claim put forth by Arenella that legal guilt requires compliance with all the rules that restrict government in executing its law enforcement responsibilities.[110] It also is too modest to support the argument that the exclusionary rule is vital to the integrity of the criminal justice system.

In a free and just society, democratic or republican ideology and notions of human dignity provide limits on what government may do to solve crime. This is why our society, like so many others, prohibits the police from using physical force to obtain confessions, from exercising unfettered discretion in searches and seizures, and from broadly using certain intrusive investigative techniques, such as wiretapping. Such restraints on government obviously preclude both the detection and the solution of a substantial amount of crime, and there is room in any society for debate about how severe these restraints should be. This book, for example, maintains that the restrictions on police interrogation in the United States are more severe than necessary to preserve our commitment to freedom and human dignity. For present purposes, however, it suffices to observe that without significant restraints in these and other areas, a society would be neither free nor just.

Every free society will thus have goals that take precedence over the desire to detect and punish crime. That these goals should be enforced by evidentiary rules in the trial of someone charged with crime is not so apparent, especially perhaps when the goals at issue have implications beyond the criminal justice system. For example, random searches for the purpose of constructing "dangerous person" files would no less violate freedom and dignity than random searches intended to uncover evidence for prosecution. That is, the Fourth Amendment may provide a civil or human right more than a criminal procedure right.[111] If this is correct, no connection between enforcement of the Fourth Amendment and a defendant's criminal trial would seem to be necessary. The absence of such a logical connection may explain why most other societies enforce their search and seizure restrictions without employing such a broad truth-defeating exclusionary remedy.

Even with respect to rules more directly related to the criminal justice system, a rational system will typically prefer to control or remedy official misbehavior by means other than the suppression of factual truth, particularly if these other means are effective. Unfortunately, our system too often seems to lack the insight, rooted in common sense, that truth should be sacrificed only for weighty reasons.[112] The presumption in the procedural system should be in favor of truth, and those who propose or defend rules that distort truth discovery should have the burden of demonstrating that such rules either are required by society's political ideology or significantly promote interests of overriding importance.

Notwithstanding this presumption, the criminal justice system will primarily be responsible for enforcing certain rules, like those relating to trial by jury or to double jeopardy, that determine the appropriate structure or operation of the criminal justice system itself and for which a remedy outside the system would not be meaningful. This will be true even when the cost of enforcement is the suppression of truth, as sometimes occurs when double jeopardy restraints preclude the prosecution of a guilty offender.[113] Similarly, when the use of evidence, and not merely the means of obtaining the evidence, violates the system's legal norms, the criminal justice system has no choice but to employ an exclusionary rule.[114] In addition, and more controversially, some official misbehavior may be regarded as so egregious, as so offensive to the society's underlying ideology, that convictions obtained thereby will seem intolerable.

Although different systems, as well as different people within systems, will differ about when and where the concern for truth must yield in these cases, the lack of a pure model of truth discovery guarantees that every system will sometimes sacrifice truth for the sake of implementing other values. Without denying this, the argument of this chapter has been that the tension between truth discovery and other goals should be resolved in a way that leaves truth a dominant goal of the procedural system.

Exclusion of Coerced Confessions

This chapter began with facts depicting a brutal murder and brutal beatings by the police to obtain confessions to the murder. The police behavior in obtaining the confessions, unlike much of the interrogation behavior that will be considered in this book, clearly violated society's norms pertaining to governmental treatment of individuals. Indeed, the police conduct itself violated the criminal law. The question raised was whether the confessions should be admitted into evidence in the defendants' trials for murder, leaving the issue of punishment for the offending officials to some other forum.

As previously suggested, the suppression of the confessions on the facts presented would be consistent with the goal of truth discovery. Because physical torture can induce persons falsely to accuse themselves, a substantial risk of unreliability is evident. Although the procedural system normally relies on the fact finder to wrestle with questions of credibility, fact finders, particularly jurors, sometimes place undue weight on confessions. Moreover, law enforcement officials gratuitously added to the risk, perhaps always present to some extent, of false self-condemnation.[115] Most importantly, the risk of mistake at issue is one of erroneous conviction, a risk our society particularly wants to avoid.

The modified case, involving corroborated confessions, is more difficult to resolve. One still may try to invoke the reliability concern by claiming that a person may know the whereabouts of, say, a murder weapon and yet not be the murderer.[116] Although this is so, the truth discovery goal, standing alone, would probably support informing the fact finder of the extremely relevant fact, confirmed by independent investigation, that the defendant knew the location of the weapon. Moreover, as previously seen, the goal of protecting the innocent does not mandate that even speculative risks of erroneous conviction be avoided.

Suppression on the facts as modified seems to require an argument unrelated to truth discovery. Of course, one can offer an argument based on constitutional premises, but the question this chapter has posed is whether an exclusionary remedy would be desirable absent an existing constitutional requirement. In support of an affirmative answer, one may argue that evidentiary use of the resulting confessions in the case at issue might be interpreted as judicial acquiescence in, or even condonation of, the offensive misconduct, an impression that should especially be avoided when police conduct is so clearly antithetical to the basic norms of society. One may also argue that our system of criminal justice should make manifest the unacceptability of particularly egregious police conduct—especially police criminal conduct—by condemning it at every possible turn, and that an exclusionary remedy does precisely this.

Common to such arguments, which have been sketched in only the barest detail, is the view that confessions procured by physical force should be inadmissible without regard to their reliability or to the existence of alternative means of controlling and punishing the police. Carrying considerable force, these arguments suggest that exclusion on the facts presented in this chapter is at least defensible, arguably correct, and perhaps even dictated by American political ideology. The arguments do not demonstrate, however, that such exclusion is the only choice that a free society could possibly make. Indeed, once it is acknowledged, as it generally is, that a "fruit of the poisonous tree" doctrine is not an inevitable choice for a free society, the admissibility of the corroborated confession along with the corroborating fruit cannot be deemed unthinkable.[117]

CHAPTER 2   **Ill-Conceived Objections to Police Interrogation**

The previous chapter considered the basic objectives of criminal procedure. This chapter discusses policy arguments for restricting the institution of police interrogation and attempts to evaluate these arguments against the objectives previously considered. Recommendations for restricting police interrogation often stem from an underlying hostility either to the institution itself or to reliance on a suspect's admissions as proof of guilt. The thesis of this chapter is that the arguments that might be made to support such hostility are unsound. By removing the underlying presumption of suspicion that the institution frequently encounters, this chapter should help cast in a different light the specific issues pertaining to police interrogation that subsequent chapters will discuss.

Because the inquiry in this chapter is one of policy, constitutional arguments once again will be held in abeyance. Without intending to minimize constitutional concerns, this approach offers two important advantages. First, it has the liberating effect of permitting unfettered consideration of the competing policies. As Judge Henry Friendly once wrote in a related context, "the opportunity to approach these problems on their merits, free from the compulsion of precedent and the cacophony of cliches, is exhilarating; one feels as if he had emerged from a fog bank and entered clear mountain air."[1] Second, as subsequent chapters will demonstrate, the Constitution's text, history, and underlying policy concerns have been subject to competing interpretations. This has led many to endorse judicial imposition of value choices on the nation, choices too often expected to express moral disapproval of police interrogation. This chapter should demonstrate that even under such an unrestrained approach to constitutional interpretation, the case for curtailing the effectiveness of police interrogation has not been made.

Notwithstanding the intended policy approach, the Constitution will cast its shadow on much of the analysis that follows. This is because arguments against police interrogation often claim to rest on constitutional policies, particularly those supposedly underlying the Fifth

27

Amendment's ban on compelling an individual to become a witness against himself in a criminal case—what we loosely call the privilege against self-incrimination. In criticizing these arguments, some of what follows may seem like a brief against the Fifth Amendment itself. To some extent it unavoidably is, but this is not the purpose of the discussion. Other analysts, including most recently Professor David Dolinko, have concluded that while "the privilege in American law can be explained by specific historical developments, [it] cannot be justified either functionally or conceptually."[2] Although this chapter may give support to such contentions, the objective is to demonstrate only the more limited proposition that sound policy arguments do not justify the hostility to police interrogation that is apparent in much of the literature and even in court opinions.

The Fair Chance or "Fox-Hunter's" Argument

In *Escobedo v. Illinois*,[3] the Supreme Court, over strong dissenting opinions, overruled previous cases[4] and held that a suspect, at least in certain circumstances, has a right to counsel during custodial interrogation.[5] Because the Constitution's text did not dictate its conclusion, the Court found it necessary to rely on policy reasons to justify such an expansive interpretation. Among other things, the Court observed that Escobedo's first admission relating to the murder in question occurred only after the police confronted him with another individual who accused him of the shooting; admitting complicity in the crime, Escobedo asserted that the other individual, not he, had done the actual shooting. In the Court's empathetic view, Escobedo may not have known that admitting complicity in the murder was legally as damaging as admitting that he was the actual killer.[6]

Disapprovingly noting that the purpose of the police interrogation was to get Escobedo to confess,[7] the Court also opined that Escobedo needed a lawyer's assistance because what occurred at the police station could affect his subsequent trial.[8] Absent a lawyer's assistance, the trial might be "no more than an appeal from the interrogation," with conviction virtually assured by the suspect's confession.[9] The Court even conjured up a prosecutor cynically supporting the right to counsel at trial with the observation that the most illustrious trial lawyer would not be able to save a suspect who had already confessed.[10]

Academic commentators have frequently echoed *Escobedo*'s arguments. Professor Welsh White has insisted that a suspect should have a right to counsel's assistance during police interrogation "to protect his chances at the forthcoming trial."[11] Along similar lines, Professor

George Dix has argued that defendants should have the same opportunity to reflect on their situation before offering a confession as they would have before entering a guilty plea.[12] Professor Peter Arenella approvingly has observed that the Supreme Court has protected suspects from the "pressures to confess that may thwart the need for an independent adjudication of guilt at trial."[13] Speaking more broadly of self-incrimination in general, and not just of confessions, Professors Yale and Irene Rosenberg have admiringly asserted that Talmudic law, which they claim prohibited even voluntary self-incrimination, prevented "reliance on evidence that is almost instinctively regarded as dispositive," thus assuring "that no shortcuts would be taken in the fact-finding process."[14] In their somewhat different ways, each of these commentators, like the Court in *Escobedo,* has expressed concern that a suspect's confession will virtually assure conviction and thereby render the subsequent trial a meaningless exercise.

The last mentioned professors have suggested that we should strive for a legal system that is "worthy of a mature and civilized society nearing the twenty-first century."[15] The question that must be asked, however, is why a mature and civilized society, regardless of the century, would base its law on the sentiments and concerns expressed in the preceding paragraphs. Derisively calling this entire line of reasoning the "fox-hunter's argument," Bentham asserted that the argument was premised on "the idea of *fairness*, in the sense in which the word is used by sportsmen":[16]

> The fox is to have a fair chance for his life: he must have (so close is the analogy) what is called *law*: leave to run a certain length of way, for the express purpose of giving him a chance for escape. While under pursuit, he must not be shot: it would be as *unfair* as convicting him of burglary on a hen-roost, in five minutes' time, in a court of conscience.[17]

Bentham sarcastically observed that this concern about the accused's likelihood of success at trial can be rational only under a sporting code that has amusement rather than justice as its end.[18] As sometimes was his wont, Bentham may have been a bit harsh in this criticism. Whatever was the case in Bentham's day, we should be reluctant to conclude that the majority in *Escobedo* and the commentators who supported *Escobedo*'s reasoning were seeking mere entertainment as their objective. Nevertheless, the obscurity of the objective supposedly reflected in the fair chance argument virtually invites such a mocking response, for, standing alone, the proposition that we should regret the assurance of a guilty defendant's conviction at trial seems terribly counterintuitive. In any event, the underlying basis of the fair chance argument, not having been articulated, can only be surmised.

Two somewhat different concerns may be reflected in the fair chance argument. The first, systemic in nature, may be that defendants who have confessed, believing that it would be futile to contest guilt, will plead guilty and thereby defeat the system's preference that guilt be decided by an adversary process. The second, individual in nature, may relate to the perceived unfairness—not in Bentham's derisive sense—in depriving the accused of a meaningful opportunity for acquittal. Neither concern withstands analysis.

The problem with the first concern lies in the supposition that the system prefers guilt to be determined by an adversary contest. Plea bargaining is generally recognized as the most prevalent means of resolving criminal cases in the United States,[19] and the Supreme Court's primary reason for upholding plea bargaining, even when the prosecutor has offered bargains almost too good to refuse,[20] has been the importance, in its view, of maintaining the high rate of guilty pleas.[21] Even while advocating an injection of accusatorial procedures into the pretrial process, many commentators, such as Professor Arenella, have conceded that abolishing plea bargaining is not feasible in view of the system's need for guilty pleas.[22] Many who disagree nevertheless insist, and seem prepared to accept, that the guilty plea rate would remain high without such bargaining.[23] Wherever one stands on the plea bargaining debate, one cannot seriously contend that a system that disposes of the vast majority of its cases by guilty plea has a preference for a contested mode of guilt determination. From a systemic perspective, therefore, not only is it not regrettable that a confession may convince a defendant of the futility of contesting guilt at trial, but the opposite most likely is true: the preference for guilty pleas makes confessions desirable.[24]

To be plausible, therefore, the fair chance argument must reflect a concern about individual fairness. The problem, however, with rooting the argument in fairness concerns is that such a strategy inevitably reduces the fair chance argument to some other argument that requires justification in its own right. For example, one may assert that the fair chance argument is intended to assure that innocent defendants will have a fair chance of acquittal at trial. This goal, of course, is uncontroversial, but to contend that innocent foxes should escape is not to suggest that those who have been eating chickens should also escape. In any event, as will soon be discussed, to embrace this reason for opposing effective police interrogation requires one to show both that this institution carries with it a high risk of unreliability and that restricting the ability to obtain reliable confessions is necessary to prevent unreliable ones.

One may likewise contend that obtaining confessions that assure conviction is unfair because it is cruel to make the defendant the source of his or her own demise. This too is a different argument than the fair chance or fox-hunter's argument baldly stated. Accordingly, it too needs justification because, as we will see, the cruelty of the matter is not obvious.

If the fair chance argument had any independent validity as an argument of its own, the criminal justice system would have to forbid or restrict capturing the defendant at the scene of the crime, matching the defendant's fingerprints with those left by the offender, searches that are a bit too successful, the employment of undercover informants, and the use of electronic equipment that can capture and record the accused in the act of committing the crime. With regard to each of these law enforcement techniques, it can frequently be said that a trial will be no more than an appeal from the technique employed, with conviction virtually assured by the evidence obtained.[25] With regard to each, one may imagine a prosecutor cynically supporting a right to counsel for the defendant at trial because even an illustrious lawyer would not be able to save the defendant from conviction.[26] Yet outside the realm of confessions, one does not encounter the view that certain techniques of law enforcement should be abandoned or curtailed simply because they are too successful in convicting guilty defendants.

The absurdity of its logical consequences is not the only reason for rejecting the fair chance argument. In a system dedicated to truth, it should be cause for celebration, not lamentation, that Escobedo's confession helped to assure his conviction. Admittedly, as seen in the last chapter, other values may sometimes compete with the desire to discover truth, but no such values support the fair chance argument. First, no essential tenet of American ideology mandates giving guilty defendants a sporting chance of acquittal.[27] Second, as previously discussed, the fair chance argument as such has nothing to do with the view that it is better that x number of guilty defendants escape than that one innocent person be convicted. Third, standing alone, the fair chance argument is based on neither a concern to prevent official misconduct nor a desire to protect the dignity of the accused. Lacking independent justification, the fair chance argument must accordingly be seen as indefensibly inconsistent with the truth-seeking goals of criminal procedure. No good reason can be given for structuring the procedural system with the express purpose of increasing the likelihood that guilty defendants, such as Escobedo, will have a fair chance of winning an erroneous acquittal.

What earned the fair chance argument Bentham's derisive fox-hunter's label was its suggestion that, as an end in itself, even guilty defendants should have a fair chance for acquittal. Nevertheless, one may be tempted to respond that both Bentham's critique and the present discussion set up a straw man to be easily crushed, for stated in such terms, the fair chance argument against police interrogation, or against self-incrimination in general, has never had serious support. Indeed, a number of commentators who have examined the possible justifications for the protection against compulsory self-incrimination have acknowledged that the fair chance or fox-hunter's argument lacks validity.[28]

Although there is some merit in the view that the importance of the fair chance argument should not be overemphasized, strains of this argument are unmistakably present, as we have seen, in *Escobedo* and in the writings of many commentators who support that decision and other decisions that have taken a dim view of confessions. The fair chance argument should be a straw man, but the influence of this argument on judicial and academic reasoning cannot be denied. Even though the label typically is missing, the argument definitely is there. In considering the merits of police interrogation, it therefore is an important first step to recognize that fair chance or fox-hunter's reasoning, however it may be disguised, warrants repudiation.

The Equality Arguments

Two different equality arguments have been offered to support restrictions on police interrogation. The first reflects concern about the perceived inequality between the interrogating officers and the hapless defendant, while the second reflects concern about inequality among defendants. The first requires only brief discussion, because it is the fair chance or fox-hunter's argument dressed in different garb. Although the second equality argument is emotionally seductive, it too, when carefully analyzed, fails to perform the task assigned to it.

Both the courts and academic commentators have expressed concern about the inequality that exists between suspects and their interrogators. Dissenting from a denial of certiorari in *Little v. Arkansas*,[29] Justice Marshall advocated that a minor should receive the advice of an adult before confessing so that he would be less on an unequal footing with his interrogators.[30] To support this position, Justice Marshall relied on statements in prior Supreme Court decisions observing that a minor typically is no match for the police during interrogation.[31]

Though not labeled as such, this equality argument can also be identified in *Escobedo*'s observation that counsel's advice is needed during custodial interrogation because such interrogation produces many confessions. As the Court saw it, "[t]here is necessarily a direct relationship between the importance of a stage to the police in their quest for a confession and the criticalness of that stage to the accused in his need for legal advice."[32] The equality argument can similarly be found lurking behind the claim in *Miranda v. Arizona*[33] that one purpose of the Fifth Amendment is to maintain a "fair state-individual balance."

Academic commentators have also deplored the unequal positions of defendants and interrogators. For example, citing, among other things, "the relative strengths of the suspect and the police in this context," Professor White has endorsed the right to counsel during police interrogation and denounced the use of trickery.[34] Echoing earlier statements by Justice Fortas, Professors Irene and Yale Rosenberg have defended *Miranda*'s insistence on "the equality of the individual and the state."[35] In support of their "modest" proposal to make all custodial statements inadmissible, they have argued that "[i]f a purpose of the privilege is to create a parity of sorts between the individual and the state, it must be recognized that, in the confines of the stationhouse or its functional equivalent, there is no equality, gross or otherwise."[36] In essential agreement, Professor Arenella has lamented that "*Miranda*'s promise of putting the suspect on an equal footing with the police" has failed to materialize.[37]

Judge Friendly responded to the state-individual equality argument by suggesting that the state's obligation to pursue justice rather than simply to prevail imposes duties on it that are not shared by the "equal" defendant.[38] To the extent his response was meant to suggest that the balance of advantage lies with the defendant, it was somewhat wide of the mark. Wherever the advantage may lie in other stages of the process, it cannot be denied that many if not most suspects are not an equal match for their interrogators in the police station. The more apt response to the equality argument is to ask why this kind of inequality should be of concern.

Because the adversary system depends on the parties for the presentation of proof, a "parity of sorts between the individual and the state" is necessary at trial to reduce the possibility of a mistaken verdict. "The innocent defendant who has no tools for investigation, no skills for the organization and presentation of his story or for the cross-examination of his accusers, and who lacks the knowledge of the relevant rules of procedural and substantive law, may quickly find himself unjustly convicted."[39] Police interrogation, however, is not an institution designed for dispute resolution.

Unlike a trial, police interrogation does not involve two parties trying to persuade a third party to adopt a certain view. Rather, police interrogation involves one party trying to learn the truth from the other party, who typically does not want to reveal it.[40] Equality in the police station would thwart the search for truth, because guilty defendants who are an equal match for their interrogators will know that it is generally not in their interest to cooperate and will resist the psychological pressures that often prompt suspects to offer explanations that eventually lead to their undoing.[41] If we want guilty defendants to confess, equality between defendants and interrogators is antithetical to our goal.

Care must be taken, however, not to dismiss the state-individual equality argument too casually. In the juvenile cases previously mentioned, the Supreme Court's concern may have been that an outmatched minor can easily be coerced and possibly even confused into admitting things that are not true.[42] More broadly, the concern for state-individual equality in general, even when adult defendants are involved, may reflect either a desire to promote truth by avoiding the risk of false confessions or a concern that outmatched, isolated defendants will not be able to prevent police tactics that "go too far."[43] Arguments along these lines, however, make equality between the state and the individual an instrumental value rather than an end in itself. The end to be furthered in such an argument is not equality but rather the achievement of truth or the prevention of inappropriate police tactics. To be convincing, therefore, the argument must demonstrate that parity between the parties in the police station is necessary to assure trustworthiness or to prevent the undesirable police conduct. If the evils that drive the argument can be prevented by less drastic means, the equality argument, under the interpretation now being considered, loses all its force.

For present purposes, it suffices to recognize that equality between the state and the individual in the police station cannot be defended as an end in itself. Indeed, to require such equality for its own sake is to express indifference about the outcome, an indifference that is irreconcilable with the procedural system's truth discovery objective. Once the reliability and abuse concerns are adequately addressed—and these still have to be discussed—equality between the state and the individual will only assure that even guilty defendants have a fair chance of avoiding conviction. Thus exposed, the equality argument has all the attributes, and all the deficiencies, of the fair chance or fox-hunter's argument previously considered.[44] In Professor Kent Greenawalt's words, the equality or fair state-individual balance argument either uses shorthand labels for some other argument or substitutes "conclusory rhetoric for analysis."[45]

The tendency to substitute rhetoric for analysis increases when the equality argument is framed not in terms of the inequality between the defendant and the interrogating officers but rather in terms of the inequality among defendants. Professor Greenawalt, for example, has deplored the use of deception during interrogation because such a tactic "work[s] unevenly by undermining the inexperienced and ignorant [while] having little effect on the hardened criminal."[46] Attacking a proposal to permit a period of custodial interrogation after a suspect's arrest, Judge David Bazelon argued several years ago that such interrogation would "primarily affect the poor and, in particular, the poor Negro citizen."[47]

In his defense of *Miranda,* Professor Dorsey Ellis, Jr., similarly observed that a minority of suspects "enjoys special advantages over the much more typical arrestee who is 'likely to be a member of the lowest social and economic groups in the country, poorly educated and perhaps unemployed, unmarried, reared in a broken home, and to have a prior criminal record.'"[48] In Ellis's view, the important interest in crime control cannot justify the inequality that stems from the police taking advantage of a suspect's ignorance.[49] Continuing the same theme, Professors Irene and Yale Rosenberg recently lamented that "perhaps the saddest facet" of the Supreme Court's recent "assault" on *Miranda* "is that it often comes in the form of a denial of information and an exploitation of ignorance that have the effect of excluding the poor and uneducated from Fifth Amendment protection."[50]

Although *Escobedo* was decided on Sixth Amendment right to counsel grounds and *Miranda* on Fifth Amendment compulsory self-incrimination grounds, the egalitarian concerns expressed by the above commentators are evident in both opinions. In *Escobedo,* the Court noted that the defendant was a "22-year old of Mexican extraction with no record of previous experience with the police," speculated that, as a layman, he was probably unaware that an admission of complicity was as damaging as an admission of being the shooter, and made reference to the inequities that face the poor in the criminal justice system.[51] Noting that a request requirement would favor sophisticated over uneducated and poor defendants, the Court in *Miranda* declined to make the rights it fashioned contingent on the suspect's request; similarly, it included a right to counsel in its new package of rights because an "admonishment of the right to remain silent without more would 'benefit only the recidivist and the professional.'"[52] The *Miranda* Court also provided a right to appointed counsel for indigent defendants, noting that without this additional benefit the right to counsel would be meaningless in the "vast majority of confession cases" involving poor defendants.[53]

Perhaps because egalitarian appeals exert such a powerful tug on the emotions of so many, efforts to distinguish good and bad egalitarian arguments are often not made. This is unfortunate, for some egalitarian arguments warrant unequivocal rejection. In particular, the argument for equality of results among defendants subject to police interrogation is ill-conceived. Assume it is true both that defendants from the professional and business classes seldom confess and that those who talk— those who get "caught in the web"—typically are "the frightened, the insecure, the weak, the untrained, the bewildered, the stupid, the naive, [and] the credulous."[54] The question that requires analysis is why this disparity, absent either abusive interrogation techniques or intentionally discriminatory law enforcement, should cause the system to frown on police interrogation and confessions.

Former Attorney General Nicholas Katzenbach rhetorically asked "why the gangster should be made the model and all others raised, in the name of equality, to his level of success in suppressing evidence."[55] As Professor David Robinson, Jr., observed, Katzenbach's point is no less well-taken if the comparison is stated in terms of the disadvantaged and the advantaged:

> Surely it does not follow that because skilled burglars carefully wipe their fingerprints off safe dials, that society must outlaw the use of all fingerprint evidence lest there be discriminatory utilization of such evidence against the "poor, the ignorant, the numerically weak, the friendless, and the powerless." It surely will not do to argue that because some clever or wealthy criminals avoid conviction that all should do so. The lack of professionalism of many of those engaged in criminal conduct is a resource which society should be able to utilize. There seems to be no justifiable end in equal acquittal of the guilty.[56]

In reality, law enforcement exploits at every turn the "lack of professionalism" of the majority of criminals. Not only are less experienced and less advantaged offenders more likely, as Professor Robinson noted, to leave clues at the scene of the crime; they also are more likely to take inadequate precautions against informants and wiretapping, to volunteer admissions to acquaintances,[57] and to fall victim to skillful cross-examination at trial. It may even be true that, given the nature of their crimes or simply a lack of foresight, defendants in this group are more likely to retain evidence that can be uncovered in searches and seizures. None of this should be a source of regret. Rather, what should be a source of regret is that some offenders are sufficiently sophisticated to escape the techniques of law enforcement and prosecution that successfully bring other defendants to book. The moral acceptability of a police practice, or a prosecution tactic at trial, cannot depend on whether the practice attains an equal distribution of success across all subgroups of offenders. In former Attorney General Katzenbach's words, "absolute equality of result could be achieved in the investigatory stage . . . only by deliberately foregoing reliable evidence and releasing guilty men."[58]

To this point, the response to the equality argument has been too easy. This may be, as some would charge, because the response distorted the argument. As Professor Yale Kamisar argued some years ago, the relevant issue is not whether convicting an offender on the basis of fingerprints the offender stupidly left at the crime scene is unfair; it is whether "we should *deprive* [the poor and ignorant] of rights and privileges they are entitled to in the abstract."[59] Surely Professor Kamisar is correct in observing that an inequality in the availability of legal rights is significantly different than an inequality that exists because some defendants, lacking sophistication, are easier to convict than others. Accordingly, while it should not concern us that unsophisticated defendants convict themselves by mistakes that sophisticated defendants would not make, it should concern us if the legal system recognizes a right to counsel but affords the right only to the wealthy or the sophisticated. In Professor Kamisar's words, "[t]o the extent that the Constitution and statutory law *entitles* the wealthy and educated to 'beat the rap,' if that's what you want to call it, why shouldn't all defendants be given a like opportunity?"[60]

Although former Attorney General Katzenbach heroically tried,[61] no easy answer can be given to Professor Kamisar's argument. If rich people have a *right* to bring a lawyer to the police station, the denial of legal assistance to indigents, simply because they cannot afford counsel, or to uneducated persons, simply because they are unaware of their right, understandably will strike many as a denial of equal justice under the law. This merely highlights, however, the advantage of considering policy arguments free from the influence of existing constitutional doctrine. The purpose of this chapter is to consider what rights we would provide during custodial interrogation if we could start from scratch with only sound policy as our guide. For purposes of this chapter, it begs the question to begin with a preexisting right to counsel for anyone in the police station.

Inequality of legal entitlement obviously cannot exist if no defendant, rich or poor, sophisticated or unsophisticated, has a right to counsel's assistance in the police station. Similarly, if the Fifth Amendment, properly construed, protects defendants only against certain compelling pressures and does not create a right to silence as such, inequality of legal rights cannot exist as long as the designated pressures are impermissible for all defendants. Of course, some subgroups of defendants may confess more readily than others even without impermissible pressure, but as we have seen, inequality of this nature should be of no concern. Professor Kamisar's troubling equality of rights argument needs to be confronted only if an independent reason can be given for recognizing a right to counsel or a broad self-incrimination protection in the first place.[62]

It will be the burden of subsequent chapters to show that such rights should not be recognized under our Constitution. For present purposes, however, it is adequate to observe that unless one of these rights is first established, the equality of rights argument simply is inapposite. Stated differently, the reasons for granting the defendant protection from the inherent pressures of police interrogation cannot be found in the equality argument.[63]

The Cruelty or Human Dignity Argument

It is sometimes said that requiring individuals to give incriminating evidence against themselves constitutes cruelty or a violation of human dignity. Even were this true, it would not follow that the mere act of asking questions that seek incriminating answers also is cruel, for we often are asked questions by people who have no legal entitlement to an answer. It does seem to follow, however, that if requiring truthful but self-incriminating responses is not cruel, then interrogation as such cannot be cruel either. That the former would be cruel or inhumane is not easy to demonstrate.

The so-called cruel trilemma is often cited as a justification for the legal protection against being required to become a witness against oneself in a criminal trial. Confronted with such a requirement, guilty persons must choose (1) to answer truthfully and bring unpleasant and possibly severe criminal sanctions upon themselves, (2) to dissemble and face the penalties of perjury, or (3) to refuse to answer and be punished for failing to obey the requirement that they answer.[64] All subpoenaed witnesses, however, face the second and third prongs of the trilemma, and confronting them with this choice is not deemed cruel.[65] Moreover, an analogous trilemma confronts both witnesses in criminal cases who are asked to provide damaging evidence against family members or close friends and parties in civil cases who are required to testify against themselves.[66] Indeed, a virtually indistinguishable trilemma confronts fearful witnesses who are forced to testify over an objection that they or their families will be killed or harmed if they testify truthfully.[67] Nevertheless, the legal system has not deemed it cruel to require witnesses and parties to confront these trilemmas and make a choice. Apparently cruelty exists only when the witness faces a criminal penalty—no matter how small—because of a truthful answer.

That the trilemma can be cruel in only this instance seems dubious. Indeed, once the above analogies are considered, it seems dubious that the perceived cruelty in compulsory self-incrimination arises from the trilemma. That is, instead of perceiving as unacceptably cruel the temptation to commit perjury to save oneself,[68] those who defend the protection against compulsory self-incrimination may deem it cruel simply to force the individual to "partake in his own undoing."[69] If this is the cruelty that justifies the protection, then the trilemma is irrelevant, and one does not have to worry about distinguishing other trilemmas that are closely analogous but not deemed cruel.

Putting the cruelty argument in these terms has an advantage for those who want to curtail police interrogation. Because the police do not generally have authority either to compel a response or to penalize false answers, the trilemma argument is not easily applied to police interrogation. Commentators have had to strain to get over this hurdle. For example, Professor Kamisar has argued that the pressures of the custodial environment will induce a defendant to assume that the police have a legal right to an answer, or at least that there will be "an *extralegal* sanction for contumacy."[70] Professor Peter Westen has similarly stated that courts eventually recognized that "although the police did not have de jure authority to compel incriminating statements, the police did possess de facto authority to do so."[71] Though not without some force, these arguments are not fully satisfactory, because even if a de facto requirement is equivalent to a legal requirement—and the existence of a de facto requirement would require empirical verification—the arguments ignore the perjury prong of the trilemma. As long as the individual has what is tantamount to a right to lie, the cruelty typically associated with the trilemma is not apparent.[72] Under the cruelty argument as modified, however, the failure to satisfy the perjury prong of the trilemma makes no difference.

This is not to say that the cruelty argument without reference to the trilemma lacks difficulties, for it is not immediately apparent why requiring people to partake in their own undoing by telling the truth is cruel, inhumane, or a violation of human dignity. Referring to this argument in now outdated terminology as the "old woman's reason,"[73] and alternatively and perhaps "with much more propriety" as "the lawyer's reason,"[74] Bentham argued that punishing people for what they reveal from their own mouths is no more cruel than punishing them for what someone else reveals. If anything, Bentham contended, self-incriminating statements are likely to be more trustworthy than the statements of witnesses.[75]

Bentham's critique notwithstanding, the cruelty argument is more difficult to refute unequivocally than the fair chance and equality arguments, for ultimately one's sense of what is cruel, inhumane, and a violation of human dignity may be more a product of predisposition than of rational analysis. Indeed, some may be tempted to agree with Justice Field's assertion years ago that the cruelty of compelling people to expose their own guilt is too "obvious" and "plain" to warrant analysis.[76] Such an assertion ultimately proves unsatisfactory, however, not only because it forecloses rational discourse but also because it is empirically false: too many people have found Bentham's criticisms persuasive to claim that the existence of cruelty is obvious.[77] Indeed, far from being plain, the claim of cruelty is unpersuasive.

First, one cannot denounce the cruelty of required self-incrimination without comparing it with alternative techniques of discovering the truth. As Bentham recognized, the cruelty argument rings hollow as long as other harsher procedures are deemed acceptable:

> You know of such or such a paper; tell us where it may be found. A request thus simple, your tenderness shudders at the thoughts of putting to a man . . . . [B]ut what you scruple not to do . . . is, to dispatch your emissaries in the dead of night to his house, to that house which you call his castle, to break it open, and seize the documents by force.
>
> Not that, in any such act of violence, considered as a necessary means to a necessary end, there is any thing to blame: it is on the score of inconsistency, and that alone, that it is here worth mentioning. Two means to the same end: the one violent, the other free from violence. The quiet one is too violent for you: you embrace the violent one; and not only in preference to the other, but to the exclusion of it: and this is your delicacy, your tenderness.[78]

Of course, one may try to respond that searches and seizures, as well as other intrusive law enforcement techniques, should also be deemed cruel and impermissible. Few seriously make such claims, however, and for good reason. If all harsh, painful, or intrusive means of law enforcement were prohibited, law enforcement would be impossible. Thus, searches must be reasonable, but a search, even of a person's "castle," is not unreasonable simply because it significantly intrudes on the individual's privacy and autonomy interests. Because an intrusive search, as Bentham recognized, seems more "cruel" than requiring suspects arrested on probable cause to answer questions, the advocates of the cruelty argument, if they are to prevail, must explain why this is not so. Faced with the acceptability of these other intrusive practices, they cannot, as the *Miranda* Court did, simply posit that the foundation of the protection against compulsory self-incrimination is "the respect a government . . . must accord to the dignity and integrity of its citizens."[79]

Second, requiring an individual to tell the truth, even if self-incrimination and punishment results, may actually be consistent with the individual's moral obligation not to cause unwarranted harm to others. To take the easiest case, few would dispute that a guilty individual has a moral obligation to confess when his confession is necessary to prevent an innocent person from being convicted for a crime. Similarly, even aside from the possibility of erroneous conviction, a person has a moral obligation to admit that he has falsely accused another, for only by so confessing can the person hope to remove the harm wrongly caused to the other's good name.[80] Generalizing from these examples, one should be able to state uncontroversially that a person has a moral obligation to confess when confessing is "necessary to provide restitution, to prevent his commission of future similar acts, or to avoid injustice to others."[81] If such a generalization is valid, it cannot be considered cruel—not, at least, without more elaboration than the advocates of the cruelty argument have provided—to require an individual to confess in those instances to which the generalization applies.

The more difficult question is whether one can defend a broader moral obligation to confess. Professor Alan Donagan has denied that such an obligation exists. In his view, although individuals have a moral obligation to be contrite and to render satisfaction for their crimes, an obligation that arises because crimes typically are moral wrongs, individuals have no obligation to confess when these objectives can be achieved without confessing. The individual's duty to society is only to conform to its institutions and laws, such as by not resisting arrest, not committing perjury, and submitting to conviction and punishment. This limited obligation to society, in Donagan's view, is "consistent with concealing crimes which you repent and for which you have made amends."[82]

Donagan's argument, though itself controversial, at least refutes Justice Fortas's more extreme defense of the protection against compulsory self-incrimination, but by doing so, it rendered dubious the distinctions it set out to support. Before becoming a member of the Supreme Court, Fortas had argued that the individual has a sovereign right "to defend himself by all means within his power" and that the state "has no right to compel the sovereign individual to surrender or impair his right of self-defense."[83] If this argument had validity, the state would have no right to prohibit such things as perjury, subornation of perjury, bribery, destruction of evidence, resistance to arrest, violation of bail, and prison escape. Stated more broadly, were the individual sovereign, the state would have no right to require him to submit to conviction and punishment.[84]

That the state, as Donagan recognized, appropriately and uncontroversially may require the individual to refrain from these self-defense strategies casts doubt on Donagan's assertion that the state has no right to demand honest responses that would be self-incriminating. Because escape and perjury, no less than silence, at least sometimes may coexist with contrition and satisfaction, the individual's obligation not to escape or commit perjury in these instances must depend entirely on the general moral obligation to obey society's laws. If this is correct, it is not apparent why the individual would not similarly have a duty to obey a law requiring truthful answers to properly asked questions. Indeed, Donagan seemed to recognize this, for he acknowledged that his claim that individuals are not generally obligated to incriminate themselves "presupposes that they are not lawfully asked questions which they are lawfully bound to answer."[85]

The analysis thus far supports the following conclusions. First, an individual has a moral obligation at least in some circumstances to confess wrongdoing. Second, when contrition and satisfaction are possible without confessing, an individual arguably does not have a moral obligation to confess wrongdoing.[86] Whether the risk of convicting an innocent person places all cases actually or prophylactically under the umbrella of the first conclusion will not be pursued here other than to note that a positive answer would cast further doubt on Professor Donagan's argument. Third, an individual, at least in a just society, has a general obligation to obey society's valid laws. Fourth, and logically compelled by the third conclusion, an individual would be obligated to obey a valid (i.e., justifiable, not cruel) societal requirement to answer truthfully investigative questions. Fifth, a societal requirement of truthful answers would not be cruel, inhumane, or a violation of human dignity at least in those cases (few or great in number depending on how the tension in the first two conclusions is resolved) in which the requirement coincides with the individual's moral obligation to tell the truth.

Although broad in scope, these conclusions are not without bounds. For example, the analysis has not refuted that reasons unrelated to cruelty may warrant denying the state authority to require truthful answers. That is, even when an individual may have a moral obligation to tell the truth, the legal system may have reasons unrelated to the cruelty or human dignity argument for providing a legal right not to do so.[87] Such reasons, however, must be articulated and not simply surmised to exist. In addition, the analysis has not refuted that it may be cruel for the state to require truthful answers under those circumstances, if any, in which the individual is not under an independent moral obligation to tell the truth.

Nevertheless, a claim of cruelty even as limited to this last instance is not easy to defend. Such a claim cannot be derived as a matter of logical imperative from a more general premise relating to individual autonomy, for the state frequently and uncontroversially demands that individuals engage in virtuous conduct that is not morally required. Moreover, as previously suggested, if the state's interest in successful law enforcement permits it to demand that individuals submit to conviction and punishment, even when they have no independent moral obligation to do so, the same interest would seem to permit the state to require other sacrifices, such as truthful responses to investigative questions. Though compliance with such a requirement would be difficult and even painful, the law frequently imposes exacting and unpleasant standards of conduct. Requirements of self-sacrifice are evident, for example, in the general unavailability of the duress defense in murder cases or when the threat is only to property, in restrictions on an aggressor's ability to rely on self-defense, and in the requirement that even defendants on trial for their lives must tell the truth if they choose to testify.[88]

As Professor Dolinko has argued, requirements thought desirable because they cause individuals to harm themselves are morally distinguishable from requirements that serve legitimate purposes and cause self-harm as an incidental side effect. Cruelty would be apparent, for example, in requiring condemned people to dig their own graves or to pull the switch for their executions. Similarly, one might condemn as cruel a requirement of truth telling imposed for the purpose of gratuitously assuring self-imposed harm. When the self-harm is "merely a side-effect" of complying with the state's otherwise laudable goal of ascertaining the truth, however, a requirement of truth telling should not be deemed cruel.[89]

In short, whatever reasons may exist for opposing a legal requirement of truthful answers when the individual is not morally obligated to confess, those reasons are unlikely to be rooted in the cruelty and human dignity argument. Nevertheless, the law in the United States is unlikely to change to require suspects to tell the truth in response to questions. Recognizing this, however, does not strip the above analysis of practical significance, for if it would not be cruel for the state to require suspects to tell the truth in response to questions, it would not seem cruel for the state to take the lesser step of subjecting suspects to questioning without obligating them to respond.

But what if the above argument is flawed and requiring truthful answers is always, or at least sometimes, cruel and inhumane? Even with such an assumption, it does not follow that the mere asking of questions would be similarly cruel. Although he has controversially argued that asking questions on meager suspicion, particularly when the relationship between the parties is close, improperly expresses a lack of trust in the person questioned, Professor Greenawalt has convincingly argued that even a close relationship does not render questions grounded on solid suspicion morally inappropriate.[90] Indeed, as Greenawalt observed, such questioning "is more respectful of [the person's] dignity and autonomy than most alternative approaches to discovering the truth."[91]

Under Greenawalt's approach, which itself arguably is more restrictive than warranted, police questioning of arrested suspects should not be problematic. First, the relationship between the government and a citizen is not analogous to those close relationships that in Greenawalt's view demand special trust. Moreover, custodial interrogation typically occurs only after an arrest based on probable cause.[92] Finally, as discussed in the previous chapter, the state's interest in discovering the truth is exceedingly strong. Thus, whatever may be said of interrogation by friends and family members, cruelty or an affront to human dignity is not apparent when society seeks the truth from a person for whom probable cause of wrongdoing exists.

Some may doubt, however, whether a legal system can consistently maintain that suspects are under no legal obligation to respond while it permits police interrogation to occur. At the least, it might be argued that consistency would require such a legal system to adopt procedures, perhaps like those judicially mandated in the United States, to assure that interrogation does not interfere with the suspect's "right of silence." The flaw in this argument, however, is in confusing a direct or positive right of silence with a right of silence that exists only in the weak or indirect sense that the person cannot be required or compelled to answer questions.[93] Because the two are not necessarily equivalent, a system that permits questioning without obligating suspects to respond need not find it morally troublesome either that officials encourage suspects to tell the truth or that suspects respond to such encouragement with truthful self-incrimination.[94] On the contrary, the suspect's cooperation may appropriately be cause for societal celebration in such a system. Indeed, undoubtedly because of their normative view "that the accused should co-operate in the discovery of truth," continental systems, which contrary to common perception do not obligate the accused to answer questions, have rejected rigid procedural devices that would discourage self-incrimination in response to official questioning.[95]

It remains possible, of course, that specific interrogation conditions or tactics may be cruel and inhumane. Although disagreement may exist over the propriety of particular police stratagems, limits assuredly exist, as the previous chapter argued, on the conduct a free society will tolerate from its officials even in the pursuit of truth. The present discussion should have demonstrated, however, that the interrogation environment should not be considered cruel merely because it encourages the suspect to tell the truth.

All interrogation necessarily includes certain inherent pressures, pressures that are likely to be especially keen for suspects in custody who know they have committed the crime under investigation. Standing alone, however, the inherent pressures of interrogation should be troublesome only in a system that views it as undesirable for suspects to choose to cooperate in the investigation. Moreover, once it is recognized that encouraging suspects to cooperate is not cruel, there should be no reluctance on cruelty grounds to deny suspects assistance, such as advice of counsel, that will discourage their cooperation. On the contrary, it demonstrates uncertainty of purpose—something readily apparent in American confessions law—simultaneously to strive to encourage and to discourage confessions.

Regardless of the argument's force, some may find it difficult to jettison the belief that it is cruel to influence a suspect to act against the suspect's best interests.[96] Such a belief, of course, limits its focus to the suspect's material as opposed to moral interests. This response aside, the logic of such a belief, as already indicated, would require the state to permit many of the self-defense strategies, like escape and perjury, that it now uncontroversially prohibits. Moreover, unless rational debate is to be eschewed, the advocates of the cruelty argument must respond to the moral claims of their critics. At some point, that is, those who persist in the cruelty argument must either yield to the force of the counterargument or demonstrate where the latter has gone astray.[97]

The claim of this section is that it is neither cruel nor a violation of human dignity for the state to encourage or influence people to tell the truth, even when that truth is self-incriminating and might help produce the speaker's conviction. With only slight modification, what the Supreme Court recently said with regard to the Fifth Amendment's application in grand jury proceedings fairly summarizes the proper response to the cruelty or human dignity argument against police interrogation:

The [concept of human dignity] does not prohibit every element which influences a criminal suspect to make incriminating admissions. Of course, for many witnesses the grand jury room engenders an atmosphere conducive to truthtelling, for it is likely that upon being brought before such a body of neighbors and fellow citizens, and having been placed under a solemn oath to tell the truth, many witnesses will feel obliged to do just that. But it does not offend the [concept of human dignity] if in that setting a witness is more likely to tell the truth than in less solemn surroundings.[98]

The Accusatorial System Argument

In the previous chapter, the claim that our criminal justice system is adversarial or accusatorial rather than inquisitorial was sidestepped with the observation that, whatever these ambiguous terms may mean, the tendency of a legal system to lean toward one characterization or the other depends on society's underlying political ideology. Nevertheless, the claim that ours is an adversarial or accusatorial system, almost always made approvingly, plays too large a role in the debate about police interrogation to permit this response to suffice. The objective here is to show that this claim, though frequently and passionately made, does not support those who would limit the effectiveness of police interrogation.

In numerous cases, especially when it has sought to justify the invalidation of a government practice on Fifth Amendment grounds, the United States Supreme Court has solemnly intoned that "ours is the accusatorial as opposed to the inquisitorial system."[99] Rooting itself in history, the Court has insisted that Anglo-American procedure has been accusatorial since the English eliminated the Star Chamber and with it the inquisitorial practices that had been borrowed from the Continent. Even when rejecting an individual's Fifth Amendment challenge, the Court has often felt constrained to defend its holdings as consistent with the accusatorial nature of our system.[100] Just as often, dissenting opinions have claimed that decisions rejecting constitutional challenges have condoned the inquisitorial procedures that our accusatorial system was designed to avoid.[101]

Justice Stevens's dissent in *Moran v. Burbine*[102] illustrates particularly well how the claim that ours is an accusatorial rather than an inquisitorial system can be put to rhetorical use. Finding violations of neither the Sixth Amendment right to counsel nor the Fifth Amendment protection against compulsory self-incrimination, the majority condoned the use of a confession by a custodial suspect who waived his *Miranda* rights without being informed that a lawyer retained by his sister had telephoned the police station. Justice Stevens began his dissent by attacking the majority's opinion as a "startling departure from [the] basic insight" that "'ours is an accusatorial and not an inquisitorial system,'" and he concluded it by similarly asserting that the Court had "flouted the spirit of our accusatorial system."[103]

Between start and finish, Stevens elaborated this theme. While he conceded that requiring the police to inform a suspect of a lawyer's call would decrease the likelihood of obtaining confessions, he described this cost as "necessary to preserve the character of our free society and our rejection of an inquisitorial system."[104] Accusing the majority of fearing that suspects will exercise their rights, Stevens derided this concern as invalid in an accusatorial as opposed to an inquisitorial system.[105] He also insisted that lawyers, though viewed as "nettlesome obstacle[s]" to the discovery of truth in an inquisitorial system, were regarded as protectors of rights in an accusatorial system.[106] Finally, Justice Stevens castigated the majority for failing "to appreciate the value of the liberty that an accusatorial system seeks to protect."[107]

Much like the wartime reassurance that "God is on our side," the Stevens dissent kindles allegiance by contrasting good (us) and evil (them): our accusatorial system cherishes freedom, liberty, and individual rights; their inquisitorial system sacrifices these values in its headlong pursuit of truth. Though this contrast lacks factual support, many will find it persuasive, for the term *inquisitorial* readily conjures up images of the Star Chamber, the Spanish Inquisition, and the *ancien régime*, institutions associated with torture and browbeating.[108] Moreover, many also will regard Justice Stevens's claim that the practices at issue in *Burbine* were inquisitorial as undiminished by his failure to articulate, except in the abstract way discussed below, just what distinguishes an accusatorial from an inquisitorial system. For those prepared to accept both the major premise that inquisitorial practices necessarily are bad and the minor premise that the interrogation conduct at issue was inquisitorial, Justice Stevens's condemnation of the police conduct in *Burbine* is validated by the rules of rudimentary logic.

In reality, of course, Justice Stevens's condemnation of the police conduct in *Burbine* is no stronger than his unsupported premises. Because the claim that our system is accusatorial "is not so much analytically precise as it is hortatory and rhetorical, aimed at mobilizing consent and at winning points in legal argumentation,"[109] it would seem "more suitable," as Justice Walter Schaefer argued years ago, "for Law Day speeches than for analytical judicial opinions."[110] Thus, if our system is not accusatorial in all its various aspects, Stevens's argument collapses with the loss of its major premise. Moreover, unless one can identify the essential attributes and institutional arrangements of the competing systems, the analysis of concrete issues cannot be facilitated by positing that a given system or a particular practice is accusatorial rather than inquisitorial.[111] Thus, even with regard to its minor premise, the Stevens dissent does little more than illustrate that whether a particular police practice "is characterized as 'inquisitorial' seems to depend on whether the writer disapproves of the practice and desires to argue his position with emotive language."[112]

The possibility remains, of course, that an accusatorial system argument can be made that remedies the deficiencies in Justice Stevens's *Burbine* dissent. Initially, however, one must identify precisely what is being contrasted. Often, and probably inaccurately, the terms *adversarial* and *accusatorial* are used interchangeably to describe the opposite of *inquisitorial*.[113] Responding to an earlier published defense of police interrogation that failed to distinguish these terms, Professor Peter Arenella insisted that "[o]ne may concede . . . that it is inappropriate to apply *adversarial* procedures to police practices without accepting . . . that *accusatorial* norms do not apply to the investigatory process."[114] In Arenella's view, "accusatorial procedure encompasses not only an adversarial trial procedure but other fundamental norms . . . that regulate the balance of advantage between the state and the accused throughout the criminal process."[115] Thus, while the adversarial process may best be described as a contest that "unfolds as an engagement of two adversaries before a relatively passive decision maker,"[116] the accusatorial system may entail much more, such as the bedrock presumption of innocence.[117] Presumably, Arenella believes that the inquisitorial system not only proceeds without such an adversary contest but also fails to advance at least some of these basic norms.

Conceding to Professor Arenella that *accusatorial* is a more encompassing term than *adversarial*, one must still conclude that the purported dichotomy between the accusatorial system and its inquisitorial counterpart at best represents "the distance between the old continental inquisitorial procedure at its historic worst, and a variable selection of somewhat idealized features of modern American criminal proceedings."[118] Stated differently, perhaps beyond some core meaning for each concept, clear criteria do not exist to classify procedural attributes as belonging to one or the other system.[119] One commentator has even suggested that the only two essential attributes of inquisitorial procedure are the "officialization of all the important phases" of the criminal process and the duty of official bodies "to investigate judicially . . . and to establish the substantive facts and the objective truth."[120] In any event, American procedure, as we will see, has many "inquisitorial" attributes, while modern "inquisitorial" procedures on the Continent, which vary from one country to another, include many "accusatorial" ideas. [121]

To say that we lack criteria to define the competing systems is not to deny that many have tried, at least in terms of broad outlines. For example, while Justice Stevens in his *Burbine* dissent did not define the distinguishing characteristics of each system, he did in a footnote quote from a 1949 Supreme Court opinion that had sketched the general characteristics of the accusatorial system:

> Under our system society carries the burden of proving its charge against the accused not out of his own mouth. It must establish its case, not by interrogation of the accused even under judicial safeguards, but by evidence independently secured through skillful investigation. . . . The requirement of specific charges, their proof beyond a reasonable doubt, the protection of the accused from confessions extorted through whatever form of police pressures, the right to a prompt hearing before a magistrate, the right to assistance of counsel, to be supplied by government when circumstances make it necessary, the duty to advise an accused of his constitutional rights—these are all characteristics of the accusatorial system and manifestations of its demands. [122]

Unfortunately for those seeking to rely on the accusatorial system argument, this passage neither helps in distinguishing accusatorial from inquisitorial systems nor provides the necessary particulars to resolve concrete issues.

With regard to the description's failure meaningfully to differentiate the competing systems, many of the so-called characteristics or manifestations of our accusatorial system could be used just as accurately to describe inquisitorial systems. Continental systems also require specific charges, [123] and they adhere to the axiom that the defendant "should be accorded the benefit of factual doubt."[124] To this extent, at least, both systems recognize a presumption of innocence. [125] Indeed, "[t]hat continental criminal law has discarded guilt-presumptive devices while common law courts frequently operate with them is by now a cliche of comparative law."[126] In addition, the claim that a right to appointed counsel in serious cases is a characteristic of the accusatorial system is historically inaccurate given that such a right was a late arrival both in England and in this country. [127] In any event, continental systems also recognize a right to appointed counsel, and in some jurisdictions, though not all, this right applies even to preliminary interrogations of the accused. [128] Continental systems, like virtually all modern systems, prohibit coerced confessions,[129] and at least two commentators have suggested that confessions obtained by the police play a larger role in American than in continental cases.[130] Moreover, although virtually all continental systems permit judicial examination of the accused, most of them also now recognize, in contrast to their medieval predecessors, that the accused cannot be required to answer questions.[131]

Even if one assumes that the passage quoted by Justice Stevens somehow captures the distinctive flavor of the accusatorial system, it cannot help in resolving concrete issues. While the passage makes reference to the right to counsel and to the duty to advise individuals of their constitutional rights, it neither defines when the right to counsel attaches nor particularizes what constitutional rights individuals have, other than the right not to be forced to answer questions. This is significant, especially when one recalls that the passage was written in 1949, when the Supreme Court neither recognized a right to counsel during police interrogation nor required the police to give the suspect warnings of any kind. What the Supreme Court found subversive of the accusatorial system in the particular case was the "protracted, systematic, and uncontrolled subjection" of the defendant to police questioning for more than a week,[132] something that modern inquisitorial systems also would condemn.

In 1958, nine years after the quoted passage was written, the Supreme Court upheld the use of a confession even though the police denied the defendant access to a lawyer who, unlike the lawyer in *Burbine,* actually came to the police station demanding to see his client.[133] As late as 1961, Justice Frankfurter, the author of the passage that Justice Stevens quoted, accurately observed that the Supreme Court's cases provided no litmus test for impermissible interrogation: neither extensive cross-questioning, failure to provide warnings, nor denial of consultation with friends or counsel sufficed to render a confession inadmissible. The decisive question, said Frankfurter, was whether the suspect's will had been overborne.[134] Given this background, it should be apparent that Justice Stevens's dissenting position in *Burbine* was not dictated by the Court's, or by anyone else's, historical understanding of the essential attributes of the accusatorial system.

Because of the thesis, defended above, that precise definitions are lacking, it may seem incongruous to describe here "inquisitorial" features of American criminal procedure. Nevertheless, if the term *inquisitorial* includes not only judicial interrogation of the accused but other investigative procedures designed to obtain information from perhaps unwilling suspects, then numerous aspects of American procedure can be seen as having inquisitorial characteristics. Without doubt, the investigative grand jury stands out as an inquisitorial institution, one described by the Supreme Court as a "grand inquest . . . with powers of investigation and inquisition."[135] Searches and seizures, the use of informants, and electronic surveillance are more inquisitorial than accusatorial, the latter two procedures especially in view of their function to obtain information the suspect would not knowingly communicate to the government.[136]

Similarly inquisitorial is the modern common-law requirement that an accused who chooses to testify must do so under oath, a requirement that some continentals, who lack a legal basis to prosecute the defendant for perjury, have described as unfair and inhumane.[137] More significantly, both plea bargaining and the American reliance on the guilty plea, which requires the defendant to admit guilt in open court and to respond to judicial questioning intended to establish a factual basis for the plea, can be described as inquisitorial. Expressing just this view, one commentator, who elsewhere has observed that "our accusatorial rhetoric has been one thing and our inquisitorial practices another,"[138] has even suggested that our system, through its reliance on guilty pleas, "has become more dependent on proving guilt from the defendant's own mouth than any European 'inquisitorial' system."[139]

Miranda has become so familiar that we sometimes forget that its warning requirement in the custodial context is an exception to the general rule that individuals must take the initiative in asserting the Fifth Amendment if they do not want to incriminate themselves. Until an individual makes such an assertion, the government may simply interrogate.[140] Even Justice Marshall, a staunch supporter of broad Fifth Amendment interpretations, has observed that requiring warnings whenever the government makes inquiries would conflict with "the fact that, in general, governments have the right to everyone's testimony."[141] Thus, unless compulsion is used, the state may generally prove its case in our "accusatorial" system, just as it may on the Continent, with evidence out of an individual's own mouth.

The above examples should discredit the frequently expressed notion that in an accusatorial system, the government "must shoulder the entire load" in proving the defendant's guilt.[142] These examples, however, tell only part of the story. American law actually permits the state to compel individuals to produce evidence against themselves. Having taken the position that the Fifth Amendment prohibits only compelled disclosure of evidence that is testimonial in nature, the Supreme Court has permitted the government to require the defendant not only to participate passively in a lineup but to utter the words used by the offender; to provide blood, fingerprint, handwriting, and voice samples; to provide pretrial disclosure of certain defenses and witnesses; and to respond to certain subpoenas for documentary evidence.[143] More recently, the Court upheld, with only Justice Stevens dissenting, a court order requiring a target of a grand jury investigation to sign consent directives authorizing foreign banks to disclose any accounts over which he had a right of withdrawal.[144] Relying on its past cases, the Court rejected the argument that "compelling a suspect to make a nonfactual statement that facilitates the production of evidence by someone else" is not permitted.[145]

One may object that the above paragraph proves little given the Court's interpretation of the Fifth Amendment as protecting only testimonial evidence. On the contrary, the paragraph appropriately raises the question why a truly accusatorial system would protect only testimonial evidence from compulsory disclosure. Moreover, the paragraph illustrates just how circular and question-begging the accusatorial system argument is. Typically, as in Justice Stevens's *Burbine* dissent, expansive interpretations of the Fifth and Sixth Amendments are justified by the claim that ours is an accusatorial not an inquisitorial system. When inquisitorial elements are identified in our system, however, the temptation is to respond that these elements are not really inquisitorial because the Constitution permits them. The obvious circularity comes from attempting both to define the Constitution by reference to our accusatorial system and to define our accusatorial system by reference to the Constitution. Accordingly, the question of the Constitution's meaning cannot be settled by invoking the policy claim that ours is an accusatorial system, for "[l]anguage like this, no matter how often repeated, no matter how eloquently intoned, is merely restatement of the privilege itself; it provides no illumination how the privilege works."[146]

Nor can one further analysis by stating, as Professor Arenella once did, that "[t]he fact that the government need not shoulder the *entire* load does not negate its accusatorial obligation to carry most of it."[147] The issue is the meaning and content of "most," and our ill-defined notion of what it means to have an accusatorial as opposed to an inquisitorial system cannot answer this. Try as one might to adjust the argument, there simply is no way to refute Professor Greenawalt's observation that the accusatorial system argument, like the state-individual equality argument, represents either some other argument in disguise or the substitution of "conclusory rhetoric for analysis."[148]

Miscellaneous Arguments

Some commentators have asserted that the Fifth Amendment's protection against compulsory self-incrimination protects privacy interests,[149] and by extension it might be argued that the interest in preserving privacy warrants the curtailment of police interrogation. Of course, the Fifth Amendment is *not* intended to protect privacy, for once immunity is given, the individual can be forced to disclose private information.[150] Moreover, both the Fifth Amendment and the limits placed on police interrogation restrict the government's ability to obtain information from the defendant's own mouth but not from other sources,[151] and a broader privacy protection is impossible in a system committed to the successful prosecution of criminals.

Because the concern thus seems to be that the individual not become the source of incriminating information that is otherwise desirable to obtain, the privacy argument is difficult to distinguish from the cruelty or human dignity argument previously considered. Moreover, police interrogation of suspects would seem no more intrusive on privacy interests than searches and seizures, which are permissible on reasonable cause.[152] Accordingly, those inclined to embrace the privacy argument must explain why privacy should take on absolute dimensions only in the context of police interrogation. Or, to use Judge Henry Friendly's words, they must reconcile "an uncompromising rigidity concerning what can be taken from a man's mouth in the form of speech with [the] commonsensible view concerning what can be taken from it in the form of saliva."[153]

Another possible argument is that severe restrictions on police interrogation are desirable to limit the potential for police abuse. Typically, however, only extraordinary situations justify throwing the baby out with the bath. Although identification procedures are fraught with peril, our society has appropriately chosen to address the risks and abuses without either banning the procedures themselves or rendering them ineffectual. Similarly, despite the danger of abuse, our society has not prohibited searches and seizures but has required only that they be "reasonable." The same commonsense approach should be taken with respect to police interrogation. We have the legal tools to address the possible abuses,[154] and we have the imagination and ability to acquire new tools if the present ones are thought inadequate.

Professors Yale and Irene Rosenberg have argued, however, that one must be naive or disingenuous regarding what occurs in the police station to maintain either that police persuasion of a suspect to cooperate is not coercive or that a voluntariness test can monitor police overreaching. "The recent videotape of several white Los Angeles police officers *publicly* beating and kicking a prone black motorist . . . makes it clear that restraints on the police in the *privacy* of the stationhouse cannot be in the form of a fluid, ad hoc totality of the circumstances standard."[155]

In their view, "[t]he only way to prevent coercion absolutely is to make the confession valueless from an evidentiary standpoint."[156]

Of course, that police sometimes seriously misbehave lends no support to the view that police efforts at persuasion must be viewed as coercive. Moreover, no rule regarding confessions would have prevented the violence in the Los Angeles incident, which did not involve police interrogation; even in the police station, the *Miranda* rule is no more effective than the voluntariness rule in deterring officers who are determined to beat the defendant, and a rule banning confessions altogether would not deter officers inclined to beat the defendant for personal satisfaction or for useful information regardless of its admissibility in court. The "only way to prevent coercion absolutely" is not to end the use of confessions but to end law enforcement. For society to authorize the police to engage in arrests, stops, and searches; to carry nightsticks and guns; to employ informants and wiretaps; and to question witnesses and suspects is virtually to assure that some abuses will occur, for zero risk or absolute protection against abuse in these areas can be obtained only by eliminating the procedures altogether. This is a cost that no viable society can afford.

The above should also provide an adequate response to Professor Stephen Schulhofer's effort to defend the "privilege" by positing a "link between a constitutionally protected right to silence and prevention of abusive interrogation."[157] The potential for abuse cannot be eliminated by recognizing a right of silence, because many, perhaps most, interrogations involve efforts by the police to persuade suspects who are falsely denying responsibility to tell the truth.[158] The risk of abuse can be eliminated only by prohibiting police interrogation. This is a cost Professor Schulhofer, like the Rosenbergs, might be willing to bear,[159] but given that it has rejected similar costs in contexts where the potential for abuse is equally as great, such as lineups and searches and seizures, society is not likely to agree.

Another possible argument, similar in structure to the last, is that severe restrictions on police interrogation are desirable to protect the innocent. As the previous argument was premised on the risk of police abuse, this argument is premised on the risk that a suspect may give a false confession either deliberately—for example, to shield the real offender—or because of an infirm mind.[160] Like the previous argument, this argument reflects a willingness to sacrifice many reliable confessions to prevent some unreliable ones.

Were the risk of unreliable confessions substantial, the argument might have more force. As Dean Charles McCormick observed years ago, however, instances of "abnormal self-accusation . . . are much more often encountered by the doctors than by the police; and . . . when they do come before the police, they are usually, though not always, recognizable as abnormal by experienced officers."[161] No empirical evidence exists to cast doubt on this observation. As discussed in the previous chapter, however, we do have evidence documenting the risks of unreliability that attend eyewitness identification testimony. Nevertheless, as already noted, we permit witnesses to identify the defendant in court, and we permit the police to add to the risk by employing identification procedures, even suggestive ones in emergency situations. Professor Robinson stated it well when he observed that "[i]f unreliability of confessions requires their exclusion, a fortiori, it would appear that eyewitness testimony should also be excluded."[162]

Speaking of the Fifth Amendment, Dean Robert McKay, a friend of the privilege, acknowledged that "there is little doubt that the truth-finding function would be more often served than misled by required (but not coerced) testimony."[163] The same holds true with respect to police interrogation. Still, because police interrogation is bound to produce some untruthful confessions, some critics may insist that society's special concern for preventing false convictions—a concern that leads to the tolerance of false acquittals—supports a hostile attitude toward confessions. This argument would be persuasive only if we truly believed that we should bear any cost in the goal of protecting the innocent. As we saw in the previous chapter, however, a rational system must place some limit on the number of false acquittals that it will tolerate for the sake of protecting the innocent. Absent evidence that the risk of unreliability is substantially greater than what is commonly assumed, draconian measures that would eliminate or sharply reduce the number of reliable confessions produced by police interrogation cannot be defended.

But what of the argument that forcing those who are innocent "to run the gauntlet of adversarial cross-examination can fairly be characterized as inhumane or cruel"?[164] Unlike the cruelty argument previously considered, this argument sees cruelty not in seeking to persuade a guilty person to admit guilt but rather in subjecting an innocent person to practices that might persuade a guilty person to confess. As Professor Schulhofer has stated, "[i]t is easy to imagine why an innocent person might fear the consequences of such a process and regard silence as a preferable course."[165] This argument might have merit if cruelty were judged exclusively from the perspective of the individual. It is not. *Ex ante,* the police cannot be certain about guilt or innocence. The real issue, therefore, is whether it is cruel or inhumane to allow the police to interrogate defendants, some of whom may be innocent, when probable cause of their wrongdoing exists and the police are acting in good faith. This is the same question, of course, that the previous analysis of the cruelty argument answered.

Summary

In *Miranda,* the Supreme Court spoke of the Fifth Amendment protection against compulsory self-incrimination as reflecting the individual's right "to a private enclave where he may lead a private life." The Court referred to this protection as the "essential mainstay of our adversary system." It also invoked a complex of values underlying the Fifth Amendment, such as the respect a government must accord to the dignity of its citizens and the inviolability of the human personality, the need to maintain a fair state-individual balance, and the belief that the government should shoulder the entire load.[166]

Without addressing the Fifth Amendment's proper interpretation as such, this chapter has considered and rejected each of these points as possible justifications for legal hostility to the institution of police interrogation. The privacy argument required little time, for privacy simply cannot be the underlying concern in this area. The adversary (or, more strongly, accusatorial) system argument is too devoid of content to provide an answer, other than a question-begging one, with respect to how one should regard the institution of police interrogation. The related notion that the government must bear the entire load is simply incorrect as an unqualified proposition. The fair state-individual balance argument—one of the equality arguments—is misdirected when applied to the investigative process and antithetical to the goals, as outlined in the previous chapter, that a rational system of criminal justice must pursue. The human dignity (or cruelty) argument, on the other hand, does have merit, but not when applied to prevent the encouragement of suspects to respond truthfully to police questioning. On the contrary, attempting to persuade or influence suspected offenders to cooperate may comport with respecting them as responsible human beings. To the extent, therefore, that *Miranda* relied on the policies stated above as justification for the unprecedented restrictions it imposed on police interrogation, it failed—and terribly so—to make its case.

Having listed what it perceived to be the controlling policies, the Court in *Miranda* said that our system will not permit the government to resort to the expedient of compelling individuals to speak against themselves. Without a doubt, the human dignity argument makes certain interrogation tactics unacceptable in a decent society. The debate over the institution of police interrogation should be waged in terms of identifying these tactics—of identifying, among other things, what constitutes *compulsion*. The analysis in this chapter has attempted to show that those who engage in this debate should not premise their arguments on a presumptive bias against successful police interrogation.

CHAPTER 3

The Voluntariness Concept in the Law of Confessions

During the eighteenth century, English courts developed the rule that an accused's out-of-court statements, made in response to official questioning, had to be voluntary to be admissible in evidence against him.[1] The United States Supreme Court accepted this common-law evidentiary requirement late in the nineteenth century in *Hopt v. Utah*,[2] its first case dealing with the admissibility of a confession. While the English cases, however, focused almost exclusively on whether the defendant had confessed under circumstances that made the confession's trustworthiness suspect,[3] the Supreme Court from the very beginning injected notions of free and overborne wills into voluntariness analysis. Thus, *Hopt* indicated that a confession was inadmissible when made in response to threats, promises, or inducements that deprived the defendant "of that freedom of will or self-control essential to make his confession voluntary within the meaning of the law."[4]

Even after the Supreme Court constitutionalized the requirement of voluntariness—in federal cases relying on the Fifth Amendment self-incrimination clause[5] and in state cases relying on the Fourteenth Amendment due process clause[6]—it continued to define voluntariness in terms of the accused's freedom of the will.[7] It was no secret, of course, that considerations relating to the risk of unreliability and to the acceptability of the police interrogation practices influenced the Court in deciding whether a particular confession was voluntary or involuntary.[8] Nevertheless, overborne will rhetoric defined the Court's black-letter pronouncements. In 1961, in an exhaustive exegesis on voluntariness, Justice Frankfurter succinctly and accurately summarized the relationship the Court had established between the concepts of voluntariness and overborne wills:

> The ultimate test remains that which has been the only clearly established test in Anglo-American courts for two hundred years: the test of voluntariness. Is the confession the product of an essentially free and unconstrained choice by its maker? If it is, if he has

willed to confess, it may be used against him. If it is not, if his will has been overborne and his capacity for self-determination critically impaired, the use of his confession offends due process.[9]

Though accurate as a summary of the Supreme Court's numerous black-letter elaborations of the voluntariness requirement, Justice Frankfurter's statement did little to further analysis in concrete cases.[10] The reason is that ambiguity inheres in such terms as "product," "essentially free and unconstrained choice," "overborne will," and "critically impaired capacity for self-determination." Moreover, it should be apparent that some of these terms may have different meanings. For example, it would seem that a person's capacity for self-determination may be "critically impaired" without the person's will being "overborne." Similarly, a confession that results from a "constrained" choice may not be equivalent to one that results from an "overborne will." If differences in fact exist, we need to know which terms and meanings really define the law of confessions; if, on the other hand, the various terms are intended to be synonymous, we need to ascertain their common meaning.

This chapter attempts to address these questions by dissecting the voluntariness and involuntariness concepts as they are used in the law in general and in the confessions context in particular. At the outset, it should be recognized that these concepts have been used to address issues of both volitional and cognitive impairment. In its volitional aspect, to which the overborne will rhetoric seems most relevant, voluntariness stresses control of the will.[11] For example, if, as in *Brown v. Mississippi*,[12] the police hang a suspect to a tree and beat him repeatedly until he confesses, common language usage permits us to describe the suspect's decision to confess as involuntary; in such a case, we are apt to say that the suspect's decision resulted from police coercion rather than from his own free will. The defense of duress in the substantive criminal law reflects a similar concern with volitional freedom.[13] Sometimes, however, the concepts of voluntariness and involuntariness are used both in ordinary discourse and in the law to address the question of cognitive impairment. Thus, we may sometimes say that *B* acted involuntarily if *B* was unaware of certain facts that would have prompted him to act otherwise or if *B* did not fully appreciate what he actually was doing.[14]

The thesis of this chapter is that the issue of voluntariness, in all its component parts, requires normative rather than empirical judgments. The chapter discusses, in turn, the inutility of the notion of overborne wills, the inherently normative nature of inquiries into volitional impairment, the threat-offer distinction that has received considerable attention in the philosophical literature, the issue of causation, and, finally, the cognitive aspect of the voluntariness concept and its relationship to considerations of unfair influence or improper exploitation.

Volitional Impairment and Overborne Wills

The effort to distinguish voluntary from involuntary actions dates back at least to Aristotle. Claiming that a student of virtue must distinguish between voluntary and involuntary actions, Aristotle defined a voluntary action as one in which the initiative *at the time of the action* comes from the agent and an involuntary action as one in which this initiative comes from outside the agent.[15] More particularly, Aristotle described an involuntary act as one in which "the agent or the person acted upon contributes nothing."[16] To elucidate his definition of involuntary action, Aristotle provided the example of a person, presumably in a boat, taken by the wind in an undesired direction, and he contrasted this example with that of a person jettisoning a boat's cargo during a storm to save the lives of passengers. The latter person, Aristotle claimed, acts voluntarily "because the initiative in moving the parts of the body which act as instruments rests with the agent himself."[17] Similarly, a person acts voluntarily by acceding to a terrorist's command to commit a crime or face the death of family members, for such a command requires the person to choose between competing alternatives.[18]

Although our linguistic usages of the involuntariness concept ordinarily are not so narrow, Aristotle's definitions are comprehensible and, depending on the analytic context, even of some utility.[19] Nevertheless, for purposes of assessing blame and praise, we would find our standards of moral accountability intolerably severe were voluntariness under Aristotle's definitions the only relevant consideration. Aristotle recognized that the problem of moral accountability cannot be resolved by definition, for he went on to claim that a person who responds to a severe strain or threat of harm, such as the terrorist's unhappy agent in the above example, should often be excused for a base deed. Still, much as duress is not available as a defense to murder in many jurisdictions today,[20] Aristotle also expressed the view that some acts, such as matricide, should never be excused. Aristotle insisted that the person should accept the most terrible suffering and even death rather than commit such acts.[21]

Were we to take it literally, the overborne will language would seem to correspond with Aristotle's definition of involuntary action. Indeed, some modern commentators seem on occasion to equate these concepts.

In the course of discussing moral responsibility, for example, Professor Harry Frankfurt has argued that a threat can coerce an individual only when it "appeals to desires or motives which are beyond the victim's ability to control, or when the victim is convinced that this is the case." To be coercive, Frankfurt has said, a threat must arouse a desire "so powerful that it will move [the victim] to perform the required action regardless of whether he wants to perform it or considers that it would be reasonable for him to do so."[22] Similarly, Professor Michael Philips, after praising the Supreme Court for articulating in *Haynes v. Washington*[23] "the plausible view that a defendant confesses involuntarily if his will is overborne"—meaning to Philips that he "is incapable of making a rational choice" or "of acting on such a choice"—went on to criticize the Court for finding the confession at issue involuntary merely because the police subjected the defendant to some form of compulsion.[24] "Most of us," Philips insisted, "are stronger than this."[25]

As Aristotle recognized, but as we too often overlook today, arguments at this definitional level have only limited utility in moral philosophy and law. That they have some utility, however, cannot be denied. Because it would be morally indefensible to assess blame and punishment when an actor is literally as helpless as Aristotle's wind-carried person, it is important to appreciate that a person acting under duress, unlike the person in the boat, almost always, if not always, "voluntarily" makes a choice in yielding to the coercer's threat. The refusal of many jurisdictions to permit duress to excuse murder is defensible only with this understanding. That definitional strategies have only limited utility, however, is apparent both in Aristotle's treatment of excused conduct and in the continuing debate over whether duress should be permitted as a defense to murder. Aristotle's definition of voluntary action permits us to punish the actor, but it cannot preclude moral and legal arguments that the law nevertheless should be more accepting of human weakness.[26] The issue whether to excuse thus requires a moral or normative judgment; it cannot be resolved by positing definitions of voluntariness.[27]

This is true in all areas of the law in which the voluntariness concept is important to individual responsibility or accountability, whether it be criminal law, contracts, wills, torts, plea bargaining, or, of course, confessions. While the courts in each of these areas continue to engender confusion by employing the rhetoric of overborne wills, in each they relieve actors of responsibility for agreements or conduct even though the actors clearly had the ability to resist the pressures to which they responded.[28] In the substantive criminal law, as Professor Herbert Fingarette has demonstrated, the language of overborne wills leads down a "blind alley" if we take its legal significance "as arising out of some subjective condition of inner psychic trauma or breakdown."[29] Similarly, as Professor Alan Wertheimer has observed, "despite frequent *references* to 'overborne wills,' that notion *seems* to do relatively little work" in contracts cases dealing with the doctrine of duress.[30] Even Justice Frankfurter, who employed the language of overborne wills to describe the Supreme Court's black-letter law of confessions, correctly observed that a civilized society cannot regard a confession as "voluntary" simply because it results from a "sentient choice."[31] In each of these legal areas, then, "[t]o say a person has been 'coerced' into doing something presupposes an act of will on his part";[32] it does not and cannot mean that the person's will has been overborne in any literal sense.[33]

What has been said should dispose of the notion that voluntariness inquiries are or can be empirical in nature.[34] Such an empirical inquiry would be possible only under two definitional approaches, both of which, though linguistically acceptable, would not be appropriate for achieving the goals of the law. Professors Bator and Vorenberg stated the point well with regard to confessions:

> Except where a person is unconscious or drugged or otherwise lacks capacity for conscious choice, all incriminating statements—even those made under brutal treatment—are "voluntary" in the sense of representing a choice of alternatives. On the other hand, if "voluntariness" incorporates notions of "but-for" cause, the question should be whether the statement would have been made even absent inquiry or other official action. Under such a test, virtually no statement would be voluntary because very few people give incriminating statements in the absence of official action of some kind.[35]

Even were it possible in some moral or legal contexts to take literally the notion of an overborne will,[36] we do not have the tools to make such an empirical inquiry. Like the rest of us, "the courts have found no rational formula, no criteria or paradigmatic patterns of evidence that unambiguously lead to a reasoned conclusion on the question."[37] In *Brown,* for example, no one can know whether the hangings and whipping constituted truly irresistible pressures or barely resistible pressures that the defendant chose not to resist any longer.[38] What we can know, however, is that the law will (should) not accept a confession procured by such means.

This analysis suggests that it probably would be best for the courts to drop the overborne will language not only in the law of confessions but in other legal contexts as well. Given the absence of an analytic construct of the will as an entity that can be coerced, the term arguably adds nothing, other than confusion, to our efforts to solve concrete problems. On the other hand, as Professor George Fletcher has argued with regard to the law of duress, it may be that the "metaphoric language" of the will being overborne "is one effective way to state the true ground" of the law's concern.[39] Such language, at the least, is "rhetorically rich," even if it is totally devoid of objective meaning.[40] Still, as Professor Peter Westen has said of the term *coercion,* the concept is as "rhetorically treacherous" as it is rhetorically useful.[41] If no one were misled into thinking that a psychological or empirical inquiry could displace the need for normative evaluation, such language might be useful. Unfortunately, in the law of confessions, like in other legal contexts, experience has shown that the rhetorical force of the overborne will language too frequently comes "not by facilitating argument, but by bypassing it."[42]

The Normative Inquiry into Volitional Impairment

As discussed, the overborne will approach to voluntariness, if taken literally, would prevent the law of confessions from condemning coercive police practices that impair volitional freedom without destroying the individual's will. The polar opposite approach, which regards a confession as involuntary whenever the police increase, however slightly, the defendant's psychic strain, would require the law to condemn the institution of police interrogation as such.[43] For the reasons discussed in the following chapters, our law has never been willing to go this far, and it is unlikely to do so in the future. With these extreme positions eliminated, the only remaining possibility is that the voluntariness doctrine in the law of confessions, at least to the extent that it addresses volitional freedom, must be concerned with the kind and degree of volitional impairment that should relieve defendants from being held accountable for their statements. That is, the relevant inquiry, in Justice Harlan's words, must be *"how much* pressure on the suspect [will be] permissible,"[44] or, from the other direction, how much will be "undue."[45] Whether pressure is too much or undue obviously requires a normative judgment.

Part of the difficulty with such a normative inquiry is that each individual can be expected to approach the issue with a somewhat different bent of severity or leniency.[46] Professor George Dix has suggested that the choice of what police tactics to permit "must be made intuitively and depends almost entirely upon the view that is taken of the importance of the individual's dignity."[47] In his view, this issue "is not . . . susceptible to logical debate or empirical inquiry."[48] Even were this true—and one might recall the human dignity argument considered in the last chapter—the constitutional inquiry regarding voluntariness, as the next chapter will develop, may be less indeterminate or relativistic than the inquiry made solely from a normative perspective. Nevertheless, even from a purely normative perspective, an examination of the nature of a voluntariness claim should bring into sharper focus the precise points of normative disagreement.

At the outset, the utility of examining the nature of a voluntariness claim may be questioned. If the issue is normative rather than empirical, analysis should arguably concentrate exclusively on underlying norms and policies without concern about the nature of the voluntariness concept as such. Indeed, most commentators would insist that the Supreme Court's persistent failure to articulate such underlying norms and policies accounted for the voluntariness doctrine's long-criticized vagueness and uncertainty in the law of confessions.[49] Moreover, many commentators attributed the Court's failure to articulate policy to the voluntariness concept itself, a concept variously described as "elusive,"[50] "useless,"[51] "troublesome," a phrase whose "era is past,"[52] and, perhaps more kindly, "a colorful method of expressing ultimate conclusions . . . a bit of harmless legal 'double-talk.'"[53] As others have done regarding overborne will terminology, many commentators have urged the courts to cease using the voluntariness concept and to state their "real reasons" for excluding particular confessions.[54]

In the view of most commentators, courts have had two real reasons for excluding confessions as involuntary: (1) a desire, surviving from the common-law approach, to eliminate untrustworthy confessions and (2) a desire to control offensive police practices. Emphasizing the second of these reasons, Professor Yale Kamisar summarized the argument against voluntariness terminology with two rhetorical questions:

> Is "involuntariness" or "coercion" or "breaking the will" (or its synonyms) little more than a fiction intended to vilify certain "effective" interrogation methods? Is "voluntariness" or "mental freedom" or "self-determination" (or its equivalents) little more than a fiction designed to beautify certain other interrogation techniques?[55]

One cannot examine the Supreme Court's numerous cases concerning the admissibility of confessions and not conclude that Professor Kamisar's observations have substantial merit. Moreover, a similarly valid observation could be made in virtually every area of the law in which the voluntariness concept is important. As Professor Wertheimer has shown, all successful legal claims of coercion involve, as one necessary element, a judicial conclusion that the coercer engaged in "wrongful" behavior.[56] To this extent, a court that decides a voluntariness issue necessarily makes a judgment about the propriety of the behavior that induced the actor's conduct. Still, as Professor Wertheimer has observed, directly responding to Professor Kamisar, "the voluntariness principle captures important underlying values which the 'reliability' and 'proper technique' tests do not."[57] Making much the same point, Professor Fingarette has observed that "there is in law no tight or necessary connection between the word 'unfairness' and involuntariness."[58]

This suggests that the voluntariness concept, though requiring a normative judgment about the alleged coercer's conduct, expresses an important, even if not a completely independent, moral concern about the impairment of volitional freedom, a concern that might lose its intellectual force were voluntariness terminology to be abandoned and "fairness," as such, to become analytically dominant. Unlike the notion of overborne wills, which may cause more harm than good, voluntariness and coercion terminology need not be a mask for the real reasons that prompt courts to admit or suppress confessions. On the contrary, the elimination of this terminology could very likely cause "the problems which haunt its specification [to] reappear under another heading."[59]

To say that voluntariness terminology is useful is not to suggest that one should revert to the previously criticized viewpoint that this terminology standing alone can do all the necessary work. From a linguistic standpoint, there are many appropriate usages of terms such as *involuntary* and *coercion*.[60] For example, a court may deem a confession involuntary that the police obtained after making threats, but the suspect's codefendants, implicated by the confession, just as appropriately may reject, at least in terms of language usage, the claim of coercion and hold the suspect accountable for the choice to confess.[61] In other cases, perhaps in the interest of urging certain reforms, critics may find it appropriate to use the term *coercion* to describe what occurred in the police station even though the law, with a different purpose, just as appropriately may find the defendant's confession to be voluntary and admissible in evidence.

These seemingly conflicting usages of these terms are perfectly understandable, for the task of courts in assessing the voluntariness of a confession is not to assess the linguistic truth of a coercion claim but rather to determine whether the alleged coercion by the police should relieve the defendant from being held accountable for the confession.[62] It bears repeating that the law need not find a confession to be involuntary merely because the police exerted some pressure on the suspect to confess. Part of the question that must be addressed in the law's normative inquiry is whether the police "hit below the belt" in exerting the particular pressure.[63] The beginning of understanding in this area is to recognize that the difference between the legal concepts of involuntariness and coercion, on the one hand, and the mere linguistic concept of psychological pressure or compulsion, on the other, "is one of *kind*, not degree."[64]

What, then, does a claim of coercion entail that distinguishes it from other claims? Reviewing several areas of the law in which coercion or duress can relieve an actor from responsibility or accountability for conduct, Professor Wertheimer has shown that such legal claims involve at least two prongs, each of which is necessary for the claim to succeed. First, B, the party alleging coercion, must show that A's allegedly coercive conduct (typically a threat) left B "no reasonable choice" or "no acceptable alternative" but to do what A wanted. This prong is evident, for example, in the treatment of duress both in the substantive criminal law and in contracts.[65] Second, as previously mentioned, B must show that the pressure that A applied (typically a threat) to get B to comply was "wrongful."[66] Again, this prong is evident in the criminal law of duress, which requires a threat of "unlawful force," and in the law of duress in contracts, which requires an "improper" threat.[67]

The first prong, what Wertheimer labels the choice-prong, helps to convey the sense of both urgency and impairment of volitional freedom that typically characterizes a claim of coercion. The necessity of this prong, and more importantly of the sense of stress that it helps to convey, is what compels the rejection of proposals, like that put forward by Professor Kamisar, that the law of confessions eschew voluntariness terminology and concentrate solely on the propriety or impropriety of the police interrogation practices at issue. The latter, of course, must be part of the analysis, for the difficulty of a person's choice, standing alone, does not amount to coercion.[68] Nevertheless, wrongful police conduct that does not impair volitional choice to some extent cannot make out a cognizable claim of coercion.

It warrants observation at this point that no agenda is hidden in this analysis. Professor Wertheimer has shown that both prongs require normative judgments. That is, we remain free to decide both what conduct should be regarded as wrongful and what alternatives available to the actor should be regarded as reasonable.[69] Those who are hostile to police interrogation remain free to argue that even the slightest pressure is "wrongful" and that such pressure confronts the defendant with "unacceptable" alternatives.[70] While the aim of this book is to defend a contrary viewpoint, the debate cannot be resolved, although it may be clarified, by the way the analysis is structured in this chapter.

With this much recognized, it should be apparent that the law's treatment of involuntariness claims in other legal contexts can have only limited utility in the law of confessions. While the defining characteristics of the concepts of involuntariness and coercion may be the same from one legal context to another, the application of these concepts or, more precisely, the norms that they encompass can be expected to vary.[71] To take an obvious example, suppose that A threatens to break B's thumb unless B sets fire to a crowded hospital and that B sets the fire, killing many patients.[72] For purposes of determining B's criminal responsibility, many jurisdictions would simply refuse to recognize duress as a defense in these circumstances, but even in those with a contrary view, a jury might reject the defense by concluding that A's threat was insufficiently coercive to relieve B of responsibility.[73] Either way, the law would be saying that B had a reasonable alternative, which was to accept the broken thumb rather than commit the heinous crime. Suppose now that a police officer threatens to break D's thumb if D does not confess, and D, having good reason to believe that the threat is credible, confesses. Confronted with such facts, virtually every court in the country would find the confession involuntary and inadmissible.[74] The different results in these two contexts reflect not inconsistency but only that the law of confessions—quite properly, given its different objectives—requires less for a finding of involuntariness than does the substantive criminal law.[75]

More broadly, no area of the law can unthinkingly borrow from another its treatment of coercion claims, for the normative judgments in each area are different. Justice Harlan reflected this basic insight when he once stated that the "question of 'voluntariness' for purposes of assessing the validity of a guilty plea . . . must be distinguished from the question of 'voluntariness' for purposes of assessing reprosecutability under the Double Jeopardy Clause."[76] Likewise, coercion claims in the criminal law may be more difficult in general to establish than such claims in the civil law.[77] Even within a given legal context, coercion claims may be treated differently depending on the underlying policy objectives. For example, one empirical study of undue influence claims in the law of wills concluded that such claims prevailed against nonrelatives more readily than they did against relatives, reflecting a "policy of preserving wealth for the bloodline."[78] Applications of the coercion doctrine within a given legal context may similarly change as underlying policies change. Thus, while courts, desirous of preventing illegitimacy status for offspring, may once have been reluctant to void certain marriages on grounds of duress, courts today, less concerned about this consequence, may more readily find duress.[79]

Although this may seem to labor the obvious, commentators frequently make the mistake of criticizing the voluntariness doctrine in one area of the law by relying on the voluntariness doctrine from another. Thus, Professor Philips found incongruous the Supreme Court's finding of involuntariness in *Garrity v. New Jersey*,[80] which involved a Fifth Amendment claim by a public employee who agreed to testify after being threatened with discharge, and its finding of voluntariness in *North Carolina v. Alford*,[81] which involved a Fifth Amendment claim by a defendant who, protesting his innocence, nevertheless pleaded guilty to avoid a possible death sentence. "Alford's rock," Philips observed, "was harder than Garrity's and his whirlpool more deadly."[82] In a well-known passage criticizing the law of confessions, Professor Sutherland made a similar error. Conjuring up a kidnapped testatrix, and equating the pressures on her to those confronting an arrested suspect, Sutherland rhetorically asked, "Would any judge of probate accept the will so procured as the 'voluntary' act of the testatrix?"[83]

More recently, in defending the view of compulsion set forth in *Miranda v. Arizona*,[84] Professor Schulhofer fell into the same error by arguing that "[i]f a comment on silence generates impermissible pressure to speak at trial (where the comment adds only marginally to inferences the jury will draw anyway), can we say that a police officer's request for information, addressed to an unwarned suspect in custody, does not create impermissible pressure?"[85] Unless the normative and policy considerations are identical in both legal contexts—which they may or may not be—the clear answer to Schulhofer is, yes.[86]

Offers versus Threats

A significant issue in philosophical discussions of coercion is whether offers, like threats, can coerce. In his 1987 book, Professor Wertheimer defends the proposition that only threats can coerce.[87] Professor Nozick's "inclination" is to agree, but he is content to leave the issue in some doubt.[88] Others have labored to show that offers can be coercive.[89]

Part of the difficulty with the issue is definitional. Although generalizations are hazardous, it seems fair to say that an offer proposes to better the recipient's situation if the recipient does what the person making the offer wants, while a threat proposes to worsen the recipient's situation unless the recipient performs the desired conduct. The distinction is relevant to the coercion issue because offers supposedly enhance freedom by expanding existing options to achieve what the recipient regards as desirable, while threats limit freedom by proposing to take away something the recipient regards as important.

Better and worse, however, are relative concepts that require some baseline of comparison. What has troubled philosophers is whether this baseline should be defined in factual or moral terms.[90] To take an example frequently discussed in the literature, suppose that A proposes to save B from drowning only if B will agree to pay A a large sum of money. With a factual or statistical approach to the baseline question, the issue of whether A's proposal is an offer or a threat turns on the likelihood in the particular society of the rescue being made without such a demand. If the greater likelihood were that such a rescue would be made, then A's proposal is a threat, for A is proposing, if not paid handsomely, to make B's situation worse by withholding the rescue that B would otherwise expect. With a moral baseline, the issue turns on A's moral obligations in the particular situation. Thus, if A has no moral obligation, A is proposing to make B's situation better in return for the money, whereas if A is morally obligated to save B, A is proposing to make B's situation worse by withholding the morally required rescue absent the required payment.[91]

Proposals that many people might want to describe as coercive may nevertheless constitute offers under either baseline approach. Professor Joel Feinberg provides the example of a millionaire who proposes to provide the funds that a woman desperately needs to obtain life-saving surgery for her daughter, the proposal being contingent on the woman's agreement to become his mistress.[92] Because people ordinarily do not pay for the medical needs of strangers and because the wealthy in our society are neither morally nor legally obligated to make such payments, the proposal to pay for the surgery seems to be an offer under both baseline approaches. Under either a factual or moral baseline, the woman's expectations are that her daughter will die; the millionaire's proposal, however obnoxious it may be, has provided the woman an opportunity to improve on the expected course of events. Thus, if only threats can coerce, the woman's agreement, despite the intense and urgent pressure the millionaire has generated, cannot be regarded as coerced or involuntary.[93]

Hypotheticals such as these tempt one to agree with Professor Westen that the issue whether offers can coerce is largely semantic.[94] Nevertheless, the distinction between offers and threats may be important in some areas of the law, such as in the criminal law defense of duress, where we may have good reasons not to excuse conduct done in response to offers that are "too good to refuse."[95] Whatever the correct answer in the criminal law, or in other legal contexts, however, it seems virtually certain that an offer by interrogating officers along the lines of the millionaire's proposal would prompt courts to find the resulting confession involuntary because of coercion.

Consider, for example, this interrogation hypothetical. During postarrest questioning on minor theft charges, the police inform D that they will drop unrelated but properly initiated murder charges against S, D's son, if D confesses to the theft. Because the police in the normal course of events would be expected to prosecute S for the murder, and because they are legally and morally entitled to do so, the interrogation proposal extends the promise of a benefit to D and, thus, constitutes an offer under both baseline approaches in the above analysis. Nevertheless, it seems doubtful that any American court would listen seriously to an argument that the facts do not even state a claim of coercion.[96]

While the facts in the last hypothetical may seem farfetched, consider the facts in *Lynumn v. Illinois*,[97] where the police told the defendant after her arrest that she could get ten years' imprisonment for selling narcotics, that her Aid to Dependent Children benefits would probably be cut off, that she would probably lose custody of her two young children, but that "it would go light on her" if she cooperated.[98] Assuming both that the indicated consequences were likely to result from conviction on the designated charge and that the police did not renege on their promise to recommend leniency—and the Court did not question either of these assumptions[99]—the police proposal to recommend leniency in return for cooperation, a proposal they were not morally obligated to make, was an offer rather than a threat under both baseline approaches discussed above. Nevertheless, the Supreme Court unanimously concluded that the defendant's confession was "not voluntary, but coerced."[100] Of course, we might want to conclude on careful consideration that the Court decided *Lynumn* incorrectly, but such a contention based entirely on the offer-threat distinction rings rather hollow.

Perhaps the above examples suggest that whether a proposal is coercive requires a judgment not simply about the nature of the proposal in isolation (the offer-threat distinction) but rather about the propriety of conditioning the proposal on the recipient's performance of the desired action.[101] Such an approach to the question of coercion may hold promise, but to embrace it fully, one would need to develop a "theory of the morality of proposals."[102] This book is not the place to develop such a theory.

Nevertheless, it is useful to consider how such an approach would affect the analysis. In Feinberg's millionaire hypothetical, for example, the proposal to pay the woman for her daughter's surgery might be treated as a threat—or more importantly, for present purposes, as coercive—because the millionaire had a moral obligation not to condition his offer to pay on compliance with the particular demand that he made.[103] Likewise, the police proposal in the interrogation hypothetical may be wrongful, and hence possibly coercive, not in and of itself, as there is nothing inherently improper in offering not to pursue a prosecution, but in conditioning the offer not to prosecute the son for serious charges on the father's agreement to confess on unrelated minor charges. Whether the wrongfulness of coupling these matters stems from the close family relationship, from the substantial disparities between the theft and the murder charges, or from some combination of the two would have to be explored.

Finally, although the analysis seems somewhat less satisfying, the police proposal in *Lynumn* perhaps was improper, and hence potentially coercive, because it exploited a mother's natural concern for her children by conditioning the promise of a continued family relationship on the defendant's agreement to confess. What is not immediately apparent, however, especially if the police did not lie about either their intentions or the possible consequences of conviction without leniency, is why we should want to regard the police conduct at issue in *Lynumn* as improper.[104]

As will shortly be discussed, the voluntariness concept encompasses concerns other than the impairment of volitional freedom. Possibly, therefore, the interrogation cases that involve offers rather than threats, and even the millionaire hypothetical, could be viewed as involving noncoercive exploitation or undue influence.[105] In this borderline area where the concepts of coercion and noncoercive exploitation seem to perform much the same work, we can ordinarily—but not always—expect the results in actual cases to be the same regardless of how we conceptualize the issue.

Nevertheless, there may be merit in using the concept of coercion for police inducements that make it difficult for the defendant in a volitional sense to choose other than to confess and the concept of improper exploitation or unfair influence for inducements that inappropriately take advantage of the defendant's cognitive handicaps. First, proceeding along these lines comports with the historical willingness of courts in confessions cases to consider claims of coercion in situations involving offers.[106] Just as importantly, it comports with our ordinary linguistic usage, for it allows us to rely on our natural inclination to speak of coercion in situations like that presented by the millionaire and interrogation hypotheticals considered above. At least with regard to the law of confessions, the case for not distinguishing threats and offers seems stronger than the case in favor.

Volitional Impairment and Causation

In the course of elaborating its overborne will test, the Supreme Court has made statements to the effect that the police may neither "induce" a confession by hope or fear[107] nor "bring about confessions not freely self-determined."[108] Similarly, the Court has said that a confession, to be considered voluntary, must be the "product" of a free will[109] and must not be "extracted" or "obtained" by improper influence.[110] Explaining his overborne will approach in *Culombe v. Connecticut*,[111] Justice Frankfurter indicated that the "line of distinction" between voluntary and involuntary confessions is "that at which governing self-direction is lost and compulsion, of whatever nature or however infused, propels or helps to propel the confession."[112]

The significant concepts in these sentences—*induce, bring about, produce, extract, obtain, compel, propel*—all pertain to causation.[113] These concepts suggest that no claim of involuntariness is possible unless the police have *caused* the defendant to confess.[114] The issue that warrants analysis is the meaning of causation in this context.

At the outset, it may be objected that the use of the word *causation* is inappropriate when speaking about volitional human activity, for we do not speak of human actions as being caused the same way we speak of physical occurrences as being caused.[115] When we speak of human actions, "we have to deal with the concept of *reasons* for action rather than *causes* of events."[116] Professor Sanford Kadish has gone even further in objecting to the use of causal language in this context:

> In a word, every volitional actor is a wild card; he need never act in a certain way. He responds as he chooses to influences and appeals. . . . Sine qua non in the physical causation sense, therefore, does not exist in any account of human actions. . . . [T]here are no sufficient conditions for an act of will; nor are there any necessary conditions, save those like knowledge and nonconstraint, without which there can be no free act of will at all.[117]

Given what has been said about the notion of overborne wills, there is a sense in which Professor Kadish is correct: occurrences external to an actor cannot be a sufficient cause for an actor's volitional conduct. Kadish insisted, however, that "[n]o matter how well or fully we learn the antecedent facts, we can never say of a voluntary action that it had to be the case that the person would choose to act in a certain way."[118] Professor Kadish provided no support for such a powerful claim.[119] Indeed, the correctness of his claim seems to imply a rejection of determinism and an acceptance of indeterminism or free will theory, a thicket that Kadish purported not to be entering.[120] It may be, as Kadish claimed, that every volitional actor is a "wild card," but to build an entire legal or moral edifice on such a controversial and unverifiable premise seems both hazardous and unnecessary.[121]

If we admit at least the possibility that the "wild card" premise may be wrong, Professor Kadish's argument against the use of the word *causation* in the context of human volition is reduced to an argument concerning the appropriate use of language. Indeed, at one point Kadish purported not to be claiming that the use of causal language as such was inappropriate in this context; rather, he posited the more limited proposition that "the way in which a person's acts produce results in the physical world is significantly different from the way in which a person's acts produce results that take the form of the volitional acts of others."[122] In other words, Kadish's argument pertained to the use of a particular conception of causation.

In analyzing volitional conduct, we could, of course, choose to speak of *reasons, inducements,* or *influences* instead of causes, but as Professor Joshua Dressler has indicated in response to Professor Kadish, the issues of responsibility and accountability that motivated the causal inquiry in the first place remain the same regardless of the label.[123] In the confessions context, the question that must be answered is not which word to use but whether defendants should be relieved of accountability for their statements because the police improperly constrained their choice not to talk. For purposes of answering this question, the language of causation is not, as Kadish had to concede, inappropriate.

Because, as already discussed and as Professor Kadish would obviously agree, the defendant's choice to confess is a necessary cause of virtually every confession, grossly improper police interrogation conduct, considered in isolation, will rarely be a sufficient cause.[124] Unless the voluntariness doctrine is to accept confessions obtained by police brutality, it must follow that such a demanding level of causation (or influence) cannot be required to support a finding of involuntariness. Likewise, however, except for the rare individuals who surrender to the police to bare their souls, virtually all police interrogation must be regarded, contrary to what Professor Kadish has suggested, as a necessary or but-for cause of the statements it produces. Unless police interrogation is to be abolished altogether, it must also follow that a confession cannot be deemed involuntary merely because it is the product, in this but-for sense, of the interrogation process.

We have seen, however, that the concept of coercion requires a conclusion that the alleged coercer engaged in improper pressure. This suggests that the inquiry should focus not on the interrogation as such but on the improper aspects of the interrogation process. The question that requires examination, therefore, is the kind of causal connection that must exist between the improper police conduct and the confession before a finding of involuntariness is warranted. [125]

The necessity of at least but-for causation can easily be demonstrated:

1. Police officers arrested D for robbery and brought D to the station for interrogation. When D refused to answer questions, the officers viciously beat D. D, however, persisted in refusing to answer until the officers finally abandoned their efforts to obtain a confession. At D's subsequent trial, the prosecutor relied on other evidence independently obtained.

Given the absence of a confession in this illustration, there obviously are no issues of causation and voluntariness. The police terribly misbehaved, and if D can prove these facts, they have made themselves liable to both civil damages and criminal penalties. In D's criminal trial for robbery, however, D has no remedy for the police misconduct, for there is no confession to suppress, and our procedural law, even in the interest of deterrence, has never been willing to suppress either the entire prosecution[126] or items of evidence totally unrelated in a causal sense to the police misconduct. [127]

Consider now a slightly modified set of facts:

2. Police officers arrested D for robbery and brought D to the station for interrogation. When D refused to acknowledge guilt, other officers went to D's home to interrogate D's spouse. Finding D's spouse equally uncooperative, the officers responded by beating the spouse. In the meantime, D, who was neither mistreated nor cognizant of the events at D's home, had a change of heart and confessed. At D's subsequent trial, the prosecutor relied on D's confession as well as other evidence.

Although this second illustration involves a confession, it is similar to the first in lacking a causal nexus between the police misconduct and the evidence obtained. While the police misconduct should again be subject to sanctions, *D*'s confession is voluntary and, like other evidence independently obtained, is admissible in *D*'s criminal trial.[128] Indeed, were the law to exclude the confession in a case such as this, ordinary language usage would require that it do so for a reason other than the confession's alleged involuntariness. Without any causal connection between the police misconduct and the confession, without the former being a "reason" for the latter, it would not be intelligible to claim that the police coerced *D* into confessing.

Because the existence of but-for causation is an empirical question, some commentators have been led to believe that the causation component of voluntariness inquiries essentially is empirical in nature. In his book on coercion, for example, Professor Wertheimer stated that "B's motivations are essentially a matter of *fact*."[129] Similarly, after stating that "[r]eceiving a coercive proposal and having no acceptable alternative . . . but to succumb to the proposal are each necessary and jointly sufficient to establish that A coerces B," Professor Wertheimer indicated in a footnote that this statement necessarily assumes that B does X "in response to and because of A's proposal."[130] Again, this suggests that the causation issue essentially is factual in nature.

Under Professor Wertheimer's view, then, coercion or involuntariness exists when an improper proposal has factually caused the recipient of the proposal to take some action, provided that the recipient had no reasonable alternative but to act as he did. Because the latter part of the inquiry is "moralized," what this really means to Wertheimer is that the recipient was morally entitled to yield to rather than to resist the proposal.[131] This account, which reduces the causal element to a factual issue, seems to lose something that is essential to the concept of coercion.

To see this, it helps first to consider an illustration in which Wertheimer's account seems satisfactory:

> 3. Police officers arrested *D* for robbery and brought *D* to the station for interrogation. When *D* refused to answer questions, the officers threatened to beat *D*. *D*, visibly shaking and begging the police to refrain, immediately confessed.

The improper proposal in this hypothetical is the conditional threat to beat *D*. With respect to causation, the nature and sequence of events should leave us sufficiently confident that the threat caused (influenced) *D* to confess, at least in a but-for sense. Finally, employing Wertheimer's "moralized" approach to the choice prong of his inquiry, few would deny that *D* was entitled to yield to the threat rather than resist the demand and seek some other remedy for the beating D expected. Thus, Wertheimer's approach yields the readily acceptable conclusion in this illustration that the police coerced D into confessing, meaning that D confessed involuntarily.

Consider, now, this more troubling variation of the illustration:

4. Prior to being arrested for robbery, D indicated in a recorded statement to a friend that D was 98 percent sure that D would surrender and confess. Before D took any action, however, police officers arrested D for the robbery, took D to an interrogation room, and immediately indicated that they would beat D unless D truthfully answered their questions. D, visibly shaking and begging the police to refrain, responded that it was unnecessary for the police to engage in threats because D was inclined to confess all along. D then confessed, and a subsequent polygraph examination confirmed that the police threat had only a slight impact on D's decision to confess.

Under Professor Wertheimer's analysis, this illustration is analytically indistinguishable from the previous one. That is, taking as given, as the facts are intended to require, both that D at the time of arrest remained 98 percent convinced to confess and that the police threat merely helped to remove the remaining doubt, we must conclude that the police misconduct constituted a necessary cause of the confession, for without the threat, D would not have confessed at that time. Nevertheless, although all Wertheimer's criteria are as satisfied in this illustration as in the last, the conclusion that the police coerced D into confessing does not seem so obviously correct.[132]

The claim in the previous sentence is not that a conclusion of coercion would necessarily be unwarranted but only that such a conclusion is not as obviously correct as in the previous illustration. In the substantive criminal law, for example, we might be reluctant to recognize a claim of duress if we knew for certain that the recipient of the threat was 98 percent predisposed to commit the crime before the threat.[133] The concept of coercion ordinarily conveys some sense of force or of "overpowering" pressure,[134] a sense insufficiently captured in Wertheimer's analysis, which looks only to the reasonableness of the actor's decision under the circumstances. When this sense of volitional impairment, or interference with autonomy, seems lacking, we may hesitate, at least without further thought, to embrace a finding of coercion.[135]

Other commentators have tried to capture this sense in their discussions of coercion. Professor Frankfurt, for example, has claimed that a coercive threat must be irresistible.[136] In discussing the concept of victimization, which he regards as encompassing the concept of coercion, Professor Fingarette less demandingly has stated that the victimizer must provide the victim a "crucial reason" for acting.[137] Professor Murphy similarly has indicated that the coercer's threat must be a "paramount reason" for the recipient's action.[138] Recognizing that people typically have multiple reasons for acting and that these reasons may have more or less influence in different instances, Professor Nozick has come closer to the mark in suggesting that "one might begin to speak of someone's being partially coerced, slightly coerced, [and] almost fully coerced into doing something."[139]

None of this holds much promise for illuminating the concept of causation in the law of confessions unless one also recalls that the ultimate issue is whether the police should be blamed, or the defendant held accountable, for the defendant's confession. Given their different underlying purposes, the criminal law of duress might conceivably require a more significant causal connection between the improper threat and the conduct at issue than does the law of confessions. Indeed, depending on how its purposes are defined, the law of confessions might demand no more than a minimal causal link, conceivably no more than but-for causation, for a finding of involuntariness.[140] This is why a finding of coercion cannot be considered outside the bounds of possibility in the last illustration.[141]

What Professor Wertheimer missed in his analysis is that the issue of causation, like the other issues pertaining to coercion, necessarily involves normative judgments, at least once but-for causation is established. The necessity for normative judgment should be apparent once it is realized that in identifying the cause of an event—in this case, of a confession—a court must isolate for special consideration one causal factor from a set of causal factors that are sufficient only in combination.[142] When a court concludes that improper police conduct caused—induced, brought about, extracted, compelled, influenced—the defendant's confession, it necessarily makes a choice based on some normative criterion.

In rebuttal, it may be asserted that if the law of confessions were to require only but-for causation, the inquiry in any particular case would essentially be empirical. Although this is true, it remains the case that the choice to require only but-for causation requires a normative defense. Given, as we saw from the second illustration, that a defendant will be held fully accountable for a confession that has no causal link to police impropriety, those who would defend a test requiring only but-for causation must be prepared to argue that the defendant should be relieved of accountability when the causal link barely crosses the but-for threshold.[143]

This chapter is not the place to settle such a controversy. For present purposes, it suffices to recognize that one's attitude about police interrogation, confessions in general, and the wisdom of using the criminal justice system to remedy police abuse will largely determine one's views on the issue of causation. In all their constituent parts, therefore, the definitions of coercion and involuntariness as volitional concepts require normative judgments.

Voluntariness and Unfair Advantage

The Supreme Court has not limited its examination of police interrogation practices to concerns about coercion or volitional impairment.[144] On the contrary, the Court has also spoken of the need to protect against fundamental unfairness[145] and to promote a "sense of fair play."[146] Reflecting these latter concerns, the Court in *Spano v. New York*[147] condemned a confession partly because the defendant's friend, at the behest of the police, persuaded the defendant to confess by falsely arousing sympathy for himself. Similarly, denying that freedom of the will is the sole interest at stake, the Court in *Blackburn v. Alabama*[148] invalidated a confession that the police obtained from a defendant who was insane and legally incompetent when he confessed. Moreover, the Court in numerous cases has referred to the defendant's age, education, and mental condition as part of the relevant background, factors that while sometimes relevant to the issue of volitional impairment more significantly bear on the issue whether the police unfairly took advantage of, or improperly exploited, the defendant's cognitive deficiencies.[149]

In *Blackburn,* the Court observed that the concept of an involuntary confession reflects "a complex of values," including a strong conviction that our system of law enforcement should not take advantage of an accused in certain ways.[150] Thus, instead of choosing terminology to differentiate underlying interests, the Court has encompassed both the interest in preventing coercion and the interest in preventing unfairness or improper exploitation under the same voluntariness rubric. This has not helped to advance understanding. For example, insufficiently appreciating that voluntariness terminology may be appropriate even when volitional impairment is absent, commentators have disputed whether a confession obtained by a police officer posing as a member of the clergy can appropriately be characterized as involuntary.[151] The answer is both yes and no, depending on one's definition of voluntariness.

From the standpoint of acceptable language usage, action undertaken in ignorance may sometimes be described as involuntary. Aristotle, for example, said that acts due to ignorance are involuntary when they bring sorrow and regret.[152] Thus, if A tells B that he has a new pet food that B should try on her pet, and if A then gives B poison, which B gives to her pet, it would be acceptable to say that B involuntarily poisoned her pet. Likewise, if B confesses to a police officer posing as a priest or a lawyer, B's confession may be said to be involuntary in this broad sense of the term.

The involuntariness in these situations, however, differs from the involuntariness that would be involved if B knowingly poisoned her pet or deliberately chose to confess because A had a gun to B's head or subjected B to some other conditional threat. Cases involving cognitive impairment present different moral and legal issues than cases involving volitional impairment. For example, unless B was at fault in not learning the facts, it would be difficult to blame B for unknowingly poisoning her pet in the above hypothetical. On the other hand, depending on the nature of the threat to which B responded, B's choice to poison her pet rather than accept A's threatened consequences might be blameworthy. Similarly, while certain interrogation pressures may be viewed as improperly coercive, it is at least conceivable that some deceptive strategies will not be viewed as unfairly exploitative. The use of undifferentiating voluntariness terminology blurs the possible distinctions in these situations.

There is reason to doubt, however, that a call for a different nomenclature will fall on receptive ears. First, courts have long used the voluntariness concept to embrace more than volitional freedom. In addition, courts and commentators may sometimes have difficulty distinguishing cognitive and volitional concerns. Some might contend, for example, that if P falsely tells D that D's codefendant has confessed, P not only has distorted D's cognitive awareness but also has added to the coercive atmosphere compelling D to confess. Nevertheless, the virtue in employing terminology that differentiates the underlying concerns is that courts and commentators would have to think more clearly about how to characterize the issues raised by particular police practices, and this would clarify the points of disagreement in the debate over the propriety of these practices.

Whether or not the terminology is changed, clarity in analysis requires separate consideration of the interest in preventing coercion and the interest in preventing unfair advantage or improper exploitation. Under an undiscriminating totality of circumstances approach, a conclusion on voluntariness is expected to emerge from a hopper into which all factors, volitional and cognitive, are randomly thrown. Indeed, under the totality approach, cognitive factors, such as those relating to the defendant's educational deficiencies or mental deficiencies, sometimes seem employed more to induce an emotional reaction than to further careful analysis of whether the defendant was either coerced or unfairly exploited. Thus, although it might be difficult to maintain persuasively that facts A through C amount to coercion or that facts D through F amount to improper exploitation, the totality of circumstances approach often enables one to assert with confidence, if not with adequate explanation, that facts A through F in combination support a finding of involuntariness. Obfuscation such as this can be avoided only by focusing on unfair advantage as a distinct concern.

It remains to consider the meaning of concepts such as unfair advantage or improper exploitation. Unlike the concept of coercion, these concepts on their face implicate normative judgments, for one may take advantage of or exploit another's situation without engaging in "unfairness" or "impropriety."[153] The obviousness of this point, however, should not detract from its importance. Just as a claim of undue influence in contracts law will not succeed simply because one party was at a bargaining disadvantage with regard to the other,[154] so too in the law of confessions it cannot be assumed, as it sometimes is, that the defendant should prevail with a claim of unfairness simply because the defendant was no intellectual match for the police. It may be that such inequality should be a legal concern, but as we saw in the last chapter, such a claim is difficult to defend.

Although the concept of fairness may seem hopelessly subjective, some insights are possible. We may say, for example, that a procedure or tactic is fair when it is consistent with the rules that govern the institution in which it is employed.[155] Thus, because the rules of cross-examination permit a lawyer to attempt to catch a witness in a lie, cross-examination designed to do this, however much it may embarrass or offend the witness, is fair, at least as long as it stays within the bounds of other rules that may also apply. Similarly, we may agree that the failure of the police to abide by the rules governing the interrogation process is unfair. This analysis, however, essentially is unhelpful when the question to be answered is whether the rules that govern the institution themselves are fair.

To a large extent, the fairness of the rules governing an institution depends on the institution's purpose and function. If the institution of boxing is intended to allow for competition in fighting skills, a rule permitting a heavyweight to compete with a featherweight would be unfair, for rather than testing comparative skill, such a contest would permit skill to be overwhelmed by sheer strength. On the other hand, were boxing purposely designed to compare the relative importance of strength and skill, there would be nothing unfair in such a fight. Similarly, a grade of A may be unfair on a test designed to measure skill on some objective scale and yet be fair on a test designed to measure overall improvement in a course.[156]

This suggests that whether the rules governing police interrogation are fair depends, at least to some extent, on the purpose and function of this institution. Putting aside the interrogation of mere witnesses, police interrogation is generally intended to obtain from guilty suspects self-incriminating statements and clues to additional evidence or other suspects. Like the criminal justice system of which it is a part, therefore, police interrogation is intended to facilitate the ascertainment of truth.[157] Moreover, society's undeviating acceptance of this institution over the years demonstrates that self-incrimination as such, at least from society's perspective, is not unfair.

Nevertheless, like most institutions, including the criminal justice system as a whole, police interrogation has multiple and competing goals. Because ascertaining truth cannot be its sole desideratum, police interrogation cannot be analogized to combat and war, where the rules impose only minimal restraints on the steps that may be taken to achieve one's objectives. On the other hand, as already indicated, the very existence of the institution suggests that police interrogation cannot be analogized to a sporting contest in which the aim is to make the competing parties as evenly matched as possible. The fairness limitations on police interrogation, therefore, must stem from a conviction that while we want the police to succeed in ascertaining the truth, our morality places limits on the means that may be used to achieve this end. Respect for the individual as an individual, as a member of humanity, yields limits on what will be permitted in the otherwise laudable search for truth.

This is not to suggest that this interest in protecting human dignity yields easy or noncontextual answers. In combat or war, for example, the concern for human dignity is not strong enough to condemn some practices that would be forthrightly condemned in virtually every other context. Likewise, it is at least conceivable that practices considered undue or unfair in contracts or wills may not be so considered in police interrogation. This is simply to say, of course, that the normative question in police interrogation necessarily is *how far* the police may go in taking advantage of a suspect before their tactics will be condemned as unfair.

Individuals will differ in responding to this question. While Professor Kauper, for example, has described many assertions of unfairness as "simply a maudlin sympathy for inexperienced but guilty persons,"[158] Professor White has condemned virtually all police practices that in any way deceive the accused.[159] These competing positions need to be discussed. For current purposes, however, it suffices to observe once again that voluntariness as a normative concept is necessarily concerned with questions of degree, and this holds true whether the concern is coercion or unfair exploitation of cognitive deficiencies.

Part 2
Constitutional Considerations

CHAPTER 4

The Due Process Requirement
of Voluntariness

The previous normative inquiry regarding both the criminal justice system in general and police interrogation in particular supports the conclusion that a confession or statement should not be considered involuntary merely because it results from police interrogation, police encouragement to tell the truth, or police interrogation strategies that succeed in their objective. Modest though it may be, this conclusion is not trivial, for it necessarily negates the premise that self-incrimination and police interrogation are inherently suspect as such.

Such a negative premise about police interrogation is inherent in much of the academic literature. Few commentators, however, have been as forthright as Professors Irene and Yale Rosenberg both in acknowledging a "philosophical predilection" for the view that *all* confessions—voluntary or compelled, reliable or spontaneous, custodial or noncustodial—should be inadmissible and in doubting that "any statements to government officials can be deemed noncompelled."[1] Still, similar if not identical premises seem implicit in the frequently heard lament that *Miranda* did not go far enough.[2]

The previous discussion also casts doubt on arguments to restrict police practices that add only marginally to the inherent psychological pressures on the suspect to tell the truth. This too is significant, for although some commentators might concede that "zero-value pressure conditions" are impossible to obtain, many also remain predisposed to disallow any pressure that exerts even the slightest "tug" on the suspect to cooperate.[3]

To extend the inquiry beyond the basic desirability of police interrogation and confessions, the focus now shifts from normative to constitutional considerations. Resuming where the last chapter ended, this chapter returns to the question of voluntariness, but now in the context of the due process voluntariness doctrine. As previously indicated, the Supreme Court first used the Fourteenth Amendment's due process clause in the 1930s to give federal constitutional stature at least to certain aspects of the common-law voluntariness requirement in state criminal cases. Along with other constitutional doctrines that subsequent chapters will discuss, the due process voluntariness requirement, albeit frequently criticized, continues to play an important role in the law of confessions.

Several reasons explain the continuing importance of the voluntariness doctrine.[4] First, the voluntariness requirement applies to police interrogation contexts not covered by *Miranda,* and even when *Miranda* applies, the voluntariness requirement governs the validity of most *Miranda* waivers.[5] In addition, the prosecution may impeach a testifying defendant's credibility with a statement taken in violation of *Miranda,* but only if the statement is voluntary.[6] Similarly, the "fruit of the poisonous tree" doctrine applies with less rigor when a mere *Miranda* violation has occurred than when the defendant's statement is truly involuntary.[7] Of potentially broad significance, the voluntariness doctrine seems to brook no exceptions, while *Miranda* may at least sometimes be deemed inapplicable because its perceived costs substantially outweigh its perceived benefits.[8] Apart from these reasons, however, the voluntariness doctrine is of critical importance in this book because of the thesis, elaborated in subsequent chapters, that the Fifth and Sixth Amendments should not be read as imposing restraints on police interrogation that exceed those imposed by the voluntariness requirement.

The shift in this chapter to a constitutional focus warrants explanation. Most obviously, the strategy in the first three chapters of putting aside constitutional issues, though useful for obtaining perspective, must eventually respond to the objection that constitutional requirements necessarily trump conflicting normative conclusions. Truth may be an important desideratum in the abstract, but if the Constitution requires us to sacrifice truth, we must comply. Moreover, the normative analysis in the previous chapters has reached the point of diminishing returns, for the more one reaches back to justify essential premises, the more one appreciates that normative analysis ultimately depends on the predilections—or on the unprovable axioms or first principles—of those who undertake it. Thus, one who begins from a deontological conviction that lying always is morally wrong may reach radically different conclusions about interrogation trickery than one who embraces a utilitarian calculus or a different deontological premise. This is not to claim that constitutional analysis has escaped the influence of personal predilection, subjective judgment, or philosophical predisposition but only to suggest that the constitutional text may support less extensive, or at least different, restrictions on police interrogation than what some commentators would derive from purely normative or moral discourse. The next section further develops this theme.

The Interpretational Difficulty

The Fifth and Fourteenth Amendment due process clauses, respectively and in virtually identical terms, preclude the federal government and the states from depriving any person of life, liberty, or property "without due process of law."[9] Because neither due process clause says anything about voluntariness or confessions, a stranger to our system might be perplexed by talk of a due process voluntariness requirement. The interpretational difficulty of deriving such a requirement from the constitutional text is the subject of this section, and its consideration requires some attention to the Supreme Court's development of due process doctrine in general.

With roots traceable both to King John's thirteenth-century sealed promise in Magna Charta that a free man would not be seized, imprisoned, dispossessed, outlawed, or prosecuted except "by the lawful judgment of his peers and by the law of the land"[10] and to the later statutory commitment in the reign of Edward III that similar actions would not occur unless the individual "be brought to answer by due process of law,"[11] the constitutional due process requirement has long troubled American courts.[12] Disagreement has existed over such issues as whether the constitutional drafters and ratifiers meant "due process" to be synonymous with the "law of the land," intended "due process" to have a fixed or definite meaning, sought to restrain the legislature as well as the executive and the courts, and expected courts to use "due process" to impose substantive as well as procedural constraints on governmental action.[13] Disagreement over these questions persists to this day.

In *Murray v. Hoboken Land and Improvement Co.*,[14] decided in 1856, the Supreme Court interpreted the Fifth Amendment's due process clause to permit the seizure and sale of property under a Treasury Department distress warrant issued pursuant to an Act of Congress. Equating "due process" and "law of the land," the Court observed that the Fifth Amendment failed to specify the processes that were either permitted or disallowed. The Court concluded, however, that the Fifth Amendment precluded Congress from having final say on the process that was due.[15] The "law of the land," in the Court's view, could not be simply the law as established by Congress, even if that law complied with all other constitutional constraints.

Given that the English Parliament after Magna Charta had defined the process that was due through a series of statutes,[16] *Murray*'s conclusion on this point required justification, which the Court did not provide. More importantly for present purposes, however, the Court's conclusion raised important questions about the American judiciary's role in defining the meaning of due process. Absent textual guidance, some source of judgment had to be identified unless courts, through the vehicle of the due process requirement, were prepared merely to substitute their own normative views for those of the legislature.

In *Murray,* the Court identified two sources of interpretational judgment. First, stating the obvious and making the due process requirement redundant, the Court indicated that processes authorized by Congress could not conflict with any of the Constitution's other provisions.[17] Second, and less obvious, the Court said it would look to "those settled usages and modes of proceeding existing in the common and statute law of England, before the emigration of our ancestors, and which are shown not to have been unsuited to their civil and political condition by having been acted on by them after their settlement of this country."[18] In the Court's view, the distress warrant procedure at issue in *Murray* passed due process muster because it was consistent with common-law modes of procedure.

However dubious the Court's interpretation of due process may have been,[19] its analysis put it on the road, albeit in a procedural context, of examining sources outside the Constitution's text for possible due process restraints on government.[20] The road has been one of uncertainty and conflict ever since. In 1884, almost thirty years after *Murray,* the Court confronted a Fourteenth Amendment due process challenge to California's reform legislation that substituted prosecution by information for prosecution by grand jury indictment. Claiming that due process had a "fixed, definite, and technical meaning," and relying on the settled usage language in *Murray,* the appellant argued that the requirement of grand jury indictment was a settled mode of procedure at common law that crossed the Atlantic with the colonists.[21] Correctly concerned that such an approach to due process would "stamp upon our jurisprudence the unchangeableness attributed to the laws of the Medes and Persians," the Court responded that settled usage was sufficient to establish due process, as it did in *Murray,* but not a requisite of due process.[22]

What, then, did due process require, if not those processes with a lineage firmly rooted in history and tradition? Remarking that the Constitution was "made for an undefined and expanding future," the Court concluded that the due process requirement assures adherence to the "law of the land of each state," as long as that law is "within the limits of those fundamental principles of liberty and justice which lie at the base of all our civil and political institutions."[23] Rather portentously, the Court also intimated in dictum that substantive law representing little more than an exercise of arbitrary power could not be considered "law" within the meaning of the due process clauses.[24]

Before the century ended, the Court acted on the latter suggestion by using the Fourteenth Amendment's due process clause to prohibit certain state interferences with "the right to make all proper contracts."[25] Shortly thereafter, the Court in *Lochner v. New York*[26] reaffirmed this doctrine of "substantive due process" by invalidating a law that imposed a limit on the number of hours a person could be employed in a bakery. With these decisions, the Court abandoned the effort to define due process in terms of its text and historical roots, for as Professor Edward Corwin wrote in 1911, such decisions represented "nothing less than the elimination of the very phrase under construction ['without due process of law'] from the constitutional clause in which it occurs."[27] What offended the Court in these cases was not the deprivation of liberty without appropriate process but rather the deprivation of liberty as such.

At the beginning of what is sometimes called the *Lochner* era, the Court, somewhat ironically, continued to invoke history to support narrow understandings of procedural due process. In *Twining v. New Jersey*,[28] just three years after *Lochner*, the Court read due process as historically requiring little beyond notice of the charge and an opportunity to be heard. Nevertheless, rejecting the claim that protection from compulsory self-incrimination was required in state courts as an element of procedural due process, the Court, in language reminiscent of its substantive due process reasoning, also concluded that such protection was not "an immutable principle of justice which is the inalienable possession of every citizen of a free government."[29]

Although the Court generally treated procedural due process less expansively than substantive due process during this era, not all of its procedural decisions rejected the claim that due process had been denied. For example, describing the need for notice and an opportunity to be heard as an immutable principle of justice, the Court in *Powell v. Alabama*,[30] in 1932, held that due process required, at least on the facts of the particular case, the timely appointment of counsel for indigent defendants. *Powell,* and other cases before and after it, established that a state failed to comply with the "fundamental conceptions of justice" embodied in due process when it contrived a conviction through the pretense of a trial.[31]

By the middle of the 1930's, therefore, the Court was defining due process in terms of immutable principles of justice, principles that it considered fundamental to a free society. Of course, the Court's soon-to-end substantive due process invalidation of state economic legislation hardly reflected immutable principles of justice,[32] but on both the procedural and substantive sides, the Court emphatically disclaimed, as it still does today, authority simply to substitute its own judgment of right and wrong for that of the states. Thus, on the substantive side, Justice Holmes wrote for the Court that the danger in not allowing differences of view among the states is that "instead of embodying only relatively fundamental rules of right," the Constitution will "become the partisan of a particular set of ethical or economic opinions, which by no means are held *semper ubique et ab omnibus*."[33] Even the *Lochner* Court strained to deny that it was "substituting [its] judgment . . . for that of the legislature."[34] On the procedural side, Justice Cardozo similarly wrote that a procedure does not violate due process simply "because another method may seem to our thinking to be fairer or wiser or to give a surer promise of protection to the prisoner."[35] In short, under the Court's due process doctrine, states could modify their substantive and procedural laws as long as they did not offend "some principle of justice so rooted in the traditions and conscience of our people as to be ranked as fundamental."[36]

It was during this era that the Court, in *Brown v. Mississippi*,[37] for the first time employed the Fourteenth Amendment's due process clause to invalidate a state conviction based on a coerced confession. *Brown*, which involved the admitted hanging and whipping of the defendants described in chapter 1, was not difficult for the Court under its due process precedents. Indeed, although the Court at the time was still bitterly divided over the constitutionality of President Roosevelt's New Deal legislation and still at odds over the legitimacy of substantive due process, it was unanimous in finding a due process violation in *Brown*. Stressing that the prerogative of the states to define their own procedures is limited by the fundamental principles of justice that are rooted in the traditions and conscience of the people, the Court concluded that a trial becomes a "mere pretense where the state authorities have contrived a conviction resting solely upon confessions obtained by violence." The Court added that "[i]t would be difficult to conceive of methods more revolting to the sense of justice than those taken to procure the confessions of these petitioners."[38]

Brown did not, as is sometimes thought, establish a due process voluntariness requirement. In fact, the words *voluntary* and *involuntary* appear in the opinion not in passages containing the Court's due process analysis but only in quotations from the state court dissenting opinion, and no mention whatsoever is made of overborne wills.[39] Four years later, however, shortly before it sounded the death knell for the first era of substantive due process,[40] the Court in *Chambers v. Florida*[41] read

Brown as based on the conclusion that the confessions in that case "were the result of compulsion." Finding "compulsion" in the case before it, the *Chambers* Court condemned the "relentless tenacity which 'broke' petitioners' will."[42] Nevertheless, even without the defendant's allegations of physical brutality, which the Court put aside, the facts in *Chambers* were sufficiently egregious to preclude any dissenting objection that the Court's finding of a due process violation conflicted with the Court's due process precedent.

After *Chambers*, the Supreme Court's review of state confession cases began to focus increasingly on the concepts of compulsion, voluntariness, mental freedom, and overborne wills.[43] This trend might not have been troublesome had these concepts not caused the Court gradually to disregard the earlier precedent limiting the due process inquiry to whether the state's method of obtaining the conviction offended some fundamental principle of justice rooted in the traditions and conscience of the country.[44] Stated differently, the Court's confession cases demonstrated the validity of Justice Cardozo's earlier admonition about the tyranny of labels:

> A fertile source of perversion in constitutional theory is the tyranny of labels. Out of the vague precepts of the Fourteenth Amendment a court frames a rule which is general in form, though it has been wrought under the pressure of particular situations. Forthwith another situation is placed under the rule because it is fitted to the words, though related faintly, if at all, to the reasons that brought the rule into existence.[45]

That the Court fell victim to this tyranny is evident from the evolution that occurred over the years in its confession cases. In the early post-*Brown* cases, the Court appropriately recognized that the "voluntariness," as such, of a confession was an issue not of federal constitutional law but rather of state or federal evidentiary law, depending on the jurisdiction involved.[46] Each state was at liberty "to adopt, by statute or decision, and to enforce such rule as she elect[ed], whether it conform[ed] to that applied in the federal or in other state courts," as long as its rule did not offend immutable principles of justice or notions of "fundamental fairness essential to the very concept of justice."[47] Moreover, the Court recognized the general impropriety of using the Fourteenth Amendment to impose stricter voluntariness standards on the states than common-law evidentiary principles required.[48]

Under the Court's approach, a finding of due process involuntariness required not merely disapproval of the police behavior but a conclusion that such behavior was clearly beyond the pale of acceptable conduct in a free society. As Justice Jackson observed, albeit in a dissenting opinion, any broader application of the due process clause to negate a state's employment of effective police interrogation practices was "as dangerous and delicate a use of federal judicial power" as the substantive use of the due process clause "to disable [the states] from social or economic experimentation,"[49] a use of due process that the late New Deal Court had explicitly repudiated.

As the voluntariness doctrine took on a life of its own, however, the Court increasingly seemed willing, at least if judged by its actions, simply to substitute its own normative judgments for those of the state courts.[50] Failing to heed Justice Cardozo's warning, the Court brought new situations under the voluntariness umbrella without seriously considering whether they truly implicated the limited concerns that had given life to the due process voluntariness rule in the first place. Nevertheless, in words and sometimes even in deeds, the Court has continued to deny that it may simply write into due process its own standards of fairness. Thus, though it expressed "distaste" for police deception of an attorney who had attempted to protect the accused from interrogation, the Court in 1986 held that this deception fell "short of the kind of misbehavior that so shocks the sensibilities of civilized society as to warrant a federal intrusion into the criminal processes of the States."[51]

Such judicial disclaimers notwithstanding, a textualist or originalist with regard to constitutional interpretation might still dispute the authority of courts to engage in any extratextual search for fundamental or immutable principles of justice.[52] Under this view, the imposition of personal values is evident in the Court's very use of the due process clauses to create a nontextually based voluntariness requirement for confessions. That this argument merits a response should be apparent from the above discussion. Nevertheless, for the reasons developed below, this chapter will not consider the validity of such a frontal assault on the due process voluntariness requirement.

First, whether right or wrong from the standpoint of interpretational methodology, such an argument would not be taken seriously at this late date, except perhaps in academic debate.[53] The force of stare decisis cannot be treated casually even in constitutional law,[54] and although later chapters will argue that the Court should overrule *Miranda*, the roots of the voluntariness doctrine are considerably older and deeper than *Miranda*'s. Second, one cannot reject the due process voluntariness doctrine on textualist or historical grounds without also rejecting substantive due process, for the two doctrines, as should be apparent from the above discussion, share salient characteristics and similar vulnerabilities. Although a second judicial interment of substantive due process might be a welcome development, questions of such magnitude go to the very heart of the current debate about constitutional interpretation.[55] Important and relevant as they are, such questions cannot be addressed with sufficient adequacy in this book.[56] Finally, whatever the arguments, the Court, regardless of its makeup, is not going to abrogate the voluntariness doctrine.

The extreme opposite position, that the due process clauses should be read as inviting judges simply to write their own moral preferences into the Constitution, is even less appealing. As Professor John Ely has observed, anyone attracted to such a view immediately confronts "the immense and obvious problem of reconciling [it] with the basic democratic theory of our government."[57] Not surprisingly, therefore, academic commentators have "seldom endorsed in so many words" such a methodology of judicial review.[58] Even more significantly, judges have always denied, as the above discussion indicates, that they possess the authority to give constitutional stature to their own moral preferences. To paraphrase Professor Ely, one cannot find Supreme Court opinions that say, "We think the state conduct at issue is morally unacceptable, the dissenters think it is morally acceptable, we win five to four."[59] When the constitutional text itself does not supply the premise for their reasoning, judges invariably invoke sources that they want us to believe lie outside their personal values.

The only remaining course for this chapter, therefore, is to attempt to steer between the two unacceptable interpretational poles of complete abrogation of the due process voluntariness doctrine on the one hand and overt judicial infusion of personal values into the meaning of voluntariness on the other. The voluntariness doctrine, in the words of the Court's early due process decisions, should be premised on notions of fundamental fairness that are rooted in some "objective" source, such as tradition or the concepts of ordered liberty and justice.[60]

Of course, such an approach immediately confronts the objection that no middle ground really exists. Professor Ely has argued, for example, that "although the judge or commentator in question may be talking in terms of some 'objective,' nonpersonal method of identification, what he is really likely to be 'discovering,' whether or not he is fully aware of it, are his own values."[61] This argument, of course, echoes the familiar and persistent argument of the late Justice Hugo Black, who insisted that a fundamental rights or fundamental fairness view of due process invites judges to "roam at will in the limitless area of their own beliefs."[62]

The Supreme Court's recent revival of substantive due process gives powerful support to the Black-Ely argument.[63] Nevertheless, sincere and respected judges have insisted that the search for principles of fundamental fairness need not "imply that judges are wholly at large."[64] For example, Justice Felix Frankfurter maintained that in the search for fundamental principles of justice, judges "may not draw on . . . merely personal and private notions and disregard the limits that bind judges in their judicial function."[65] He added,

> To practice the requisite detachment and to achieve sufficient objectivity no doubt demands of judges the habit of self-discipline and self-criticism, incertitude that one's own views are incontestable and alert tolerance toward views not shared. But these are precisely the presuppositions of our judicial process. They are precisely the qualities society has a right to expect from those entrusted with ultimate judicial power. . . . The faculties of the Due Process Clause may be indefinite and vague, but the mode of their ascertainment is not self-willed.[66]

Likewise, denying that a flexible approach to due process leaves judges "free to roam where unguided speculation may take them,"[67] the late Justice John Harlan cautioned that the proper judicial restraint in this area requires a "continual insistence upon respect for the teachings of history, solid recognition of the basic values that underlie our society, and wise appreciation of the great roles that the doctrines of federalism and separation of powers have played in establishing and preserving American freedoms."[68]

Somewhat paradoxically, Justice Harlan adhered to his flexible approach to due process while insisting that the Court, with the constitutional text as its "only commission," has authority to interfere with state prerogatives "[o]nly to the extent that the Constitution so requires."[69] The seeming contradiction, of course, is that the text cannot be the Court's only commission when the Court defines and protects rights that cannot be found in the text. The contradiction exists, however, only if one rejects the premise that the Constitution itself assumes the existence of fundamental but unenumerated rights that government may not violate.[70] Harlan's approach requires such a controversial premise both to give unenumerated rights jurisprudence legitimacy as constitutional law and to distinguish this jurisprudence from the mere imposition of personal values.

In the current era—one defined by the United States Senate's recent rejection of a textualist or originalist approach to constitutional interpretation[71] and by the Supreme Court's unwillingness, despite its supposedly "conservative" judicial philosophy, to disavow unenumerated rights methodology[72]—the moderate judicial philosophy of Justices Frankfurter and Harlan may provide the second best solution for those who want the Constitution's text to remain substantially relevant to constitutional law.[73] Although both jurists embraced a flexible approach to due process, they also recognized, as Holmes had before them, the need for ample restraint, lest judges exceed the proper scope of their authority. Perhaps as much as Justice Black, both were determined to prevent constitutional law from degenerating into a battle of personal preferences among judges.

Still, the Frankfurter-Harlan position can be coherent only if it actually is possible to identify objective sources of judgment outside the judge's set of personal values. When the Court goes beyond the constitutional text, it typically attempts to ground its analysis in history and tradition, immutable principles of justice, or principles of justice that, if not immutable and universal, at least are basic to the American system of justice.[74] Each of these potential sources of judgment admittedly has serious ontological and epistemological problems.[75] Yet, ambivalent and manipulable as these sources may be, each suggests an obligation to search for principles that have been vital in giving shape to the American system of government and that have a pedigree considerably stronger than the contemporary musings of philosophical and academic discourse. Whether or not these sources can actually be "discovered," the Court's perceived need to invoke them conveys a symbolic but important reminder that judges should begin their inquiry, in Frankfurter's words, with "incertitude that one's own views are incontestable" and, in Holmes's words, with understanding that the Constitution is not "the partisan of a particular set of ethical . . . opinions, which by no means are held *semper ubique et ab omnibus*.[76]

As part of an attempt to convey such a message, Justice Frankfurter once described a particular course of police conduct not merely as offensive to "some fastidious squeamishness or private sentimentalism about combatting crime too energetically" but as conduct that "shocks the conscience."[77] Although Professor Laurence Benner, like others, has argued that "shocks the conscience" terminology "ransoms due process to the personal values of five members of the Court,"[78] the apt question is, Compared to what? Compared to approaches that would have the Court make judgments about fairness simpliciter, or that would invite the Court to "civilize" the meaning of due process,[79] the notion that judicial intervention requires a shocked judicial conscience conveys a message of judicial restraint, one instructing judges to refrain from relying on their private notions of fairness or right and wrong.

To appreciate this, one must read the "shocks the conscience" language in the context of the broader discussion in which Frankfurter used it. Frankfurter began his analysis with the reminder, too often ignored today, that federal judges must be "deeply mindful of the responsibilities of the States for the enforcement of criminal laws," and he warned against turning the due process requirement "into a destructive dogma against the States in the administration of their systems of criminal justice."[80] Describing the Court's scrutiny of state convictions under the due process clause as "very narrow," Frankfurter characterized due process as protecting only those principles of justice that are "so rooted in the traditions and conscience of our people as to be ranked as fundamental"; he likewise spoke of principles of justice that are "implicit in the concept of ordered liberty."[81] Before using the "shocks the conscience" language, Frankfurter further cautioned, in words quoted earlier in this chapter, that due process analysis must not be self-willed.[82] Placed in context, therefore, the "shocks the conscience" language did not invite judges to search their own consciences. On the contrary, Frankfurter took pains to emphasize that the personal consciences of federal judges were insufficient to justify a judicial override of state court judgments.

Viewed in these terms, the "shocks the conscience" concept is useful not as a black-letter test, which it cannot be, but as a symbolic reminder. The concept suggests that federal judges must always strive to distinguish broadly contestable, moral judgments, which they have no authority to impose on the states no matter how strongly held, and society's bedrock moral or political principles, which the due process clause may arguably protect.[83] This is a distinction we all can understand, even if we disagree on particulars. As Justice Harlan described it, due process analysis "recognizes, what a reasonable and sensitive judgment must, that certain interests require particularly careful scrutiny of the state needs asserted to justify their abridgment."[84] For those inclined to accept the legitimacy of substantive due process—which need not follow from the above analysis—the point may be made by observing that a claimed right of married couples to use contraceptives is qualitatively different in our society than a claimed right of an individual to drive without a seat belt.[85] While the better interpretational view may be that the constitution we have speaks to neither, an advanced degree is not needed to appreciate that our society does not view, and has not viewed, these claims as equally compelling.

It would be incorrect to contend at this point that the proffered analysis fully answers the objection that, left this untethered, judges will yield to the powerful temptation to describe their personal values as constitutionally required, a temptation that also exists, however, in approaches that are textually based. As Justice Frankfurter conceded, no appeal exists, short of impeachment or constitutional amendment, from Supreme Court decisions.[86] Ultimately, self-restraint must be relied on in a system that essentially overlooked the need for checks and balances on the judiciary. Stated bluntly, more than interpretational methodology distinguished Justice Harlan from Justices Brennan and Blackmun.

The analysis in this section has attempted to demonstrate that Justices Frankfurter's and Harlan's restrained nontextualist approach has much to commend it as an acceptable first alternative to textualism, at least in this context where we are trying to give meaning to an existing and deeply rooted voluntariness requirement under the due process clauses. In addition, the analysis has attempted to show that, whatever its faults, the application to the voluntariness issue of such a restrained approach is consistent with the Court's longstanding view of due process analysis in general. Though the activists will surely want more and their opponents less, the suggested approach has the virtue of at least trying to come to terms with the Fourteenth Amendment's intended purpose of protecting basic individual rights without radically altering the federal-state balance of authority. Adhering to this purpose, this section has sought, just as the Supreme Court originally did, to justify some federal intervention or oversight in this area without depriving the states, within narrowly defined limits, of the authority to determine their own voluntariness standards. The remainder of this chapter will attempt to demonstrate that a properly limited due process approach necessarily generates far fewer restraints on police interrogation than many academic commentators would like.

The Volitional or Mental Freedom Concern

As discussed in chapter 3, the concept of involuntariness or coercion has at least two and perhaps three component parts: (1) a claim that the alleged coercer engaged in wrongful conduct, (2) a claim that this wrongful conduct left the allegedly coerced party with no reasonable choice or no acceptable alternative but to comply with the coercer's wishes, and (3) a claim that the wrongful conduct caused the coerced party to comply with the coercer's wishes. Although, as we have seen, some dispute exists about whether and how the third component adds to the second, this dispute does not alter the conclusion that each part of the voluntariness inquiry demands normative judgments.

Professor George Dix has argued that because they are necessarily intuitive, the normative judgments in the voluntariness inquiry do not lend themselves to logical debate or empirical inquiry.[87] We have seen, however, that the set of normative judgments that due process analysis justifiably permits courts to impose on the police and state courts must necessarily be more modest in size and less contestable in content than the set of normative judgments that compete for recognition in philosophical discourse. Outside this relatively small set of federal due process constraints, state courts should be free, as earlier Supreme Court cases recognized, to make voluntariness judgments in accordance with their own views about state law. In Justice Frankfurter's words, the scope of due process review should be "very narrow," the goal being only to establish a floor beneath which the states may not go.[88]

That some constitutional notion of voluntariness should limit police interrogation seems to be taken as a given, at least once the obstacle of interpretational methodology discussed in the last section is hurdled.[89] Thus, few would challenge the abstract statement that interrogation conduct is constitutionally wrongful if by duress it unduly impairs the defendant's volitional freedom. The problem, of course, is that the words *duress* and *unduly* make questions of degree inevitable. Still, the abstract statement suggests that interrogation tactics at some undefined point may involve such an assault on the defendant's autonomy and dignity that constitutional intervention, through the vehicle of the due process voluntariness requirement, becomes appropriate.

To begin to move beyond abstract statements, it helps to consider cases that lie at or close to opposite ends of the voluntariness spectrum. At one end of the spectrum are cases like *Brown v. Mississippi*,[90] the case described in chapter 1, which involved the hanging and beating of the defendants to get confessions. At the other end are cases like *Miranda v. Arizona*,[91] which involved little more than the inherent pressures of a short custodial interrogation. Incontestably, *Brown* is the easier case in terms of supporting a conclusion of constitutional involuntariness.

Why is this so? Primarily because we can convincingly claim that torture—meaning, for present purposes, physical violence against defendants to procure confessions or information—violates fundamental principles of justice that are deeply rooted in the traditions and conscience of our nation.[92] This is not to say that torture has always been condemned. On the contrary, European countries between the twelfth and eighteenth centuries authorized and regularly used torture to procure confessions. During the eighteenth century, however, and within the space of one generation, most European countries made such torture illegal.[93] It may be, as Professor John Langbein has argued, that abolition occurred not in response to humanitarian arguments but because changes in the law of proof made confessions less important in obtaining convictions.[94] Whether or not this is so, the fact remains that European countries, which had previously institutionalized the practice of physical torture to obtain confessions, decisively made torture unlawful during the eighteenth century, and ever since the international condemnation of torture has been uncompromising.[95]

Given its ties to and influence on American procedure, common-law English procedure is particularly relevant in the search for principles rooted in the history and conscience of our nation. Although instances of torture occurred in practice, the English legal system, unlike its Continental counterparts, never systematized the use of torture to obtain confessions, and English writers boasted about this difference.[96] Moreover, English criminal procedure formally condemned the use of torture a century before Continental countries did.[97] Of equal relevance, both English and American cases during the eighteenth century consistently enforced a voluntariness requirement for confessions, a requirement now reflected in English statutory provisions making statements inadmissible that have been obtained by torture, violence, or threats of violence.[98]

The prohibition on the use of torture, or physical violence, to procure confessions stems primarily from broadly shared community beliefs concerning the inherent dignity and autonomy of human beings.[99] Perhaps these beliefs stem in turn from even more basic beliefs relating to the notions of free will and individual responsibility, beliefs that seem to underlie much of our legal system and that often incline us to excuse those who have been "forced" to act against their wishes.[100] In addition, the denunciation of torture stems from broadly shared perceptions about what it means to be a free and democratic society. The use of torture to procure confessions is, we believe, a hallmark of totalitarian societies.

The rejection of torture as a means of procuring confessions also reflects societal commitment to the basic principle, discussed in chapter 1, that the conviction of an innocent person is a greater evil than the acquittal of a guilty person. As Dean Charles McCormick once observed, the risk of unreliability is grave because the defendant's "reluctance to make a confession which in the long run will lose him life or liberty is converted to a willingness to accept this hazard whose consequence is deferred, in order to escape a more terrifying immediate evil."[101] Of course, even the pre-eighteenth-century European architects of the law of torture expressed concern about the risk of unreliability in physically coerced confessions,[102] but unlike them, post-Enlightenment democratic societies have rejected the fictions that cloaked the seriousness of the danger.[103]

Against this background, the Court's unanimous due process condemnation of the police violence in *Brown* seems unremarkable. Even as
it reaffirmed the then-prevailing view that the Fifth Amendment's self-
incrimination clause did not apply to the states, the Court insisted that
"[c]ompulsion by torture to extort a confession is a different matter."[104]
Observing that state procedures must comport "with the fundamental
principles of liberty and justice which lie at the base of all our civil and
political institutions," and describing the use of coerced confessions as
the "curse of all countries," the Court readily concluded that it could
hardly "conceive of methods more revolting to the sense of justice than
those taken to procure the confessions" in this case.[105] The freedom of
the state in devising its own rules and procedures is "the freedom of
constitutional government"; constitutional government has no freedom
to substitute the rack and the torture chamber for the witness stand.[106]

Miranda and *Brown* are fish from very different kettles. According
to the Court, Miranda, an indigent, twenty-three-year-old Mexican
male with an eighth grade education and "pronounced" sexual fantasies,
was arrested at his home and taken to a police interrogation room, where
two police officers questioned him. Without employing force, threats,
or promises, the officers in two hours obtained Miranda's signed confession to rape.[107] Nevertheless, despite the absence of police impropriety—
unless one considers custodial interrogation itself improper—the Supreme Court held that Miranda's confession should not have been admitted into evidence.

Not surprisingly, the Court conceded with magnificent understate-
ment that it might not have found Miranda's statement "to have been
involuntary in traditional terms."[108] Using more forceful language, Justice Harlan accused the Court majority of sacrificing truth to its "own
finespun conception of fairness," and he expressed astonishment "that
the Constitution [could] be read to produce this result."[109] Of course,
the Court relied on the Fifth Amendment self-incrimination clause—
which will be discussed in the next chapter—and not on the due process
voluntariness doctrine as such, but this does not detract from the point
that a judgment of involuntariness in *Miranda,* though perhaps plausible
to some as a matter of personal moral philosophy, would be indefensible
under a due process analysis rooted in the traditions and fundamental
principles of the nation rather than in the personal moral preferences of
the judges. The normative concerns so apparent in *Miranda* just do not
have the same universality or moral hold as those that were apparent in
Brown. Indeed, far from being fundamentally wrong, the police conduct
in *Miranda* would win moral approval under the arguments presented in
the previous chapters of this book.

Between the polar extremes of the police practices in *Brown* and those in *Miranda* lie a spectrum of police practices that vary according to their perceived impropriety and the amount of pressure or duress they impose. Torture, of course, can be psychological as well as physical.[110] Like actual violence, the threat of violence may cause defendants to experience substantial anguish, to relinquish their preferences out of fear, and even falsely to condemn themselves. Moreover, a defendant threatened with violence should not be expected to wait for the first blow before deciding that capitulation to the police demands may be the safer and wiser course. Thus, if the use of physical violence to procure confessions is constitutionally impermissible, the threat to employ such violence should be equally impermissible, and confessions that result from such threats should be deemed constitutionally involuntary.

The threat of violence need not be explicit to have its intended effect. In *Malinski v. New York*,[111] for example, the defendant was stripped and kept naked for three hours, after which he was permitted to put on socks, shoes, and underwear and to wrap himself in a blanket. Kept in this state of partial undress the next seven hours, he finally confessed. The prosecutor described the police conduct as good psychology: "let him sit around with a blanket on him, humiliate him there for a while; let him sit in the corner, let him think he is going to get a shellacking."[112] The police, however, are not authorized to punish or to humiliate suspects, either gratuitously or for the purpose of finding evidence. Whether the primary concern is human dignity or autonomy, the defining characteristics of a free and democratic society, or the material risk of false confessions, such degrading and intimidating police conduct, with or without the prosecutor's comments, violates the fundamental norms of our society. Moreover, although the police conduct in *Malinski* did not literally overbear the defendant's will, we can regard as eminently reasonable the defendant's decision to succumb.[113] Appropriately, therefore, the Court in *Malinski*, although divided on other points, unanimously condemned the defendant's confession as constitutionally involuntary.

Protracted, incommunicado custodial questioning also can violate precepts that can be described as fundamental with little controversy. In *Chambers v. Florida*,[114] the Supreme Court described five days of questioning that culminated in a successful all-night session as violative of due process:

The very circumstances surrounding their confinement and their questioning without any formal charges having been brought, were such as to fill petitioners with terror and frightful misgivings. . . . From virtually the moment of their arrest until their eventual confessions, they never knew just when anyone would be called back to the fourth floor room, and there, surrounded by his accusers and others, interrogated by men who held their very lives . . . in the balance.[115]

The Court relied not only on the element of fear, as discussed in the above quotation, but also on the "fundamental idea that no man's life, liberty or property should be forfeited" in a free society absent a proper charge and a fair and public trial.[116] Unremarkably, the Roosevelt-packed *Chambers* Court, which certainly had come to understand the limits of due process analysis, again was unanimous in finding a due process voluntariness violation.

On the surface, the Court's nonunanimous opinion in *Ashcraft v. Tennessee*[117] may seem more difficult to justify. Acting in relays, various police officers continuously interrogated the defendant from 7:00 P.M. Saturday to 9:30 A.M. the following Monday, a period of thirty-six hours. Describing the situation as "so inherently coercive that its very existence is irreconcilable with the possession of mental freedom," the Supreme Court concluded that the defendant's confession was not voluntary.[118] This reasoning prompted a dissent from Justice Jackson, who argued that the Court must always determine whether the defendant's confession "was obtained by pressures so strong that it was *in fact* involuntarily made."[119] In effect, Jackson accused the majority of abandoning the voluntariness inquiry with its inherent coercion approach.

The answer to Justice Jackson's objection lies in the component elements of the voluntariness inquiry. The first element requires a normative judgment at the constitutional level about the interrogation conduct of the police. For many of the reasons given in the immediately preceding paragraphs, the combination of incommunicado detention, denial of sleep or even rest, and relentless interrogation can be condemned not simply in terms of private sentimentalism but as a matter of fundamental constitutional principle.[120] The second element requires a judgment as to whether the coercive conduct of the police left the defendant with "no reasonable choice" or "no acceptable alternative" but to confess.[121] As we saw in the last chapter, this prong of the inquiry is not factual, as Justice Jackson mistakenly suggested in his *Ashcraft* dissent, but normative. The stronger the pressure created by the impermissible interrogation conduct and the greater the degree of impropriety, the more inclined we are to empathize with the defendant's decision to extricate himself from the interrogation. Indeed, we might even go so far as to say that Ashcraft's decision to succumb after thirty-six hours of relentless interrogation was justified, not merely reasonable or under-standable, in the sense that we may actually want to encourage cost-free compliance when the situation is so severe.[122]

The third element of the inquiry, assuming that it exists as a sepa-rate component and is not subsumed in the second, requires a decision regarding causation. Because the defendant persisted in proclaiming his innocence throughout the thirty-six hour ordeal, but-for causation, at the very least, is easy to infer. Moreover, on facts as egregious as these, it may be defensible to conclude that more than but-for causation is unnecessary. In any event, the Court clearly did not require more than but-for causation to support its finding of involuntariness. It seems erro-neous, however, to conclude, as some have done, that the Court's inher-ent compulsion analysis necessarily dispensed with a causation require-ment altogether.[123]

A more sensible reading of *Ashcraft*—and one that preserves the significance of voluntariness terminology—is that fundamentally inap-propriate police conduct did in fact put pressure on (cause) the defen-dant to confess, something he did not want to do. The tougher problem is in deciding what factors are relevant in answering the normative question about the reasonableness of the defendant's position to succumb to the impermissible pressure. The Court's inherent compulsion ap-proach suggested, in effect, that because pressure like that in *Ashcraft* always makes the decision to surrender the most reasonable course of action, an analysis of other factual details is unnecessary. While some might dispute this normative conclusion, the normative nature of the inquiry makes it linguistically appropriate for those who agree with the majority to describe Ashcraft's confession as involuntary. Whether the confession was involuntary in a constitutional sense is, of course, an-other matter. Nevertheless, given the rather extreme facts, *Ashcraft* would not seem to rank as one of the Court's more troubling due process decisions.

There may be an inclination at this point to ask what the second prong of the analysis really adds. Why not always limit the inquiry to the propriety of the police conduct, at least once but-for causation between that conduct and the confession can be established? Such a narrowed focus might seem particularly appropriate given that the police practices inquiry often seems to do most of the analytic work in the cases. Part of the answer, as explained in the last chapter, is that a police practices approach standing alone cannot capture the essence of a claim of in-voluntariness, a claim that has independent moral force. Second, cases may exist in which the second prong of the inquiry interplays with the first to justify a finding of involuntariness. Third, in some cases

Ashcraft's per se approach may be normatively unacceptable in that the perceived reasonableness of the defendant's alternatives may depend, in part, on the defendant's characteristics: under similar circumstances, what may be regarded as involuntary surrender by one defendant may be treated as voluntary cooperation by another.

The difficult case of *Lynumn v. Illinois*,[124] discussed in the last chapter, perhaps illustrates the possible interplay of the first two prongs. It will be recalled that the police in *Lynumn* informed the defendant that, if convicted, she could be incarcerated for ten years, that her welfare would be terminated, and that she would probably lose custody of her children. They also suggested to her that "it would go light on her" if she cooperated. The difficulty encountered in the last chapter was in identifying precisely what made the police conduct wrongful, particularly absent any suggestion that the police had lied about the likely consequences. Even were this difficulty surmounted at the purely normative level, it would remain difficult to perceive how the police conduct violated an immutable principle of justice or a principle of justice rooted in the traditions and conscience of our nation.

The normative judgment we can more readily make in *Lynumn*, however, is that the defendant, as a parent, had no reasonable alternative but to comply when the police suggested that she could preserve custody of her children only by "cooperating." This judgment, if valid, casts the question about the propriety of the police practices in a different light. That is, because of the interplay of the two prongs of the voluntariness inquiry, we may now claim that the police acted improperly in seeking self-incriminating cooperation by offering Lynumn a deal that a decent parent would find too good to refuse. Viewed in this light, the unanimous finding of constitutional involuntariness in *Lynumn* may be explained on the ground that it violates a fundamental precept of American justice for the police to put a parent to the wrenching choice of self-destruction or loss of her children.[125] Of course, for *Lynumn* to be right as a constitutional decision, at least under the approach advocated in this chapter, this conclusion must be something more than a personal moral preference of the judges. Nevertheless, whatever one's ultimate conclusion about *Lynumn*, there should be little quarrel with the general proposition that even in the search for truth, some police "offers" impose choices on defendants that are beyond the constitutional pale.[126]

In many cases, the impropriety of the police conduct, if present at all, is not of sufficient magnitude to justify an automatic conclusion that the defendant had no choice but to succumb by confessing. Nevertheless, facts relating to the particular defendant may make such a conclusion warranted. As Justice Jackson observed in his *Ashcraft* dissent, unfortunately in the context of discussing overborne wills, "the Court always has considered the confessor's strength or weakness, whether he was educated or illiterate, intelligent or moronic, well or ill, Negro or white."[127] For example, a false statement that the defendant will get the death penalty for robbery if the defendant fails to cooperate will be more coercive to a defendant who is ignorant of the law than to one who knows it. In the former case but not in the latter, we may want to conclude that the police gave the defendant no reasonable choice but to confess.

In *Haley v. Ohio*,[128] the police arrested a fifteen-year-old black male for murder. Five or six officers, in one or two person teams, then questioned the defendant in relays from midnight until five o'clock in the morning, when he confessed. The Court stated that the defendant's youth was relevant to the voluntariness inquiry: "That which would leave a man cold and unimpressed can overawe and overwhelm a lad in his early teens."[129] The Court added that while a mature person might withstand such an ordeal, a fifteen year old, held incommunicado in a police station, is likely to respond to a relentless midnight inquisition with fear and even panic.[130] Restated in the terminology under discussion, the Court's opinion concluded, in effect, that the interrogation at issue was improper and, given the fear that it induced, left this particular defendant (but not necessarily all defendants) no reasonable course of action except to confess.

This interpretation of *Haley* should not be misunderstood. No claim is being made that the interrogation was wrongful simply because it exerted some pressure on Haley to confess. As previously observed, pressure is a legitimate purpose of interrogation, not something to be condemned. Indeed, supplying the necessary fifth vote in *Haley,* Justice Frankfurter approvingly observed that the very purpose of interrogation is to put pressure on the suspect to talk, and he distinguished ordinary pressures from "coercion."[131] Nor is any claim being made that Haley's will was overborne, for such a statement, as we have seen, would be meaningless. Haley clearly had the capacity to resist his interrogators, but he chose not to. What is being claimed is that the involuntariness of Haley's confession can be supported by two normative judgments: first, that the interrogation imposed undue or impermissible pressure on Haley and, second, that such undue pressure made confessing Haley's only reasonable option. The normative judgments required to make a voluntariness inquiry necessarily involve questions of degree, and personal characteristics of the defendant, such as age, may be relevant to these questions.

What must yet be considered is whether the normative judgments necessary to defend the holding in *Haley* can be supported at the constitutional level. This question is important because, as we have seen, a proper understanding of due process should leave the states free, within narrowly defined limits, to define their own standards of voluntariness. More so than the majority opinion, Justice Frankfurter's concurring opinion saw the need to address this question. Seeking to justify the Court's intrusion into the Ohio criminal justice system, he insisted, as he always did, that the Court's judgments had to be based on more than "merely private notions" or "personal bias."[132] Nevertheless, he concluded that this case involved "sentiments deeply embedded in the feelings of our people."[133] He added,

> It would disregard standards that we cherish as part of our faith in the strength and well-being of a rational civilized society to hold that a confession is "voluntary" simply because the confession is the product of a sentient choice. . . . In concluding that a statement is not voluntary which results from pressures such as were exerted in this case . . . I do not believe I express a merely personal bias against such a procedure. Such a finding, I believe, reflects those fundamental notions of fairness and justice . . . which lie embedded in the feelings of the American people and are enshrined in the Due Process Clause. . . .[134]

Unfortunately, Justice Frankfurter did not explain what made his and the Court's conclusion on voluntariness reflective of fundamental American values, and his mere denial would seem insufficient to negate an accusation that he relied merely on personal sentiments. Moreover, that four justices dissented suggests that the majority's normative judgments were highly contestable rather than reflective of broadly shared, fundamental values. The dissenters insisted that the facts, as ascertained by the lower court, precluded a judgment "that this was a confession wrung from a child by means which the law should not sanction."[135] This is not to say that due process violations cannot be ascertained by divided votes. Nevertheless, especially when the Court is closely divided, those who would find a constitutional violation should be obligated to explain how they have determined that *fundamental* principles are implicated. Because Frankfurter did not and perhaps could not do this, the possibility cannot be dismissed that *Haley* was wrongly decided as a due process case.[136]

While age, intelligence, physical health, and mental illness may sometimes be relevant in making the normative judgments that the due process voluntariness inquiry requires, the defendant's actual guilt or innocence is an individual characteristic that should be ignored. As a practical matter, of course, the defendant's guilt or innocence cannot be known with certainty either at the time of the police interrogation or when the pretrial motion to suppress the statement is made and decided. In any event, the Supreme Court's cases have long taken the view that the actual reliability of the defendant's statement is irrelevant to the due process inquiry.[137] This approach is essentially correct. The due process voluntariness doctrine imposes limits on what the police may do even in the search for truth. It would accordingly make little sense to permit truth to justify or excuse police conduct that otherwise would be subject to constitutional condemnation. Any lingering doubt on this score should be removed by recalling that what offended fundamental values in *Brown, Ashcraft,* and *Lynumn* had nothing to do with the guilt or innocence of the defendants.

The Unfair Advantage or Improper Exploitation Concern

As explained in the last chapter, the concepts of voluntariness and involuntariness have been used, rightly or wrongly, to address questions not only of duress or coercion but also of unfair advantage or improper exploitation. Although often melded together in the Court's opinions, these two concerns should be considered separately for analytic clarity. For purposes of the due process voluntariness doctrine, however, the governing approach must be the same: unless the principle of fairness at issue is so rooted in the traditions and conscience of the nation that it may properly be viewed as fundamental, a due process finding of involuntariness cannot be justified.

Professor Fred Inbau has long advocated the view that while the police should be permitted to employ both "fair" and "unfair" interrogation practices, they should not be permitted to do anything that would be likely to make an innocent person confess.[138] Nevertheless, Professor Inbau has also recognized that some police trickery may be impermissible simply because it "shocks the conscience." To illustrate his point, Professor Inbau indicated that a police officer may not procure a suspect's confession by pretending to be a chaplain or a defense lawyer.[139]

Why not? Given that the pressure to confess from the defendant's perspective does not depend on whether the lawyer or chaplain is an imposter or real, such trickery does not seem to involve a question of coercion. To use the terminology from the previous section, it is difficult to see why the deception in Inbau's hypotheticals would leave a defendant with no reasonable alternative but to confess. This is not to say that deceit may never create an issue of coercion-involuntariness but only that the imposter situation more clearly seems to raise an issue of possible unfairness or improper exploitation. The question that must be addressed is why the perceived unfairness in the hypotheticals, unlike that arguably present in other kinds of deception, rises to the constitutional level.

The answer lies in the special significance our society long has attached to individual relationships with lawyers and members of the clergy. The lawyer's obligation of loyalty to his or her client extends back to Roman law, and this obligation is reflected both in the legal profession's ethical standards and in the attorney-client privilege that developed at common law and that every American state now recognizes.[140] The legal status of relationships with the clergy is, if anything, even stronger. Although English case law abandoned the clergy-communicant privilege after the Reformation, New York started the American trend in favor of this privilege well before the Fourteenth Amendment was added to the Constitution, and today virtually every American jurisdiction recognizes such a privilege.[141] Of course, the wisdom of these privileges, particularly the attorney-client privilege, has always been subject to dispute.[142] Still, despite even harsh criticism stressing that these two privileges, like all privileges, impede the search for truth, both remain firmly rooted in American law.

Police impersonation of a defense lawyer or a member of the clergy would necessarily intrude on the special trust that individuals place in such professional people for the confidentiality of communications, a trust that our law broadly seeks to encourage. If the police cannot require lawyers and members of the clergy to disclose confessions, they should not be able to obtain confessions directly from defendants by exploiting such relationships of trust. As Professor Inbau put it, such deception "shocks the conscience." Stated in less subjective terms, deception of this nature, even in the search for truth, violates a fundamental principle, one that history and the available data inform us is strongly grounded in the traditions and conscience of our nation.

Police deception involving other professional relationships may raise similar concerns. In *Leyra v. Denno*,[143] police persistently interrogated the fifty-year-old defendant for several days in connection with the murder of his parents. Having promised to obtain a doctor to relieve the defendant from the severe pain of a sinus attack, the police summoned a psychiatrist who, rather than providing medical assistance, questioned the defendant for an hour and a half, using both suggestive and hypnotic techniques. As the Court concluded, the undisputed facts were more than adequate to demonstrate coercion-involuntariness at the constitutional level. For purposes of this section, however, the more interesting question is whether such use of a doctor or psychiatrist, even absent the facts showing coercion, would constitute improper exploitation-involuntariness in violation of due process.

While the common law did not recognize an evidentiary privilege for private disclosures to physicians, confidentiality was the norm of practice, and English case law even suggested that a doctor's honor precluded voluntary disclosure of medical secrets.[144] Well before the adoption of the Fourteenth Amendment, New York started the American movement toward the recognition of a general physician-patient privilege, and today the majority of states recognize this privilege.[145] The psychotherapist-patient privilege also did not exist at common law, nor did it widely exist until rather recently. Nevertheless, today a privilege for communications to psychiatrists and psychotherapists is more in favor than the ordinary physician-patient privilege.[146]

Of course, that a principle has broad contemporary support does not necessarily mean that it is firmly rooted in the traditions and conscience of the nation. It is equally true, however, that the law of evidence is only one datum concerning the status of specific relationships in our society. Doctors and psychiatrists have traditionally earned the public's trust by respecting the confidences of their patients, and largely because of this trust, a substantial segment of the public will reveal secrets to these professionals that it will not reveal to others.[147] Indeed, some commentators have gone so far as to suggest that the expectations of privacy in these relationships are sufficiently great to justify constitutional protection for private communications.[148]

In *Leyra,* the police exploited the trust that inheres in the physician-patient relationship. Recognizing that he needed help, and after much coaxing, Leyra talked to a person whom he perceived to be a treating doctor, and he was persuaded by this person to confess. Were the law to state, in effect, that Leyra had to assume the risk that his "doctor" was working as a police agent—or worse, was not even a doctor at all—it would significantly damage the public trust in doctors that is so essential to the physician-patient relationship. More important than this utilitarian concern, however, was the fundamental unfairness, rooted in the way our society traditionally has viewed the physician-patient relationship, in deceptively providing Leyra a doctor who intended to act against his interests rather than for his well-being.[149] Totally aside from the issue of coercion-involuntariness, therefore, the use of the psychiatrist in *Leyra* violated the unfair advantage or improper exploitation strand of the due process voluntariness doctrine.

The police deception in *Leyra* and in Inbau's hypotheticals should be distinguished from the police use of jail plants and other informants to gain information from defendants. As the Supreme Court recently indicated, the Constitution does not forbid "strategic deception by taking advantage of a suspect's misplaced trust in one he supposes to be a fellow prisoner."[150] Absent coercion, "[p]loys to mislead a suspect or lull him into a false sense of security" are not prohibited.[151] Nothing in our tradition would equate the suspect-acquaintance relationship, or the prisoner-cellmate relationship, to relationships that individuals have with lawyers, doctors, and members of the clergy.

As the last paragraph suggests, skillfully employed deception often is an important interrogation tool for learning the truth. Such deception may take many forms in addition to the use of informants. The interrogator may feign sympathy with the defendant, cast aspersions on the victim, or falsely state that a codefendant has confessed and implicated the defendant. Likewise, the interrogator may claim that the defendant's fingerprints have been found, that witnesses have identified him, or that the police have other information linking the defendant to the crime.[152] If the defendant gives an alibi, the interrogator may invent a fact, such as a traffic tie-up caused by an accident at the alleged alibi site, to see how the defendant responds.[153] Because a defendant who is fabricating an alibi cannot know whether the interrogator is telling the truth about the mentioned event, such police deceit can be quite effective in trapping the defendant in lies and in helping to persuade the defendant to tell the truth.

In a particularly poignant example of police deceit, Professor Inbau tells of a police officer who was interrogating one suspect while a companion suspect waited outside the interrogation room. Even though the interrogation was not going well, the officer walked into the waiting room and asked his secretary to bring a note pad into the interrogation room. Shortly thereafter, the secretary returned to a desk in the waiting room and started to type from what appeared to be notes. At one point, the secretary even asked the companion suspect how his friend spelled his name. Shortly thereafter, the interrogator returned the first suspect to the waiting room and called the companion suspect in to be questioned. Erroneously thinking that his friend had talked, the companion quickly confessed.[154]

Through such deception, police officers often outsmart defendants, who typically are ill-equipped to deal with these tactics. Viewing this as a problem, many commentators have condemned either trickery in general or various of the techniques described in the preceding two paragraphs. Over thirty years ago, Bernard Weisberg expressed the view that courts might bar deception by developing "civilized standards of procedure."[155] More recently, focusing on particular deceptive practices, Professor Welsh White condemned as unfair "any tactic that challenges a suspect's honor or dignity."[156] To Professor Kent Greenawalt, tactics that play on a suspect's weaknesses or that deceive a suspect about crucial facts, such as whether a codefendant has confessed, do not accord with the suspect's "autonomy and dignity."[157] Professor George Dix has perhaps been most forceful in arguing this position:

> [T]he defendant's decision whether or not to confess [should be] as fully informed and reasoned as possible . . . . [E]xploitation of a subject's ignorance or mistake . . . should be condemned insofar as this can be done without incurring excessive countervailing costs. Moreover, this is true whether the ignorance or mistake concerns the existence of an abstract legal right, the law relating to implementation of that right, or facts that influence the tactical decision to exercise that right.[158]

Many of these condemnations of police trickery reflect the foxhunter's, equality, and human dignity arguments reviewed and criticized in chapter 2. The dignity argument, however, has a dimension in this context that has not yet been considered. Instead of making the broad and unconvincing claim that it violates human dignity to induce or encourage defendants to incriminate themselves, the opponents of deception can make the narrower and more plausible claim that this particular police strategy impermissibly violates human dignity.

That this claim is plausible, however, does not mean that it is persuasive. If our morality really opposed manipulation and deception, we would not permit practices like wiretapping and the use of undercover informants. These practices by their very nature intrude on human dignity. Moreover, whatever the scope of their proper use, these practices can be dangerous because of the risk of abuse. Yet, as Professor H. Richard Uviller has reminded us, "the potential abuse of an investigative technique is never a ground for abandonment lest we be rendered utterly helpless against the onslaught of crime."[159]

Many Americans—more likely, most—would undoubtedly share Professor Uviller's belief that "without some strenuous efforts to discover crime and identify, catch, and punish the perpetrators, lawful society would be the hopeless captive of the lawless."[160] As Professor Jan Gorecki has observed, although torture is generally considered unfair, "many relatively innocent police tactics, such as false sympathy or the 'Mutt and Jeff' technique, do not seem to invite general contempt, especially when applied to solve a major crime."[161] Going further, many might even say that "[i]t is consonant with good morals . . . to exploit a criminal's ignorance or stupidity."[162]

While such views may reflect utilitarian arguments that are out of fashion in some circles, our society has taken a utilitarian approach to lying and deception in general, as evidenced by the persistence of such notions as white lies, polite lies, excusable lies, and even justifiable lies. No evidence exists to suggest that it would not apply similar utilitarian thinking in the context of police interrogation.[163] Simply put, if the goal of police interrogation is to learn the truth, this goal will not be accomplished by seeking to make the "defendant's decision whether or not to confess as fully informed and reasoned as possible." On the contrary, "trickery and deceit are at times indispensable to the criminal interrogation process."[164]

But what if a judge fervently believes, perhaps because of a nonutilitarian outlook, that the critics of police deception have the better moral argument? This is where the limited nature of the due process inquiry comes into play. Whatever one's personal moral views, it cannot plausibly be claimed that police deception violates a principle of justice rooted in the traditions and conscience of our nation. Were material misrepresentation suddenly to constitute a constitutional wrong, contemporary judges would have to "invalidate many transactions accepted, indeed approved by courts for ages."[165] Indeed, even Professor Dix has acknowledged, although with dismay, that American courts readily adopted the view of the English treatise writers that fraud does not make a confession inadmissible.[166] Though the critics of police deception might be the vanguard of a new morality, they cannot claim to speak for our nation's fundamental values.

An important caveat needs to be mentioned. Police may not deceive defendants about the nature or scope of their legal rights.[167] While this limitation on the police may be stated in terms of a fundamental principle of justice, it actually reflects a more basic notion: the police do not afford defendants the legal process that is due when they deceive them about available rights or the applicable law. Thus, it would violate due process to tell suspects that they are obligated to answer questions or that only statements made under oath are legally admissible.[168] Similarly, as long as the law recognizes a right to counsel during police interrogation, the police may not suggest to defendants that they have no such right.

Trustworthiness and Other Possible
Due Process Concerns

Given that the voluntariness test at common law originally reflected concern about trustworthiness,[169] it would be inappropriate to ignore trustworthiness as a possible due process concern. As discussed in chapter 1, concern about convicting the innocent is strongly rooted in our history and tradition. Our legal system, however, generally leaves it to the trier of fact to assess the reliability of evidence. Nevertheless, it is one thing to tolerate the inherent unreliability risks of an evidentiary system and another thing to tolerate police practices that gratuitously add to those risks.[170]

This much recognized, the need to have a separate reliability strand of the due process voluntariness doctrine may still be doubted. Under the approaches already considered, the risk of the defendant making an unreliable confession would be a factor in considering whether the defendant had no reasonable choice but to confess (coercion-involuntariness) or whether the police obtained the confession by taking unfair advantage of the defendant (improper exploitation-involuntariness). Thus, although a defendant need not show a risk of unreliability to make out a due process violation, a police practice that created a serious risk of unreliability on the facts of a given case almost certainly would violate one of the other two strands of the voluntariness doctrine. Nevertheless, those who prefer to focus on reliability as a third strand of the doctrine would not be wrong for doing so.

Some may criticize the analysis so far offered for ignoring our society's commitment to an accusatorial system as a fundamental principle of justice. Chapter 2 concluded, however, that the argument distinguishing "our" accusatorial system from "their" inquisitorial system not only is incapable of solving concrete issues but also substitutes conclusory rhetoric for analysis.[171] If this is true at the mere policy level, it necessarily is true at the due process level. No fundamental principle of justice can tell us just how accusatorial state criminal justice systems must be.

Some may also contend that the protection against compulsory self-incrimination is a fundamental principle of American justice that has been ignored in this chapter. This protection, explicitly mentioned in the Fifth Amendment, is discussed in the next chapter. The purpose of this chapter has been to show that due process standing alone at best supports a voluntariness doctrine that is considerably narrower than many commentators advocate.

Objections to the Voluntariness Doctrine

Many commentators are likely to be troubled by the discussion in the preceding sections. Past criticisms of the voluntariness test make it reasonable to anticipate objections both that any voluntariness approach is inherently unworkable and that, in any event, the test proposed in this chapter is too narrow in scope.[172] In a well-known criticism of the voluntariness test three decades ago, Professor Yale Kamisar described efforts to achieve precision regarding the meaning of voluntariness as attempts "to do the impossible."[173] More recently warning against proposals to replace *Miranda* with a voluntariness test, Professor Stephen J. Schulhofer elaborated on six major defects that Kamisar and other writers had supposedly proved to be inherent in the voluntariness test. In Schulhofer's view, these defects were that the test (1) left the police without adequate guidance, (2) impaired judicial review, (3) depended on a swearing contest about what had occurred, (4) allowed considerable pressure to be placed on the accused, (5) allowed the weak to be manipulated, and (6) failed adequately to check physical brutality.[174]

Schulhofer's third and sixth objections are easily answered. Because all legal tests, including *Miranda*'s, depend on sworn testimony, we still have "swearing contests" about what was said and done during police interrogation. This is a serious issue that needs to be addressed, but it is not addressed by replacing the voluntariness test with some other test of admissibility. Similarly, no test, including *Miranda*'s, can provide a complete check against police brutality. The brutality concern could be alleviated, however, by providing a solution, such as video- or audio-tape recording, for the swearing contest problem. Ignoring similar defects in the *Miranda* approach, Schulhofer revealed a broader agenda by suggesting that the voluntariness test permitted brutality to go unchecked because it "encouraged the questioning process itself."[175] Fortunately for society, however, Schulhofer's hostility to police interrogation is not reflected in the due process clauses or anywhere else in our national Constitution.

Schulhofer's fifth objection, that the voluntariness test allowed the weak to be manipulated, was criticized in chapter 2 as reflective of an ill-conceived equality argument. Indeed, specifically complaining that the "vulnerable were more likely to be on the losing end of a successful police interrogation," Schulhofer asserted "that we do (and should) find it unseemly for government officials systematically to seek out and take advantage of the psychological vulnerabilities of a citizen."[176] Schulhofer obviously holds this moral belief, but he neglected to state who else comprises the "we." Moreover, to say a practice is unseemly is a far cry from claiming and demonstrating that the practice violates a principle of justice deeply rooted in our nation's traditions and conscience. In any event, the weak and the unsophisticated undoubtedly also waive *Miranda* rights more readily than the sophisticated. Schulhofer's concern for the weak can be adequately addressed only by prohibiting police interrogation altogether, a goal that would apparently not trouble him.

Schulhofer's remaining objections reveal a lack of sensitivity to the need to take federalism into account and to the necessarily limited nature of the due process inquiry. By faulting the voluntariness test for not adequately guiding the police and for allowing considerable pressure, Schulhofer ignored the imperatives of our constitutionally mandated federal system, a system that leaves the general business of regulating the police and determining policy to the respective states.[177] Because the United States Supreme Court is not the highest appellate court of the various state judicial systems, it has no common-law authority over state courts or state instrumentalities of government. With some obvious lapses, the Court's due process doctrine in general and its voluntariness doctrine in particular have recognized this. Thus, as already discussed, the Court early recognized that voluntariness as such was for the states to define for themselves. The due process voluntariness doctrine was intended to have only the very limited purpose of protecting those truly fundamental principles that no state could ignore in devising its own test.

In complaining that the voluntariness test impaired judicial review, Schulhofer asserted that judges "were virtually invited to give weight to their subjective preferences when performing the elusive task of balancing."[178] The due process approach discussed in this chapter, which does not require "balancing," makes no such invitation. Of course, even under a limited due process approach, close cases will arise in which reasonable judges may disagree about whether truly fundamental principles have been violated. Disagreement in close cases, however, is not something to bemoan.[179] In the narrow borderland between moral principles that are personal or broadly contestable and those that are fundamental in the sense discussed in this chapter, there is little reason to be concerned about differences of opinion.

Still, the desire of commentators like Kamisar and Schulhofer for more detailed rules cannot be dismissed altogether. Nothing in this chapter, however, would prevent the adoption of specific rules defining what the police may and may not do, for to say that the due process voluntariness test should be narrow in scope is not to say that the public debate about police interrogation practices should be similarly confined. Indeed, it is quite arguable that the *Miranda* approach, which both

Kamisar and Schulhofer have supported, has contributed to the failure to adopt more specific rules in the United States. As Professor Mark Berger has observed, "[t]he constitutional law focus of the American confession law debate has diverted attention from the substantive police interrogation issues that society should address."[180]

Lacking such a constitutional emphasis, the British, by contrast, have "confronted directly what goes on during police questioning and enacted legislation recasting the system from the ground up."[181] The British experience indicates that "interrogation issues can be legislatively addressed in a manner that is not limited to framing a standard for admitting confessions."[182] Those, like Kamisar and Schulhofer, who disagree with the police tactics that this book would permit, and with the morality that these tactics reflect, need only understand that their battle should be waged not in the United States Supreme Court but in some other forum.

CHAPTER 5   **The Protection against Compulsory**
Self-Incrimination

During a seven-year period in the 1960s, the Warren Court issued a spate of decisions that revolutionized criminal procedure (and constitutional law) in the United States. Although its impact was enormous, the revolution was relatively short-lived. Indeed, its momentum had largely ebbed even before "conservative" Warren Burger replaced "liberal" Earl Warren as Chief Justice in 1969. In the last twenty years, moreover, the judicial pendulum has noticeably moved in the opposite direction, with the Court increasingly manifesting disaffection for Warren Court opinions. Nevertheless, although many commentators are inclined to suggest otherwise, the Court over the last two decades has not engaged in a counterrevolution. Notwithstanding some changes, primarily although not entirely at the margins, the Court today essentially operates under the rules it created during the aberrational years of the Warren Court.[1] This is especially true in the law governing police interrogation and confessions.

Under the Court's due process doctrine, which dominated the constitutional law of confessions until the 1960s, neither custodial interrogation nor the denial of a suspect's request for a lawyer alone or together sufficed to render a confession involuntary. Indeed, in 1958, during its first phase, the Warren Court decided two cases that upheld the admissibility of confessions from custodial suspects whose requests for counsel had been denied.[2] In 1964, however, having entered its second and revolutionary phase, the Warren Court overruled these decisions and held that the Sixth Amendment right to counsel applies to police interrogation.[3]

The Court has since reduced the role of the Sixth Amendment in police interrogation. This has not had much practical significance, however, because the Court in *Miranda v. Arizona*[4] used the Fifth Amendment's self-incrimination clause to make custodial interrogation inherently suspect, to require that certain warnings precede custodial interrogation, and in general to provide custodial suspects with a panoply of rights, including the right to a lawyer's presence during interrogation.

Miranda's Fifth Amendment right to counsel and the other rights that it created remain in place today.

Although the rights that *Miranda* created were unprecedented in federal constitutional law, the Court's conclusion that the Fifth Amendment's protection from compulsory self-incrimination is "fully applicable during a period of custodial interrogation"[5] was perhaps even more significant from a jurisprudential standpoint. By thus leaving the due process "totality of circumstances" approach behind, the Court enabled itself to fashion a detailed code of interrogation rules that due process jurisprudence could never have supported. Moreover, by shifting constitutional gears from Fourteenth Amendment due process to Fifth Amendment self-incrimination, the Court avoided the need formally to overrule decades of due process precedent that had rejected litmus tests for the admissibility of confessions.

This chapter begins by questioning the Court's reliance on the Fifth Amendment in *Miranda*. This is done by examining both the Court's application of the Fifth Amendment's self-incrimination clause to the states and its use of this clause to address the problem of police interrogation. This discussion is useful for perspective even though the Court is not likely at this date to permit the merits of the matter to drive the Fifth Amendment from the arena. After reviewing these issues, the chapter turns to an issue that we need not yet regard as permanently settled: the Fifth Amendment's proper meaning in the context of police interrogation. The thesis the chapter defends is that *Miranda* took an excessively expansive view of the Fifth Amendment. Properly understood, the Fifth Amendment should not limit police interrogation practices more broadly than does the mental freedom strand of the due process voluntariness doctrine.

The Incorporation Issue

As already indicated, the Court in *Miranda* based its decision on the Fifth Amendment's guarantee that no person "shall be compelled in any criminal case to be a witness against himself."[6] Directing his ire both at the Court's extension of the Fifth Amendment to police interrogation and at its failure to demonstrate that the Fifth Amendment, even if applicable, mandated its new rules, dissenting Justice Harlan derided the Court's reliance on the Fifth Amendment as "a *trompe l'oeil*."[7] Were it not for a case decided two years earlier over his dissent,[8] Harlan might also have seen a sleight of hand in the Court's reliance on the Fifth Amendment in a state rather than a federal case.

The Court has always recognized that the Bill of Rights, including the Fifth Amendment's protection against compulsory self-incrimination, was enacted to restrain the federal government but not the states.[9] Nevertheless, in the first heyday of substantive due process, and with the reluctant concurrences of Justices Holmes and Brandeis—both of whom essentially opposed substantive due process—the Court concluded that speech, which is specifically protected against federal abridgement by the First Amendment, is a liberty interest that the Fourteenth Amendment's due process clause substantively protects against the states.[10] Since that time, and notwithstanding the first demise of substantive due process in the 1940s, it has been generally accepted judicial doctrine that the Fourteenth Amendment, in effect, incorporates and makes applicable to the states the First Amendment's protection of speech.

Perhaps because the due process incorporation doctrine raises all the difficult interpretational questions discussed in the last chapter,[11] incorporation did not go much beyond speech until the 1960s, when the Court, overruling numerous precedents, selectively applied almost all the provisions of the Bill of Rights to the states.[12] With regard to the Fifth Amendment's protection against compulsory self-incrimination in particular, the Court, before the 1960s, twice refused to apply this protection to the states. In *Twining v. New Jersey,*[13] the Court's review of history led it to the "irresistible" conclusion that "the privilege, if fundamental in any sense, is not fundamental in due process of law, nor an essential part of it."[14] Looking beyond Anglo-American history, the *Twining* Court also declined the culturally myopic invitation to declare the Fifth Amendment's protection an "immutable principle of justice which is the inalienable possession of every citizen of a free government."[15]

Four decades later, the Court affirmed *Twining* in *Adamson v. California.*[16] *Adamson* distinguished physical and psychological coercion, which the due process voluntariness doctrine prohibited, from legal compulsion to testify, which the Fifth Amendment prohibited in federal cases but the due process clause permitted in state cases.[17] Concurring in *Adamson,* Justice Frankfurter characterized *Twining* as "one of the outstanding opinions in the history of the Court."[18]

Had *Twining* and *Adamson* remained the law, *Miranda*'s reliance on the Fifth Amendment would not have been possible; instead, the states would have retained the right to decide for themselves whether, to what extent, and in what contexts to recognize the protection against compulsory self-incrimination. In *Malloy v. Hogan,*[19] however, the Court, obviously disagreeing with Frankfurter's characterization, overruled both these cases and applied the Fifth Amendment's self-incrimination clause to the states. Performing what even Professor Yale Kamisar concedes may be described as "a shotgun wedding of the privilege to the confessions rule,"[20] the Court concluded that its coerced confession cases demonstrated, contrary to what *Adamson* had said, that the due process voluntariness doctrine had come to reflect Fifth Amendment principles.[21] The Court also relied on the view suggested in *Mapp v. Ohio*[22] that the Fifth and Fourth amendments "conjoined" in the Fourteenth Amendment to make the federal search and seizure exclusionary rule applicable to the states.[23] Finally, the Court garnered support from judicial statements describing the American system of justice as accusatorial and the Fifth Amendment self-incrimination clause as one of the principles of free government.[24]

All of the Court's reasoning in *Malloy* can be rebutted. First, because the previous confession cases had explicitly excluded the Fifth Amendment from their rationale,[25] they supported rather than undermined *Twining* and *Adamson*. Second, to the extent that *Mapp* made more than passing reference to the Fifth Amendment, the exclusionary rule's "connection to the privilege is now viewed as utterly untenable."[26] The Fifth Amendment protects against neither the compulsory disclosure of physical evidence nor the discovery of evidence by search and seizure,[27] and even if it did, one could not find compulsory self-incrimination only in cases involving *illegal* searches. Moreover, it may be appropriate to note that *Mapp* itself was a Warren Court decision that discarded well-established precedent.[28]

For the reasons discussed in chapter 2, the accusatorial-inquisitorial distinction added no support to the Court's decision in *Malloy*. More significantly, because the issue before the Court was whether the federal Constitution imposed a uniform model of procedure on the states, the Court begged the question by positing "that the American system of criminal prosecution is accusatorial, not inquisitorial."[29] Finally, the Court simply erred in describing the protection against compulsory self-incrimination as a basic principle of free government. While a society cannot be free unless it provides some protection against the suppression of political speech and arbitrary arrest and search, a society can very well be free and yet require those under suspicion to answer questions posed in an orderly proceeding. Unlike the speech and search and seizure protections, the Fifth Amendment's restriction on government does not embody a fundamental principle of justice.[30]

In short, Professor Donald Dripps's description of *Malloy* as "an extraordinarily weak opinion" is difficult to resist.[31] Nevertheless, Professor Dripps's proposal that the Court overrule *Malloy* and reinstate *Twining* and *Adamson* is likely to be perceived as too radical, or too late in the day, to garner majority support on the Court. It may not be too late, however, for the Court to disinter Justice Harlan's view—a view first suggested by Justice Holmes—that an incorporated provision should apply to the states with more flexibility than it does to the federal government.[32] Of course, the Holmes-Harlan approach would be logically indefensible under Justice Black's theory that the framers of the Fourteenth Amendment intended to apply all of the Bill of Rights to the states, for incorporation under this theory has nothing to do with a particular right being viewed as fundamental.[33] Under the Court's selective incorporation approach, however, which applied to the states not all Bill of Rights provisions but only those that reflected, in the Court's view, fundamental principles of justice, the application of nonfundamental aspects of incorporated provisions is logically incoherent. Justice Brennan's retort that the Court would not apply to the states a "watered-down, subjective version" of a Bill of Rights provision, though colorful and seductive, simply ignored the due process theory under which incorporation proceeded.[34]

Under the Holmes-Harlan approach, which has yet to be relegated to history,[35] the Court would be justified in binding the states only to those aspects of Fifth Amendment interrogation law that can truly be regarded as fundamental, as that term is used in due process jurisprudence. Thus, even if *Miranda*'s reading of the Fifth Amendment could somehow be defended, the states, if not the federal government, would be freed from all *Miranda* requirements that do not reflect fundamental aspects of the Fifth Amendment's protection. Requirements as unprecedented and controversial as most of *Miranda*'s would be difficult to defend in such terms.[36]

The Fifth Amendment and the Admissibility of Confessions

The incorporation issue aside, *Miranda* still had to confront the question whether the Fifth Amendment applies to the issue of coerced confessions. Unlike *Malloy,* however, which had to justify a sharp break with both old and recent incorporation precedent, the *Miranda* Court was able to invoke a nineteenth-century precedent that had used the Fifth Amendment to address the problem of coerced confessions. In *Bram v. United States,*[37] decided in 1897, the Supreme Court said that the voluntariness of confessions in federal trials was to be decided under the Fifth Amendment's self-incrimination clause.[38] The *Bram* Court justified this conclusion by asserting that the Fifth Amendment's protection against compelling individuals to become witnesses against themselves was "but a crystallization of the [common-law voluntariness] doctrine as to confessions," and it described the Fifth Amendment as "comprehensive enough to exclude all manifestations of compulsion, whether arising from torture or from moral causes."[39]

Criticizing *Bram* many years ago, Professor Wigmore claimed that "no assertions could be more unfounded."[40] Observing, as was noted in chapter 3, that the common-law voluntariness rule for confessions reflected a concern about trustworthiness, Wigmore succinctly summarized the distinction between the two rules: "the confession-rule aims to exclude self-incriminating statements which are *false,* while the privilege-rule gives the option of excluding those which are *true.*"[41] Referring to *Bram*'s use of history as "inexcusable," and suggesting that it had to be "specially repudiated,"[42] Wigmore contended that "the *history* of the two principles is wide apart, differing by one hundred years in origin, and derived through separate lines of precedents."[43]

In support of this claim, Wigmore observed that the protection against compulsory self-incrimination developed during the tangled, protracted, several-century struggle against the religious and political persecutions carried out by the ecclesiastical courts, the High Commission, and the Star Chamber. Resistance to the mandatory ex officio oaths used by these institutions, on the ground that no one was bound to engage in self-accusation, played a significant role in this struggle. The dissidents ultimately prevailed in the middle of the seventeenth century when Parliament abolished the High Commission and the Star Chamber and barred the ecclesiastical courts from administering mandatory oaths. Nevertheless, broader claims persisted that individuals could not be re vquired to answer incriminating questions even if they were not under oath, and "creeping in by indirection," the protection against compulsory self-incrimination gradually came to be viewed as a bar to judicial questioning of the accused in the common-law courts, although its full scope in these courts was not resolved for many years.[44]

By contrast, Wigmore noted, the voluntariness rule for extrajudicial confessions did not develop until some time in the eighteenth century, well after the protection against compulsory self-incrimination, at least in its early form, had been established. Significantly, the courts that gave birth to this rule did not rely on the protection against compulsory self-incrimination. As Wigmore put it, "[i]f the privilege, fully established by 1680, had sufficed for both classes of cases, there would have been no need in 1780 for creating the distinct rule about confessions."[45]

Wigmore's assertion that the two rules had "no connection"[46] has been a frequent target of criticism. Most notably, Professors Edmund Morgan and John Maguire have found fault with at least certain aspects of Wigmore's discussion.[47] Relying in part on these two scholars, historian Leonard Levy has stated flatly that Wigmore was "wrong."[48] More recently, Professor Laurence Benner, coming from a somewhat different direction, has added his voice to those contending that Wigmore engaged in "too narrow a reading of history."[49] None of his detractors, however, has been able to discredit Wigmore's basic criticism of *Bram*.

Noting that Wigmore had conceded the application of the privilege in administrative proceedings, Professor Morgan found it curious that Wigmore nonetheless insisted that the "privilege" did not apply to confessions coerced by the police.[50] The basis for this criticism is not altogether clear, however, for the issue whether an agency—including the police—has a right to require answers or evidence from a person (the privilege issue)[51] is different from the issue of whether certain interrogation methods are likely to produce false answers or are offensive to moral norms (the coercion or voluntariness issue). Hence, no inconsistency exists in saying that the privilege applies in administrative proceedings but does not govern the issue of coerced confessions.

In any event, Professor Morgan acknowledged that "[n]o one will quarrel with [Wigmore's] assertions that the privilege and the rule as to confessions have separate histories and that they are not coincident in area or in details of application."[52] Morgan also acknowledged—and he wrote almost twenty years after Wigmore—that "in countless cases where the admissibility of a confession is in issue, no mention is made of the privilege."[53] While Morgan did cite several cases that had taken conflicting positions on whether the privilege applied to the issue of coerced confessions, all the cited cases that invoked the privilege, with the exception of *Bram* itself, were decided many years after *Bram*.[54]

Writing five years after Morgan, and citing him, Professor John Maguire made the rather odd statement that both the privilege and the voluntariness rule have a "common general aim—personal protection."[55] Many procedural rules, however, such as the speedy trial rule, have the protection of the accused as their broad, abstract aim, but this does not imply that all such rules have something to do with the protection against compulsory self-incrimination.[56] Moreover, Maguire, like Morgan, conceded that the privilege and the voluntariness rule had "different causes and times of their origination."[57]

Professor Levy, as already noted, relied in part on Morgan and Maguire. He also relied on Professor Charles McCormick who, though conceding that *Bram* was guilty of a "historical blunder," thought that "the kinship of the two rules is too apparent for denial."[58] Maintaining that opponents of English procedure regarded compulsory self-incrimination as a "species of torture," Levy insisted that sixteenth- and seventeenth-century arguments against torture, compulsory self-incrimination, and coerced confessions "overlapped."[59] Of course, the term "species of torture" in this argument might be regarded as somewhat unilluminating, for a legal requirement that a person answer questions is not really analogous to practices like stretching a person on the rack.[60] Prolonged pretrial detention might just as readily be described as "a species of torture," but this would not establish a connection between restraints on such detention and the privilege. Moreover, Levy elsewhere acknowledged that torture played an insignificant role in English law and, although understating the point, he also acknowledged that "the right against self-incrimination was not solely responsible for the disuse of torture to get confessions."[61]

Levy also seems to have conceded that the rule against coerced confessions emerged in the eighteenth century, as Wigmore had claimed, to protect against untrustworthy evidence.[62] Rather than prompting Levy to endorse Wigmore's criticism of *Bram*, however, this concession inspired Levy to insist that the historical blunder was made not by *Bram* but "by the English courts of the eighteenth century when they divorced the confessions rule from the self-incrimination rule."[63] That *Bram* did not purport to criticize the English voluntariness cases—indeed, that it cited them favorably—is only a minor objection to Levy's claim. More damaging is the change of hats that the argument betrays, for by proffering the rationale that English courts, in his opinion, should have used, Levy ceased to analyze the law as a pure historian. From the perspective of historical criticism, one cannot persuasively fault Wigmore's condemnation of *Bram* by wishing that the eighteenth-century courts, which after all developed the voluntariness rule, had relied on a different rationale than they did.[64]

Professor Benner's more recent criticism of Wigmore differed somewhat from that of his predecessors. Benner faulted Wigmore for planting the roots of the privilege in the jurisdictional power struggles that culminated in the religious and political strife of the seventeenth century.[65] In Benner's view, Wigmore overlooked the "policies of individual freedom and dignity" that motivated the early protests against compulsory self-incrimination.[66] Yet, Benner also attacked *Bram* for perpetuating a "veil of ignorance, by engrafting the common-law voluntariness rule onto the Fifth Amendment and virtually equating the two."[67] This prompted courts, in Benner's view, to think of the privilege as a utilitarian principle concerned with trustworthiness, which was the focus of the common-law voluntariness doctrine, rather than as a deontological principle "grounded in the nature of the relationship between the individual and the state."[68] "[L]ike unwanted baggage," Benner complained, "the trustworthiness rationale . . . quietly accompanied the common law voluntariness doctrine when it became interwoven with the fabric of the Fifth Amendment."[69]

While applauding *Bram*'s willingness to fashion a test of compulsion "heavily weighted in favor of the accused,"[70] Benner, it should be apparent, essentially endorsed Wigmore's historical criticism of *Bram*'s attempt to define Fifth Amendment compulsion in terms of the common-law voluntariness rule. Whereas Wigmore believed, however, that *Bram*'s historical blunder led to an unwarranted expansion of the Fifth Amendment's scope, Benner attributed to *Bram* an unduly narrow understanding of the Fifth Amendment. In Benner's view, *Bram* caused the "true origins of the privilege to become lost in the shadows of history."[71]

Benner, unlike Wigmore, thus endorsed the use of the Fifth Amendment to determine the admissibility of confessions, claiming, in essence, that neither *Bram* nor *Miranda* went far enough in restricting police interrogation. In Benner's view, *Bram*'s fundamental error, which *Miranda* duplicated, was in perceiving the Fifth Amendment issue in terms of compulsion.[72] The privilege, Benner argued, encompasses a cluster of rights, with the protection against compelled self-incrimination being merely an element of this cluster, "an important corollary of the 'privilege.'"[73]

Benner acknowledged that the Fifth Amendment's text speaks only of compelling individuals to become witnesses against themselves. He maintained, however, that the text reflects "careless drafting," which is partly responsible for the "present bankruptcy of theory."[74] The framers used "highly stylistic and picturesque phraseology," seeing no need for precise drafting because they fully understood the privilege.[75] In support of this last point, Benner invoked the following passage from Levy:

> The clause itself . . . might have been so imprecisely stated, or misstated, as to raise vital questions of intent, meaning and purpose. But constitution-makers, in that day at least, did not regard themselves as framers of detailed codes. To them the statement of a bare principle was sufficient, and they were content to put it spaciously, if somewhat ambiguously, in order to allow for its expansion as the need might arise.[76]

Arguments that slight the constraints of constitutional text make rebuttal difficult except at the policy level. Under the Levy-Benner approach to constitutional interpretation, one cannot really criticize *Bram* or *Miranda* for yielding incorrect interpretations of the Fifth Amendment; all one can do is disagree about whether there was a "need" for "expansion"—by judges, not the people, of course—of the constitutional provision at issue. Ironically, however, the quotation from Levy itself invoked a framers' intent argument, for it claimed that the framers, regarding themselves as drafters of bare principles rather than legal rules, intended that future interpreters would supply the necessary content of what they wrote. That the Convention added the precise words "in any criminal case" to prevent Madison's original self-incrimination proposal from applying to civil proceedings[77] apparently did not give Levy or Benner any pause in making this claim.

Benner's argument, however, relied only in part on the desirability of permitting judges to expand the constitutional principle at issue. Regarding the privilege as historically broader than the Fifth Amendment's text, Benner more forcefully argued that the framers intended to constitutionalize the historical privilege. In Benner's view, the privilege underwent two stages of development: the first establishing a right to a formal charge, supported by oath or indictment, before one could be held to answer; the second establishing initially a right not to be questioned under oath and ultimately a right not to be judicially questioned at all.[78] Benner also claimed that the voluntariness doctrine in the eighteenth and nineteenth centuries, reflecting the same concern for fairness toward the individual as the privilege, virtually barred any interrogation of a prisoner.[79]

Benner suggested that to be true to the values of the historical privilege, the Court should mandate that no waiver of rights can occur unless the accused has first consulted with counsel.[80] Furthering the values of the ancient privilege, counsel would provide notice of the offense and assure that probable cause existed to detain the accused. Furthering the privilege's corollary right to be free from coercion, counsel would negate the inherently compelling influences of police interrogation.[81]

The problem with Benner's analysis is that it inflated the content of the "historical privilege." While Benner cited twelfth-century objections to questioning by the ecclesiastical courts absent formal charge and notice, by his own admission these objections were rejected in statutes passed in the fifteenth and sixteenth centuries.[82] Benner admitted that after Queen Elizabeth I the focus of the attack shifted to the oath ex officio, but wishing, like Levy, that history were different, he lamented that the "subsequent blending of the 'privilege' with the development of this new corollary 'right' against compulsory self-incrimination has resulted in a tangled confusion of thought ever since."[83]

Like Levy, Benner also viewed the seventeenth-century struggle as one to make common-law principles applicable to the ecclesiastical courts and Star Chamber,[84] but as Professor Helmholz has recently argued, it is not clear that the arguments for the privilege were rooted in the common law at all.[85] In any event, not only was the precise source of the rule that developed in the seventeenth century obscure, but "[i]ts exact reach was debatable, its interpretation required knowledge of the intricacies of the *ius commune,* and there were aspects of the subject open to dispute."[86]

The uncertainty about the scope of the seventeenth-century right continued after the abolition of the High Commission, the Star Chamber, and the oath ex officio. Acknowledging the continuing use of the Marian statutes from the sixteenth century that had authorized justices of the peace to question criminal defendants at pretrial examinations,[87] Benner nevertheless insisted that the practice of questioning the accused, even without oath, was "antithetical to this new stage in the development of the privilege."[88] In an attempt to reduce the significance of this continuing practice, Benner also suggested that the practice exceeded what Parliament had intended, demonstrating "how easily the inquisitorial method is spawned when an avenue is left open to it."[89] Inquisitorial or not, however, the fact remains that the British judges, initially at least, saw no inconsistency between the newly recognized privilege and the practice of questioning the accused, without oath, at the pretrial examination.

Benner correctly noted that English judges in the nineteenth century came to regard it as their duty to advise suspects at the pretrial examination that they need not respond to questions, a requirement ultimately codified in 1848.[90] Because these developments occurred after the Fifth Amendment's adoption, however, they do not shed much light on the principle that the framers thought they were constitutionalizing.[91] Moreover, judicial questioning of the accused at the preliminary examination persisted in some American states, such as New York, until the middle of the nineteenth century.[92] At least one commentator has speculated that the privilege came to be viewed as a bar to judicial questioning at the pretrial examination only after the examination court ceased to perform an investigatory function and assumed more of an ordinary judicial role.[93] This thesis finds support in the observation of a British Home Office working group that the nineteenth-century development of organized police forces made possible the separation of the investigative and judicial functions that had previously been combined in the pretrial examination court.[94]

That the historic privilege was not as broad as Benner would have readers believe is supported by Levy:

The fact must be emphasized that the right in question was a right against *compulsory* self-incrimination, and . . . the right had to be claimed by the defendant. . . . It vested an option to refuse to answer but did not bar interrogation nor taint a voluntary confession as improper evidence. Incriminating statements made by a suspect at the preliminary examination or even at arraignment could always be used with devastating effect at his trial. That a man might unwittingly incriminate himself when questioned in no way impaired his legal right to refuse answer. He lacked the right to be warned that he need not answer. . . . That reform did not come in England until . . . 1848, and in the United States more than a century later the matter was still a subject of acute constitutional controversy.[95]

Finally, one must take exception to Benner's claim that the English voluntariness doctrine during the eighteenth and nineteenth centuries evolved into a rule "virtually barring any interrogation of a prisoner."[96] Preliminarily, as already noted, the voluntariness rule was not premised on the protection against compulsory self-incrimination and thus has little bearing on the meaning and scope of the Fifth Amendment. Even if this objection is put aside, however, the voluntariness rule never was as broad as Benner suggested. Indeed, in the section of his article providing supporting citations, Benner more carefully acknowledged that prior to *Bram* in 1897, "no British appellate decision had authoritatively ruled on the issue of custodial interrogation," and statements casting doubt on the practice of police interrogation were no more than "expressions from individual justices."[97]

It should not be surprising, moreover, that the mid-nineteenth-century statutory restrictions on judicial questioning of the accused created in some quarters "a sense of resistance to police interrogation";[98] in Professor Mark Berger's words, "[h]aving given up the role of interrogator, the justices of the peace were uncertain whether police could be allowed to perform that function."[99] As already seen, however, the development of organized police forces and the concomitant ban on judicial questioning, at least at the pretrial examination, did not take hold either in Britain or in this country until well after the Fifth Amendment was adopted. In any event, uncertainty about the propriety of police interrogation and a ban on police interrogation are two different matters, and the former never evolved into the latter. On the contrary, as Professor George Dix has documented, nineteenth-century voluntariness law in England tolerated confessions induced by trickery and made exceptions to the rule excluding confessions induced by promises, while American courts displayed even "less enthusiasm" for the common-law rules.[100]

The foregoing should make apparent that *Bram* and *Miranda* erred, at least from a historical perspective, in perceiving an "intimate connection"[101] between the privilege, which prohibited compulsory oaths and mandatory judicial questioning of the accused, and the issues pertaining to the admissibility of extrajudicial confessions. Just as *Bram* had erred, as Wigmore correctly perceived, in treating the Fifth Amendment as a "crystallization" of the common-law voluntariness rule, so also did *Miranda* err in concluding "that all the principles embodied in the privilege apply to informal compulsion exerted by law-enforcement officers during in-custody questioning."[102] Although the common law had developed a voluntariness requirement for confessions prior to the adoption of the Fifth Amendment, neither the voluntariness rule nor its underlying trustworthiness rationale referred to the protection against compulsory self-incrimination. Concededly, some voices did question how police interrogation could be deemed consistent with the mid-nineteenth-century ban on mandatory judicial questioning of the accused at the pretrial examination, but in neither Great Britain nor the United States did the voluntariness rule or the privilege evolve to the point of prohibiting police interrogation. Indeed, not even *Bram* or *Miranda* went that far.

Compulsion, Coercion, and Involuntariness

The argument in the preceding section will not fully satisfy many who support *Miranda's* application of the protection against compulsory self-incrimination to police interrogation. Professor Yale Kamisar, for example, has challenged Professor Wigmore's conclusions without really challenging his history:

> I do not contend that "the implication[s] of a tangled and obscure history" dictate that the privilege apply to the police station, only that they permit it. I do not claim that this long and involved history displaces judgment, only that it liberates it. I do not say that the distinct origins of the confession and self-incrimination rules are irrelevant, only that it is more important (if we share Dean Charles T. McCormick's views) that "the kinship of the two rules is too apparent for denial" . . . .[103]

To respond to Kamisar's argument, one must consider what it means for the privilege to apply to the police station. Assuming the Fifth

Amendment's appropriate application to the states, as we are doing in this section, one might be prepared to concede that the Fifth Amendment would prohibit a law requiring suspects to answer police interrogatories. Even without an oath requirement, such a law would be in tension with the plain language of the Fifth Amendment and with the late-seventeenth-century view that the privilege made it unlawful to require persons to answer incriminating questions. Those who defend *Miranda* want far more than this interpretation, however, for the police have never enjoyed or asserted a legal entitlement to answers; all the police have had, and feel a need to retain, is a right to ask questions.

Some may contend that the privilege, if applied to the police station, should make police-initiated interrogation unlawful.[104] This would make the privilege in the police station coextensive with the privilege at trial, where both the prosecutor and judge are forbidden from questioning an accused who does not "waive" Fifth Amendment rights by taking the stand in his own defense.[105] If this is the privilege to be applied, however, the "kinship" between it and the common-law voluntariness rule, far from being "too apparent for denial," is difficult to fathom, for the common-law voluntariness rule, as the previous section indicated, never condemned police interrogation as such.

Still, some may find it incongruous to bar interrogation at trial but to permit police questioning before trial. Several years ago, for example, Bernard Weisberg complained in an influential article that we "would be hard put to explain to visitors from a legal Mars how . . . secret questioning in a police station fits into a system of criminal law which recognizes the privilege against self-incrimination," and he specifically contrasted the scope of an accused's protections at trial with the absence of corresponding protections in the police station.[106] Building on this theme, Professor Kamisar similarly contrasted in colorful, metaphoric prose the "show in the gatehouse," where "ideals are checked at the door and 'realities' faced," and the "show in the mansion," where "the defendant is 'even dignified, the public invited, and a stirring ceremony in honor of individual freedom from law enforcement celebrated.'"[107] These arguments of course resemble those of the nineteenth-century jurists who pondered whether police interrogation could be deemed consistent with the new ban on interrogation by justices of the peace at the pretrial examination.[108]

The answer to the charge of incongruity is rooted both in history and in the "realities" that Professor Kamisar disparagingly referred to. Despite the questions that were raised, nineteenth-century courts in both Great Britain and this country refused to prohibit police interrogation or to render it ineffective by onerous restrictions. Although debate has never abated, courts in both countries, particularly in recent years, have continued to recognize the importance of police interrogation.[109] Indeed, as was suggested in the previous section of this chapter, the transformation of the judicial role that occurred in the nineteenth century was probably made possible by the development of police forces that assumed the investigative function previously performed by the pretrial examination court.

Anglo-American systems have not been alone in recognizing the need for practical accommodation of the competing interests. Procedural reforms in some continental countries have provided "a full panoply of safeguards for the defendant during the pre-trial judicial investigation, while allowing crucial incriminating statements to be obtained from the suspect by the police."[110] Countries that have significantly restricted the investigative role of the judiciary have "shift[ed] the bulk of actual investigative activity to the preceding 'informal' investigative activities of the police, so much so that the latter overshadow in importance the judicial investigation."[111] One commentator has observed, for example, that the French accommodation has been to provide considerable powers to those involved in investigation as "adversary" elements have been introduced in later judicial stages: "the further the French criminal process progresses, from the initial police inquiries through the intermediate stage of the preliminary judicial investigation to the trial, the greater the adversary elements allowed for."[112]

The division of the investigative and adjudicative functions makes sense from a separation of powers perspective.[113] Moreover, reflecting their own perceptions of fairness, American criminal justice systems in particular have deemed it important to separate the prosecutorial and the judicial roles.[114] Whatever a system's structure or underlying ideology, however, the investigative authority must be lodged somewhere for the system to be viable. Because successful investigation often depends on the questioning of reluctant witnesses and suspects, and on other intrusive strategies as well, the investigative stage, as a practical matter, cannot be subject to the same restraints that govern the adjudicative stage.[115] The operative rules will be different because the institutions that dominate the successive stages of the process have dissimilar functions and responsibilities. Simply put, an investigation is not, and cannot be, a trial.

Taking into account the need for investigative questioning of suspects, many American commentators over a wide span of years have proposed reforms that in essence would substitute judicial questioning of the accused for the secretive and potentially abusive process of police interrogation.[116] Although some of these reforms would have reduced the risk of police abuse, Professor Kamisar is correct in observing that they have always provoked cries of unconstitutionality.[117] In addition, such reforms have not been able to overcome our society's strong ideological beliefs about the proper distribution and separation of power. None of this, however, counts as a persuasive argument against police interrogation. We saw in chapter 1 that the existence of constitutional or ideological barriers to certain truth-enhancing reforms does not negate truth discovery as one of the dominant objectives of the criminal justice system. Similarly, the existence of constitutional or ideological barriers to perhaps a preferable system of pretrial interrogation does not make invalid the existing system.

One might still object, however, that an argument invoking history and practical considerations does not provide a principled response to the gatehouse-mansion dichotomy.[118] After all, the fact remains that the accused is not subject to interrogation at trial unless he elects to testify, and on principle the institution of police interrogation seems inconsistent with this limitation. The answer to this is that the alleged inconsistency is not nearly as obvious as it seems. Rather than referring to a single rule, the "privilege . . . embraces several distinct rules of law, each having an independent development."[119] Nonetheless, in most situations, the "privilege is merely an *option of refusal,* not a prohibition of inquiry."[120]

Thus, taxpayers may be compelled to answer questions on tax returns, and if they fear incrimination, they must affirmatively assert the privilege with regard to specific requests for information.[121] The same rule applies to witnesses in general.[122] "[I]f a witness under compulsion to testify makes disclosures instead of claiming the privilege, the government has not 'compelled' him to incriminate himself."[123] More on point, a grand jury may subpoena even a target of its investigation, and the targeted individual has the burden of invoking the privilege on a question-by-question basis.[124] Similarly, even under *Miranda,* targets of police interrogation who are not in custody are not entitled to warnings and have the burden of affirmatively invoking the privilege when questioned.[125] Indeed, based on the law in most other contexts, one might be justified in claiming that the defendant's immunity from having to invoke the privilege at trial is itself inconsistent with general Fifth Amendment doctrine, a doctrine reflected in pre-*Miranda* and even some post-*Miranda* confessions law.[126]

If the privilege cannot plausibly be viewed as a ban on police-initiated questioning, what can it mean in the context of police interrogation, and what establishes its "kinship" to the voluntariness rule for confessions? We have already seen that despite the historical importance of the oath ex officio, one might concede that the privilege would prohibit any attempt formally to require suspects, in custody or not, to answer questions. Such a prohibition would be vacuous, however, if governmental officials could force suspects to answer questions by the use of physical or psychological coercion. Not surprisingly, therefore, although the privilege did not play a significant role in the abolition of torture to secure statements in English procedure, various individuals on both sides of the Atlantic came to regard torture as inconsistent with the privilege.[127] Viewed in this light, an obvious kinship exists between the privilege and the voluntariness requirement; indeed, had a voluntariness requirement not independently developed, one might early have been inferred as a logical imperative of the privilege. All this leads, however, to the unremarkable conclusion that the Fifth Amendment, if properly applied to police interrogation at all, prohibits coerced or involuntary confessions. That is, in the context of police interrogation, to "compel" a suspect to become a witness against himself can only mean to "coerce" a suspect to become a witness against himself.

This conclusion, however, is bothersome for *Miranda*'s supporters. For example, Professors Irene and Yale Rosenberg have asserted that "it seems unlikely that the long struggle culminating in the incorporation of the Fifth Amendment prohibition against compelled testimony could have been simply an heroic effort to provide an official synonym for involuntariness."[128] Likewise, regarding it as almost self-evident that the privilege was "more than the 'voluntary' test masquerading under a different label," Professor Kamisar has declared that it takes "real dexterity" to purport to apply the Fifth Amendment to the police station and "yet conclude that this . . . does not change things very much."[129] But, to repeat, unless the Fifth Amendment is read as a prohibition on all police questioning, custodial and noncustodial, it can be read in the context of police interrogation only as providing protection against involuntariness or coercion. Indeed, the *Miranda* Court read the Fifth Amendment this way, for it found the Fifth Amendment applicable to the "informal compulsion" exerted by the police, concluded that "custodial" interrogation was "inherently compelling," and distinguished on-the-scene questioning, which it exempted from its holding, on the ground that "the compelling atmosphere inherent in the process of in-custody interrogation is not necessarily present."[130]

The possibility remains, of course, that *coercion* for Fifth Amendment purposes should be a less demanding concept than *coercion* for due process purposes and that, accordingly, *involuntariness* should have different meanings under the two amendments. The Court in *Miranda* took such an approach, for none of its previous due process voluntariness cases had sought to protect the suspect merely from the inherent pressures of custodial questioning. Indeed, the Court candidly admitted, even if it understated the point, that it "might not find the defendants' statements to have been involuntary in traditional terms."[131] The question that *Miranda* did not answer, however, is why the concepts of coercion and involuntariness should have different meanings in the Fifth Amendment and due process contexts.

Fifth Amendment precedent did not support *Miranda*'s desire to negate the mere inherent pressures of custodial interrogation or otherwise to change the meaning of voluntariness. True enough, *Bram* had equated the Fifth Amendment with the common-law voluntariness requirement, and in some respects the common-law rule did not require as much for a finding of involuntariness as the due process rule that later developed. *Bram,* however, also recognized "that the mere fact that the confession is made to a police officer, while the accused was under arrest in or out of prison, or was drawn out by his questions, does not necessarily render the confession involuntary."[132] In other federal confession cases both before and shortly after *Bram,* the Court likewise treated the voluntariness requirement as not prohibiting, nor even rendering suspect, the use of confessions obtained by custodial questioning.[133] The Court's rule for pretrial judicial proceedings was no different. In cases involving judicial and prosecutorial questioning of the accused at the preliminary hearing, the Court rejected both warning and counsel requirements and found the defendants' statements to be voluntary and admissible.[134]

Bram, of course, preceded the Court's development of the due process voluntariness doctrine by almost forty years, but once this had occurred, the Court did not seem to regard the two voluntariness standards as different. In *Ashcraft v. Tennessee,*[135] for example, the Court characterized the issue in *Bram* as whether the defendant "had been compelled or coerced," described the due process issue before it as whether the defendant "similarly was coerced," and, taking *Bram* "together" with an earlier due process case, declared that "a coerced or compelled confession cannot be used to convict a defendant in any state or federal court."[136] This is not to say that the Court found the Fifth Amendment's self-incrimination clause, as such and with all its variant meanings, applicable in state cases, for we know from the previous discussion that this was not the case. It is to suggest, however, that the Court did not regard the Fifth Amendment voluntariness requirement as imposing a different or tougher standard than the Fourteenth Amendment voluntariness requirement.[137]

Even the Warren Court—except in *Miranda*—seemed to equate the two voluntariness standards. In *Shotwell Manufacturing Co. v. United*

States,[138] for example, the Court cited both *Bram* and a due process voluntariness case in upholding against Fifth Amendment challenge a Treasury Department policy encouraging delinquent taxpayers to come clean.[139] The majority obviously knew what it was doing, for the dissent specifically criticized its reliance on the due process case, claiming that the Fifth Amendment standard should be regarded as more precise.[140] Similarly, in post-*Miranda* confession cases, in which the Fifth Amendment but not *Miranda* applied under then prevailing retroactivity doctrine, the Warren Court applied a voluntariness test and relied on due process precedent for its meaning.[141]

The post-Warren Court has continued to adhere to the same approach. In *Beckwith v. United States*,[142] the Court reaffirmed that the voluntariness test rather than *Miranda* governs noncustodial interrogation, and it cited due process voluntariness cases as supplying the applicable standard.[143] Because the Fifth Amendment applies in a noncustodial context—the government surely cannot compel a noncustodial suspect to answer incriminating questions—*Beckwith* necessarily supports the conclusion that the Fifth Amendment voluntariness standard is no tougher than the due process voluntariness standard. Similarly, after recognizing that the Fifth Amendment applies to grand jury questioning of a target witness, the Court in *United States v. Washington*[144] cited a due process voluntariness case as defining the applicable voluntariness standard.[145]

Professor Schulhofer has nevertheless argued that the Fifth Amendment and due process standards must be different because the Court in various Fifth Amendment contexts has found compulsion when it was not plausible to conclude that the individual's will was overborne.[146] The mistake in this argument, however, is the assumption that the due process cases really required an *overborne will*. On the contrary, as indicated in chapters 3 and 4, a literal finding of an overborne will was implausible in each of the Court's cases—including *Brown*—that found a defendant's confession to be involuntary on due process grounds. Anticipating this response, Schulhofer suggested that those who would reject a literal overborne will test must then concede that even "mild pressures" can render a confession involuntary.[147] No such concession is required, however, for in assessing a claim of involuntariness, one need not regard mild pressure as undue pressure. This aside, the claim here is that, whatever the standard, the Court's Fifth Amendment and due process voluntariness cases have given identical treatment to the issue of what constitutes undue pressure.

Concededly, just as a few due process cases went far in protecting the defendant from mild pressures, some Fifth Amendment cases did the same thing. *Griffin v. California*,[148] which held that judicial and prosecutorial comment on a defendant's failure to testify at trial violates the Fifth Amendment, is one such case. Professor Schulhofer has argued that *Miranda*'s finding of inherent compulsion in custodial interrogation follows *a fortiori* from *Griffin*'s holding: "If a comment on silence generates impermissible pressure to speak at trial (where the comment adds only marginally to inferences the jury will draw anyway), can we say that a police officer's request for information, addressed to an unwarned suspect in custody, does not create impermissible pressure?"[149]

Schulhofer's argument, however, overlooks that *Griffin* involved that aspect of Fifth Amendment doctrine that governs the trial, a context, unlike most, in which the accused need not even assert the privilege, and it is significant in this regard that the Court has since limited *Griffin* to the trial context.[150] In addition, the comment on the defendant's failure to testify in *Griffin* could conceivably be seen as implying that the defendant was obligated to testify; so understood, it would have violated the Fifth Amendment's core prohibition without requiring any inquiry into voluntariness.[151] Finally, the possibility should not be overlooked that *Griffin*, which preceded *Miranda* by one year, was itself wrongly decided.[152] It has been argued, for example, that *Griffin*'s holding was neither "required by the Constitution" nor "warranted as a matter of policy."[153] In England, moreover, the privilege is not understood as prohibiting judicial comment on the accused's failure to testify.[154] In any event, even read as Schulhofer would read it, *Griffin* standing alone is insufficient to negate the cases, decided both before and after it over a period of several decades, that have equated Fifth Amendment and due process voluntariness standards.

"Of course, debate about the meaning of compulsion cannot be settled simply by resort to *stare decisis*."[155] The still unanswered question is whether Fifth Amendment "involuntariness" *should* have a different meaning than its due process counterpart, one that makes the admissibility of confessions more difficult to achieve. The reader will recall from chapter 3 that a claim of wrongful conduct is a necessary element in any allegation of coercion. The more precise question, then, is whether, notwithstanding the lack of textual or historical support, we should regard police practices as wrongful under the Fifth Amendment that would be insufficiently wrongful to make out a due process claim of involuntariness.

Miranda, in essence, treated the inherent pressure of the least stressful custodial interrogation as wrongful, for under *Miranda*, as Justice White explained in dissent, a suspect's incriminating response to only one custodial question—such as, "Did you kill your wife?"—"has somehow been compelled," at least if that case's warning and waiver requirements have not been satisfied. "Common sense," Justice White insisted, "informs us to the contrary."[156] Justice White was correct. Common sense rejects *Miranda*'s conclusion regarding compulsion because we lack good reasons for regarding the inherent pressure of a custodial question as wrongful. Indeed, demonstrating this point was a large part of the burden of chapter 2, which considered and rejected various policy arguments against police interrogation. The "fair chance," "equality," "human dignity," and "accusatorial system" arguments, as well as some others, fail to make a persuasive case for indulging a presumptive bias against police interrogation.

Even if those arguments against police interrogation are not persuasive in their own right, one might contend that they reflect the policies that underlie the Fifth Amendment and should accordingly sway the judiciary. This argument loses its force, however, when one recalls not only that the meaning and scope of the privilege were far from settled when the Fifth Amendment was adopted but also that the privilege evolved as a "procedural remedy for a substantive wrong"—that being the religious and political persecutions in the High Commission and Star Chamber courts previously discussed—and that the normative policies that supposedly underlie it are "ahistorical."[157] The policies typically presented as justifications for the privilege are after-the-event formulations,[158] and if these policies are unsound, as chapter 2 argued they generally are, we have no reason to rely on them for expansive interpretations of the self-incrimination protection.

Sound underlying policies, as Wigmore argued, might support the Fifth Amendment's "wide extension," but unsound policies—especially unsound ahistorical ones—make a case for its "close restriction."[159] Thus, although the Fifth Amendment's text and underlying history preclude any reform, even if thought desirable, that would require the defendant to testify at trial, our hands are not similarly tied concerning what constitutes coercion in police interrogation. Those who support *Miranda* cannot argue that decades, if not centuries, of contrary precedent should be ignored and then insist that critics of the decision are somehow constrained from rejecting *Miranda*'s underlying policies.

Professor Kamisar has explained that *Miranda* regarded as compulsion any police tactic likely to exert "a tug" on suspects to incriminate themselves.[160] Of course, if *Miranda*'s purpose really was to eliminate such tugs, it failed, for as Professor Kamisar elsewhere acknowledged, "[z]ero-value pressure conditions" are impossible as long as police interrogation is permitted to exist.[161] Even if this was *Miranda*'s purpose, however, no good reason exists to regard it as the Fifth Amendment's purpose. On the contrary, as was previously discussed, encouraging defendants to tell the truth is desirable. The Constitution, the Supreme Court has recently reminded us, does not prohibit every element that influences truth telling, and a particular practice does not offend the Fifth Amendment simply because it increases the likelihood that a person will tell the truth.[162] "[F]ar from being prohibited by the Constitution, admissions of guilt by wrongdoers, if not coerced, are inherently desirable."[163]

But when should an admission of guilt be regarded as coerced? More precisely, what tugs, pressures, or influences should be regarded as wrongful for Fifth Amendment voluntariness purposes? These questions present the identical problem of distinguishing constitutional law from subjective value judgments that chapter 4 encountered. Were it up to Professor Schulhofer, for example, the slightest pressure intended to discourage silence would not be permitted.[164] What needs consideration, however, is why Professor Schulhofer—more accurately, why judges who think like him—should get to impose such a controversial value judgment on each of the states in the nation.

In the absence of textual guidance, judges should impose normative judgments on the country as a matter of constitutional fiat only, if at all, when those judgments embody truly fundamental values rooted in some objective source. As the analysis in chapter 4 sought to demonstrate, to give judges broader authority than this—and even this may go too far—is to allow judges to impose their personal values on the country in the name of constitutional law. Were this approach followed with regard to the Fifth Amendment issue of voluntariness, the resulting constitutional limitations would correspond to those derived from the due process voluntariness approach discussed in the last chapter—an approach, though not itself without difficulties, based on normative values that can plausibly be rooted in the nation's history or traditions.

Besides limiting judges, the above approach has three additional virtues. First, it would tie up another loose end by properly limiting incorporation, at least in this one context, to the fundamental aspects of the incorporated provision. Second, its results would be consistent with the many precedents both before and after *Miranda* that equated Fifth and Fourteenth Amendment voluntariness standards. Third, it would make it unnecessary for judges to engage in the task of defending a Fifth Amendment line for wrongful police behavior that differs from the Fourteenth Amendment line, an exercise destined to be futile and ad hoc given the complete lack of textual guidance in either case.

"Distinguishing degrees," Professor Kamisar has acknowledged, "is inherent in the process of defining 'compel.'"[165] Given that compulsion cannot realistically be defined so as to make any amount or kind of pressure unlawful, Kamisar is obviously correct. What Kamisar and others have failed to show, however, is that the task of distinguishing degrees should produce different lines, or can do so on a principled and constitutionally defensible basis, in the Fifth and Fourteenth Amendment contexts.

A persuasive argument cannot be made that the Constitution mandates different lines. Moreover, the nature and content of the different lines that are possible cannot possibly be derived from the relevant constitutional texts. Neither textual nor historical analysis can demonstrate, for example, that although the Fourteenth Amendment voluntariness requirement would not be an obstacle in either case, the pressures inherent in custodial interrogation violate the Fifth Amendment voluntariness requirement but that the pressures inherent in noncustodial interrogation do not. Without the text for support, one must turn to policy arguments, but unfortunately for those who dislike police interrogation, good policy reasons do not exist for drawing different lines, especially at the constitutional level. Indeed, the important goal of truth discovery strongly favors an approach that countenances interrogation strategies that do not offend fundamental values.

Although this argument obviously takes issue with *Miranda*, it is not a call for a radical, new approach. On the contrary, the argument is that the Supreme Court, with the exception of *Miranda* (and possibly *Griffin*), has had it right over the years: Fifth Amendment voluntariness and Fourteenth Amendment voluntariness should have the same meaning.

The Absence of a Right to Silence

In opposition to the argument in the previous section, one might counter that *Miranda* protected the defendant's Fifth Amendment right of silence. Indeed, *Miranda*'s first requirement was that a person subjected to custodial interrogation be informed "in clear and unequivocal terms that he has the right to remain silent."[166] By combining warning and waiver requirements, *Miranda* seemingly sought to protect against unintelligent waivers of this Fifth Amendment right. If this is correct, the above focus on coercion or voluntariness is misplaced.

The answer to the right-of-silence argument is implicit in what has been said so far. Nevertheless, because this argument demonstrates how easily the mischaracterization of a principle can lead to faulty conclusions, it needs to be directly confronted.[167] The Fifth Amendment confers a right not to be compelled to answer questions; it does not confer a substantive or formal right of silence. Concededly, the former right does give rise to a right of silence in "the very weak sense" that a person has "a right to silence on every subject": a person who cannot lawfully be coerced into speaking can, of course, remain silent.[168] Still, as Judge Friendly observed shortly after *Miranda* was decided, the "distinction is not mere semantics; it goes to the very core of the problem."[169] The reason is that while the notion of waiving a right of silence is intelligible, the notion of waiving a right not to be compelled, especially when compel is a synonym for coerce, is not. "If the right is one not to be *compelled* to speak, rather than a right to remain silent *simpliciter,* the issues of waiver and consequently of the need for warning should not be reached."[170]

Justice Marshall, an ardent supporter of *Miranda,* essentially conceded this point on one occasion:

> The inquiry in a case where a confession is challenged as having been elicited in an unconstitutional manner is, therefore, whether the behavior of the police amounted to compulsion of the defendant. Because of the nature of the right to be free from compulsion, it would be pointless to ask whether a defendant knew of it before he made a statement; no sane man would knowingly relinquish a right to be free of compulsion. Thus, the questions of compulsion and of violation of the right itself are inextricably intertwined. The cases involving coerced confessions, therefore, pass over the question of knowledge of that right as irrelevant, and turn directly to the questions of compulsion.[171]

Marshall also conceded that *Miranda*'s waiver requirement went only to "the rights [defendants] are informed of by police warnings" and not to the underlying right, which *Miranda* was seeking to protect, to be free of coercion.[172]

If the Fifth Amendment really conferred a substantive or formal right of silence, the police, contrary to what even *Miranda* recognized, might have to stop and caution "a person who enters a police station and states that he wishes to confess,"[173] for the issue whether the right of silence was knowingly waived would be present in all such cases. In addition, the very act of asking questions would seem to infringe such a right, whether or not the person is in custody.[174] At the very least, all questioning would have to be preceded by a valid waiver, a result inconsistent with *Miranda,* Fifth Amendment precedent in general, and the historical understanding that a person, in almost all contexts other than trial, must affirmatively assert the privilege or lose it. The waiver requirement could not be limited to the custodial context, as *Miranda* limited it, because the Fifth Amendment, as previously indicated, applies even to noncustodial interrogation.

Finally, only the absence of a substantive or formal right of silence can make sense of the cases allowing the defendant's silence both before and after arrest to be used for impeachment purposes, provided that the police have not possibly induced that silence by providing *Miranda* warnings.[175] If the defendant had a substantive or formal right of silence, these cases would be wrong. Although some commentators might be happy to see the impeachment cases reconsidered, they are consistent with the view that the Fifth Amendment provides only a right not to be compelled to answer—which in the context of police interrogation is synonymous with a right not to be coerced into answering.

These considerations support the unremarkable conclusion that the Fifth Amendment actually means what it says. To speak of a right of silence as such may be a convenient shorthand at times, but this is not the right that the Fifth Amendment, or *Miranda* for that matter, actually protects.

CHAPTER 6

The Right to Counsel

Although both have played a significant role in the modern constitutional law governing police interrogation, the Fifth Amendment's self-incrimination clause and the Sixth Amendment's right to counsel protect different interests and reflect different concerns. The Fifth Amendment, as chapter 5 discussed, is concerned with protecting defendants from being compelled to become witnesses against themselves, and in the context of police interrogation, this translates, as *Miranda* itself recognized, into a concern about protecting defendants from being coerced into answering questions. Reflecting this concern, *Miranda* created what is tantamount to a Fifth Amendment right to counsel to protect defendants from the inherent pressures of custodial interrogation. Not limited like the Fifth Amendment to protecting against coercion, the Sixth Amendment's concern is providing legal help or assistance to defendants in their confrontations with the prosecution.[1]

By arguing that the inherent pressure of custodial interrogation is inadequate to implicate Fifth Amendment concerns, the previous discussion has undermined the basis for *Miranda*'s Fifth Amendment right to counsel. The possibility remains, however, that the Sixth Amendment could be used to fill the void that the rejection of *Miranda* would create. Arguably, defendants should have a right to counsel's help or advice when they are being interrogated by the police. Under a Sixth Amendment rationale, the reason for providing counsel would not be to protect custodial suspects from undue pressure, although that might be an incidental benefit, but rather to protect them from making unwise or strategically bad decisions.

Although critical analysis of the Sixth Amendment argument could appropriately begin with the incorporation issue, the discussion would essentially cover the same ground that was covered in chapter 5. Moreover, if we view the Court's selective incorporation doctrine as a given part of the legal landscape,[2] the Sixth Amendment right to counsel, at least as it applies at trial, is a considerably stronger candidate for application to the states than the Fifth Amendment's self-incrimination clause.[3] The right to counsel can easily be viewed as an essential component of the right to a fair trial. As the Court stated in *Powell v. Alabama*[4] in 1932, "[e]ven the intelligent and educated layman" may have trouble in evaluating the charge, applying the rules of evidence, and otherwise preparing and presenting an available defense.[5]

Indeed, without relying on the Sixth Amendment at all, a right to counsel at trial could be derived directly from the requirement of procedural due process. The "law of the land," which is the historical source of the due process requirement, has long been viewed as "a law which hears before it condemns."[6] Stated in nineteenth-century terminology, the rights to notice and to be heard on the charges rank, if any rights do, among the "'immutable principles of justice which inhere in the very idea of free government which no member of the Union may disregard.'"[7] *Powell* merely contributed the rather unremarkable insight, which the Court used in *Gideon v. Wainwright*,[8] that "[t]he right to be heard would be, in many cases, of little avail if it did not comprehend the right to be heard by counsel."[9]

The reluctance to reexamine the incorporation of the Sixth Amendment in greater depth should not be misunderstood as suggesting that this issue ought to be ignored in the effort to reform the current law governing police interrogation. As the last chapter discussed in connection with the Fifth Amendment, the doctrine of selective incorporation that the Supreme Court has espoused should make applicable to the states only the fundamental aspects of incorporated provisions. The thesis of this chapter is that the Sixth Amendment, properly construed, does not afford a right to counsel during police interrogation. If it does nothing else, the argument in defense of this thesis should demonstrate at least that such a right is not rooted in our nation's history and traditions. While the Sixth Amendment right to counsel at trial may be fundamental for purposes of incorporation, the right to counsel during interrogation is not. Accordingly, the Court should free the states from this requirement even if it is not prepared to change the law regarding the federal government.[10]

A second preliminary issue that might warrant critical analysis is whether the Court properly construed the Sixth Amendment as affording a right to appointed counsel for indigent defendants. The Court so interpreted the Sixth Amendment in *Johnson v. Zerbst*,[11] a case that at least one commentator accused of ignoring history.[12] Even if this criticism has validity, however, the principle that the right to counsel, when it exists, should not depend on one's financial ability to retain counsel is now solidly ingrained in our constitutional law. Of course, it might be argued that this principle may be valid at trial and yet not carry similar weight in the context of police interrogation.[13] Nevertheless, in dismissing the equality arguments often made for restricting police interrogation, chapter 2 conceded that inequality among defendants relating to the availability of legal rights—in contrast to inequality relating to personal sophistication—is a matter of legitimate concern. The burden of this chapter, therefore, is to argue that under our Constitution even defendants with their own lawyers should not have a right to counsel's assistance during police interrogation.

The above thesis is not as radical as it may seem. First, from a Sixth Amendment perspective, the thesis, for all practical purposes, conforms rather closely to the current state of the law. Under current doctrine, most custodial suspects have only a Fifth Amendment right to counsel when they are interrogated. Were the problem of coercion to be addressed by other means, or were *Miranda* to be overruled, these suspects would have no right to counsel under existing law. Second, the thesis merely advocates a return to the constitutional law that historically governed this area until the aberrational Supreme Court opinions that came down in the 1960s. Third, the thesis is consistent with the original meaning of the constitutional text and with the policy goals that the procedural system should be attempting to further.

This chapter begins by reviewing the original state of the law in this area. Concentrating on the Sixth Amendment, it next considers the dramatic doctrinal expansion that occurred in the 1960s and the significant although far from total contraction that has taken place since 1972, when the Supreme Court limited the Sixth Amendment right to counsel to confrontations that occur after the start of adversary judicial proceedings. The thesis presented here, as already indicated, is that neither the constitutional text nor sound policy supports a right to have counsel's assistance during police interrogation.

The inquiry next turns to the Court's reasons for applying the Sixth Amendment after the start of adversary judicial proceedings. Although the above analysis will have refuted the Sixth Amendment's application even in this limited context, an argument is presented defending the Court's adversary judicial proceeding requirement, formalistic as it may seem, as preferable to an approach that would once again expand the Sixth Amendment's application to precharge interrogation.

The chapter closes by arguing that the discussion in previous chapters has undermined the basis for a separate Fifth Amendment right to counsel. By eliminating this right, the Court could restore the historical view of the right to counsel, at least for the vast majority of cases.

The Supreme Court's Original Position

On March 17, 1947, Charles Kittush was shot and killed during the robbery of his dry goods store in Newark, New Jersey. On Saturday,

December 17, 1949, more than two years later, the police received an important break when the wife of one of the robbers implicated her husband, another individual, and Vincent Cicenia in the crime. That same day, the police informed Cicenia's parents that he should report to the local police station on Sunday. After consulting a lawyer, Cicenia, who was then 20 years old, reported to the station as directed, accompanied by his brother and father. The police then separated Cicenia from his relatives and took him to Newark police headquarters, where, after interrogating him between two o'clock in the afternoon and nine-thirty at night, they emerged with a signed, detailed confession. During this period, both Cicenia and his lawyer, who had arrived at the Newark headquarters, requested to communicate with each other, but the police denied these requests until they had finished taking the signed confession.

After failing to get the New Jersey courts to suppress his confession, Cicenia pleaded *non vult* and received a life sentence. Cicenia then unsuccessfully challenged his plea in the state courts on the ground that the plea was based on an unlawfully obtained confession. Thereafter, raising the same issue, Cicenia unsuccessfully petitioned for a writ of habeas corpus in federal district court and unsuccessfully appealed to the federal court of appeals. In 1958, during the early years or the first phase of the Warren Court, the Supreme Court, in a five-to-three decision written by Justice Harlan, affirmed the decisions of these lower federal courts.[14]

Because Cicenia had abandoned his claim that his confession was coerced—a claim that the lower court had rejected as not substantiated—the Supreme Court was able to focus squarely on whether a voluntary confession should be excluded from evidence when the police deny a suspect's request to consult with counsel. Recognizing the reality that lawyers often advise suspects not to cooperate, the Court observed that a right to counsel during police interrogation "in many instances might impair [the police's] ability to solve difficult cases."[15] It would do this, the Court remarked in a companion case, by precluding in effect all police interrogation, "*fair as well as unfair.*"[16] The Court also commented that Cicenia's right to counsel argument would require it "to apply the Fourteenth Amendment in a manner that would be foreign both to the spirit in which it was conceived and the way in which it has been implemented by this Court."[17] The Court was obviously correct in this assertion, as should have been made apparent in chapter 4.

The Court's resolution of the right to counsel issue was hardly an innovation. Prior to *Cicenia*, the Court had never indicated that a denial of counsel to a suspect was enough by itself to render a confession inadmissible. On the contrary, the Court had consistently said that lack of counsel was merely a factor to consider in assessing voluntariness.[18] Indeed, in *Wilson v. United States*,[19] almost three-quarters of a century earlier, the Court had held that, even in combination, custody, a lack of counsel, and the absence of warnings did not render inadmissible a defendant's postarrest responses to questioning by a United States Commissioner.[20]

That *Wilson* seems not to have been decided on constitutional grounds should not detract from the force of its holding, especially when one recalls that *Bram v. United States*,[21] decided the next year, equated the Fifth Amendment and the common-law voluntariness requirements and that *Ashcraft v. Tennessee*,[22] decided several years later, equated the Fifth Amendment and the Fourteenth Amendment voluntariness requirements. That is, whether it premised its analysis on the common law, the Fifth Amendment, or the Fourteenth Amendment, the Court always rejected the argument that a defendant had a right to counsel during police interrogation. As late as 1961, Justice Frankfurter could accurately say both that the Court had never developed a "single litmus-paper test for constitutionally impermissible interrogation" and that police refusal to permit a suspect to communicate with friends or legal counsel was not enough by itself to render a confession constitutionally infirm.[23]

The Court in *Cicenia* also pointed to another consideration: "the 'very essence of our federalism [is] that the States should have the widest latitude in the administration of their own systems of criminal justice.'"[24] The question, therefore, was not whether the federal judges personally approved the denial of counsel to Cicenia but whether the federal Constitution made impermissible New Jersey's view of what the law in its state should be.[25] In this regard, it is worth noting that just a few years earlier the New Jersey Supreme Court had reaffirmed its view that the right to counsel did not apply to police interrogation.[26] Similarly, in the companion case that came to the United States Supreme Court with *Cicenia*, the California Supreme Court had also reaffirmed its view that a denial of counsel to a suspect, under both federal and state law, was merely a factor to consider in assessing voluntariness.[27]

Far from being deviational, these cases reflected the view that state and federal courts had historically taken. One survey of cases published in 1923, for example, reported that state courts had uniformly rejected claims that a denial of counsel to a suspect was sufficient by itself to render a confession inadmissible.[28] The first suggestion in a state case that an accused should be afforded counsel in *postcharge* interrogation occurred in a dissenting opinion in *People v. Spano*,[29] a case decided by the New York Court of Appeals in 1958. Although embraced by the New York Court of Appeals two years later,[30] even this limited position did not find much favor in other courts.[31] Thus, it would have been quite remarkable, and even presumptuous, for the Supreme Court to have decided *Cicenia* other than the way it did.

Expansion and Contraction of the Sixth Amendment Right

Although the Supreme Court did not abandon *Cicenia* and its historical approach to the right to counsel issue until the 1960s, the seeds for change were planted the year after that case was decided when newly appointed Justice Potter Stewart expressed partial support for the position of the *Cicenia* dissenters. When *Spano,* mentioned in the last section, came up to the Supreme Court, Chief Justice Warren, who was one of the *Cicenia* dissenters, curiously avoided the right to counsel issue and instead wrote a majority opinion reversing the conviction on voluntariness grounds.[32] In a separate concurring opinion, however, Justice Stewart wrote that the interrogation without counsel, after the defendant had been indicted, violated the Constitution.[33] Justice Stewart saw no need to quarrel with *Cicenia* itself, however, because that case involved police interrogation "in the course of investigating an unsolved crime" rather than postindictment interrogation.[34] Because the Court had not yet applied the Sixth Amendment right to counsel to the states, Justice Stewart had to base his argument squarely on the due process clause, a curious grounding given that no state, not even New York, had yet embraced that position.

Five years later, relying on the Sixth Amendment in a federal case, Justice Stewart converted his *Spano* concurrence into a majority opinion. In *Massiah v. United States,*[35] an "oddball Sixth Amendment–'confession' case,"[36] the Court held that the postindictment use of an informant to obtain incriminating statements from the defendant violated the right to counsel. Justice Stewart's opinion tracked his concurrence in *Spano:* "the confession had been deliberately elicited by the police after the defendant had been indicted, and therefore at a time when he was clearly entitled to a lawyer's help"; in our system an indictment is to "be followed by a trial, 'in an orderly courtroom, presided over by a judge, open to the public, and protected by all the procedural safeguards of the law.'"[37] Besides relying on his own previously stated views, Justice Stewart could find support for the Court's opinion only in decisions from New York, the New York Court of Appeals having reversed itself after *Spano.*[38]

The opinion's emphasis on Massiah's right to a lawyer's *help* was significant, because *Massiah* was not plausibly a case in which a lawyer could be viewed as a safeguard against coercion. Massiah thought that he was talking to a friend, not an agent of the state whom he might have had reason to fear.[39] Concern about coercion, however, lurked underneath the surface in *Escobedo v. Illinois*,[40] a straightforward police interrogation case that the Court decided just a month after *Massiah* and shortly after it had "incorporated" both the Sixth Amendment's counsel clause and the Fifth Amendment's self-incrimination clause.[41] The significant facts were a virtual carbon copy of those in *Cicenia:* the police, questioning the defendant about a murder before indictment or the start of judicial proceedings, denied both the defendant and his lawyer permission to consult with each other. To dissenting Justice Stewart's consternation, the majority relied on the Sixth Amendment and *Massiah* in overturning Escobedo's conviction and in overruling *Cicenia.*[42]

The *Escobedo* majority stated that it would "exalt form over substance" to have the Sixth Amendment right to counsel depend on whether the defendant was formally charged.[43] Employing reasoning already reviewed in chapter 2,[44] the Court concluded that Escobedo's need for a lawyer's help and advice was no less than Massiah's.[45] The Court felt that unless a defendant has a right to counsel's assistance during interrogation, the trial might become a mere formality, with conviction assured by a confession.[46] Notwithstanding this emphasis on the need for legal advice, however, the majority opinion also referred to the protection against compulsory self-incrimination, the absence of a warning about the "absolute right to remain silent," the "fear" a defendant might have that remaining silent will imply guilt, and the potential for police abuse during the interrogation process.[47]

Justice Stewart based his dissent solely on the fact that the interrogation, like that in *Cicenia,* had occurred before the start of adversary judicial proceedings.[48] Rejecting the view that this exalted form over substance, Stewart insisted that Sixth Amendment rights simply do not attach before this point.[49] Stewart did not address the separate argument, alluded to in parts of the majority opinion, that counsel's services might be needed not only to give advice (a Sixth Amendment concern) but also to protect against coercion (a Fifth Amendment concern). There may be two reasons for this omission. First, despite evident concern about coercion and sporadic references to the Fifth Amendment, the Court based its decision squarely on the Sixth Amendment.[50] In addition, the Court not only failed to respond to Justice Stewart's claim that Escobedo's confession was voluntary;[51] it also gave this claim credence by observing that the lower court had reached this very conclusion.[52]

Second, as is perhaps suggested by his dissenting vote in *Miranda*, it may not have occurred to Justice Stewart—or to anyone else then on the Court—that a right to counsel having nothing to do with the Sixth Amendment might be grounded in the Fifth Amendment's self-incrimination clause. That is, Stewart may have thought that whatever the underlying concern, a right to counsel had to be grounded in the Sixth Amendment, an amendment that simply did not become operational, in his view, until the start of formal judicial proceedings.[53]

Recognizing that *Escobedo* raised as many questions as it answered,[54] the Supreme Court promptly granted certiorari in four cases, which collectively became known as *Miranda v. Arizona*,[55] "further to explore some facets of the problems . . . of applying *the privilege against self-incrimination* to in-custody interrogation."[56] Thus, in its first reference to *Escobedo*, *Miranda* surprisingly described that case as involving Fifth Amendment issues. In a second reference, however, *Miranda* ambiguously described *Escobedo* as an "explication" of both Fifth and Sixth Amendment rights.[57] The third reference had no ambiguity: as the Court now described it, the police failure to remove the anxieties that they had created and their denial of Escobedo's request to consult with counsel "heightened his dilemma, and made his later statements the product of this compulsion."[58] The effect of this passage, of course, was to transform *Escobedo* into a Fifth Amendment case, which made it fully compatible with *Miranda*'s Fifth Amendment grounding.

For those who supported the doctrinal changes that were rapidly occurring, *Escobedo*'s metamorphosis was of no moment. After all, by requiring detailed warnings for custodial suspects before interrogation, providing a right to appointed counsel for indigent defendants, and imposing rigorous waiver requirements, *Miranda* significantly expanded *Escobedo*'s holding.[59] Likewise, *Massiah*, which had taken but a step in the direction of overturning *Cicenia*, quickly became "lost in the shuffle of fast-moving events that reshaped constitutional-criminal procedure in the 1960s."[60] Given *Miranda*'s scope, *Massiah*'s conceivable potential for expanding the restrictions on the police through the Sixth Amendment was limited to the postarrest but precharge use of informants[61] and to those noncustodial interrogations to which *Miranda*, by its terms, did not apply. With all that was going on at the time, these were not front-burner issues.[62]

Eight years after *Massiah* and *Escobedo*, and six years after *Miranda*, Justice Stewart saw his views on the scope of the Sixth Amendment right to counsel prevail. The case had nothing—but really everything—to do with police interrogation. Following his arrest, Thomas Kirby, who had not been advised that he had a right to counsel, was identified in a police station showup by a robbery victim. Relying on *United States v. Wade*,[63] another revolutionary decision that had applied the Sixth Amendment's counsel requirement to a postindictment lineup, Kirby argued that the showup violated the Sixth Amendment. Justice Stewart's plurality opinion rejected this argument, holding that the Sixth Amendment simply did not apply because the showup had occurred before the start of adversary judicial proceedings against the accused.

The *Kirby* plurality correctly stated that *Miranda* did not conflict with this holding, because *Miranda*'s right to counsel was based entirely on the Fifth Amendment's self-incrimination clause, which had no bearing on the showup issue.[64] All of the Court's other—one might say all of its true—right to counsel cases, with the exception of *Escobedo*, had reflected the adversary judicial proceeding limitation. With regard to *Escobedo*, the plurality noted that the Court in retrospect had determined that *Escobedo*'s primary purpose "was not to vindicate the constitutional right to counsel as such, but, like *Miranda*, 'to guarantee full effectuation of the privilege against self-incrimination.'"[65] In support of this statement, Justice Stewart cited *Johnson v. New Jersey*,[66] a case that determined that *Escobedo* and *Miranda* would not be given retroactive effect, but as we have seen, he could have relied here on *Miranda* itself.[67] Second, and less significantly for doctrinal purposes, the plurality noted that *Escobedo*'s holding had been limited to its facts.

That the Sixth Amendment, as elaborated in *Massiah*, still carried force after *Kirby* became apparent in *Brewer v. Williams*,[68] a five-to-four decision that Justice Stewart wrote. *Williams* overturned a murder conviction because the police, in the absence of counsel and without obtaining a waiver, deliberately elicited statements from the defendant after formal proceedings were initiated against him. That the adversary proceeding limitation also had teeth, however, became apparent almost a decade after *Williams* in *Moran v. Burbine*.[69]

The relevant facts in *Burbine* are not a carbon copy of those in *Cicenia* and *Escobedo*, but they are close; indeed, given the Court's opinion, the factual differences almost certainly are irrelevant. Questioned about a murder following his arrest, Brian Burbine was informed of his *Miranda* rights but not of the fact that a lawyer, retained by his sister, had phoned the police station offering to represent him if he was questioned. Burbine argued that this failure violated both *Miranda*'s Fifth Amendment right to counsel and the Sixth Amendment, but the Court rejected both arguments.

Regarding the latter argument, the Court held that Burbine did not have a Sixth Amendment right to counsel because the interrogation had occurred before the start of adversary judicial proceedings.[70] Reiterating that *Escobedo* has no remaining vitality as a Sixth Amendment case, the Court stated that it would make "little sense to say that the Sixth Amendment right to counsel attaches at different times depending on the fortuity of whether the suspect or his family happens to have retained counsel prior to interrogation."[71] The Court acknowledged both that legal assistance would be "of value" to suspects in Burbine's position and that trial counsel's case at trial is made more difficult when the defendant has confessed. As the Court saw it, however, these considerations were irrelevant: "For an interrogation, no more or less than for any other 'critical' pretrial event, the possibility that the encounter may have important consequences at trial, standing alone, is insufficient to trigger the Sixth Amendment right to counsel."[72]

One might attempt to distinguish *Burbine* and *Escobedo* by noting that the defendant in the latter case actually requested the assistance of a lawyer whom he, not a third party, had personally retained. The Court's reasoning, however, to say nothing of its holding, strongly suggests that such factual distinctions do not matter. Were they to matter, the right to counsel would turn on the "fortuity" of the suspect retaining counsel prior to the interrogation. As Professor Yale Kamisar has commented, "such a rule would seem to favor the 'professional criminal' most of all."[73]

In any event, Justice Stewart, who more than any other justice influenced doctrinal development in this area, clearly thought it irrelevant that the suspect retained and requested counsel, for Stewart dissented in *Escobedo,* which presented those very facts. Justice Stewart never abandoned his *Escobedo* dissent, and his plurality opinion in *Kirby,* which the Court often quotes,[74] in fact is little more than an echo of that dissent.[75] What *Burbine* indicates is that a majority of the Court has now fully embraced the position that Justice Stewart consistently advocated from *Spano* to *Kirby* and *Williams:* questions pertaining to the defendant's need or desire for counsel's assistance simply should not be discussed unless adversary judicial proceedings have commenced.

Nevertheless, under the current state of the law, the defendants in *Cicenia* and *Escobedo*—but not *Burbine*[76]—would still win their cases. They would win, however, solely because of *Miranda* and its Fifth Amendment rationale. They would not win because they needed the "guiding hand of counsel" or because police interrogation is a "'stage when legal aid and advice'" are critical.[77] Nor would they win because they were entitled to have counsel act as a "medium" between the state and themselves.[78] These critical stage arguments would fail today in cases like *Cicenia* and *Escobedo* not because they lack persuasive force—which they do—but rather because they are simply irrelevant prior to the initiation of adversary judicial proceedings. Thus, the only remaining obstacle to the disinterment of *Cicenia*'s actual holding, and the historical approach it represented, is *Miranda*'s inherent compulsion rationale, a rationale that has already been found deficient in this book.

The Sixth Amendment and Police Interrogation

Before evaluating the Court's current doctrine in this area, we should consider the more basic question of whether the Sixth Amendment's right to have counsel's assistance should be understood as applying at all to police interrogation. By its terms, the Sixth Amendment provides "the accused" "in all criminal prosecutions" the right "to have the assistance of counsel for his defence."[79] In the present context, the constitutional text raises questions about whether a suspect or an arrestee is an "accused," whether police interrogation is part of the "criminal prosecution," and whether counsel's advice to the defendant during police interrogation is "assistance . . . for his defence." We have seen, for example, that Justice Stewart, in essence, did not believe that a suspect could become the accused or that an investigation could become part of the criminal prosecution until the start of adversary judicial proceedings, and this is now the Court's position. The Court in *Escobedo*, on the other hand, maintained that a person subjected to custodial interrogation has "for all practical purposes already been charged" and thus has "become the accused."[80] Stewart apparently agreed with *Escobedo*, however, that counsel's advice during an interrogation, at least one that occurs after the start of adversary judicial proceedings, does constitute "assistance for [the accused's] defense."

One does not do violence to the bare language of the text in supporting either Justice Stewart's or *Escobedo*'s position regarding who is an accused or what is a criminal prosecution.[81] This is not to deny that one reading of the text may be better, in the sense of truer to its intended purpose, than the other; indeed, the next section of this chapter argues that Stewart's reading of the text is the more defensible of the two. This section, however, defends a broader thesis: that counsel's help to a defendant during police interrogation is not the "assistance" the amendment was intended to assure. Such help differs not only in degree but in kind from the "assistance" assured by the Sixth Amendment, and it goes far beyond the amendment's purpose.

The Sixth Amendment was enacted in reaction to English law, which until 1836 did not provide felony defendants the right to have retained counsel assist them in presenting a defense at trial.[82] After the

American Revolution, and even before, most of the American states rejected the English rule, and some even granted unrepresented defendants a right to appointed counsel, a right that English statutory law did not provide until 1903.[83] Those who drafted and ratified the Sixth Amendment wanted to assure that the American rather than the English rule would prevail in the federal courts, at least with respect to the right to be represented by retained counsel.[84] As one Sixth Amendment scholar noted in commenting on the amendment's intended scope,

> There was no feeling before 1938 that defendants who pleaded guilty, or those who failed to request counsel, had a constitutional right to be advised and offered counsel, or that a conviction without counsel was void. History denied such a meaning to the counsel provision of the Sixth Amendment, and no responsible authority, scholarly or judicial, had held it to be within the scope of the Amendment.[85]

As indicated previously, the intention here is not to quarrel with *Johnson,* the 1938 Supreme Court decision that read the Sixth Amendment as affording indigent defendants a right to appointed counsel.[86] Indeed, unless one embraces a narrow definition of original intent, this judicial "expansion" of the right to counsel should not be all that troubling. The obvious concern that led to the nineteenth- and twentieth-century English reforms and to the American rejection of the original English rule was that many defendants with possible defenses, both legal and factual, were incapable of recognizing or presenting those defenses on their own.[87] This concern about avoiding wrongful convictions applies just as much, if not more, in the case of indigent defendants.[88] The Court's decision to read the Sixth Amendment as including a right to appointed counsel, though perhaps not anticipated by the framers, at least comported with the framers' reasons for adding the amendment to the Constitution.

The Court's expansion of the right to counsel to include certain pretrial stages can be justified by the same rationale. For example, the concern about wrongful conviction was apparent in *Hamilton v. Alabama,*[89] when the Court applied the right to counsel to a preliminary arraignment where defenses had to be raised to be preserved for use at trial.[90] Similarly, *Coleman v. Alabama*[91] recognized that counsel's presence at the preliminary examination was important both to expose weaknesses in the state's case, thereby possibly saving the accused from the ordeal of trial, and to develop and preserve evidence that might establish a defense at trial. As the Court recognized in these cases, although the core purpose of the Sixth Amendment was to provide assistance at trial, this purpose would be undermined if counsel's assistance was not available at certain "pretrial events that might appropriately be considered to be parts of the trial itself."[92]

The application of the Sixth Amendment to police interrogation has little to do with the Sixth Amendment's historical purpose. The New Jersey Court of Errors and Appeals forcefully made this point back in 1915 in rejecting the "novel" claim that the right to legal assistance applied to police interrogation:

> [T]he Constitution does not provide that the defendant shall have the right to have assistance of counsel from the time of his arrest, but for his defense. Obviously, the word "defense," as here used, means that a defendant is entitled to be represented and defended by counsel when put in jeopardy on his trial, and that his counsel shall have reasonable access to the prisoner for the purpose of preparing his defense.... By no stretch of the imagination can the provision be construed to mean that one accused of crime shall have the benefit of counsel to advise him as to whether or not he shall confess. Confession is a thing entirely apart from defense upon a trial.[93]

This distinction seems to be lost on some modern commentators. Examining the history of the right to counsel shortly before the Supreme Court decided *Escobedo,* one student commentator, in a frequently cited essay, characterized counsel's role as overcoming "the original unfairness of the balance of state against individual."[94] Recognizing that counsel had historically played this role at trial, the commentator observed that in modern criminal procedure, critical confrontations occur during the investigative stages: "[t]he point at which the individual first confronts the amassed power of the state has moved back in the process from trial to the police stage."[95] This procedural change prompted the commentator to ask how the defendant was to be "defended" at the police station.[96] His answer? "[W]e might have to alter our conception of the role counsel must play to readjust the balance."[97] Heeding his own advice, the commentator then concluded that the defendant should have a right to counsel's assistance during interrogation because he is "incapable of defending himself in this moment of stress."[98] He should have this right "even if the result is the end of interrogation."[99]

Although the argument's logic may seem impeccable, its major premise is flawed. The right to counsel did not develop to address the imbalance between the state and the defendant as such but rather to address a particular imbalance at trial that led to wrongful convictions. Even the intelligent and educated layperson needs counsel's assistance at trial to counter the serious risk that truth will not emerge and that a miscarriage of justice will occur.[100] To be sure, counsel's presence at trial will sometimes produce a wrongful acquittal, but this is an unavoidable consequence of the need to prevent wrongful convictions. The purpose of providing counsel's assistance at the police station, however, at least under a Sixth Amendment rationale, is to protect the defendant from the unwise choice of revealing the truth. While counsel's presence at trial is intended to further the search for truth, counsel's presence at the police station comes "at the expense of the search for truth."[101]

For similar reasons, it does not make sense to speak of defending the defendant at the police station. At the station, in contrast to the courtroom, the defendant is confronted not with legal procedures and rules but with a question of fact concerning the defendant's involvement with a certain event.[102] Police interrogation is, among other things, an investigative tool for obtaining reliable evidence, and in this regard, it is like a search, a wiretap, a sting operation, a blood test, or an alcohol test. The Sixth Amendment was not intended to assist the individual in defending against the possibility that these investigative techniques will succeed, and outside the context of police interrogation, we seem to recognize this. If interrogation does not result in an involuntary confession, the law should regard it the same way it does a lawful search. As the New Jersey court indicated in the passage quoted above, "confession"—like a search or a blood test—"is a thing entirely apart from defense upon a trial."

This argument is not built on the premise that truth is the only goal of the procedural system—a premise that was rejected in chapter 1. As was previously discussed, our disdain for wrongful convictions is so powerful that we are willing, within bounds, to increase the overall number of wrongful outcomes so that the risk of mistake will generally fall on the prosecution. The risk of mistake is allocated by the presumption of innocence, by the requirement that the prosecutor must overcome this presumption with proof that convinces the trier of fact beyond a reasonable doubt, and by the procedural and evidentiary rules that apply. In a sense, therefore, even if the defendant is guilty, an acquittal is not really wrongful when the prosecution cannot carry its burden of persuasion in court. It is one thing, however, for counsel to test the strength of the prosecutor's proof at trial and quite another for counsel to prevent the prosecutor from obtaining reliable evidence in the first place.

Of course, some of the rules that apply at trial are intended to further policies that have nothing whatsoever to do with truth or with allocating the risk of error. Whether or not these rules are wise, defense counsel is obligated to ensure that the prosecution satisfies its burden of proof in accordance with them. This obligation of defense counsel, which is antithetical to the search for truth, does not, however, support a role for counsel in the police station. The only constitutional rule that applies in the police station is the one precluding the police from compelling the defendant to answer questions. When counsel encourages a defendant to refrain from making a voluntary statement, counsel is doing more than enforcing the applicable rule. As Judge Henry Friendly once remarked, "there is no social value in preventing uncoerced admission of the facts,"[103] and nothing in the Sixth Amendment's history compels us to accept this as its purpose or goal.

In a recent effort to rewrite and defend *Massiah*, whose own reasoning he deplored as analytically shallow, Professor James Tomkovicz acknowledged that the Sixth Amendment's historical meaning was quite limited.[104] Nevertheless, Tomkovicz contended that the "incompatibility" between the historical conception of counsel's role and "American visions and aspirations" prompted the Supreme Court, "[o]ur premier legal educator," to pursue a "'more enlightened' approach."[105] Insisting that "interpretation tied solely to . . . historical attributes would be seriously flawed," Tomkovicz contended that the Court must interpret the Sixth Amendment, "one of those great generalities," "in light of modern conditions, practices, and attitudes."[106] Tomkovicz praised the Court's "commitment to look beyond history and to interpret the promise of counsel in light of evolving conditions and attitudes."[107]

Of course, a constitutional provision does not become a great generality merely because someone labels it as such. In particular, the Sixth Amendment is a most unlikely candidate for such a characterization, given its rather specific and limited original meaning. More fundamentally, however, this open-ended approach to constitutional interpretation, which we have previously confronted in this book, deprives Supreme Court critics of a powerful basis on which to argue. Under this approach, constitutional interpretation cannot be evaluated as correct or incorrect but only as good or bad, and this latter evaluation will depend on the commentator's views of what constitutes and comports with modern, evolving, or enlightened attitudes. Thus, to the argument that cases like *Miranda, Escobedo,* and *Massiah* are historically unsound, the defender of these decisions need only respond, "Perhaps so, but they are enlightened and reflect our evolving visions and aspirations."

There is a more narrow sense, however, in which Professor Tomkovicz could be right.[108] Few would argue that a constitutional provision should have only those specific applications that the framers and ratifiers actually anticipated. To carry out the underlying purposes of a provision in light of changed conditions, a court may have to apply the provision in unanticipated ways. Thus, as discussed above, the Court's interpretations of the Sixth Amendment as affording a right to appointed counsel and as applying to certain pretrial judicial proceedings may be defended in terms of the amendment's underlying purposes. This is quite different, however, from positing more enlightened underlying purposes for the amendment, purposes that accord with "modern" thinking.

As already discussed, the Sixth Amendment's underlying purposes have little if anything to do with providing counsel during police interrogation. Describing the American system as adversarial, however, Tomkovicz referred to counsel as the "central component of the system" and as "the glue that holds it together."[109] Stating that an adversarial system is impossible without "rough equality," Tomkovicz portrayed counsel as "the equalizer [who] gives a defendant necessary parity in the battle with the state."[110] Thus, "to remedy the adversarial contest's inherent imbalance, counsel should be free to protect against all facets of the government's effort to convict and to supply any needed assistance."[111]

It should be noted that Professor Tomkovicz proceeded from a premise quite similar to that of the student commentator discussed above, and accordingly his argument suffers from the same deficiencies. Adversarial balance, or rough equality, may be the norm that dictates trial procedures, but one cannot simply posit that this norm should dictate the rules of investigation and the gathering of proof. Of course, "if we had, in fact, a completely adversarial system," the argument "would be all but unanswerable."[112] The reader will recall from chapter 2, however, that such a description of our system is untenable.[113]

As the discussion in chapter 2 showed, the adversarial—more accurately, the accusatorial—system argument cannot provide the meaning of constitutional provisions. Moreover, this argument results in circular reasoning: expansive applications of the Constitution, here the Sixth Amendment, are justified by positing that the system is accusatorial; when nonaccusatorial characteristics in the system are identified, and many exist, especially at the investigative stage, the typical response is that these are different because the Constitution permits them. One cannot both define the Constitution by relying on the characteristics of the accusatorial system and define the characteristics of the accusatorial system by relying on the Constitution.

The adversarial balance or rough equality argument posits that defendants—or certainly most guilty defendants—should be advised that it is unwise for them to answer police questions.[114] As Judge Walter Schaefer noted years ago, however, "this reasoning would apply equally to any police questioning."[115] It would beg the question to respond to Judge Schaefer that noncustodial questioning and the prearrest use of informants are not governed by the dictates of the adversarial or accusatorial system. If they are not, the question is why such adversarial or accusatorial dictates should apply to custodial questioning, or indeed to any procedure not involving the judicial process.

Professor Tomkovicz's answer was that "[a] conception of fair play as mandating equalization only after the government has become committed to conviction is reconcilable with the adversary system and its values."[116] This answer does not help for two reasons. First, and of lesser importance, the government's commitment to conviction can exist well before arrest, the triggering point for Sixth Amendment rights advocated by Professor Tomkovicz.[117] Second, and of greater importance, this answer continues to beg the question. One can just as well posit a conception of fair play that mandates equalization only at the judicial or trial-like stages of the process. Professor Tomkovicz has not shown, and indeed cannot show, that his conception of adversarial fair play is dictated by the Sixth Amendment.

Ultimately, then, those who are willing to cast aside historical understanding of constitutional text must rely on policy arguments. Even if such an approach to constitutional interpretation is legitimate, one must still ask whether the policy arguments for extending the right to counsel to police interrogation are sound. Invoking the values of individual dignity and autonomy, Professor Tomkovicz saw virtue in a "staunch refusal to take advantage of a lesser opponent" and in the belief "that no individual should be exploited."[118] Others, in agreement with *Escobedo,* have commented that counsel is needed because police interrogation can seal the defendant's fate and render the trial a mere formality.[119] For the police to seal the defendant's fate by obtaining evidence from the defendant's mouth—but apparently not from his home, person, or body[120]—is somehow supposed to leave us with a sense of unfairness, with a sense that the rules of fair play have been violated.[121]

These arguments need not be belabored, for they should be recognized as the fair-chance, equality, and human dignity arguments previously encountered in chapter 2. The fair-chance argument and the argument to equalize the positions of the defendant and the interrogating officer reflect the disreputable sporting theory of justice,[122] and neither provides a persuasive basis for protecting defendants against the unwise choice they may make to confess. As Professor H. Richard Uviller recently observed, "[t]he heavy burden of proof carried by the government is (or should be) the only edge to which the 'disadvantaged' defendant is constitutionally entitled, and it is in no sense awarded as 'compensation' for an inherently weaker position."[123] Similarly, although the human dignity argument may make certain police tactics unacceptable, it is not persuasive when used to protect defendants from unwisely confessing their deeds in response to police interrogation.

Notwithstanding the discussion in chapter 2, some may continue to feel that it is unjust, perhaps even un-American, for an interrogating officer to take advantage of an uncounseled suspect. This feeling may draw some support from the widespread acceptance, at least in the legal community, of the disciplinary rule that precludes the lawyer of one party from communicating "about the subject of the representation" with a party "represented by another lawyer in the matter," unless the latter lawyer consents.[124] Of course, a disciplinary rule is not the same thing as a constitutional requirement, but this response, although it should be adequate, may not persuade those who are predisposed to read good policies into the Sixth Amendment.

Even at the policy level, however, good reasons exist for not applying this disciplinary rule to police investigative efforts in criminal cases. As Professor Uviller has argued,

> A criminal investigation presents only a crude analogy to a civil interrogation. In criminal investigations, unlike their civil counterparts, public policy favors full prosecutorial investigation while powerful constraints limit unfair or coercive police methods. The disciplinary rule makes little sense in this setting, and unthinking application may achieve intolerable results. . . . [125]

Moreover, as Professor Roger Cramton and attorney Lisa Udell have noted, allowing a disciplinary rule to dictate the limits on investigative efforts in criminal cases would be "unwise" because such rules, promulgated by bar associations, "rarely take into account the full range of interests that should govern the uneasy balance between effective law enforcement and a defendant's . . . rights."[126]

Other considerations also support a limited role for the anticontact disciplinary rule in criminal cases. First, the rule "presupposes two parties, each represented by counsel loyal only to her client," and thus "reinforces mutual professional comity customary in civil matters."[127] In criminal cases, however, "[t]he amorphous nature of the prosecutor's 'client'" allows defense lawyers to communicate whenever they choose with law enforcement officials and prosecution witnesses.[128] One might add here that police officers are not lawyers, and the case for regarding them as mere agents or alter egos of the prosecutor needs to be made, not simply posited.[129] Second, the rule in any event permits a lawyer to communicate with a represented party when "authorized by law to do so," an exception to the general prohibition that seems to make sense only in the criminal context.[130] Third, if applied to criminal cases, the rule's mandate would conceivably apply to represented suspects against whom there is suspicion but not probable cause to arrest, an application that would make much law enforcement activity virtually impossible. "Indeed, any person operating on the shady side of the law might retain counsel on an ongoing basis and thereby insulate himself completely from any government efforts, overt or covert, to obtain oral evidence from him."[131]

Finally, to read the disciplinary rule as defining the constitutional standard would be to create the very inequality that critics of police interrogation usually decry, because the rule applies only when the party to be interviewed is actually represented by a lawyer. The inequality thus created would be more than a matter of rich defendants having greater constitutional entitlements than poor ones. As Professor Uviller has observed, "the professional criminal and the affluent, corrupt official [would] obtain a significant evidentiary immunity not available to the single offender who does not need or receive professional service until indicted—an intolerable disparity."[132] Of course, the inequality regarding legal entitlement could be avoided by making counsel available to poor and less sophisticated defendants who are not already represented at the time of the police interview. Such a maneuver, however, would give the disciplinary rule, in effect, considerably broader scope in criminal cases than in civil ones, a perverse result given that the rule is uncontroversially applicable only on the civil side.

The disciplinary rule thus provides little support for a right to counsel in cases like *Cicenia, Escobedo,* and *Burbine.* Properly construed, the rule should have no, or at best limited, application in criminal cases. Even if applicable, the rule supports an interpretation that exempts police interrogation from its general mandate. Finally, whatever its technical application and scope in local disciplinary matters, policy reasons suggest that the rule should not be read as defining the constitutional standard. In short, the argument for affording defendants in criminal cases a Sixth Amendment right to counsel "receives no support from the parallel maxim that a lawyer for a civil party may not speak to a represented adverse party without the permission of her opposite number."[133]

The foregoing analysis supports the conclusion that a right to have counsel's assistance in trying to avoid unwise self-incrimination during police interrogation cannot be justified by the Sixth Amendment's text, its historical purpose, or sound policy. This conclusion merely affirms that the Supreme Court correctly decided those cases, both before and after *Escobedo,* in which it found the right to counsel inapplicable to police interrogation. *Escobedo,* which reached a contrary conclusion, was an aberration as a Sixth Amendment case, and it was, as the Court now recognizes, constitutionally indefensible on such grounds. What remains is to examine the Court's argument for applying the Sixth Amendment to police interrogations that take place after the start of adversary judicial proceedings against the accused.

The Adversary Judicial Proceeding Line

As previously discussed, Justice Stewart was the architect of the Court's current position that the Sixth Amendment right to counsel applies only to those critical police-suspect encounters that occur after the start of adversary judicial proceedings. Not surprisingly, we must turn to him for the explanation why it should apply even then. If, as the Court's cases now recognize, a defendant has no right to counsel's assistance during police interrogation that occurs before formal proceedings are initiated, why does the defendant have a right to such assistance when the interrogation occurs after such proceedings begin?

In *Spano,* which provided his first occasion to write on the subject, Justice Stewart argued that "[u]nder our system of justice an indictment is supposed to be followed by an arraignment and a trial . . . in an orderly courtroom, presided over by a judge, open to the public, and protected by all the procedural safeguards of the law," not by "an all-night inquisition in a prosecutor's office, a police station, and an automobile."[134] Five years later in *Massiah,* Justice Stewart elaborated the same theme. Relying on *Powell v. Alabama,*[135] he also reasoned that defendants need counsel's consultative and investigative skills not just at trial but "'during perhaps the most critical period of the proceedings,'" meaning "'from the time of their arraignment until the beginning of their trial.'"[136]

In his dissent in *Escobedo,* Justice Stewart made clear that the defendant's need for counsel's help was not an independent rationale. Indeed, responding to the Court's observation that a defendant's confession can affect his trial, Stewart stated that he "had always supposed that the whole purpose of a police investigation of a murder was to 'affect' the trial of the murderer, and that it would be only an incompetent, unsuccessful, or corrupt investigation which would not do so."[137] Distinguishing *Spano* and *Massiah,* Stewart insisted that "the institution of formal, meaningful judicial proceedings . . . marks the point at which a criminal investigation has ended and adversary proceedings have commenced."[138] This is the point at which Sixth Amendment rights— speedy trial, confrontation, the right to counsel—apply.[139] By importing "concepts historically applicable only after the onset of formal prosecutorial proceedings," the Court had converted "a routine police investigation of an unsolved murder into a distorted analogue of a judicial trial."[140] It thus had "frustrate[d] the vital interests of society in preserving the legitimate and proper function of honest and purposeful police investigation."[141]

Justice Stewart built his Sixth Amendment jurisprudence, therefore, not on the premise that defendants need help in confronting their interrogators—Escobedo needed help as much as Spano and Massiah— but on the view that the Constitution structured the criminal justice system into two distinct phases. In the investigative phase, the police and other investigative bodies have considerable leeway as long as they do not coerce the defendant. In the judicial phase, which marks the end of the investigative phase, the state's agents may not approach the accused unless they do so in a way that accords with the procedural protections that govern the accusatorial, judicial process. Thus, once the judicial phase begins, state officials may not confront the accused, at least absent counsel's involvement, with extrajudicial procedures such as police interrogation, surreptitious interrogation, or presumably grand jury questioning.[142] After his arrest, Escobedo could appropriately expect the police to subject him to noncoercive questioning; by contrast, after their indictments, Spano and Massiah could appropriately expect the rules of open courtroom proceedings to apply.

The question is whether Justice Stewart's argument requires a modification of the previously reached conclusion that the Sixth Amendment, understood in light of its history and underlying purposes, should not be deemed to apply to police interrogation. It is difficult to see that it does. As then Justice Rehnquist once observed, nothing in the Constitution dictates "a rigid dichotomy between the types of police activities that are permissible before commencement of formal criminal proceedings and those that are subsequently permissible."[143]

Moreover, nothing implicit in the structure of the American system suggests "that once the adversary process formally begins the government may not make any effort to obtain incriminating evidence from the accused when counsel is not present."[144] If Justice Stewart's arguments were valid, searches and seizures after the commencement of judicial proceedings would seem as impermissible as police interrogation.[145] A postcharge search for evidence, at least absent counsel's consent, does not seem to square with the view that the filing of formal charges marks the point at which the investigation is supposed to end and the rules of the judicial process are to take over. Yet, courts have apparently not barred postcharge searches, and the Supreme Court's recent case that distinguished, for Sixth Amendment purposes, a passive informant from one who deliberately elicits statements suggests that it would be wrong to do so.[146] Justice Stewart never explained why the Sixth Amendment—not the Fifth Amendment—should be viewed as barring only efforts to elicit evidence from the accused's mouth.

Justice Stewart's argument also is vulnerable, as Professor Uviller has observed, because "it allows some and precludes other access to the mind of an uncounseled suspect without a principled basis for the demarcation."[147] The resulting formalism perhaps is nowhere more apparent than in *Brewer v. Williams*.[148] In that case, the defendant surrendered to police in Davenport, Iowa, after the police in Des Moines obtained a warrant to arrest him for child abduction. Before the Des Moines police arrived in Davenport to take charge of the defendant, the Davenport police brought him to a Davenport courtroom for a preliminary arraignment on the arrest warrant. In the police car on the ride back to Des Moines, Detective Leaming gave Williams the famous "Christian burial speech," which apparently later prompted Williams to take the police to the abducted girl's body.

As noted earlier, Justice Stewart's bare majority opinion found a violation of the Sixth Amendment right to counsel. Williams had retained a lawyer in Des Moines and had consulted another lawyer in Davenport, but these facts, as we know, would not have been relevant to Justice Stewart, and they were not stressed in his opinion. Why then did the Sixth Amendment apply? Justice Stewart's answer was brief. After noting that the Sixth Amendment entitles a defendant to a lawyer's help at or after the commencement of judicial proceedings, "'whether by way of formal charge, preliminary hearing, indictment, information, or arraignment,'"[149] Justice Stewart added,

> There can be no doubt in the present case that judicial proceedings had been initiated against Williams before the start of the automobile ride from Davenport to Des Moines. A warrant had been issued for his arrest, he had been arraigned on that warrant before a judge in a Davenport courtroom, and he had been committed by the court to confinement in jail.[150]

The obvious implication is that if the Davenport police had not made the "mistake" of arraigning Williams, and thus initiating judicial proceedings against him, Detective Leaming's speech would not have violated the Sixth Amendment. Of course, Williams's need for counsel's help in the police car did not depend on the arraignment having occurred, and for the case to turn on this fact cannot help but strike many as formalistic.[151] Moreover, many will readily agree with Professor Yale Kamisar that the right to counsel should not depend on "a point that can often be manipulated by law enforcement authorities."[152] Although not devoid of logic and intellectual appeal, Justice Stewart's rigid demarcation between the investigative and judicial phases seems too abstruse when one confronts the hard realities of concrete cases.

Along with the arguments previously considered, the formalism of the current approach supports the view that the Court should go one step further and completely withdraw the Sixth Amendment from the subject of police interrogation. If the Court does not take this step, the existing formalism does not present a reason for disinterring *Escobedo* and moving the right to counsel line back to arrest. That is, the current approach, with all its defects, is preferable to one that would make the right to counsel more broadly applicable.

First, a revival of *Escobedo* would not eliminate the formalism and the risk of police manipulation. In *Hoffa v. United States*,[153] for example, the government employed Jimmy Hoffa's friend as an informant to learn whether Hoffa was trying to tamper with a jury in an on-going trial. Relying on *Massiah* and *Escobedo*, Hoffa argued that this violated his Sixth Amendment right to counsel, but the Court curtly responded that it was not prepared to create what in effect would amount to a right to be arrested under the Sixth Amendment.[154] From the standpoint of needing legal assistance, however, Hoffa's situation was no different from Massiah's, against whom the government had used precisely the same investigative approach.[155]

Moreover, if the Court revived *Escobedo*, *Hoffa* might tempt the police to manipulate the point of arrest to avoid the counsel requirement. This risk would not be limited to cases involving the use of informants, for just as the police can avoid *Miranda*'s requirements by questioning a suspect at home or by "inviting" the suspect to come to the station,[156] they would likewise be able to avoid a Sixth Amendment right that comes into being on arrest. There may be less room for manipulation under a rule that triggers Sixth Amendment rights at arrest rather than at the commencement of judicial proceedings, but room there undeniably still is.

A more radical change to avoid the formalism and the risk of manipulation in the current approach would be to move the Sixth Amendment line back to the point that an investigation begins to focus on a particular suspect. Under such an approach, of course, the government

168 · *Confessions, Truth, and the Law*

would have been barred from using any informants in *Hoffa*. Indeed, such an approach would virtually eliminate all undercover police work. Whatever might be said in defense of dealing such a drastic blow to law enforcement, the Sixth Amendment is a bizarre vehicle to bring about such a result. It should not be surprising, therefore, that even the Court that decided *Massiah*, *Escobedo*, and *Miranda* refused to take such an argument seriously in *Hoffa*.

To avoid such a radical result, one might argue that the right to counsel should attach at different times for different police procedures[157]—for example, at arrest for the use of informants but at focus for direct questioning. This approach would revive *Escobedo* without undermining *Hoffa*. At this point, however, one must step back and ask what goal one is seeking to accomplish. The question that prompted the current analysis was whether, despite the general conclusion that the right to counsel should not apply to police interrogation, a case could be made for applying the Sixth Amendment to interrogations after the start of judicial proceedings. It would be perverse to use deficiencies in the argument for an exception to the general rule to undermine the rule rather than the exception. If one accepts, as has been argued in this chapter, that *Massiah* was both a constitutional and a policy mistake, an approach that strains and maneuvers to give that decision the fullest conceivable scope makes substantially less sense than an approach that confines the decision, as the Court has done, to limited if difficult to rationalize circumstances. Stated differently, the problem of apparent formalism, which cannot be eliminated even by extending the right to counsel, is a far lesser evil than the elimination of police interrogation.

Finally, if the Court is going to retain a limited role for the Sixth Amendment in this context, a positive argument of sorts can be made for the adversary judicial proceeding requirement.[158] As Justice Stewart stated in his plurality opinion in *Kirby*,

> The initiation of criminal proceedings is far from a mere formalism. It is the starting point of our whole system of adversary criminal justice. For it is only then that the Government has committed itself to prosecute, and only then that the adverse positions of Government and defendant have solidified. It is then that a defendant finds himself faced with the prosecutorial forces of organized society, and immersed in the intricacies of substantive and procedural criminal law. It is this point, therefore, that marks the commencement of the "criminal prosecutions" to which alone the explicit guarantees of the Sixth Amendment are applicable.[159]

Although Professor Uviller has failed to find anything of substance beneath this "rhetorical polish,"[160] the filing of a formal charge, which typically involves the prosecutor,[161] represents more of a commitment to prosecute than does a police decision to arrest. True enough, although Justice Stewart thought otherwise, an arrested person under interrogation may well feel that the government's adverse position against him has "solidified." Nevertheless, as Stewart recognized, the fact remains that defendants do not have to make decisions involving the intricacies of substantive and procedural criminal law until judicial proceedings are initiated; only then do they have to consider whether to waive preliminary examination or indictment; whether to move to reduce bail; whether to seek discovery; what plea to enter; what pretrial motions, if any, to file; and what defenses to present. Moreover, and textually most important, the rights contained in the Sixth Amendment *are* trial rights; they are rights that pertain to the "criminal prosecution." The rights to jury trial, to public trial, to notice of the accusation, to confrontation of adverse witnesses, and to compulsory process apply either at trial or to earlier judicial phases of a formally initiated prosecution. Even the right to a speedy trial, which the Court, perhaps incorrectly, has held to be triggered by an arrest,[162] is a right that pertains to trials.

Although it did not recognize a right to counsel during police interrogation even after the filing of formal charges, the New Jersey Court of Errors and Appeals, in the 1915 case previously quoted in this chapter, did grasp the significance and scope of the bundle of rights provided by the Sixth Amendment:

> It clearly appears that the rights thus intended to be secured to a criminal defendant are rights arising from a criminal prosecution; that is, a trial upon an indictment. A prisoner making a confession is not confronted with any witnesses, at least never in the sense that they are examined in his presence, he can have no process for witnesses in his favor upon such an occasion, and, consequently, he is not entitled to the assistance of counsel to save him from himself. That is done later by the trial court if the confession was unlawfully obtained.[163]

The Fifth Amendment Right to Counsel

In *Miranda v. Arizona*,[164] the Court concluded that advice from an interrogating officer to a custodial suspect that he has a right to remain silent and that anything he says can be used against him in court is insufficient to protect the suspect from being compelled to become a witness against himself:

> The circumstances surrounding in-custody interrogation can oper-
> ate very quickly to overbear the will of one merely made aware of
> his privilege by his interrogators. Therefore, the right to have coun-
> sel present at the interrogation is indispensable to the protection of
> the Fifth Amendment privilege under the system we delineate to-
> day.[165]

Thus did the Court give birth to what Justice White in dissent aptly labeled "a limited Fifth Amendment right to counsel,"[166] a right that applies to all custodial interrogation, even that preceding the initiation of adversary, judicial proceedings.

It should be stressed that *Miranda*'s justification for recognizing a right to counsel has nothing to do with helping the defendant to make strategically wise decisions. To be sure, *Miranda* did recognize that coun-sel's presence at the interrogation "may serve several significant subsidiary functions as well," such as assuring that the accused gives an accurate statement and that the police record it accurately.[167] These "subsidiary" functions do not provide the constitutional justification for the right. Under *Miranda*'s Fifth Amendment rationale, counsel is provided to pre-vent compelled self-incrimination, not to prevent unwise self-incrimina-tion.[168]

Several cases subsequent to *Miranda* have confirmed the limited Fifth Amendment basis of its right to counsel. For example, in *Kirby*, the previously discussed case that limited the Sixth Amendment right to counsel to confrontations occurring after the start of judicial proceed-ings, the Court found *Miranda*'s right to counsel totally irrelevant to the issue of a precharge custodial identification. *Miranda*, the Court said, was based "exclusively" on the Fifth Amendment, "upon the theory that custodial *interrogation* is inherently coercive."[169] Likewise, in *Burbine*, whose Sixth Amendment holding was also previously discussed, the Court rejected the defendant's argument that the police tainted his waiver of *Miranda* rights by not informing him of the call from the lawyer his sister had retained. The Court's reasoning reiterated the limited nature of the Fifth Amendment right to counsel:

> No doubt the additional information would have been useful to
> respondent; perhaps even it might have affected his decision to
> confess. *But we have never read the Constitution to require that the*

police supply a suspect with a flow of information to help him calibrate his self-interest in deciding whether to speak or stand by his rights. . . . Once it is determined that a suspect's decision not to rely on his rights was uncoerced . . . the analysis is complete . . . .[170]

In *Connecticut v. Barrett,*[171] the Court rejected a *Miranda* challenge to an oral statement given by a defendant who had said he would not give a written statement without counsel. That the defendant's decision may have been "illogical" was "irrelevant" to the Court, for it had "never 'embraced the theory that a defendant's ignorance of the full consequences of his decisions vitiates their voluntariness.'"[172] Similarly, in *Colorado v. Spring,*[173] the Court rejected an argument that *Miranda* required the defendant to be informed of the crimes about which he was to be questioned. The Court stated that this information "could affect only the wisdom of a *Miranda* waiver, not its essentially voluntary and knowing nature."[174]

The difference in the supporting rationale for the Sixth Amendment right to counsel that *Escobedo* had embraced, before its transmogrification into a Fifth Amendment case, and the supporting rationale for the Fifth Amendment right to counsel that *Miranda* created could not be more apparent. In *Escobedo,* the Court was concerned with helping the accused to calibrate his self-interest and with protecting him from unwise decisions. It voiced concern, for example, that Escobedo might not have known that it was just as damaging to admit complicity in the murder as to admit that he was the shooter.[175] It also worried that his confession could affect the whole trial, that it could assure his conviction, leaving little for counsel to do at trial.[176] In short, *Escobedo,* unlike *Miranda,* gave the accused a right to "the Assistance of Counsel."[177]

Perhaps no case illustrates the difference in the respective rationales as much as *Illinois v. Perkins,*[178] which held that *Miranda* did not apply to the questioning of a defendant by an undercover agent who had been placed in the defendant's cell. Had this questioning occurred after the start of formal, judicial proceedings, the defendant would have been entitled to a lawyer's help under *Massiah.* Because formal proceedings had not commenced, however, the defendant could rely only on *Miranda.* The Court rejected this argument because "*Miranda* forbids coercion, not mere strategic deception."[179] The Court added that "[p]loys to mislead a suspect or lull him into a false sense of security that do not rise to the level of compulsion or coercion to speak are not within *Miranda*'s concerns."[180] After *Perkins,* therefore, there can be no doubt that *Mi-*

randa's right to counsel—which is the only right to counsel that applies in the precharge context—is concerned with preventing coerced self-incrimination, not unwise self-incrimination.

Chapter 5 argued that *Miranda* erred in equating the mere inherent pressures of custodial interrogation with compulsion under the Fifth Amendment. Indeed, as that chapter showed, the Court, until *Miranda*, had always and appropriately treated Fifth Amendment compulsion as synonymous with Fourteenth Amendment coercion. If these conclusions are correct, *Miranda* also erred in creating a Fifth Amendment right to counsel to protect the defendant from the mere inherent pressures of custodial interrogation. Under a Fifth Amendment rationale, protecting the defendant from voluntary statements cannot be justified.

Nor can *Miranda*'s right to counsel be justified on the ground that the defendant needs help in deciding whether to assert the right to silence. First, such an "assistance" rationale seems more akin to Sixth Amendment rather than to Fifth Amendment thinking, and the Sixth Amendment does not apply in the precharge context. Second, as argued in chapter 5, the Fifth Amendment provides not a right of silence as such but rather a right not to be compelled to speak. As Judge Henry Friendly noted years ago, "[t]his distinction is not mere semantics; it goes to the very core of the problem."[181] A correct characterization of the issue, as previously discussed, eliminates the issue of waiver. More importantly, it suggests that we should search for a way to avoid the evil—coercive interrogation techniques—other than through a device that by preventing the "fair as well as unfair"[182] reduces the likelihood of obtaining voluntary statements in the search for truth.

With *Miranda*'s limited Fifth Amendment right to counsel abrogated, the law regarding the right to counsel during police interrogation, at least at the precharge stage, would return to what it was before 1964. What remains to be considered, however, is whether *Miranda*'s right to counsel can be justified as a prophylactic protection against real compulsion. This is the subject of the next chapter.

CHAPTER 7

Miranda **as a Prophylactic Decision**

Compared to most of its constitutional law opinions, the Supreme Court's opinion in *Miranda v. Arizona*[1] is exceedingly atypical. The typical opinion begins with a succinct statement of the relevant facts and of the issues the facts have generated. The opinion then discusses the arguably relevant principles and precedent and reasons to a holding that is tied, sometimes more tightly than others, to the concrete issues the Court has identified. Not so *Miranda*.

Miranda's opening paragraph informed the reader that the case had something to do with the Fifth Amendment and the admissibility of statements produced by custodial interrogation.[2] Without describing the specifics of what the police had done in the four cases before the Court, subsequent pages of the opinion then introduced and summarized the holding, reviewed precedent, analyzed the history of the Fifth Amendment, surveyed police manuals to present a general picture of police interrogation, imposed various mandates by way of dicta, elaborated and again summarized the holding, and examined the law in other countries to show that the holding was really not that extreme.[3] After more than fifty pages, the opinion acknowledged that the preceding discussion, which included all the Court's new rules, had occurred without "specific concentration on the facts of the cases before us."[4] Belatedly turning to the facts, the opinion then spent only eight pages in concluding that the police in each case had obtained the confession in violation of the new rules.[5] While the opinion obviously dealt with police interrogation, it left the impression, as Justice White complained, that the Court had "not examined a single transcript of any police interrogation, let alone the interrogation that took place in any one of [the four] cases."[6]

Miranda's legislative quality, however, stems from more than an appearance that the Court addressed what it felt to be a societal problem rather than a concrete legal issue raised by specific facts. Going beyond a mere conclusion that specific police conduct had violated the Constitution, the Court "legislated" a set of four specific warnings and a waiver requirement that the police would have to follow in all cases regardless of factual differences.[7] The Court even conceded that the Constitution did not necessarily require adherence to this particular scheme for protecting Fifth Amendment rights, and it encouraged Congress and the states to devise equally effective alternative schemes.[8]

Finally, as already mentioned, the Court issued numerous mandates, "a miscellany of minor directives,"[9] that were unrelated to the facts in the four cases and that addressed issues the Court would confront in subsequent years. In rank dicta, the Court indicated that statements taken in violation of its new rules could not be used to impeach a testifying defendant,[10] elaborated the requirements for a valid waiver of the new rights,[11] informed the police what they must do if a defendant actually invokes the right of silence[12] or the *Miranda* right to counsel,[13] stated that a defendant's silence would not be admissible against the defendant[14] and that a defendant would not permanently waive his rights by beginning to talk,[15] reminded federal officials that they remained bound by federal prompt arraignment rules,[16] and suggested that the new rules would not apply to on-the-scene questioning.[17]

Even apart from questions concerning the substantive validity of the new rules, such an atypically crafted opinion was bound to spark controversy in a system that generally expects federal courts to decide only the concrete cases and controversies actually before them.[18] Nevertheless, courts throughout history have succumbed to the temptation to address extraneous issues and sometimes even to legislate minicodes, and *Miranda* conceivably only carried bad existing judicial practices to a new and alarming extreme. In 1974, however, in *Michigan v. Tucker*,[19] a plurality of the Court raised a more fundamental question when it described *Miranda*'s very holding as merely a "prophylactic" safeguard for the Fifth Amendment. This statement, which a majority of the Court now accepts, raises the question not of whether the Court erred in interpreting the Fifth Amendment but of whether the Court had authority to impose *Miranda*'s prophylactic rules on the states.

The latter question is the focus of this chapter. Unlike the discussion in chapter 5, which challenged *Miranda*'s understanding of the Fifth Amendment's self-incrimination clause, the discussion in this chapter addresses the legitimacy of *Miranda* as the Court now understands what it did in that case. First, the meaning of the term *prophylactic,* as it is used in connection with *Miranda,* is explored, and in this regard, the prophylactic *Miranda* decision is contrasted with the nonprophylactic *Massiah* decision. Because some view the prophylactic reading of *Miranda* as an invention of the post-*Miranda* Court, the chapter next examines how the *Miranda* opinion itself supports the Court's current characterization of the *Miranda* rules. Finally, inquiring whether the Court had the authority to impose the prophylactic *Miranda* rules on the states, the chapter argues that a prophylactic rule decision is identical except in label to a so-called supervisory power decision. If this conclusion is correct, the Court lacked authority to do what it did in *Miranda*.

Prophylactic Rules: *Miranda* and *Massiah* Contrasted

Because the adjective *prophylactic* describes something that may be used to prevent or to defend against a certain occurrence, it has the potential for wide employment in constitutional discourse. For example, the right to have the assistance of counsel at trial can be viewed as a prophylactic device to prevent or defend against the evil of unjust convictions. Similarly, although citizen participation in the enforcement of the criminal law may be an end in itself, the right of trial by jury can also be a prophylactic measure to prevent wrongful convictions by judges subservient to the executive's wishes. These entirely correct usages of the word, however, raise no issues of particular interest, and they are not the subject of this chapter.

As used in this chapter, the term *prophylactic* has a special and narrower meaning. To illustrate, the plurality in *Tucker* thought it relevant to ask whether the police interrogation "directly infringed upon respondent's right against compulsory self-incrimination or whether it instead violated only the prophylactic rules developed to protect that right."[20] Even more clearly, the plurality concluded that the interrogation did not violate the Fifth Amendment but only the "procedural safeguards associated with that right since *Miranda*."[21] Yet again, the plurality stated that its conclusion that the police employed no compulsion "to breach the right against compulsory self-incrimination [did] not mean there was not a disregard, albeit an inadvertent disregard, of the procedural rules later established in *Miranda*."[22] Therefore, as used by the *Tucker* plurality to describe *Miranda*, prophylactic rules are not simply protective devices for constitutional provisions but more importantly— and this is the crux of the matter for the legitimacy issue—rules that may be violated without violating the Constitution. According to *Tucker*, the state's use of a defendant's confession may sometimes violate *Miranda*'s rules but not the Fifth Amendment's protection against compulsory self-incrimination.

Since *Tucker*, the Court has made plain that it views *Miranda* as prophylactic. In *New Jersey v. Portash*,[23] decided five years after *Tucker*, the Court reaffirmed its view that "a defendant's compelled statements, as opposed to statements taken in violation of *Miranda*," may not be used even for impeachment purposes at trial.[24] Similarly, in creating a public safety exception to *Miranda* a few years later, the Court in *New York v. Quarles*,[25] quoting the *Tucker* plurality, described the *Miranda* warnings as protective measures for the Fifth Amendment rather than "'rights protected by the Constitution.'"[26] Stating that "the failure to provide *Miranda* warnings in and of itself does not render a confession involuntary," the *Quarles* Court specifically denied that it was creating an exception for compelled statements.[27] Curiously, even Justice Marshall, a staunch defender of *Miranda*, acknowledged in his dissent that *Miranda* is "overbroad in that its application excludes some statements made during custodial interrogations that are not in fact coercive."[28]

Tucker, *Portash*, and *Quarles* are not isolated examples. Refusing to apply traditional "fruit of the poisonous tree" analysis in evaluating the admissibility of a second statement when the first statement was obtained in violation of *Miranda*, the Court in *Oregon v. Elstad*[29] stated that *Miranda*'s exclusionary rule "sweeps more broadly than the Fifth Amendment itself [and] may be triggered even in the absence of a Fifth Amendment violation."[30] The Court added that "*Miranda*'s preventive medicine provides a remedy even to the defendant who has suffered no identifiable constitutional harm."[31] In *Connecticut v. Barrett*,[32] the Court similarly stated that the *Miranda-Edwards* rule, which essentially prohibits further questioning once a custodial suspect asks for a lawyer,[33] "is not itself required by the Fifth Amendment's prohibition on coerced confessions, but is instead justified only by reference to [*Miranda*'s] prophylactic purpose."[34]

The Court gave this last-mentioned rule an expansive application in *Minnick v. Mississippi*.[35] Nevertheless, *Minnick* described the rule's benefits as outweighing such costs as the "'suppression of trustworthy and highly probative evidence even though the confession might be voluntary under traditional Fifth Amendment analysis,'"[36] a remarkable balancing of the interests quite apart from the implications concerning the Court's perception of its authority to reverse state convictions absent a constitutional violation.

While the Court without doubt thus views *Miranda*'s requirements as prophylactic—again meaning that they can be violated without violating the Fifth Amendment—its view of *Miranda*'s Sixth Amendment first cousin, *Massiah*, is quite different. True enough, then Justice Rehnquist once said in dissent that *Massiah* "rests on a prophylactic application of the Sixth Amendment right to counsel that . . . entirely ignores the doctrinal foundation of that right."[37] Although, as discussed in chapter 6, a persuasive case can be made that *Massiah* wrongly construed the Sixth Amendment, nothing in *Massiah* or its progeny, with a minor exception discussed below, suggests that the Court believes *Massiah*'s rule can be violated without violating the Constitution. Of course, Rehnquist may have used the term *prophylactic* differently than the Court has used it in the *Miranda* context, but if he did, he would only have reinforced the distinction between *Miranda* and *Massiah* that is being emphasized here.

The opinions in the *Massiah* line of cases demonstrate that the Court does not view *Massiah* as prophylactic. In *Massiah,* the Court said it was dealing with "the specific guarantee of the Sixth Amendment," and it held that the prosecutor's use of Massiah's statements obtained by an informant in the absence of counsel denied Massiah "the basic protections of that guarantee."[38] In *Brewer v. Williams,*[39] the Christian burial speech case discussed in the last chapter, the Court relied on *Massiah* in concluding that Williams was "deprived of . . . the right to the assistance of counsel."[40] Likewise, in *United States v. Henry,*[41] which like *Massiah* involved an informant reporting on conversations with the defendant, the Court explicitly stated that "the Government violated Henry's Sixth Amendment right to counsel."[42] Finally, in *Maine v. Moulton,*[43] another informant case, the Court held "that the State violated Moulton's Sixth Amendment right when it arranged to record conversations between Moulton and its undercover informant."[44] Interestingly, the Court in *Moulton* refused to adopt what would have been a prophylactic rule: the Court said that evidence that pertains to offenses for which Sixth Amendment rights have not yet attached need not be excluded simply because Sixth Amendment rights have attached on other charges.[45]

Nothing in these cases indicates a belief on the part of the Court that the governmental conduct at issue violated a judicially fashioned prophylactic rule but not the Constitution itself. On the contrary, the Court explicitly concluded in each case that the governmental conduct violated the defendant's Sixth Amendment right to counsel. Given what the Court has said, the basic *Massiah* rule cannot be viewed as prophylactic.

Nevertheless, the Court does view one aspect of its Sixth Amendment doctrine as prophylactic. In *Michigan v. Jackson,*[46] a Sixth Amendment case, the Court applied the *Miranda-Edwards* rule that once a defendant requests counsel, further interrogation must cease until counsel has been made available to the defendant, unless the defendant initiates further conversations with the police. Under this rigid rule, even an otherwise valid waiver of the right to counsel will not save a resulting statement if the police resume the interrogation. As previously observed, the Court has described this rule as prophylactic in the *Miranda* context,[47] and it would seem equally prophylactic in the Sixth Amendment context.

Indeed, in *Michigan v. Harvey,*[48] the Court described *Jackson* as having "superimposed" the *Edwards* prophylactic rule onto the Sixth Amendment.[49] Because *Jackson's* rule was only prophylactic, the Court in *Harvey,* following the approach it had taken with regard to *Miranda* violations,[50] permitted statements obtained in violation of *Jackson* to be used for impeachment purposes even though such statements cannot be used in the prosecution's case in chief. Significantly, however, the Court viewed the impeachment use of statements obtained without a valid waiver of Sixth Amendment rights as a different issue, one that was not before it.[51] The clear implication is that although the *Jackson* rule is a prophylactic safeguard to assure valid waivers of Sixth Amendment rights, the *Massiah, Williams, Henry,* and *Moulton* rulings are not prophylactic but instead reflect the Court's view—however misguided it may be—of what the Sixth Amendment actually requires.

According to Professor Stephen Schulhofer, "some critics" have concluded that *Miranda* is prophylactic because one can imagine at least some cases of voluntary responses to custodial interrogation that *Miranda* would bar from evidence.[52] Voluntary responses to custodial interrogation are more than imaginable, but the Court itself, not *Miranda*'s critics, determined that *Miranda* violations are not necessarily constitutional violations. *Miranda* would cease to be a prophylactic decision if the Court were to conclude, however absurd it might seem, that *every* statement obtained in violation of *Miranda* is compelled within the meaning of the Fifth Amendment. Only the Court, not its critics, can determine whether its decisions are merely prophylactic, and for better or worse, the Court has determined that *Miranda*'s requirements are prophylactic while *Massiah*'s Sixth Amendment requirements are not.[53]

The *Miranda* Opinion

Rather than blaming "some critics" for the characterization of *Miranda* as prophylactic, Professor Yale Kamisar has implied that responsibility lies with the revisionism of the Burger and Rehnquist Courts.[54] Although not as wide of the mark as the first allegation, this charge is not completely accurate either. *Tucker,* a Burger Court opinion, concededly was the first decision formally to articulate the prophylactic view of *Miranda.* Nevertheless, the *Miranda* opinion easily lent itself to such a reading. Moreover, because any other understanding of *Miranda* is implausible, a prophylactic reading of the case was virtually inevitable.

Despite its failure to rely on specific facts in the record, *Miranda* does contain some passages suggesting that a violation of its rules is a violation of the Fifth Amendment. In its strongest statement along these lines, the Court stated that "[u]nless adequate protective devices are employed to dispel the compulsion inherent in custodial surroundings, no statement obtained from the defendant can truly be the product of his free choice."[55] To the same effect, the Court also observed that "without proper safeguards the process of in-custody interrogation . . . contains inherently compelling pressures which work to undermine the individual's will to resist and to compel him to speak where he would not otherwise do so freely."[56] Moreover, rejecting an argument that it should stay its hand until others had addressed the issue of police interrogation, the Court insisted that "the issues presented are of constitutional dimension," and it asserted that it had the responsibility to deal with a claim that a statement "was obtained in violation of the defendant's constitutional rights."[57] "Where rights secured by the Constitution are involved," the Court added, "there can be no rule making or legislation which would abrogate them."[58]

Mention has already been made of both the Court's statement that the Constitution did not necessarily require its new rules and the Court's invitation to Congress and state legislatures to devise "at least as effective" alternative safeguards.[59] While this sounds like the language of prophylaxis, by itself this language is not determinative, although it certainly is relevant. Taken together with the passages cited above, this language could be read as saying that without the warnings and waiver, or some fully effective alternative, any statement that results from custodial interrogation has actually been compelled within the meaning of the Fifth Amendment. While the warnings as such may not be constitutionally required, this interpretation of *Miranda* would not have the Court reversing state convictions without finding that the defendant was compelled to be a witness against himself.[60]

Notwithstanding the existence of this inherent compulsion rationale in certain of *Miranda*'s passages, much of the opinion is written in the language of mere prophylaxis. The very first paragraph announced that the case involved the need for procedures "which assure that the individual is accorded" his Fifth Amendment rights.[61] The Court also acknowledged that it might not have found the four defendants' statements "to have been involuntary in traditional terms," but this did not lessen its concern "for adequate safeguards to protect" Fifth Amendment rights.[62] Along the same lines, the Court spoke of the "potentiality for compulsion" and of the need for the police "to afford appropriate safeguards at the outset of the interrogation to insure that the statements were truly the product of free choice."[63] To the same effect, the Court spoke of Fifth Amendment rights being "jeopardized" by custodial interrogation and of the need for "procedural safeguards . . . to protect the privilege."[64]

All this language, of course, undermined the inherent compulsion rationale: potential compulsion is different from inherent compulsion;

jeopardizing Fifth Amendment rights is different from actually violating them; and assuring that Fifth Amendment rights are protected is different from concluding that they have actually been infringed. Under the inherent compulsion rationale, every confession that results from custodial interrogation without procedural safeguards has been compelled; under the potential for compulsion rationale, at least some of these confessions have not been compelled. Therefore, the potential for compulsion rationale is prophylactic precisely in the sense that *Miranda*'s progeny used that term.

Other passages in *Miranda* also support a prophylactic rationale. For example, the Court indicated that if the police failed to give the warnings in subsequent cases, it would not inquire whether the defendant in any event knew of his rights.[65] This suggests, of course, an intent to enforce the procedural safeguards even when the right the safeguards are intended to protect has not been violated. As already indicated, the Court also canvassed interrogation manuals rather than the actual records of the four cases to find police practices of which it disapproved. Addressing those practices, the Court said that "[u]nless a proper limitation upon custodial interrogation is achieved—such as these decisions will advance—there can be no assurance that practices of this nature will be eradicated in the foreseeable future."[66] A prophylactic rule, of course, seeks to prevent constitutional violations that might occur in future cases rather than to discover whether an actual violation occurred in the case at hand.

The Court's treatment of the four cases before it also is illuminating. It found Miranda's confession inadmissible because he was not given advice concerning the right to counsel; "nor was his right not to be compelled to incriminate himself effectively protected in any other manner."[67] Quite understandably, the Court did not suggest that the two-hour interrogation, preceded by advice that he did not have to talk, actually compelled Miranda to confess. Similarly, it found defendant Vignera's confession inadmissible simply because he was not given any warnings of his rights and because "[n]o other steps were taken to protect these rights."[68] The Court did not give any indication that it thought Vignera's confession actually to be compelled.

In defendant Westover's case, the Court's opinion was somewhat ambivalent. Federal agents warned Westover of his rights before the two-hour interrogation that produced his confession. The federal interrogation, however, followed on the heels of an unsuccessful state interrogation that had occurred without any warnings, and this sequence led the Court to conclude that the federal warnings came too late.[69] "In these circumstances," added the Court, "an intelligent waiver of constitutional rights cannot be assumed."[70]

This last sentence may prompt some to conclude that the Court found an actual constitutional violation in Westover's case. Nevertheless, because the only applicable constitutional right was the Fifth Amendment right not to be compelled to speak, this is not the best reading of this sentence. The concept of waiver may make sense as applied to the protections fashioned in *Miranda,* but as discussed in chapter 5, it makes little sense if applied to the Fifth Amendment right not to be compelled. While the Court did say that the federal interrogation took place in the "same compelling surroundings" as the state interrogation,[71] its final sentence was that "[i]n these circumstances the giving of warnings alone was not sufficient to protect the privilege."[72] Thus, although the matter is not as clear as in Miranda's and Vignera's cases, it seems that the Court concluded not that the agents actually compelled Westover to speak but that they failed to take adequate steps to assure that compulsion would not materialize.

Only in defendant Stewart's case did the Court's discussion suggest the existence of actual compulsion. After arresting Stewart in connection with a series of robberies, the police interrogated him on nine different occasions during a five-day incommunicado detention. When the police arrested Stewart, they also arrested his wife and three visitors, whom they released after Stewart confessed. In the language of prophylaxis, the Court stated that it would not presume Stewart's Fifth Amendment rights had been adequately "safeguarded" absent the *Miranda* warnings or "an effective alternative."[73] In the language of actual constitutional violation, however, the Court added that "Stewart's steadfast denial of the alleged offenses through eight of the nine interrogations over a period of five days is subject to no other construction than that he was compelled by persistent interrogation to forgo his Fifth Amendment privilege."[74] Significantly, Justice Clark, who dissented regarding the other three defendants, concurred in Stewart's case because the state had failed to prove either a waiver of rights or "a totality of circumstances showing voluntariness."[75]

Still, given *Miranda*'s competing rationales, one may question why *Miranda*'s progeny chose the prophylactic reading suggesting that *Miranda* violations are not constitutional violations. After all, that the *Miranda* Court consciously sought to suggest that its new requirements could be violated without violating the Constitution seems highly improbable; that it was not even aware of the tension in its decision seems more likely. The answer may be that any other reading of *Miranda* is implausible. As discussed in chapter 5, to reject a prophylactic reading of *Miranda,* one must conclude that an unwarned suspect's incriminating response to only one custodial question in all circumstances has been compelled.[76] Such a conclusion defies common sense, for as even Professor Schulhofer, one of *Miranda*'s staunchest defenders, has acknowledged, "one can imagine a case in which a law professor-suspect knows his rights and is not in fear of abuses, in which he tells all in response to the first question, not because of any sense of pressure but simply because he wants the truth to come out."[77] Indeed, unless one holds a view of voluntariness similar to Professor Schulhofer's, one need not strain so hard to imagine, and actually to find, instances of voluntary responses to custodial interrogation.

A prophylactic reading of *Miranda* also saves the decision from being incoherent. Because *Miranda* requires both a warning and a waiver, one must conclude under the inherent compulsion rationale that even a warned suspect who confesses without giving the requisite waiver has been compelled.[78] Justice White in dissent immediately saw the contradiction: if this is correct, "how can the Court ever accept [a defendant's] negative answer to the question of whether he wants to consult his retained counsel or counsel whom the court will appoint?"[79] Under the inherent compulsion approach, no such waiver could be voluntary. Reading *Miranda* as prophylactic, however, resolves the difficulty, for no responses are necessarily compelled under this approach.

Thus, the Burger and Rehnquist Courts had abundant reason for giving *Miranda* a prophylactic reading. Rather than being revisionist, their reading of *Miranda* has such compelling force that *Miranda*'s most ardent defenders both on and off the Court have sometimes felt compelled to concede the point.[80] Even Professor Kamisar, "flabbergasted" because a prophylactic reading would have "taken aback" *Miranda*'s author,[81] has succumbed. Raising the legitimacy issue that will be discussed in the remainder of this chapter, he asked how the Court obtained the authority to impose *Miranda* on the states if a *Miranda* violation "does not, *or at least does not usually,* violate the Constitution."[82] Of course, if *Miranda* violations *usually* are constitutional violations, a conclusion that itself is dubious, they sometimes are not. No middle ground exists between rules that cannot be violated without violating the Constitution (e.g., *Massiah,* as the Court understands that decision) and rules that can sometimes be violated without violating the Constitution (e.g., *Miranda,* as the Court understands that decision). Professor Kamisar's concession may have been restrained and grudging, but it was sufficient to emphasize the legitimacy issue he sought to avoid.

The Legitimacy Issue

Imagine the following hypothetical facts. Alleging both *Miranda* violations and actual compulsion, defendant, *D*, charged with a felony in state *X*, moves to exclude his confession from evidence. The trial court denies *D*'s motion, concluding that the police neither violated *Miranda*'s rules nor actually compelled *D* to confess. Having won the suppression motion, the prosecution uses the confession both to prove *D*'s guilt in its case in chief and again to impeach *D*'s credibility after *D* testifies in his defense and denies the crime. On *D*'s appeal following conviction, state *X*'s highest court holds that the police had in fact violated *Miranda* but that the trial court was correct in finding no actual compulsion. Because of its conclusion that no constitutional violation had occurred, and because no federal statute dictates a contrary result, the state court affirms *D*'s conviction. The United States Supreme Court then grants *D*'s petition for a writ of certiorari.

Assume that the United States Supreme Court is determined not to change the applicable law and that it also agrees with state *X*'s highest court that the police violated *Miranda;* that they did not, however, actually compel *D* to confess; and that no federal statute requires suppression in state court of *D*'s voluntary confession. (Any such statute, of course, would raise its own issues of constitutionality.) With these assumptions, any law student who has taken Criminal Procedure should be able to write the Court's opinion. First, because a statement taken in violation of *Miranda* cannot be used in the prosecution's case in chief, the Court will reverse state *X*'s highest court and overturn *D*'s conviction. Second, because a statement taken in violation of *Miranda* can be used for impeachment purposes if it is not actually compelled,[83] the Court will permit the prosecution to use *D*'s statement for impeachment purposes if *D* again testifies on retrial.

The issue the hypothetical opinion raises is whether the Supreme Court has authority to reverse a state court conviction absent an actual violation of either the Constitution or some other valid federal law. At the outset, the hypothetical itself should eliminate one argument that Professor Schulhofer and others have made in support of such authority. With *Miranda* in mind, Professor Schulhofer recently defended decisions that rely on prophylactic rules as particularly appropriate "[w]hen an assessment is complex and often beyond the ken of judges."[84] Even if this argument can justify some prophylactic rules, however, it cannot justify *Miranda*. On the contrary, the Court's impeachment doctrine squarely refutes Professor Schulhofer's claim that "in any ranking of the issues that properly demand some form of prophylactic rule, the problem of determining compulsion in the context of custodial interrogation wins the prize hands down."[85] That courts are required to make assessments of compulsion or voluntariness whenever a defendant seeks to have statements excluded for all purposes, including impeachment, demonstrates that such questions are not beyond the ken of judges. Thus, properly refined, the issue is whether the Supreme Court has authority to reverse a state court conviction on *Miranda* grounds when it can readily be determined, and often will have been determined, that the defendant was *not* compelled to become a witness against himself.

When the Court holds, as it did in *Massiah*, that certain governmental conduct actually violates the Constitution, we may challenge the correctness of its decision but not, if the Court was acting in good faith, its authority to render the decision. *Marbury v. Madison*[86] established that when the written Constitution, as positive and superior law, conflicts with other law, judges are bound to follow the Constitution. Of course, conflicts may not be obvious without first interpreting the Constitution, but *Marbury*, in a memorable if question-begging line, proclaimed that "[i]t is emphatically the province and duty of the judicial department to [say] what the law is."[87]

Under *Marbury*, therefore, the Court had the authority in *Massiah*, first, to interpret the Sixth Amendment as providing a right to counsel at all postcharge interrogation and, second, to invalidate all governmental conduct that violates that right. Of course, because the Court is not infallible,[88] *Massiah* may have erred, as this book contends, in interpreting the Sixth Amendment, but this possibility notwithstanding, the legitimacy of its decision is not an open issue given the institution of judicial review that *Marbury* initiated.

When *Escobedo*, in effect, applied *Massiah* to the states and extended its application to the precharge context, the Court again acted legitimately even though, by its own later acknowledgment, it acted incorrectly.[89] While *Marbury* established the Court's authority to interpret the Constitution, *Martin v. Hunter's Lessee*[90] and *Cohens v. Virginia*[91] held that the Supreme Court and other federal courts have the authority, when jurisdiction exists, to review state court determinations of federal questions. Rejecting the argument that the states are separate sovereign entities, the Court in *Martin* reasoned that valid federal law would not be supreme, as the Constitution commands, if different state courts each had unreviewable say on its meaning.[92] For federal supremacy, "the absolute right of decision, in the last resort,"[93] had to lie in the Supreme Court rather than in the state courts. Under *Martin* and *Cohens*, therefore, the Supreme Court had authority to review the determination of the Illinois courts that Escobedo did not have a right to counsel under the federal Constitution when the police interrogated him. Moreover, as long as *Escobedo* remained good law, its holding regarding the meaning and actual requirements of the Sixth Amendment was binding on state courts that had a contrary, and in retrospect correct, view.

The state sovereignty argument still has force, however, when there is no federal law to apply. Since it is not part of any state's judicial system, the United States Supreme Court lacks authority to review state court judgments on the meaning of state law.[94] As the Court recognized in *Erie Railroad v. Tompkins*,[95] "[s]upervision over either the legislative or the judicial action of the states is in no case permissible except as to matters by the Constitution specifically authorized or delegated to the United States."[96] In the above hypothetical, therefore, the Supreme Court's authority to review the decision of state X's court would seem to have ended with its conclusion that the confession was neither compelled in violation of the Fifth Amendment nor taken and used in violation of any valid federal law.

One might respond that the confession *was* taken and used in violation of federal law: the *Miranda* rules. To "legislate" rules that go beyond constitutional requirements, however, the Supreme Court must have authority, presumably derived from the Constitution, either to create a body of federal common law that is binding on the states or—and perhaps this is another way of saying the same thing—to exercise some sort of supervisory power over state courts. That it has such authority seems doubtful.

The Illegitimacy of *Miranda*

Prophylactic Rules, Federal Common Law, and Supervisory Power

In an important article published in 1975, Professor Henry Monaghan argued that *Miranda*'s prophylactic rules are best understood as part of "a substructure of substantive, procedural, and remedial rules drawing their inspiration and authority from, but not required by, various constitutional provisions; in short, a constitutional common law."[97] *Erie Railroad v. Tompkins*,[98] of course, rejected the notion that the mere grant of jurisdiction authorizes federal courts to promulgate a "federal general common law,"[99] but Professor Monaghan, drawing on admiralty, interstate dispute, and state commerce clause cases, contended that *Erie* has not prevented federal courts from developing a "specialized" common law.[100] Like the constitutional provisions that deal with these areas, constitutional provisions that concern individual liberties may be seen as "authorizing the creation of a common law substructure to carry out the purposes and policies of those guarantees."[101]

While the existence of "specialized" federal common law cannot be disputed, Professor Monaghan's argument can. At the least significant level, one may question some of his analogies. For example, some commentators disagree that the Court is promulgating constitutional common law when it invalidates state laws based on the negative implications of the Constitution's grant of power to Congress to regulate commerce among the states.[102] Moreover, while the admiralty and interstate dispute cases do involve the promulgation of federal common law, they involve special considerations that seem inapplicable in the Fifth Amendment context. The Constitution, by granting jurisdiction to federal courts over interstate disputes, "can well be deemed to require that the federal courts should fashion law when the interstate nature of a controversy makes it inappropriate that the law of either state should govern."[103] Likewise, although the matter may be less clear, the Constitution's jurisdictional grant to federal courts in admiralty and maritime cases may implicitly convey lawmaking authority, for no state "has legislative jurisdiction to deal authoritatively with problems of maritime law generally."[104]

Of course, the Court may have erred in finding such an implication in the jurisdictional grant in admiralty cases, but even a mistaken interpretation of the Constitution, if made in good faith, solves the legitimacy problem. Federal common law in admiralty rests on the Court's belief that the Constitution implicitly granted law-making power to federal courts in this area;[105] to be analogous, *Miranda*'s common law would require a conclusion that the Fifth Amendment, or its vehicle of incorporation, the Fourteenth Amendment, conveys similar law-making power to federal courts, or at least to the Supreme Court. Unremarkably, the Court has never even hinted at such a conclusion.

The notion that the Constitution or a valid federal statute must authorize federal courts to promulgate federal common law stems from *Erie*. Of course, *Erie*'s meaning has been a subject of debate, with some commentators arguing that its limitation on the law making power of the federal courts derived more from the Court's understanding of the Rules of Decision Act[106] than from its understanding of constitutional requirements.[107] Yet, in overruling *Swift v. Tyson*,[108] which for almost a hundred years had permitted federal courts to apply federal common law in diversity cases, the *Erie* Court stated that "[i]f only a question of statutory construction were involved, we should not be prepared to abandon a doctrine so widely applied throughout nearly a century."[109] *Erie* overruled *Swift* because "the unconstitutionality of the course pursued has now been made clear";[110] *Erie* overruled *Swift* because that case had unconstitutionally permitted federal courts to apply federal common law rather than state law in diversity suits.[111]

In any event, *Erie*'s importance in recognizing limits on the law-making power of federal courts is difficult to ignore. As acknowledged by Professor Martha Field, an advocate of broad federal common-law authority, "the scheme we have inherited from *Erie* and developed since has become such a fundamental part of our way of thinking about the boundary between state and federal power that many of our suppositions, constitutional and otherwise, are built upon it."[112] In Professor Field's words, *Erie*'s limitation on the federal courts, "[e]ven if not constitutionally required in any strict sense," appears to be a permanent feature of our system.[113] What is this limitation? Simply, in Professor Field's view, "that there must be a source of authority for any given federal common law rule."[114] Under this limitation, "federal courts cannot make a rule unless they identify some enactment giving them power to do so."[115]

Of course, except in cases involving explicit grants of law-making authority, the search for authorizing provisions will raise questions of statutory and constitutional interpretation. Here, what Professor Field granted with one hand, she took back with the other. In her view, federal judges have "extreme flexibility" in finding an authorizing provision, so much so that they have "great freedom to make federal common law where they will."[116] Thus, what starts out as a two-stage inquiry—the first whether an authorizing provision exists, the second whether to use the authorization that has been found—"often merges into one."[117] In deciding whether authority to promulgate federal common law has been granted, the judiciary, Field argued, "effectively decides whether federal common law is appropriate under all the circumstances."[118]

This view, of course, renders *Erie* a nullity. The claim that *Erie*'s limitation on the federal courts is an important and permanent feature of our system must be vacuous if, in effect, federal judges can displace state law whenever they choose to do so. One can only wonder how Professor Field could have arrived at such a remarkable juxtaposition of views. Part of the answer may be that in Professor Field's jurisprudence, the interpretation of a text seems to be equivalent to the making of a policy choice.[119] This description of Professor Field's interpretational philosophy does not emanate from a strict view of strict constructionism, for in searching for the authorization that *Erie* requires, one may readily agree that implicit directives are as valid as explicit ones. Nevertheless, unless one regards the meaning of words as totally subjective, one would not state, as Professor Field did, that to require an implicit directive is to permit federal courts to create common law "when no directive really exists."[120] If language has meaning, "*x* implies *y*" must sometimes be an incorrect statement.

Concededly, Professor Field made her comments in the course of describing both a Supreme Court case that found implicit statutory authorization for judicial law making power on a rather shaky basis and a commentator's apparent approval of that case.[121] Nevertheless, Professor Field's analysis was more than descriptive. Rather than criticizing the case and the commentator's analysis, Professor Field used them to illustrate the inherent properties of an implicit authorization requirement: "[a]t most [this requirement] adds a slight emphasis to the desirability of judicial restraint in decisions about formulating federal common law."[122]

By failing to distinguish the "*creative* process of common law making from the *interpretive* process of textual construction,"[123] Professor Field did more than strain the concept of interpretation to the "linguistic and conceptual breaking point."[124] In addition, she totally undermined *Erie's* constitutional vision of federalism. Under Professor Field's approach to federal common law, a federal court could substitute a federal criminal procedure rule for a state rule, which was not unconstitutional as such, merely by identifying the Fourteenth Amendment's due process clause as authorizing federal judicial law making in the particular area. That this is not a farfetched implication of such a thesis is demonstrated by Professor Monaghan's comment, made years before Professor Field wrote, that "with ingenuity" federal courts could use the common-law power to impose on the states "the best features of the Federal Rules of Criminal Procedure and the Federal Rules of Evidence."[125] At this point, of course, the concept of federalism would retain no significance, for supervision over the judicial action of the states would be permissible in all cases without any specific constitutional authorization.[126]

There may be a temptation to respond that federalism is dead, it having suffered its "second death" when the Supreme Court held in *Garcia v. San Antonio Metropolitan Transit Authority*[127] that restraints on the exercise of Congressional power over the states must come primarily from the workings of the political process rather than from judicial review.[128] *Garcia,* however, premised its holding in large part on the ability of the states, through representation and participation, to protect their interests in the federal political process. The absence of state political involvement in the federal judiciary would suggest a lesser role for federal courts than for Congress in interfering with the traditional functions of the states.

Thus, while Congress probably has the authority under existing doctrine to adopt a national no-fault system for automobile accidents, it seems doubtful that federal courts could promulgate such a system in a diversity case.[129] This is to say only that a state's Tenth Amendment interests need not exist equally against all the branches of the federal government.[130] Indeed, as Professor Martin Redish has noted, "the disparity in the quality of the relationship with the states between the Congress and the federal courts" has prompted some scholars to conclude that *Erie*'s constitutional holding "limits only the federal judiciary."[131] Perhaps one should say more accurately that *Erie* imposes "special" limits on the federal judiciary, for the Supreme Court has made it clear since *Garcia* that the notion of state sovereignty still imposes some judicially enforced limits even on what Congress may do to the states.[132]

That *Erie*'s principle of federalism, if not *Erie* by name, places special limits on the judiciary should be apparent from the Court's treatment of its so-called supervisory power. Although the Court has largely ignored the serious separation of powers questions that the exercise of this power entails,[133] it has never suggested that it could impose a supervisory power decision on the states. On the contrary, the Court has explicitly stated that federal courts have no supervisory power over state courts. In *Smith v. Phillips*,[134] for example, the Court reversed lower court decisions granting federal habeas corpus relief to a state prisoner because the prosecutor had failed to disclose certain information about a juror. After finding that the prosecutor's inaction did not violate the Constitution, the Court added,

> Absent such a constitutional violation, it was error for the lower courts in this case to order a new trial. Even if the Court of Appeals believed . . . that prosecutorial misbehavior would "reign unchecked" unless a new trial was ordered, it had no authority to act as it did. Federal courts hold no supervisory authority over state judicial proceedings and may intervene only to correct wrongs of constitutional dimension.[135]

Although the Court did not cite *Erie*, that case's federalism principle is unmistakably present in this passage.

The supervisory power cases also help to demonstrate the counterintuitiveness of the claim that federal courts have common-law authority to impose prophylactic rules on the states. In both *McNabb v. United States*[136] and *Mallory v. United States*,[137] the Supreme Court exercised supervisory power over federal proceedings to require the exclusion of confessions that were obtained while defendants were held in violation of a Congressionally imposed prompt arraignment requirement. Both the prompt arraignment requirement and the Court's exclusionary rule reflected a concern about secret interrogations and third-degree police practices as well as a concern about illegal detentions under the Fourth Amendment.[138] Yet because the Court's rule required no inquiry into the actual voluntariness of the statements or into the constitutional legality of the detentions, it exceeded the constitutional requirements then existing, and the Court never imposed it on the states. Indeed, given the Court's statements that federal courts do not have supervisory power over state institutions, it could not have imposed *McNabb-Mallory* on the states.

Suppose, however, that the Court decided to change the label on the *McNabb-Mallory* rule. That is, suppose it decided to describe the rule not as a product of its supervisory power but as a prophylactic safeguard to protect Fourth and Fifth Amendment rights. Given the rule's original concerns, the prophylactic label would certainly seem linguistically appropriate. To be sure, some statements affected by the rule are neither compelled within the meaning of the Fifth Amendment nor obtained in violation of the Fourth Amendment, but overbreadth, by definition, is an inherent characteristic of prophylactic rules. The question that arises is whether the Court could now impose the *McNabb-Mallory* rule, with its new label, on the states. Under the arguments set forth by Professors Monaghan and Field, the answer would have to be yes. Yet it would seem obvious that the Court's disclaimers of authority to impose supervisory power decisions on the states were intended to have more significance than this, for a disclaimer accompanied by an implicit caveat for cases in which the Court is willing to change the rule's label is devoid of meaning.

In defense of the Court's authority to impose prophylactic rules on the states, it is sometimes said that such rules are ubiquitous in constitutional law.[139] Professor Monaghan, for example, has compared belief in such rules—his "constitutional common law"—to belief in infant baptism: "'Believe in it? Why, man, I've seen it . . . !'"[140] In reality, however, prophylactic rules are not nearly so pervasive as some commentators contend. One must take care not to confuse a per se rule that does not require case-by-case factual analysis with a rule that can be violated without violating the Constitution. *Gideon v. Wainwright*,[141] for example, established a per se rule that entitles all indigent defendants in felony trials to appointed counsel without regard to factual circumstances, but the Court has never said that a state can violate *Gideon* without violating the Constitution. Likewise, *Lovell v. Griffin*[142] invalidated an ordinance that gave a city manager broad discretion whether to permit the distribution of literature, but it did not, as Professor David

Strauss has contended, promulgate a "judge-made prophylactic rule" intended to ensure that permission not be withheld for "improper reasons."[143] Rather, in the Court's own words, *Lovell* found the ordinance "invalid on its face."[144]

It bears repeating that a rule is prophylactic, as that term is used in *Miranda,* not because it, or its underlying constitutional provision, instrumentally serves other ends. A rule is prophylactic only when the rule may be violated without violating the Constitution. Those who believe such rules are pervasive should list which rules, other than *Miranda,* the Court has identified as prophylactic under this standard.[145]

In any event, the ubiquitousness of prophylactic rules is not the issue; their legitimacy is. Just as the use by various presidents of electronic surveillance in internal security cases could not immunize such executive conduct from the strictures of the Fourth Amendment,[146] an unexamined judicial practice of promulgating prophylactic rules should not immunize such judicial conduct from the Constitution's limits on the federal judiciary. To be legitimate, any such rule would have to overcome both *Erie,* which precludes federal courts from imposing federal common law on the states, and the Court's numerous statements that the federal judiciary does not have supervisory power over the states.

Indeed, these two obstacles to the legitimacy of prophylactic rules undoubtedly reflect the same federalism principle. Because any supervisory power rule can be viewed as inspired by, if not really required by, the due process clause or some more specific provision in the Bill of Rights, any such rule can be relabeled, if the Court so wishes, a prophylactic rule. To permit federal courts to impose prophylactic rules on the states therefore is to say in essence that federal courts have supervisory power over state courts. One need not be familiar with *Erie* to recognize that such a power in federal courts would eviscerate the structure of federalism inherent in our Constitution.

Interstitial Interpretation and Federal Question Law Making

Because no constitution can address all the issues that will arise in constitutional litigation, filling interstices or gaps must be viewed as part of the interpretive task.[147] For example, the Sixth Amendment says nothing about whether a defendant can waive the rights it provides. If a state permits a waiver, the Supreme Court will have to decide whether any waiver at all is constitutionally permissible and, if so, whether the particular waiver is valid. The Court cannot simply avoid the first question by saying that the Sixth Amendment is silent on waiver, for such a statement is equivalent to deciding that the Sixth Amendment permits the states to allow waiver. Conceivably, the Court could allow the states to decide for themselves the requisites of a valid waiver, but even this would be to conclude that the Sixth Amendment is indifferent to the standard that is applied when its rights are relinquished. Moreover, because such a ruling would permit a mischievous state court completely to undermine federal rights, we might expect the Court to rule, as it has, that the Sixth Amendment requires any waiver to satisfy certain criteria.[148] Although such a ruling may seem like creative lawmaking, it really is an inevitable component of the interpretive task.[149]

When the Court fills in interstices by constitutional interpretation, no legitimacy question arises, for interpreting the Constitution is its task under *Marbury*. Of course, to be engaged in interpretation rather than untethered law making, the Court has an obligation to resolve the issue not in accord with its own policy preferences but "in a manner most consistent with the attainment of the policies sought to be achieved" by the provision under consideration.[150] That is, to be interpreting, the Court must tie its decision "closely and carefully to the structure, text, and purposes" of the provision at issue.[151] Still, as already indicated, the rule produced by even a poor job of interpreting the Constitution, as long as the Court has acted in good faith, is different from a prophylactic rule. What makes *Miranda* illegitimate is that the Court, by its own admission, has exceeded the bounds of what the Constitution, interpreted by the Court, actually requires.

The waiver issue is just one of many issues not explicitly addressed by the Constitution. As we saw in the last chapter, the Sixth Amendment's bare text does not define the point at which a "criminal prosecution" begins or ends; nor does it answer whether the state must appoint counsel for indigent defendants or whether the "assistance of counsel" includes the assistance of a psychiatrist. Similarly, the Constitution does not allocate the burden of proof on constitutional issues, indicate what standard shall apply to that burden, address whether the defendant, counsel, or both must participate in waiver decisions, provide a standard for review on appeal, define a standard of harmless error, or even state whether constitutional error can be harmless.

Although each of these issues could be resolved by an act of constitutional interpretation, it may be that some of them should be treated as federal questions, calling for an answer by federal courts, even in the face of complete constitutional silence. To illustrate, the Court in *Chapman v. California*[152] "preferred" its own harmless error standard to the one the state court had applied, while indicating that Congress could require it to follow a different rule.[153] The Court did not find that the state's harmless error standard was unconstitutional.

Justice Harlan accused the *Chapman* majority of exercising supervisory power over state courts, "a startling constitutional development . . . wholly out of keeping with our federal system."[154] To reject this criticism, one must conclude that the Court had authority to go beyond constitutional interpretation and to make law in *Chapman*. One must conclude, that is, that "[t]he extent to which state law may limit the impact of federal law is, under the supremacy clause of article VI, a federal question."[155] In *Chapman*, a line had to be drawn between federal constitutional error that tainted the state's conviction of the defendant and constitutional error that did not. The constitutional structure of federalism may not be threatened by the conclusion that the federal court with ultimate authority to review the federal issue, and not the state court that is alleged to have violated federal rights, should draw this line.[156]

In fact, the Supreme Court has often treated as a federal question whether state procedural rules can block the assertion of federal rights. Most particularly, under the Court's doctrine that a state procedural rule, such as a contemporaneous objection requirement, must be "adequate" to deny a federal claim by a defendant seeking federal review of a state conviction, the Court has found state rules to be inadequate without finding them to be unconstitutional.[157] Less frequently, the Court has reviewed even state substantive rulings to prevent the loss of federal rights. In *Ward v. Board of County Commissioners*,[158] for example, a state court denied relief to Native Americans who had paid state taxes on land that was constitutionally exempt from taxation; the state court ruled that the state's statutes did not provide for suits to recover taxes that had been voluntarily paid. The Supreme Court held that a state statute was unnecessary because the payment "was not voluntary, but made under compulsion."[159] The Court ruled on the voluntariness issue even though it did not find either the state's voluntariness standard, or its procedure for determining voluntariness, to be unconstitutional.[160]

In accordance with the previous discussion, however, judicial conduct cannot be its own source of justification. Rather, a federal court must identify an authorizing provision, either constitutional or statutory, before it can substitute federal common law for state law. We have seen, however, that such authorization may be implicit. When federal rights are at stake, the supremacy clause may be viewed as authorizing federal courts to assure that state courts have not transgressed those rights.[161] Professor Redish has concisely stated the argument:

Ultimately, if the result of the state court's conclusion on the substantive law issue is inconsistent with the result sought by the party asserting the federal right, the Supreme Court cannot be barred from reviewing the state court's determination on the federal issue, regardless of the adequate state ground doctrine. . . . If it concludes that the federal right has been violated, the supremacy clause requires that the result reached by the state court be overturned, regardless of its validity as a matter of state law.[162]

The impression should not be left, however, that federal question law making in cases that come from the states is not controversial. Quite arguably, if the state's procedural or substantive rule is constitutional, no violation of a federal right can have occurred. For example, if the state's harmless error rule in *Chapman* was constitutional, it is not apparent how the defendant's conviction can be viewed as violating the Constitution. Similarly, if a state's contemporaneous objection rule is constitutional, a defendant's unexcused failure to comply with the rule in asserting federal rights arguably removes those rights from the case. The point is simply that the supremacy clause argument, though not without some force, is not powerful enough to sweep away opposing viewpoints.

This question need not be resolved here, however, for federal question law making under the supremacy clause cannot support *Miranda*'s legitimacy. In the *Miranda* context, there is no state rule, procedural or substantive, preventing the assertion of an otherwise valid federal claim. On the contrary, as the impeachment cases attest, courts can, and often must, decide whether the defendant was actually compelled. *Miranda* does not displace state law so that a federal constitutional violation may be reached and remedied; rather, *Miranda* displaces state evidentiary law even when no federal constitutional violation has occurred. Through its *Miranda* decision, the United States Supreme Court, which is not part of any state's judicial system, required state courts to reverse convictions that were not obtained in violation of the federal Constitution.

Professor Redish has cautioned that if used only as "an introductory incantation . . . to get to the 'treasure' of unrestrained law creation," the concept of gap-filling "becomes nothing more than thinly disguised manipulation."[163] The same holds true with regard to the federal question doctrine discussed above. A state court's interposition of its own law to bar the enforcement of a federal right "obviously restricts that right to some degree."[164] Under the supremacy clause argument, whether the state's interests in enforcing its own law can justify the restriction of a party's federal rights may be regarded as a federal question.[165] Just as the supremacy clause can require state law to yield when it obstructs the enforcement of a party's federal rights, however, the Constitution's protection of federalism requires federal courts to yield when there are no federal rights in the case at hand to enforce. Indeed, this limit on the federal courts is itself implicit in the supremacy clause.

A Conclusive Presumption of Compulsion

While otherwise describing *Miranda* as a prophylactic decision, the Court in *Oregon v. Elstad*[166] also stated that *Miranda* created an "irrebuttable" presumption of compulsion that applies to unwarned statements obtained during custodial interrogation.[167] Though he vehemently disagreed with *Elstad's* holding and most of its reasoning, Justice Brennan found comfort in the Court's recognition "that there is an 'irrebuttable' presumption that such confessions are indeed coerced."[168] Similarly offering approval of this characterization of *Miranda*, Professor Schulhofer has admonished critics to remember that conclusive presumptions, which he describes as "aids to adjudication," pervade judicial decision making.[169] In reality, however, it only exacerbates the legitimacy problem to view *Miranda* as having created a conclusive presumption of coercion.

For discussion purposes, assume that either or both of the arguments relating to interstitial constitutional interpretation and to federal question law making can justify the Supreme Court when it reviews a state case in deciding which party has the burden of proving compulsion and the standard this burden must satisfy.[170] Whether the authority to decide these matters would also justify the Court in creating a *rebuttable* presumption of compulsion, triggered by certain facts such as the mere existence of custodial interrogation, is far from clear. Indeed, the Court's authority in this regard might depend on whether it was reviewing a federal or a state case.

In a federal case, the question of the Court's authority to adopt such an "aid to adjudication" might depend on the scope of the federal judiciary's implied or incidental authority to adopt procedural rules absent Congressional authorization. Relying in part on the fact that the necessary and proper clause[171] applies only to Congress, Professor William Van Alstyne has argued that federal courts (and the president) have only those incidental powers that are indispensable to carrying out their constitutional functions.[172] Relying in part on textual differences in the power-conveying articles of the Constitution,[173] Professor Sara Sun Beale, however, has defended broader, but by no means limitless, incidental judicial power.[174]

Whatever the proper scope of the Court's incidental power in a federal case, however, its power in a state case must be fairly narrow to preserve the constitutional structure of federalism. If the Court in a state case confronts a close question of whether a defendant's statement was compelled, it may need first to decide which party has the burden of proof, for its decision regarding compulsion may turn on this antecedent issue. Once the burden of proof issue is resolved, however, the Court can decide the compulsion issue without the aid of a rebuttable presumption. A rebuttable presumption may be conducive to, or convenient for, determining the issue of compulsion, but the question whether to use a rebuttable presumption, unlike the question of burden of proof, need not be reached to decide whether compulsion occurred.[175] Because the states in our federal system have the authority, subject only to constitutional constraints, to adopt whatever procedures and evidentiary devices they choose, it is far from obvious that the Supreme Court through the vehicle of appellate reversal should be able to force state courts to employ a rebuttable presumption they prefer not to employ.[176]

Assume that this analysis is wrong, however, and that the Court's authority to adopt a rebuttable presumption of compulsion in reviewing state convictions is no different from its authority to decide who has the burden of proving compulsion. Proceeding from this questionable assumption would still not help to justify *Miranda*'s employment of a conclusive presumption. The reason is elementary: a conclusive presumption is not an "aid to adjudication" or "a presumption at all"; rather, a conclusive presumption is a substantive rule of law.[177] To say that Y will be conclusively presumed when X is proved is to say that Y is irrelevant or immaterial and that X defines the legal standard.

A few examples should suffice to illustrate the point. McCormick cites the "conclusive presumption" that a child under seven is incapable of committing a felony. If this were a true presumption, proof that the defendant was under seven at the time of the crime would shift to the prosecution the burden of overcoming (rebutting) the presumption and proving the defendant's capacity. Being conclusive, however, the so-called presumption "simply express[es] the rule of law that someone under seven years old cannot legally be convicted of a felony."[178] Y, the fact of actual capacity, is legally immaterial when X, an age under seven, is established.

That a conclusive presumption is a substantive rule of law can be seen even more clearly by considering coexisting rights that are the opposite of each other. The Supreme Court has held that a defendant has both a right to the assistance of counsel at trial and the correlative right to waive counsel and to engage in self-representation.[179] Consistent with both rights, a court could adopt a (rebuttable) presumption that a defendant who appears unrepresented at trial has not waived the right to counsel. Under such a presumption, which would favor the right to counsel over the right to waive, a prosecutor would not be able to save the conviction of an unrepresented defendant without showing that the defendant affirmatively and knowingly elected to waive counsel and to engage in self-representation. A court could not go further, however, and adopt a conclusive presumption that an unrepresented defendant has not waived counsel, for such a "presumption" would be tantamount to a substantive rule that a waiver of counsel is impermissible, a rule that would conflict with the right of self-representation. Unlike a rebuttable or true presumption against waiver of counsel, a conclusive presumption against waiver cannot coexist with a right of self-representation.[180]

As a final example, consider a statute that adopts negligence rather than strict liability as the tort standard for a particular activity. Perhaps because of a belief that accidents do not normally occur unless the operator of the activity is negligent, a court might adopt a (rebuttable) presumption of negligence triggered by the mere occurrence of an accident. (If X, an accident, occurs, Y, the operator's negligence, will be presumed barring proof to the contrary.) While such a presumption might be unwise and empirically unsound, and while it would impose on the operator the burden of disproving negligence, it would remain consistent, in letter if not in spirit, with the statutory standard of negligence. The same could not be said about a conclusive presumption of negligence triggered by the mere occurrence of an accident. Under such a rule, liability would exist regardless of what the operator could prove, were such proof permitted, about lack of negligence. That is, Y, the operator's negligence, would now be legally immaterial. Such a "presumption" would really constitute a substantive rule of strict liability and, as such, it would represent a rejection of the statutory standard.[181]

These examples help to put in perspective what *Miranda* did if it adopted, as *Elstad* maintained, an irrebuttable or conclusive presumption of compulsion. As previously discussed, the Fifth Amendment proscribes compelled self-incrimination. It does not proscribe self-incrimination that is not compelled, nor does it proscribe custody, interrogation, or custodial interrogation as such. By supposedly adopting a conclusive presumption of compulsion (Y) from the mere fact of unwarned custodial interrogation (X), *Miranda* eliminated compulsion (Y) from the legal standard. Even if the prosecutor can convincingly demonstrate that the defendant was not compelled—and the impeachment cases inform us that lack of compulsion in unwarned custodial questioning can be proved—the conclusive presumption requires the confession to be excluded from the prosecution's case in chief.

It is apparent, therefore, that *Miranda,* as described in *Elstad,* did not adopt an aid to adjudication or a true presumption; on the contrary, it substituted for the constitutional rule a new substantive rule of its own making, one that excludes statements that the Fifth Amendment accepts. To explain, applaud, or defend *Miranda* in terms of a conclusive presumption rationale, therefore, is to assert for the Supreme Court the power of constitutional amendment. There is no other way to describe it.

Of course, the Supreme Court has arguably amended the Constitution numerous times by novel interpretations of its text. It is not apparent, however, how this could support the Court in ignoring the Fifth Amendment's requirement of compulsion—unless one abuse of authority can justify another. In any event, textual interpretations that constitute an abuse of the *Marbury* power differ from *Miranda*'s supposed use of a conclusive presumption. While *Massiah,* for example, may have employed a farfetched view of the right to counsel, it did not overtly make the constitutional standard irrelevant. If *Miranda,* however, adopted a conclusive presumption of compulsion, as *Elstad* claimed that it did, it did not render a novel interpretation of the Fifth Amendment's protection against compulsion. Rather, it simply announced that henceforth courts were to ignore the Fifth Amendment's actual standard. The Court has never sought to justify or explain its assumption of such judicial power.

CHAPTER 8

Overruling *Miranda*

The previous discussion supports the conclusion that the rules promulgated in *Miranda v. Arizona*[1] are extremely undesirable in terms of the policy objectives that the criminal justice system should be seeking to further. Moreover, although our Constitution sometimes precludes us from instituting desirable reforms, this is not true with respect to *Miranda*. Read as an interpretation of what the Fifth Amendment, even broadly construed, actually requires, *Miranda* is seriously flawed. Read as a prophylactic decision, which is how it is currently read, *Miranda* reflects an untenable and an alarming understanding of the United States Supreme Court's authority over state courts. In short, evaluated from policy and constitutional perspectives, *Miranda* is both misguided and wrong. The question that necessarily arises is, "So what?"

Miranda is now more than a quarter of a century old. When it was decided, *Miranda* might have "evoked much anger and spread much sorrow among judges, lawyers, and professors,"[2] but now, at least according to a survey conducted by a "special committee" of the American Bar Association, *Miranda*'s restrictions do not trouble a "strong majority" of prosecutors, judges, and police officers.[3] In the committee's view, moreover, *Miranda*'s "demise would do little to decrease crime or to improve the effectiveness of prosecutions."[4]

In calling for *Miranda*'s retention, the committee has some surprising allies. More than a decade ago, Chief Justice Warren Burger, hardly an admirer of the decision, stated that he "would neither overrule *Miranda*, disparage it, nor extend it at this late date."[5] Likewise, albeit with insufficient analysis, Judge Frank Easterbrook used *Miranda* as a primary example of a case that stare decisis should save.[6] Such diverse support for *Miranda*'s survival apparently reflects a shared belief that even if *Miranda* was wrongly decided, neither its "pedigree" nor its "effects" are "*sufficiently* bad" to warrant the Court in overruling its holding.[7]

Of course, as Justice Brandeis approvingly indicated years ago, the Court has always felt less constrained by stare decisis when considering whether to overrule constitutional as opposed to nonconstitutional mistakes.[8] This lesser role for stare decisis in constitutional law can be explained either by pointing to the immunity many, but not all, constitutional decisions enjoy from legislative correction or by emphasizing the written Constitution's superiority over all other forms of law, including judicial decisions.[9] Nevertheless, a role for stare decisis in constitutional adjudication can be defended. As Judge Easterbrook has succinctly stated, "[p]recedent is the device by which a sequence of cases dealing with the same problem may be called law rather than will, rules rather than results."[10]

With regard to constitutional adjudication, the perceived distinction in the public's mind between law and will may help to maintain the legitimacy of judicial review, although it seems perverse that the price of such legitimacy should be adherence to constitutionally infirm decisions.[11] In addition, as Professor Henry Monaghan has observed, "stare decisis operates to promote system-wide stability and continuity by ensuring the survival of governmental norms that have achieved unsurpassed importance in American society."[12] Thus, one cannot dismiss out of hand the above arguments that the Court should retain *Miranda* even if it now believes that case to be wrongly decided.

The purpose of this concluding chapter, however, is to present the case for overruling *Miranda*. Making the burden of persuasion more difficult, the analysis will not espouse the view that the Court should correct all or even most of its constitutional mistakes but instead will assume that stare decisis has an important role to play even in constitutional law. To proceed otherwise without begging the question about *Miranda*'s overruling would require the development of a theory of stare decisis in constitutional adjudication. This not only would be out of place here but also would leave *Miranda*'s overruling contingent on the persuasiveness of that theory. From a practical standpoint, moreover, the current Court, which most likely would not have decided *Miranda* the same way, will not be persuaded to overrule that decision simply because it was wrongly decided.[13]

The premise that stare decisis is important does not suggest the degree of importance that this doctrine should assume in actual application. Arguably, a person hostile to *Miranda* will be predisposed to find the presumption in favor of stare decisis overcome, while one sympathetic to *Miranda* will be predisposed to the opposite conclusion. Indeed, on the Court itself, stare decisis may operate "with the randomness of a lightning bolt: on occasion it may strike, but when and where can be known only after the fact."[14] As the Court recently acknowledged, its decisions on overruling customarily reflect "a series of prudential and pragmatic considerations designed to test the consistency of overruling a prior decision with the ideal of the rule of law"; they reflect, that is, a weighing of "the respective costs of reaffirming and overruling" the prior case.[15] Under such an approach, of course, it is inevitable that readers will use differently calibrated scales to weigh the adequacy of an argument in favor of overruling a particular decision. There is no remedy for this other than to let the argument stand or fall on its merits.

According to Professor Jerold Israel, when the Court decides to overrule a case, it usually relies on changed circumstances, the lessons of experience, or the requirements of later precedent.[16] Along similar if not identical lines, the Court more recently asserted that it considers whether the decision at issue defies "practical workability," whether overruling would work an undue hardship because of reliance, and whether changes in the law or the facts have left the decision without "significant application or justification."[17] Quite obviously, all these considerations are extremely subjective and manipulable, which may explain, as noted above, why the Court's applications of stare decisis seem so inconsistent and unprincipled.[18] Because they are so manipulable, the discussion that follows is not organized around these considerations, although it obviously must take them into account. Adhering to the Court's general approach, however, the discussion is intended to demonstrate the special justification that a departure from precedent requires.[19]

The first matter that warrants attention is the claim that Congress repealed *Miranda* by statute in 1968, at least for federal courts. While the 1968 statute lends support to the argument that *Miranda* should be overruled, careful analysis of this argument suggests that the statute is not sufficient to make the case for overruling. The statutory argument, however, serves to highlight the legitimacy issue discussed in chapter 7, and this issue places *Miranda* in a different category than most other wrong constitutional decisions.

After considering the statutory argument for *Miranda*'s demise, the analysis focuses on whether *Miranda*'s constitutional deficiencies are outweighed by pragmatic considerations. The thesis defended is that far from fulfilling its promise of providing workable and sensible rules, *Miranda* has produced its own muddy jurisprudence and has encouraged courts to stress form over substance. Moreover, the Court's cases reveal a philosophical tension that not only must be resolved but must be resolved against *Miranda* if the institution of police interrogation is to survive. The discussion concludes with a brief consideration of life without *Miranda*.

One claim that would provide powerful support for overruling *Miranda* is that, contrary to the Court's expectations at the time, the decision has substantially harmed legitimate law enforcement efforts. Relying on studies conducted shortly after *Miranda* was decided and on descriptions of particular cases, the Justice Department's Office of Legal Policy made such a claim a few years ago.[20] In response, and joining others who have denied that *Miranda* has had a negative impact on law enforcement, Professor Stephen Schulhofer disputed the studies, discounted the individual case descriptions, and concluded that the claim of harm was "surprisingly hollow" and "extraordinarily weak."[21]

Of course, as former Assistant Attorney General Stephen Markman has noted, part of the difficulty in assessing these competing contentions stems from our inability to count "the loss of statements that are never obtained" because of *Miranda*,[22] voluntary statements that would help a trier of fact to determine truth. Nevertheless, common sense and intuition suggest that *Miranda* (assuming the decision is wrong, of course) has caused considerable mischief in law enforcement efforts[23] and probably in the administration of the judicial system as well.[24] But precisely how much? Partly because *Miranda* forces every jurisdiction into the same mold, empirical studies cannot answer this question, at least not to the satisfaction of those on the competing sides of the claim. Rather than enter this quagmire, the analysis in this chapter, perhaps foolishly, will *not* rely on the claim that the decision has harmed law enforcement.

The Omnibus Crime Act of 1968

Two years after *Miranda,* Congress passed and President Lyndon Johnson signed the Omnibus Crime Control and Safe Streets Act of 1968, Title II of which substitutes the voluntariness test for *Miranda* in the federal courts.[25] This law, which is still on the books, requires federal judges to determine voluntariness by considering all the circumstances, including the defendant's knowledge of his rights and the presence or absence of *Miranda* warnings.[26] Nevertheless, the statute explicitly states that the defendant's lack of knowledge and the absence of warnings need not be conclusive in determining voluntariness.[27]

Because it is now accepted that the Supreme Court's interpretations of the Constitution, and not just the Constitution itself, are the supreme law of the land,[28] this aspect of the 1968 statute was largely ignored. Congress succeeded in expressing its hostility to what the Supreme Court had done, but everyone really understood that a constitutional amendment, not a mere statute, is required to overturn a decision based on the Constitution. To be sure, some scholarship tentatively suggested that Congress may have authority to reject the Supreme Court's factual conclusions, which by stretching might include the conclusion that custodial interrogation is inherently coercive.[29] Some commentators even saw in § 5 of the Fourteenth Amendment a possible corrective role for Congress in constitutional interpretation, a role that might have been of greater help had the statute been directed at the states.[30] Nevertheless, federal courts, and even the Justice Department, largely ignored the statute in actual litigation.[31]

The Court's description of *Miranda* as prophylactic—meaning, as discussed in chapter 7, that the admission of a confession at trial may violate *Miranda* without violating the Fifth Amendment—sparked renewed interest in the statute. In particular, because Congress has the ultimate authority to prescribe the rules of procedure and evidence for the federal courts,[32] the binding nature of a statute providing for the admissibility of voluntary (i.e., noncompelled) confessions might appear obvious. After all, the Supreme Court has stated that the Fifth Amendment is violated only by the introduction of a compelled statement.[33] The Office of Legal Policy succinctly made the argument:

> In 18 U.S.C. § 3501, Congress has mandated that voluntary statements be admitted despite non-compliance with *Miranda*'s rules. Applying *Miranda* in such a case accordingly requires a federal court to violate an Act of Congress, though complying with the Act would involve no violation of a constitutional right of the defendant.[34]

While its logic is essentially sound, the argument's ramifications give cause for concern. If Congress may reject *Miranda* merely by prescribing what is tantamount to a rule of evidence for federal courts, the question of a state's authority to do the same thing cannot be avoided. No less than Congress in the federal system, state legislatures and state courts have ultimate authority for prescribing the rules of evidence in the various states, provided, of course, that they stay within constitutional bounds. *Miranda* is an odd duck as a Supreme Court decision, however, if every jurisdiction that it affects may reject it simply by enacting a rule of evidence. The only way to avoid this unsatisfactory result under the argument being considered is to conclude that state institutions somehow lack the rule-making authority that Congress has, but such a conclusion seems arbitrary and equally unsatisfactory. Under either alternative, therefore, the argument that Congress can direct the federal courts to disregard *Miranda* leads to unattractive results when *Miranda*'s status in the states is considered.

This is not to suggest that the statutory argument is flawed, for the proposition that Congress can reject a judicially created rule of evidence for the federal courts is not controversial. The problem is that the Court in *Miranda* was speaking primarily to the states, only one of the four cases that constitute *Miranda* having resulted from a federal conviction. Because the reasoning of the statutory argument seems correct, however, at least given the Court's current understanding of *Miranda,* the statutory argument really raises once again the question of the Court's authority to impose *Miranda* on the states in the first place. That is, the statutory argument strengthens the legitimacy argument presented in the last chapter. Indeed, the Office of Legal Policy recognized that "*Miranda*'s continued application in state proceedings has a decidedly mysterious character," one that the Court could presumably clarify "only by holding that it has supervisory authority over the state courts."[35]

Legitimacy and Stare Decisis

The difference between a mistaken interpretation of the Constitution and an illegitimate exercise of judicial power was discussed in the last chapter. Because the Court's members are not infallible, mistaken constitutional interpretations are a regrettable but inevitable consequence of judicial review. Thus, had they held sway, the inherent compulsion passages in *Miranda,* which reflect a seriously incorrect understanding of the Fifth Amendment, would not have raised a question of judicial authority. Under an inherent compulsion rationale, *Miranda* would arguably be little different than most other wrong constitutional decisions for purposes of stare decisis.[36] The potential for compulsion rationale was present from the very beginning, however, and in the years following *Miranda,* the Court relied on this rationale, rather than the rationale of inherent compulsion, to cast *Miranda* into the mold of a prophylactic decision.

As elaborated in chapter 7, and as the quotation at the end of the last section suggests, maintaining that the Court may impose prophylactic rules on state courts is equivalent to maintaining that the Court has supervisory power over them. This is true no matter how one tries to finesse the matter by choice of words. The purpose of chapter 7 was to show that the Court has no such authority. At the very least, however, whether the federal judiciary has such extensive authority over state courts is a question of tremendous importance, one that stare decisis should not shield from careful examination. As Justice Harlan once remarked, in a context of lesser consequence, stare decisis should not constrict the Court "in a matter that goes to the very pulse of sound constitutional adjudication."[37]

This is especially so given that the Court has never seen fit to explain its source of authority to impose prophylactic rules on the states, perhaps because it may have stumbled into the prophylactic characterization of *Miranda* without giving thought to the legitimacy issue.[38] Seizing on *Miranda*'s potential for compulsion rationale, the Court in the 1970s seems to have asserted the prophylactic characterization so that it could more easily justify restrictions on *Miranda*'s scope, a laudable goal to be sure. The real irony, of course, is that a supposedly "conservative" Court wound up embracing, probably unwittingly, a judicial doctrine with the potential to destroy our system of separate federal and state courts. To appreciate this threat, one need only recall Professor Monaghan's claim, recounted in the last chapter, that "with ingenuity" federal courts could use such authority to impose "the best features of the Federal Rules of Criminal Procedure and the Federal Rules of Evidence" on the states.[39] Confronted with a choice between reading *Miranda* for all that it may be worth or claiming such expansive authority over state courts, the Court quite arguably chose the significantly greater of the two evils.

The fundamental importance of this judicially unexamined issue relating to judicial authority constitutes but one of the reasons for not allowing stare decisis to stand in the way of overruling *Miranda*. Inconsistency with earlier and later precedent is an additional reason. In cases decided both before and after *Miranda*, the Court has categorically insisted that federal courts have no supervisory authority over state courts.[40] As a prophylactic decision, *Miranda* seems openly to defy the statements in these cases. If *Miranda* is defensible as a prophylactic decision, these cases need to be overruled or at the very least satisfactorily distinguished. If, as argued in chapter 7, no persuasive distinction can be made, overruling *Miranda*, with its unsound philosophical premises, is preferable to overruling these several other decisions.

One may contend, however, that reinterpreting *Miranda* yet again would be preferable to confronting the legitimacy issue. That is, by emphasizing inherent compulsion over potential compulsion as the decision's rationale, the Court could conclude that *all Miranda* violations are, after all, constitutional violations. As a preliminary matter, this stratagem would not avoid problems relating to stare decisis, for the Court has rejected this reading of *Miranda* on several occasions.[41] Indeed, the Court has based specific holdings on the premise that *Miranda* is only prophylactic.[42] If anything, the doctrine of stare decisis counsels against an interpretation of *Miranda* that would require these later cases to be overruled.

Moreover, as maintained in chapters 5 and 7, it is implausible to contend that the unwarned response to even one custodial question is actually compelled. Indeed, the unwarned responses to more protracted sessions of custodial questioning often cannot be regarded as actually compelled. In any event, the Court could take such an expansive view of Fifth Amendment compulsion only by rejecting precedent both before and after *Miranda*. Without repeating all the discussion in chapter 5, suffice it to recall that *Bram v. United States*,[43] a late-nineteenth-century case that itself gave an expansive reading to the Fifth Amendment, specifically rejected the view that a statement is compelled simply because it is obtained by custodial questioning.[44] The Court has expressed the same view since *Miranda*. For example, the Court has held that statements taken in violation of *Miranda* may be used for impeachment purposes, but only if such statements are not compelled.[45] By applying this exception, the Court has recognized that some statements obtained through custodial interrogation are not compelled. Similarly, in creating a public safety exception to *Miranda*, the Court denied that it had created an exception for cases of actual compulsion.[46]

Understood, as it now is, as a prophylactic decision, *Miranda* presupposes federal judicial authority over state courts that is both indefensible and inconsistent with earlier and later precedent. Understood, as some commentators would like, as a decision interpreting the meaning of Fifth Amendment compulsion, *Miranda* would be both indefensible and inconsistent with earlier and later precedent. Under either view, therefore, the Court can overrule *Miranda* even "while purporting to follow the principles of stare decisis."[47] In any event, the Court is "in a position where it must choose between two lines of authority."[48] Nothing in stare decisis suggests that the Court has an obligation to favor the line of authority that is least defensible.

Miranda and the Triumph of Formalism

Dissenting from the creation of a public safety exception to *Miranda* in 1984, Justice O'Connor admonished her colleagues that *Miranda*'s rigid rules, whether right or wrong when adopted, had at least succeeded in giving clear guidance to the police and courts in dealing with custodial interrogation.[49] Similarly, Justice Marshall in the same case extolled *Miranda* for bringing "doctrinal tranquility to the field of custodial interrogations."[50] One federal appellate court, sitting en banc, even went so far as to proclaim that "[t]he rigidity of the *Miranda* rules and the way in which they are to be applied was conceived of and continues to be recognized as the decision's greatest strength."[51] If these statements have merit, overruling *Miranda* would arguably come at too high a price, for overruling, it might be claimed, would entail replacing a "rule-oriented mode of decisionmaking"[52] with the frequently litigated ambiguities of the old, case-by-case voluntariness test.[53]

Several preliminary responses may be made to this line of argument. First, even if *Miranda* added a measure of clarity to the law, the legitimacy issue concerning the scope of federal judicial authority over state courts is too foundational to be abandoned in the interest of pragmatic considerations. Second, as elaborated in chapter 4, the voluntariness test, properly understood, does not deserve the criticism that has been heaped on it. Even without the modifications urged in this book, the voluntariness test "allowed the Court to move carefully, to feel its way, and to make its judgments without fear of prematurely constitutionalizing interrogation practices."[54]

Third, as previously discussed, *Miranda* has not, in any event, freed the police and the courts from having to grapple with voluntariness issues. Because of the Court's impeachment doctrine, for example, a defendant who wants to preclude any use of his statement at trial can require the court to rule on voluntariness issues. In addition, and perhaps more significantly, the voluntariness doctrine still governs what the police may do to encourage truth telling after a custodial suspect provides a *Miranda* waiver. Thus, Professor Fred Inbau has long insisted that the police, after complying with *Miranda,* may use the same deceptive interrogation strategies that he advocated before *Miranda* was decided.[55] Whether he is right or wrong—and the voluntariness analysis in this book suggests that he is right[56]—the point remains that police and courts must still struggle with voluntariness issues. It may not be exaggeration to say, therefore, that *Miranda* merely added a rigid set of procedural requirements that must be satisfied before the voluntariness test takes over.

The argument that *Miranda*'s rigidity has brought clarity to the law may also be rebutted on its own terms. Much as Justice White predicted in his *Miranda* dissent, *Miranda* has generated considerable litigation concerning the meaning of custody and interrogation and the requirements for a valid waiver.[57] Even worse, *Miranda*'s rigidity has prompted courts to apply black-letter principles with little thought to the underlying Fifth Amendment issue that is responsible for the entire enterprise. The result has been a judicial formalism that cannot be a source of pride to American jurisprudence.[58]

Just two years after *Miranda,* the Court in *Mathis v. United States*[59] applied that decision to an Internal Revenue Service agent's interview of a person serving a sentence in state prison. Although Justice White's dissent argued that prison interviews carried less potential for coercion than police station interrogations,[60] the majority's three-page opinion did not discuss the issue in these terms but instead found *Miranda* applicable simply because the prisoner was interrogated while in custody. By thus cutting *Miranda* loose from its underlying Fifth Amendment rationale, *Mathis* committed the Court to a jurisprudence of black-letter formalism.[61]

Black-letter formalism need not always work to the advantage of the defendant. In *Oregon v. Mathiason*,[62] parolee Mathiason made incriminating statements after accepting a police invitation to come to the station for questioning about a burglary. Subsequently, Mathiason claimed that he should have received *Miranda* warnings because the interview occurred in a coercive environment. Although the state appellate court agreed, the Supreme Court concluded that *Miranda* did not apply because Mathiason was not in custody.

The *Mathiason* Court stated that "a noncustodial situation is not converted to one in which *Miranda* applies simply because a reviewing court concludes that . . . the questioning took place in a 'coercive environment.'"[63] Referring to custodial settings, the Court added that "[i]t was *that* sort of coercive environment to which *Miranda* by its terms was made applicable, and to which it is limited."[64] The Court did not explain why custodial coercive environments are more of a Fifth Amendment concern than noncustodial coercive environments. Nor did the Court acknowledge that the existence or nonexistence of custody was irrelevant to the Fifth Amendment question whether Mathiason was actually compelled to become a witness against himself. Ignoring such difficulties, the Court focused solely on "whether respondent was in custody for purposes of the *Miranda* rule."[65]

Even in black-letter terms, however, one may ask whether the Court should have found that Mathiason was in custody. The answer obviously depends on the test that is used to determine custody. Using an objective test, Justice Marshall argued in dissent that Mathiason, being a parolee and having been told that his fingerprints were found at the scene of the burglary, might reasonably have believed that he was not free to leave during the questioning.[66] Unfortunately, as Justice Marshall seemed to recognize, the only custody test that has any plausible bearing on whether the defendant actually felt compelled to speak is one that asks whether the defendant subjectively, even if unreasonably, felt that he was not free to leave.[67] Whether the hypothetical reasonable person would have felt free to leave does not provide a clue to whether the actual defendant felt compelled to answer questions.

The problem, however, as Justice Marshall may have appreciated, is that subjective tests are extremely difficult to administer, whether the focus is on the defendant's or on the officer's mind.[68] Not surprisingly, therefore, when it finally decided the issue, the Court opted for an objective test much like that advanced by Justice Marshall in *Mathiason*.[69] Of course, this test further assured that the analysis of *Miranda* issues would simply ignore the Fifth Amendment issue of compulsion.

The Court's treatment of the interrogation issue has been equally devoid of a Fifth Amendment underpinning. Although the interrogation issue had percolated in lower courts from the outset, the Court did not confront this issue until fourteen years after *Miranda*. In *Rhode Island v. Innis*,[70] the Court defined interrogation as either actual questioning or "words or actions on the part of the police (other than those normally attendant to arrest and custody) that the police should know are reasonably likely to elicit an incriminating response."[71] Curiously, the Court added in dictum that when an officer acts deliberately to elicit such a response, "it is unlikely that the practice will not also be one which the police should have known was reasonably likely to have that effect."[72]

Applying its newly coined test, the Court concluded that the police did not interrogate Innis, an arrestee they were driving to the station, when one officer said to another that it would be unfortunate if a child from a nearby school for handicapped children found the shotgun that had been used in a murder and a robbery. Although the state court had concluded that the defendant had been subject to "subtle compulsion"— arguably a Fifth Amendment concern[73]—the Court held that such compulsion was insufficient because the officer had no reason to know that his remarks were reasonably likely to elicit a self-incriminating response.[74]

This is not to suggest that *Innis* was incorrectly decided. To maintain that the brief conversation in the car actually compelled the thrice-warned defendant to reveal where he had hidden the shotgun, one would have to define the concept of compulsion as including virtually any causal influence. Under such a view, even defendants who waived their *Miranda* rights could not give a voluntary confession in response to police questioning. The point of the criticism is that the Court's approach in *Innis* made the issue of compulsion totally irrelevant. Justice Marshall, who essentially embraced the Court's black-letter test, was "at a loss" to understand how the Court could apply the test to conclude that interrogation had not occurred.[75] Reasonable people may differ over this issue, but the issue whether the defendant was compelled to be a witness against himself surely cannot depend on whether one agrees with the majority's or Justice Marshall's answer to this black-letter question. Even from a prophylactic perspective, the potential for compulsion was precisely the same under either black-letter conclusion.

That the interrogation issue is unrelated to the compulsion or potential compulsion concern was made even more apparent in *Pennsylvania v. Muniz*.[76] After taking the defendant into station house custody for drunk driving, the police, without giving *Miranda* warnings, asked him seven "booking" questions concerning his name, address, height, weight, eye color, date of birth, and current age. In responding to these questions, the defendant initially gave an incorrect age and did not recall his address without looking at his license. The booking officer then asked the defendant if he knew the date of his sixth birthday. The defendant said he did not know. A videotape of these responses was admitted into evidence at the defendant's subsequent trial.

In finding the responses to the first seven questions admissible, Justice Brennan's four-Justice plurality opinion recognized a "'routine booking question' exception which exempts from *Miranda*'s coverage questions to secure the 'biographical data necessary to complete booking or pretrial services.'"[77] The test to be applied, the plurality concluded, is whether the questions "appear reasonably related to the police's administrative concerns," as long as the questions are not designed to elicit incriminating statements.[78] The plurality found it necessary to reverse the defendant's conviction, however, apparently because the sixth birthday question did not fall within the booking question exception.[79] From the standpoint of actual or potential compulsion, of course, nothing changed between the seventh "booking" question and the eighth question concerning the defendant's sixth birthday.

In one recent case, however, the Court found the formalism of its black-letter approach too much to accept. In *Illinois v. Perkins*,[80] the Court held *Miranda* inapplicable to the state's use of an informant to elicit information from an incarcerated defendant. In a black-letter sense, of course, both custody and interrogation were present.[81] Nevertheless, the Court concluded that the coercive atmosphere that concerned *Miranda* is absent when a suspect does not know he is talking to an agent of the state.[82] The Court did not explain why a similar concern about compulsion has not been a consideration in most of its other cases dealing with custody and interrogation.[83]

Following the Supreme Court's lead, lower courts have also engaged in formalism in addressing the custody and interrogation issues. In *United States v. Conley*,[84] for example, prison guards handcuffed an inmate after a fatal stabbing, took him to an infirmary, and questioned him without *Miranda* warnings. The court recognized that *Mathis*,[85] if taken literally, would require *Miranda* warnings every time a guard asks an inmate a question, a result that would seriously impede prison administration. To deal with this dilemma, the Court decided that custody is a "relative concept," one that in the prison context depends on whether the inmate is subject to "more than the usual restraint."[86] Fortunately for the prosecution, the prison had a standard procedure of transporting inmates from one point to another in handcuffs. The Court clearly thought that the inmate's responses were voluntary,[87] but under *Miranda* it was forced to reach a black-letter conclusion about custody—a dubious conclusion at that—to permit the use of the inmate's voluntary statements.

In some cases, of course, courts have not been willing to bend the black-letter doctrine to save convictions obtained with the help of reliable, voluntary statements. *People v. Ferro*[88] is illustrative. The defendant was in a detention cell following his arrest for a residential fur robbery that resulted in a murder. Without saying anything, an officer placed furs that he had obtained from a codefendant's apartment in front of the cell. This prompted the defendant to make incriminating statements. The New York Court of Appeals reversed the resulting conviction, concluding that the statements were obtained in violation of *Miranda* and should not have been used in evidence. The defendant obviously was in custody, and the court, probably correctly from a black-letter standpoint, concluded that the act of placing the furs in front of the cell constituted interrogation within the meaning of *Innis*. To no avail, Justice Jasen protested that the court's judgment should have been based on the "right against compulsory self-incrimination, and not simply some felicitous tests uninformed by their policy purposes."[89] Justice Jason's complaint, of course, was with the United States Supreme Court, not with the New York court.

Because formalism is inherent in *Miranda*'s rigid approach, numerous cases reflect the kind of analysis that disturbed Justice Jason. Nevertheless, *United States v. Mesa*[90] is difficult to exclude from any short list of illustrative cases. Federal Bureau of Investigation agents surrounded a motel in which Mesa had barricaded himself after shooting his common-law wife and daughter the previous day. Not knowing whether Mesa held hostages (he did not), the agents summoned a special hostage negotiator who conversed with Mesa over a three-and-one-half-hour period using a mobile phone. While the negotiator made supportive comments and asked questions at appropriate times, a couple pertaining to the shooting, Mesa did most of the talking, and some of his remarks were incriminating. When Mesa finally surrendered, he thanked the negotiator for saving him from suicide.

The trial court suppressed the incriminating statements because they were obtained without *Miranda* warnings, but the Court of Appeals reversed the suppression order in a split decision with no opinion for the court. Without addressing the interrogation issue, which he labeled "difficult," Chief Judge Seitz concluded that Mesa was not in custody during the conversation.[91] Without addressing the custody issue, which he labeled "difficult" and "not free from doubt," Judge Adams concurred in reversing the trial court because the hostage negotiator, in his view, did not interrogate Mesa within the meaning of *Innis*.[92] Judge Adams, however, stated that the issue was "extremely close."[93] Judge Weiner dissented, finding both custody—Mesa could have left the motel only dead or under arrest—and interrogation.[94] On the latter question, Judge Weiner reasoned that the hostage negotiator had the "secondary purpose" of obtaining information about the shooting.[95] Moreover, the negotiator, unlike the officers in *Innis*, was aware of the defendant's unusual susceptibility to persuasion.[96]

Adding the trial judge to the appellate panel yields the following count: two judges found both custody and interrogation; one found no custody and labeled the interrogation issue difficult; one, saying the issue was close, found no interrogation and labeled the custody issue difficult. So much for the clarity and doctrinal tranquility *Miranda*'s rigid approach has supposedly brought to the law. Judge Adams candidly acknowledged that his vote on the interrogation issue was "compelled by the realization that it would be impractical and counterproductive to require *Miranda* warnings to be given in such a sensitive situation fraught with a potential for tragedy."[97] Unwilling to bend the black-letter doctrine even in the service of such a good cause, Judge Weiner nevertheless praised the hostage negotiator for getting Mesa to surrender without the use of force.[98]

Even though Judge Weiner did not conclude that Mesa actually had been compelled to incriminate himself, he felt constrained by the black letter to find a *Miranda* violation. Under *Miranda*, he accurately observed, the voluntariness of Mesa's statement was irrelevant; the issue was simply whether Mesa was subjected to custodial interrogation.[99] Unfortunately, although they voted to allow the use of Mesa's statements, Chief Judge Seitz and Judge Adams were required to address Mesa's claim in the same black-letter terms.[100] Again, of course, the degree of actual or potential compulsion in no way depended on the correct application of these black-letter concepts.

Dissenting from the denial of Mesa's petition for rehearing en banc, Judge Gibbons suggested that the solution for the hostage situation is for the police to ignore *Miranda*, as they did in *Mesa*, but for the courts to enforce *Miranda* by excluding the defendant's incriminating statements from evidence.[101] This attempt to accommodate both *Miranda* and the practical realities only highlights how stultifying *Miranda*'s formalism can be. It leaves the mistaken impression that self-incrimination as such, not just compelled self-incrimination, is the Fifth Amendment evil to be avoided. Moreover, it results in a jurisprudence that constrains judges to suppress voluntary, reliable statements even while they acknowledge that the police conduct at issue was in everyone's best interest.

Judge Gibbons apparently saw no cost in his proposed solution, for he added that the police "would not have had that evidence if they broke into the room and shot Mesa."[102] Had they done that, of course, there might not have been a need for any evidence at all. Judge Gibbons, moreover, did not consider the potential cost of losing important derivative evidence because of the "fruit of the poisonous tree" doctrine. Whatever the cost in any given case, however, the unanswered question is why the defendant should receive such a windfall when the police do precisely what a humane society wants them to do. This result alone might suggest that far from being its greatest strength,[103] *Miranda*'s rigidity is one of its great weaknesses.

Custody and interrogation are not the only *Miranda* issues that have lent themselves to a jurisprudence of formalism. In *Fare v. Michael C.*,[104] for example, the Court concluded that a juvenile did not invoke his *Miranda* rights when he asked for his probation officer rather than a lawyer to be with him during questioning. *Miranda*, of course, gave custodial defendants a right to refuse to answer questions and a right to have counsel present during interrogation; it said nothing about a defendant's right to have the assistance of a probation officer. Instead of focusing on the issue of compulsion, particularly as seen from the defendant's perspective, the Court justified its rigid adherence to *Miranda*'s black letter by distinguishing the different roles that lawyers and probation officers play in our adversary system.[105] The Court did not explain what its analysis had to do with the Fifth Amendment.

Relying on dicta in *Miranda*, the Court has imposed a rigid, per se rule that precludes further interrogation after a defendant invokes the *Miranda* right to counsel, unless the defendant initiates further conversation with the police about the investigation.[106] This rule is not as clear as it seems: *interrogation,* as discussed above, is a word of art, and a defendant's request to use the telephone would not be considered the initiation of conversation about the investigation.[107] The resulting formalism prompted Justice Powell to remark that "[c]ourts should engage in more substantive inquiries than 'who said what first.'"[108] Relying on other dicta in *Miranda,* however, the Court has refused to apply a similar per se rule for cases in which the defendant invokes the *Miranda* right to silence rather than the *Miranda* right to counsel. Here, subsequent interrogation may occur as long as the police have scrupulously honored the defendant's request to cut off questioning.[109]

The distinction between the two situations is formalistic, for it is doubtful that the average person realizes that the particular manner of invoking *Miranda* rights will matter for legal purposes.[110] Certainly nothing in the *Miranda* warnings gives a hint that this is the case. Indeed, it is probable that the particular response of a person desiring to invoke *Miranda* rights is fortuitous. More importantly, however, the black-letter rules have again drawn a distinction that has no predictive value in terms of answering whether the defendant was actually compelled to give a statement.

Even when the Court has attempted to temper the rigidity of *Miranda,* it has sometimes felt obliged to engage in less than persuasive parsing of *Miranda*'s black letter. *Miranda* stated that "a valid waiver will not be presumed simply from the silence of the accused after warnings are given *or* simply from the fact that a confession was in fact eventually obtained."[111] In *North Carolina v. Butler,*[112] however, the Court found that the defendant had waived his *Miranda* rights by agreeing to speak even though he made no express waiver of the right to counsel. The Court said that the above language in *Miranda* did "not mean that the defendant's silence, *coupled* with an understanding of his rights and a course of conduct indicating waiver," may not be enough.[113] While *Butler* commendably evidenced a preference for substance over form, *Miranda*'s language, which the Court did not repudiate, seemed to support the rigid prophylactic rule that Justice Brennan embraced in dissent.[114]

Finally, the ever present threat of formalism was apparent in *California v. Prysock,*[115] in which three dissenting Justices were prepared to reverse a murder conviction because, in their view, the fourth *Miranda* warning that the defendant received, concerning the right to the presence of appointed counsel, was not sufficiently clear.[116] That the interrogating officer went beyond *Miranda*'s requirements in cautioning the juvenile defendant, that the officer both cautioned and interrogated the defendant in the presence of his parents, and that the police recorded the interview—in short, that this was not conceivably a case in which a defendant was compelled to incriminate himself—did not affect the dissenters, who focused solely on whether the interrogating officer had adequately conveyed the information mandated by *Miranda*'s black letter.[117]

In a defense of the *Prysock* dissent that is quite revealing on the question of formalism, Professor Kamisar castigated the majority for not adopting a bright line rule "in a situation that cried for one."[118] After all these years, Kamisar insisted, police officers "surely . . . should have no great difficulty in reading the '*Miranda* card' the way it is printed."[119] Perhaps so, but it hardly follows that the Fifth Amendment requires (or should require) the reversal of a murder conviction when little possibility exists that the officer's "difficulty in reading" led to an involuntary statement.

As one may surmise from Professor Kamisar's comments, the negative effects of *Miranda*'s formalism have reached beyond the judiciary and into in the law school classroom, where future lawyers and judges are trained. Commenting on *People v. Ferro,* the fur case discussed above, and on *United States v. Thierman,*[120] a case, like *Ferro,* that grappled with the issue of interrogation, a casebook coauthored by Professor Kamisar asked the students to consider the following questions:

> Should *Ferro* have been treated as a *Mosley* case, not an *Innis* case? . . . Should *Thierman* have been treated as an *Edwards* case, not an *Innis* case? . . . In other words, should the question in a *Ferro*-type case be whether the police "scrupulously honored" the suspect's right to remain silent? And should the question in a *Thierman*-type case be: Did the police induce the suspect to change his mind after he asserted his right to counsel or did the suspect change his mind on his own initiative?[121]

The authors did not ask the students to give even a moment's thought to whether the defendants in *Ferro* and *Thierman* had actually been compelled to become witnesses against themselves. Perhaps this is understandable given that *Miranda*'s formalistic approach makes such a question irrelevant.

That the Court in 1966 foresaw the formalism that would come to characterize *Miranda*'s jurisprudence may be doubted. Nevertheless, the judicial experience since then in applying *Miranda* has exposed "the erroneous nature of the factual or policy assumption[s] upon which it was based."[122] Instead of either bringing clarity to the law or helping courts to identify situations where the potential for compulsion is great, *Miranda* has induced judges at all levels to split hairs over the meaning of black-letter rubrics. As they debate the technical requirements of the binding black letter, judges often feel obliged to ignore, as the dissenters in *Prysock* surely did, the underlying purpose of the whole enterprise— the prevention of *compelled* self-incrimination. In the eyes of far too many judges, the black letter's rigidity has become an end in itself.

Of course, *Miranda* has not proved "unworkable,"[123] if by that is meant that it is impossible to go on with the current approach. Under such a standard, of course, virtually no existing rule would be unworkable.[124] Nevertheless, *Miranda* has proved unworkable in the more relevant sense that its rigidity has produced not the intended doctrinal clarity but a perhaps unintended formalism that has reached the point of being intolerable. The judicial experience of the last quarter century, therefore, provides not an argument for adhering to *Miranda* because of stare decisis but instead yet an additional reason for overruling that decision.

Philosophical Tension in the Cases

Another reason for overruling *Miranda* is that its underlying philosophy about police interrogation is irreconcilable with the philosophy reflected in the Court's more recent cases. To appreciate *Miranda*'s outlook on police interrogation, one must examine both *Escobedo* and *Miranda*, because the Court cut both these opinions from the same philosophical cloth. It will be recalled from chapter 2 that the Court in *Escobedo* expressed concern that a defendant's confession could affect the subsequent trial. The Court submitted that the right to counsel at trial would be hollow if the prosecutor could assure the defendant's conviction before trial by obtaining a confession. In addition, the Court found it troubling that Escobedo was unaware that an admission of complicity was as damaging to him legally as an admission that he did the actual shooting. Finally, the Court viewed history as teaching the lesson that we should be wary of law enforcement systems that depend on confessions.[125]

Miranda may have shifted constitutional gears from the Sixth to the Fifth Amendment, but its view of police interrogation was essentially the same as *Escobedo*'s. The Court's opinion conceded only that "confessions *may* play an important role in *some* convictions."[126] In its very next breath, however, the Court described the four cases before it as "graphic examples of the overstatement of the 'need' for confessions."[127] While the Court in the past had expressed concern that any lawyer worthy of the name would advise the defendant not to cooperate,[128] the Court in *Miranda* said that "[t]his is not cause for considering the attorney a menace to law enforcement."[129] Stating that its concern extended beyond police misconduct, the Court found it distressing that "the very fact of custodial interrogation . . . trades on the weaknesses of individuals."[130] Along the same lines, the Court expressed concern that the defendant who does not request a lawyer's assistance "may be the person who most needs counsel."[131]

Like the cases that preceded *Escobedo* and *Miranda*, the Court's recent cases reflect neither such a negative view of police interrogation nor such concern about the defendant not being aware of information that might prompt him not to confess.[132] For example, in holding that the police did not have to advise a defendant that a lawyer had telephoned the police station on his behalf, the Court in *Moran v. Burbine*[133] said,

> No doubt the additional information would have been useful to respondent; perhaps even it might have affected his decision to confess. But we have never read the Constitution to require that the police supply a suspect with a flow of information to help him calibrate his self-interest in deciding whether to speak or stand by his rights.[134]

Similarly, in holding that the police do not have a constitutional obligation to inform the defendant of the subject matter they plan to pursue in interrogation, the Court quoted the above language from *Burbine* and said that such information would affect only the "wisdom" of the defendant's decision to cooperate.[135] In yet another case, the Court upheld the use of a defendant's oral statement that he gave immediately after refusing to give a written statement without counsel. Recognizing that some might find the defendant's actions contradictory and illogical, the Court reasoned that a defendant's ignorance of the full consequences of his decisions does not vitiate their voluntariness.[136]

In *Burbine,* the Court did not say, as *Miranda* had, that the need for police interrogation has been overstated; rather, the Court said that the need for police interrogation "cannot be doubted."[137] The Court added that confessions "are more than merely 'desirable' . . . ; they are essential to society's compelling interest in finding, convicting, and punishing those who violate the law."[138] The Court also said that the "minimal benefit" that the accused would receive in being told of his lawyer's call "would come at a substantial cost to society's legitimate and substantial interest in securing admissions of guilt."[139] A philosophical outlook more at odds with that expressed in *Escobedo* and *Miranda* is difficult to imagine.

Miranda, as its defenders like to point out, was a "compromise" between adhering to the voluntariness approach and taking an even more radical position.[140] The Court itself has acknowledged that *Miranda* declined to adopt the view that the *presence* of counsel is necessary before a *Miranda* waiver can be valid.[141] As Professor Uviller poignantly described it, "[h]aving taken us to the very edge of a confessionless abyss . . . the Court swerved, unable in the crunch to renounce alto-

218 · Confessions, Truth, and the Law

gether the product of the station house 'inquisition.'"[142] The commentators who defend *Miranda* are fully aware that its holding shortchanged its philosophical premises, for they invariably complain that the decision did not go far enough in the restrictions it imposed on the police.[143] Indeed, even *Miranda*'s critics concede that given its premises, logic and intellectual honesty require the conclusion that valid waivers are not possible in the custodial context.[144] Compromise, of course, can be a good thing even in law, but unprincipled compromise inevitably produces unprincipled and contradictory legal doctrine—precisely the point we have reached with *Miranda*.

If *Miranda*'s holding was dishonest in terms of its premises, the Court's more recent cases are even more so in failing to repudiate that decision. "[W]hat we really have is a Court that pays homage to cases that challenge the legitimacy of police interrogation but that protects police interrogation from those very same cases."[145] The current situation is doctrinally unstable, with two lines of irreconcilable cases coexisting to give the Court a choice between allowing or disallowing the police to have the necessary tools for effective interrogation. This conflict explains why even the current Court occasionally surprises observers with a decision that is hostile to police interrogation.[146] The serious threat, however, is that down the road a Court more sympathetic to *Miranda* will take its unrepudiated premises seriously and eliminate police interrogation altogether. If that day ever comes, no doubt will remain about *Miranda*'s effect on law enforcement.

The precepts of principled jurisprudence require the Court to resolve the irreconcilable tension between *Miranda* and the more recent cases. Either the Court should take *Miranda* seriously, which would mean both extending *Miranda*'s restrictions even further and rejecting the Court's more recent cases, or it should repudiate the thinking that demands such a result. If police interrogation is to survive, the Court must do the latter. To repudiate *Miranda*'s underlying thinking honestly and persuasively, however, the Court must overrule that decision, for devoid of its philosophical assumptions, *Miranda*'s holding is incomprehensible.

Living without *Miranda*

Because people have not organized their lives or their relationships around *Miranda*, it is difficult to see how reliance on that decision can count very much as an argument against overruling it. Nevertheless, there is a sense in which the proposition that the Court should overrule *Miranda* might cause one to pause with concern. Professor Stanley

Ingber has stated that *Miranda* gave blacks and indigents, among others, "a public statement of the Court's concern with police investigation and the importance of pretrial rights for defendants."[147] By, in effect, publicly reprimanding the police, the Court both assuaged those classes of people most concerned with police interrogation and notified the police that future excesses would engender even greater judicial oversight.[148] Although Ingber maintained that this was largely a symbolic gesture of ceremony and words,[149] one might contend in turn that overruling *Miranda* would have the symbolic effect of saying that the Court no longer is concerned.

As Professor Gerald Caplan has acknowledged, one can readily applaud *Miranda*'s message that limits exist on what government can do even to its "lowliest antagonist" in the war on crime.[150] That principles of morality properly limit what the police can do in the search for truth was conceded early in this book. Unfortunately, however, there is much more to *Miranda* than this lofty idea. In Professor Caplan's words, "the root idea of *Miranda* . . . is quite different and more ominous."[151] *Miranda* arose not just from a desire to curb police abuse but from "a confusion concerning the purpose behind the rules of criminal procedure."[152] *Miranda*'s antagonism to the very institution of police interrogation and its indifference to the search for truth "blur[red] the traditional and theoretical distinction between the police and the criminal."[153] As evidenced by its embrace of the fair chance, equality, and cruelty arguments discussed in chapter 2, *Miranda*, like *Escobedo*, saw the criminal, particularly the street criminal, as a victim of an oppressive society.[154] Perhaps this too was only symbolism, but it is a symbolism that a viable society, one that believes in itself and its right to punish lawlessness, can ill afford.

The virtue of the voluntariness test lies in its dual focus: its normative judgments take into account both society's legitimate interest in successfully interrogating suspects and society's democratic and moral interest in preventing police misconduct. Just as Fourth Amendment law does not consider a search to be unreasonable merely because it invades privacy, causes unpleasantness, and produces evidence to assure conviction, the voluntariness test requires something beyond these inherent attributes to make police interrogation unlawful. By giving the suspect power to prevent questioning even before it begins, however, *Miranda* gave the law of confessions a "single focus—protection of the suspect."[155] Overruling *Miranda* would not signal that anything now goes in police interrogation but would simply restore the balance, the dual focus, that cases both before and after *Miranda* have recognized must be achieved.

Even without *Miranda*, the voluntariness test would not stand alone in protecting the suspect from abuse. Whatever else it may mean, the Fifth Amendment protection against compulsory self-incrimination at its core forbids government from requiring a person to answer questions that may be incriminating. Given that the Court is not likely to change its mind on the Fifth Amendment's application to the states, any suggestion to suspects that they are required to answer would still be constitutionally condemned.[156] There is a difference, however, between trying to question someone and suggesting that an answer is required.

Professor Lawrence Herman has questioned this last point: "If they have no claim of right, what are they doing when they arrest a suspect, detain him at the police station, and subject him to 'mild pressures' or worse in order to obtain a confession?"[157] If this were correct, however, grand jury subpoenas, backed up by the contempt power, would violate the Fifth Amendment. In any event, the most that one might concede here—and the grand jury case law suggests that no concession is necessary—is the appropriateness of a warning that although the police are going to ask some questions, they have no right to require the suspect to answer. This approach would do far less damage than *Miranda*'s right to prevent interrogation altogether, a right that cannot be historically defended .

While the police thus could not suggest to suspects that they must answer, liberated from *Miranda*'s constraints, they would be free to engage in custodial interrogation without giving antecedent warnings, much as they did before 1966. Moreover, rather than being required to give advice that encourages silence, they would be permitted to encourage suspects to tell the truth. And, perhaps most importantly, custodial suspects who elect not to cooperate would no longer have the absolute right to prevent the police from trying to persuade them to change their minds.[158]

In *Miranda*'s absence, the voluntariness test would no doubt do most of the work at the constitutional level in preventing police abuse. For those who want safeguards beyond what the Constitution requires, the legislative process is always available. Indeed, as discussed at the beginning of this chapter, federal courts are required under current statutory law to take the presence or absence of police warnings into account in making voluntariness determinations.[159] State legislatures could adopt similar or more stringent restraints if such were thought desirable. Of course, some will object that few legislatures are likely to rush out in search of new ways to restrict the police. This objection may be correct in a predictive sense, but if so, it would prove only that society basically accepts the legitimacy of police interrogation and that it is not willing to saddle this institution with restraints beyond what the Constitution actually requires. That those who oppose police interrogation cannot win in the political process is not a persuasive argument for retaining *Miranda*.

One reform that deserves consideration is mandatory recording, and perhaps even videotaping, of custodial interrogation, at least when the interrogation takes place at the station house or at a regular place of detention where such recording would be practical.[160] As Professor Caplan has stated, "[a] rule mandating recording would confine extensive questioning to those cases in which it mattered most and would provide an accurate record by which the judiciary could evaluate the police pressure on the suspect."[161] On the latter point, recording would relieve courts of the need to rely on swearing contests to ascertain what actually occurred, a need that *Miranda* did absolutely nothing to remove.

Of course, such a reform would have to come from the various state legislatures, or perhaps from individual state courts. The Supreme Court has no authority to mandate such a reform, nor could it induce the states to move in this direction except perhaps by adopting a rebuttable presumption of compulsion in cases that lack a recording.[162] The last chapter expressed serious doubt that the Court has authority to employ such rebuttable presumptions in state cases. Even if the Court has this authority, the empirical basis for presuming compulsion from the absence of a tape recording seems lacking. In any event, legislatures are better equipped to deal with questions that would arise pertaining to cost, available resources, possible exemptions, and transcribing requirements.[163]

For those who find merit in the arguments expressed in this book, *Miranda*'s overruling would accomplish several salutary ends. It would nullify the Supreme Court's indefensible exercise of supervisory power over the states, restore the Fifth Amendment's correct meaning, help to reinstate the discovery of truth as a primary goal of the criminal justice system, and reestablish police interrogation as a legitimate and important means of ascertaining truth. As previously discussed, constitutional law without *Miranda* would still preclude police interrogation conduct that is likely to induce a false confession or that the judiciary finds offensive to society's truly fundamental precepts of right and wrong. It would also preclude the police from claiming that the defendant is obligated to answer.

A free and just society has no cause to view with shame or embarrassment a legal system that does not include *Miranda*. On the contrary, a legal system that provides the police a reasonable period of time to ascertain the truth by interrogating suspects arrested on probable cause, subject always to the constraints of the voluntariness doctrine, is "worthy of a mature and civilized society nearing the twenty-first century."[164] In this regard, Justice Harlan's dissenting words in *Miranda* still ring true today:

> Albeit stringently confined by the due process standards interrogation is no doubt often inconvenient and unpleasant for the suspect. However, it is no less so for a man to be arrested and jailed, to have his house searched, or to stand trial in court, yet all this may properly happen to the most innocent given probable cause, a warrant, or an indictment. Society has always paid a stiff price for law and order, and peaceful interrogation is not one of the dark moments of the law.[165]

Notes

Chapter 1

1. The exclusion of statements for violations of rules that are not constitutionally based, such as statutory prompt arraignment rules, has become less popular. *See generally* 1 W. LAFAVE & J. ISRAEL, CRIMINAL PROCEDURE 451–57 (1984).

2. Brown v. Mississippi, 297 U.S. 278 (1936) (reversing the defendants' convictions on due process grounds). The facts are taken from the United States Supreme Court opinion and from the various opinions in the two unsuccessful appeals before the Mississippi Supreme Court. *See* Brown v. State, 173 Miss. 563, 161 So. 465 (1935); Brown v. State, 173 Miss. 542, 158 So. 339 (1935).

3. The suspects were black; the victim and offending officials were white. This undoubtedly had practical importance in a case coming to the United States Supreme Court from Mississippi in the 1930s, but it is not important with regard to the issue being considered in the text.

4. The violation of a constitutional rule typically requires the exclusion of both the evidence immediately derived from the illegality and the derivative evidence, or the "fruit of the poisonous tree." *See* Nardone v. United States, 308 U.S. 338, 341 (1939) (coining the phrase). The fruits doctrine does not apply with the same rigor to mere *Miranda* violations, *see* Oregon v. Elstad, 470 U.S. 298 (1985), and it has been argued that it should not apply at all to the physical fruits of confessions, New York v. Quarles, 467 U.S. 649, 665–74 (1984) (O'Connor, J., concurring and dissenting).

5. The quotation marks are used because the word erroneous may have different meanings in this context. See notes 64–67 and accompanying text.

6. *See, e.g.,* Grano, *Implementing the Objectives of Procedural Reform: The Proposed Michigan Rules of Criminal Procedure* (pt. 1), 32 WAYNE L. REV. 1007, 1011 (1986); Steffen, *Truth as Second Fiddle: Reevaluating the Place of Truth in the Adversarial Trial Ensemble,* 1988 UTAH L. REV. 799, 803 (1988). As the discussion in the text indicates, I have found it necessary to rethink arguments I made in the 1986 article.

7. *See, e.g.,* Arenella, *Reforming the Federal Grand Jury and the State Preliminary Hearing to Prevent Conviction without Adjudication,* 78 MICH. L. REV. 463, 476–77 (1980) (criminal justice system deliberately promotes policies other than conviction of the factually guilty); Kamisar, *Remembering the "Old World" of Criminal Procedure: A Reply To Professor Grano,* 23 U. MICH. J.L. REF. 537, 541–43 (1990) (same).

8. *See, e.g.,* Arenella, *supra* note 7; Arenella, *Rethinking the Functions of Criminal Procedure: The Warren and Burger Courts' Competing Ideologies,* 72 GEO. L.J. 185,

197–202 (1983) (arguing that truth cannot be equated with empirical fact and describing power allocation and legitimation functions of criminal justice system); Goodpaster, *On the Theory of American Adversary Criminal Trial,* 78 J. CRIM. L. & CRIMINOLOGY 118, 121–24, 130–38, 143–46 (1987) (debunking truth discovery theory, reviewing other theories, and advocating "norm" theory); Kamisar, *supra* note 7, at 541–51; Rosenberg & Rosenberg, *Guilt: Henry Friendly Meets the Maharal of Prague,* 90 MICH. L. REV. 604, 614–15, 620 (1991) (maintaining that procedural rights are more important than establishing facts; suggesting that justice, in the sense of finding truth, is for God, not worldly courts); Saltzburg, *Lawyers, Clients, and the Adversary System,* 37 MERCER L. REV. 647, 650, 654 (1986) (arguing that adversary system is not based on a search for truth).

9. Goodpaster, *supra* note 8, at 144.

10. Arenella, *supra* note 8, at 186.

11. For an earlier criticism of the adversary system's disregard for truth, see J. FRANK, COURTS ON TRIAL 80–103 (1949) (chapter entitled "The 'Fight' Theory versus the 'Truth' Theory"). *See also* Vanderbilt, *The New Federal Criminal Rules,* 51 YALE L.J. 719, 720–21 (1942) (citations omitted):

The first impression concerns the enormous number of legal barnacles that encrust the subject of criminal procedure. Legal barnacles are not, however, a peculiarity of criminal procedure alone; they seem to thrive in all branches of adjective law. The first task in procedural reform is to distinguish between the essential and the adventitious and to eliminate the latter.

Judge Frank thought that trial by jury impeded the search for truth, but doubting that constitutional amendments could be passed to abolish it, he limited himself to advocating less radical reforms. J. FRANK, *supra,* at 108–45.

12. This characteristic has been criticized by Judge Marvin Frankel. *See* M. FRANKEL, PARTISAN JUSTICE 10–20, 42–43, 75–78 (1978).

13. J. FRANK, *supra* note 11, at 81.

14. Goodpaster, *supra* note 8, at 122–23.

15. Damaska, *Evidentiary Barriers to Conviction and Two Models of Criminal Procedure: A Comparative Study,* 121 U. PA. L. REV. 506, 521 (1973); id. at 523 (claiming that the "volume of American constitutional law on exclusionary rules is clearly without precedent anywhere"). *Accord* Hughes, *English Criminal Justice: Is It Better Than Ours?,* 26 ARIZ. L. REV. 507, 595–99 (1984) (claiming that English courts are more reluctant to employ exclusionary rules not based on reliability concerns).

16. *See, e.g.,* M. DAMASKA, THE FACES OF JUSTICE AND STATE AUTHORITY 112 (1986) (citing plea bargaining to support the claim that the American system "often seems satisfied with establishing merely a rough basis for punishment—sometimes a mere torso of actual wrongdoing . . . "); Alschuler, *Implementing the Criminal Defendant's Right to Trial: Alternatives to the Plea Bargaining System,* 50 U. CHI. L. REV. 931, 933 (1983).

17. M. DAMASKA, *supra* note 16, at 113, 115, 225; *cf.* J. DRESSLER, UNDERSTANDING CRIMINAL LAW 176 (1987) (defendant often has burden both of going forward and of persuasion with respect to defenses).

18. Faretta v. California, 422 U.S. 806 (1974) (finding the right to proceed *pro se* implicit in the Sixth Amendment). For a contrary view, see Grano, *The Right to Counsel: Collateral Issues Affecting Due Process,* 54 MINN. L. REV. 1175, 1179–1208 (1970). *But see* Arenella, *supra* note 8, at 201–2.

19. L. WEINREB, DENIAL OF JUSTICE 117–46 (1977).

20. Alschuler, *supra* note 16, at 995–1013. *See also supra* note 11.

21. Jackson, *Theories of Truth Finding in Criminal Procedure: An Evolutionary Approach,* 10 CARDOZO L. REV. 475, 496–527 (1988).

22. Pizzi, *Judge Frankel and the Adversary System,* 52 U. COLO. L. REV. 357, 366 (1981).

23. M. FRANKEL, *supra* note 12, at 79–86.

24. Steffen, *supra* note 6, at 822–34.

25. Goodpaster, *supra* note 8, at 124.

26. *Id.* at 122.

27. Damaska, *supra* note 15, at 580.

28. For example, Professor Weinreb has defended the constitutionality of his proposal that the judiciary assume the role of interrogating the accused, and Professor Alschuler has defended the constitutionality of his proposal that the lay jury be replaced by a mixed tribunal. L. WEINREB, *supra* note 19, at 147–64; Alschuler, *supra* note 16, at 995–98. The proposals are discussed in the text at notes 19–20, *supra.* The statement in the text about constitutional interpretation is not meant as a criticism of the constitutional arguments offered by these particular commentators.

29. M. DAMASKA, *supra* note 16, at 8–15.

30. In relying on Damaska, I am not suggesting that his two themes exhaust the domain of political ideology. Damaska claimed only that these themes best make it possible "to associate a great deal of procedural diversity—and its puzzles—with the changing structure and function of contemporary states." *Id.* at 9. Nor am I claiming that political ideology is the only influence on a society's procedural forms. Damaska himself recognized that "moral and cultural experience, the fabric of inherited beliefs, and similar considerations" play a role. *Id.* at 241; *cf.* M. TUSHNET, RED, WHITE, AND BLUE 4–17 (1988) (distinguishing the liberal and republican "traditions" in American political theory and claiming, *id.* at 6, that traditions "are not systematic, well-organized bodies of thought"). Finally, I have not seen the need in this analysis for a precise definition of ideology. *See generally* Griffiths, *Ideology in Criminal Procedure or a Third "Model" of the Criminal Process,* 79 YALE L.J. 359, 359 n.1 (1970) (referring to ideological beliefs as "pre-logical because they determine the structure of perception and consciousness and therefore are enmeshed in the factual and linguistic premises of argument").

31. M. DAMASKA, *supra* note 16, at 8–15, 16–36, 71–96 (first summarizing and then elaborating the competing ideals).

32. *Id.* at 181–239 (describing the four possible combinations and common law and European systems that evidence characteristics of each).

33. *Id.* at 218–26.

34. *Id.* at 26.

35. *Id.* at 102.

36. *Id.* at 123.

37. *Id.* at 222.

38. *Id.*

39. *Id.* at 105–6, 235. *See supra* note 18 and accompanying text.

40. J. FRANK, *supra* note 11, at 92.

41. *See also* Griffiths, *supra* note 30, at 412 ("Basic procedural questions can never be significantly understood without attention to the implications for and relation to issues of political philosophy.").

42. Only a minority of states permit a defendant to waive trial by jury, but the issue remains controversial in some places. *See, e.g.,* Grano, *supra* note 6, (pt. 2), 32 WAYNE L. REV. 1335, 1383–90. The limitation on waiver rights reflects policy-implementing influences. M. DAMASKA, *supra* note 16, at 99–100.

43. *Cf.* Goldstein, *Reflections on Two Models: Inquisitorial Themes in American Criminal Procedure,* 26 STAN. L. REV. 1009, 1018–19 (1974) (observing that the "accusatorial model closely resembles the system of private prosecution which long dominated English criminal justice").

44. Goodpaster, *supra* note 8, at 125.

45. *Id.*

46. *Cf.* S. LANDSMAN, THE ADVERSARY SYSTEM 36 (1984) (arguing that it "need not be conceded that the process is inept at finding truth").

47. *See id.*

48. Uviller, *The Advocate, the Truth, and Judicial Hackles: A Reaction to Judge Frankel's Idea,* 123 U. PA. L. REV. 1067, 1076 (1975); *see also* Jackson, *supra* note 21, at 484 (positing "differing epistemological conceptions about the meaning of truth and the kinds of truths that are most important").

49. Uviller, *supra* note 48, at 1079; Rosenberg & Rosenberg, *supra* note 8, at 613; Saltzburg, *supra* note 8, at 654.

50. Goodpaster, *supra* note 8, at 133.

51. *See* Jackson, *supra* note 21, at 513 (denying that this skepticism about knowledge necessarily leads to a "fundamental philosophical skepticism").

52. *See, e.g.,* Arenella, *supra* note 7, at 476–77 (but including questions pertaining to the defendant's intent as relevant to the inquiry into factual guilt); Arenella, *supra* note 8, at 197–98 (this time including questions of intent as relevant to the moral evaluation of the defendant's conduct); Goodpaster, *supra* note 8, at 130–33 (denying that fact and law can be radically separated); Saltzburg, *supra* note 8, at 654; Uviller, *supra* note 48, at 1076.

53. *Cf.* Jackson, *supra* note 21, at 527 (faulting the epistemological assumptions of existing adversarial and inquisitorial systems and advocating radical procedural reforms based on a dialectic theory if truth finding is to remain a serious goal).

54. Damaska, *Presentation of Evidence and Factfinding Precision,* 123 U. PA. L. REV. 1083, 1085 (1975).

55. *See generally,* J. DRESSLER, *supra* note 17, at 95–115.

56. *Id.* at 95, 102–3, 117–25.

57. Damaska, *supra* note 54, at 1085; *see also* Steffen, *supra* note 6, at 806.

58. 384 U.S. 436 (1966).

59. In one of the cases, *California v. Stewart,* the defendant was convicted of first-degree murder. The murder conviction, however, seems to have been based on the felony murder doctrine. The contested issue in the case was whether the defendant was the person who committed a series of similar robberies, one of which resulted in a death. *See* People v. Stewart, 62 Cal. 2d 571, 400 P.2d 97, 43 Cal. Rptr. 201 (1975).

60. Saltzburg, *supra* note 8, at 654.

61. Uviller, *supra* note 48, at 1076.

62. Steffen, *supra* note 6, at 806.

63. J. DRESSLER, *supra* note 17, at 191–92, 196–98, 202–3.

64. Damaska, *supra* note 54, at 1086 (suggesting that the terms in this context imply that the judgment is either coherent or incoherent "within a given framework of legal reference"). *See also supra* note 60 and accompanying text.

65. Damaska, *supra* note 54, at 1086 n.6.

66. Pound, *The Canons of Procedural Reform,* 12 A.B.A. J. 541, 543 (1926).

67. As Roscoe Pound insisted, "the end of legal procedure is to bring about results in accord with substantive law, not to afford a means of delaying or defeating substantive rights." Pound, *Some Principles of Procedural Reform,* 4 ILL. L. REV. 388, 394 (1910). *But see* Hall, *Objectives of Federal Criminal Procedural Revision,* 51 YALE L.J. 723, 724 (1942) (observing that "if the substantive laws are unduly severe, indictments will be gone over with the finest of combs").

68. Hall, *supra* note 67, at 725.

69. Professor Weinreb has stated the point succinctly:

The function of criminal process is to determine criminal guilt with a view toward imposing a penalty. If it provides a civic education for some people (which is doubtful) or a public entertainment, so much the better; but these are not its function, any more than it is the function of the judicial system to provide comfortable berths for the friends of successful politicians, as it does.

L. WEINREB, *supra* note 19, at 1–2.

70. Jescheck, *Principles of German Criminal Procedure in Comparison with American Law,* 56 VA. L. REV. 239, 240 (1970) (emphasis added).

71. *See supra* note 43 and accompanying text.

72. "I have discussed soberly and categorically which is better, to put in prison several tens or hundreds of instigators, guilty or innocent, or to lose thousands of workers and Army men. The first is better. The interest of workers . . . must win

out." V. LENIN, 23 SOCHINENIIA 241 (3d ed. 1935), *quoted in* M. DAMASKA, *supra* note 16, at 121 n.41.

73. *See* Damaska, *supra* note 15, at 576–79; Hall, *supra* note 67, at 728.

74. The hypothetical, slightly modified, comes from Jackson, *supra* note 21, at 484 n.40. *See also* Stacy, *The Search for Truth in Constitutional Criminal Procedure*, 91 COLUM. L. REV. 1369, 1407–8 (1991).

75. J. STRONG ET AL., MCCORMICK ON EVIDENCE § 341 (4th ed. 1992); Stacy, *supra* note 74, at 1405–9.

76. *See In re* Winship, 397 U.S. 358 (1970) (holding that due process requires that proof be proved beyond a reasonable doubt).

77. *See* EYEWITNESS TESTIMONY: PSYCHOLOGICAL PERSPECTIVES (G. Wells & E. Loftus eds. 1984); E. LOFTUS, EYEWITNESS TESTIMONY (1979); *see also* E. BORCHARD, CONVICTING THE INNOCENT (1932).

78. *See, e.g.,* Manson v. Brathwaite, 432 U.S. 98 (1977).

79. *See infra* chapters 3 and 4.

80. C. ALLEN, LEGAL DUTIES 286–87 (1931) (emphasis in original). According to Allen, the common law originally posited twenty to one as the acceptable ratio of false negative to false positive verdicts, Hale reduced this ratio to five to one, and a consensus eventually compromised on ten to one. *Id.* at 257–58. Blackstone adopted the latter as the appropriate ratio. 4 W. BLACKSTONE, COMMENTARIES ON THE LAWS OF ENGLAND 358 (1765).

81. Damaska, *supra* note 15, at 576 (emphasis in original).

82. *Id.*

83. H. PACKER, THE LIMITS OF THE CRIMINAL SANCTION (1968); *see also* Packer, *Two Models of the Criminal Process*, 113 U. PA. L. REV. 1 (1964).

84. H. PACKER, *supra* note 83, at 163–73.

85. *Id.* at 158–63.

86. *Id.* at 153–54.

87. Damaska, *supra* note 15, at 575.

88. *Id.*

89. Arenella, *supra* note 8, at 211.

90. *Id.* For additional criticism, see Griffiths, *supra* note 30, at 362–71; Reed, *In Defense of the Social Learning Model: A Synthesis of the Packer-Griffiths Ideologies*, 9 INT'L J. COMP. & APPLIED CRIM. JUST. 141 (1985); Reed & Gaines, *Criminal Justice Models As a Function of Ideological Images: A Social Learning Alternative to Packer*, 6 INT'L J. COMP. & APPLIED CRIM. JUST. 213 (1982).

91. Packer's mistake may have been in choosing the term model to discuss values that always coexist in tension. Packer recognized that "[a] person who subscribed to all of the values underlying one model to the exclusion of all of the values underlying the other would rightly be viewed as a fanatic." H. PACKER, *supra* note 83, at 154. On the other hand, the concept of models was important to Packer's effort. *See* Griffiths, *supra* note 30, at 362 n.14 ("Much of the awesomeness of his claim evaporates if one translates his . . . title into language with which we are more familiar: 'Two Perspectives on the Criminal Process'.").

92. Arenella, *supra* note 8, at 213–22.

93. *Id.* at 214.

94. See *supra* notes 48–70 and accompanying text.

95. Arenella, *supra* note 8, at 200, 224–28.

96. Arenella, *supra* note 7, at 477 (emphasis added) (citations omitted).

97. *See supra* note 87 and accompanying text.

98. Nor does it work, except in a question-begging way, to posit due process procedures as part of the underlying purposes of the substantive criminal law. Similarly unconvincing is the claim that one purpose of the substantive criminal law is "to minimize social interference in the lives of citizens." Griffiths, *supra* note 30, at 366–67. The purpose of the substantive criminal law is to prohibit and punish certain behavior. *See supra* note 69. Political ideology decides those areas into which the state should not intrude.

99. Damaska, *supra* note 15, at 575.

100. *See* Grano, *Probable Cause and Common Sense: A Reply to the Critics of* Illinois v. Gates, 17 U. Mich. J.L. Ref. 465, 519–20 (1984).

101. Arenella, *supra* note 8, at 202.

102. *Id.* at 203.

103. *Id.*

104. *Id.* at 205.

105. *See, e.g.,* Rochin v. California, 342 U.S. 165 (1952) (employing a "shock the conscience" test to exclude evidence).

106. 5 J. Bentham, A Rationale of Judicial Evidence, bk. 9, pt. 2, ch. 3, at 490 (1827).

107. Even when such exclusionary rules are employed in other countries, their scope is narrower than that of the American rule. *See, e.g.,* Bradley, *The Emerging International Consensus as to Criminal Procedure Rules,* 14 Mich. J. Int'l. L. 171 (1993); Bradley, *The Exclusionary Rule in Germany,* 96 Harv. L. Rev. 1032 (1983); Harnon & Horowitz, *Exclusionary Rules within the Israeli Legal System* (monograph), *reprinted from* Israeli Reports to the xiii International Congress of Comparative Law (1990); Hughes, *supra* note 15, at 595–99 (1984).

108. Arenella, *supra* note 8, at 205–8.

109. *Id.* at 208 (emphasis added). Arenella set up a straw man by contending that critics imply "that criminal procedure should focus *exclusively* on the reliable adjudication of substantive guilt." *Id.* at 205 (emphasis added).

110. If Arenella did not intend to make such a broad claim, then he must resolve the tension between truth discovery and other goals with regard to any particular rule. Legal guilt would thus be reduced to guilt determined by procedures and rules that the system chooses to enforce. So defined, the concept would do little work, which is not what Arenella had in mind.

111. *Cf.* United States v. Verdugo-Urquidez, 494 U.S. 259, 264 (1990) (Fourth Amendment prohibits unreasonable searches and seizures "whether or not the evidence is sought to be used in a criminal trial"; Fourth Amendment violation is fully accomplished at time of search).

112. This was a frequently voiced and valid complaint of Attorney General Edwin Meese III. *See, e.g.,* Meese, *Promoting Truth in the Courtroom,* 40 VAND. L. REV. 271 (1987).

113. Although finding that truth and fairness would be promoted by the government's right to appeal from erroneous acquittals, the Office of Legal Policy in the Justice Department recently concluded "that a general rule authorizing the government to appeal all acquittals—at least to the extent such appeals would result in new trials—must be rejected on constitutional grounds." OFFICE OF LEGAL POLICY, U.S. DEP'T OF JUSTICE, "TRUTH IN CRIMINAL JUSTICE" SERIES, Report No. 6, *Double Jeopardy and Government Appeals* 7–26, 54–57 (1987), *reprinted in* 22 U. MICH. J.L. REF. 831, 843–61, 889–93 (1989).

114. *See* Loewy, *Police-Obtained Evidence and the Constitution: Distinguishing Unconstitutionally Obtained Evidence from Unconstitutionally Used Evidence,* 87 MICH. L. REV. 907 (1989). *See also* United States v. Verdugo-Urquidez, 494 U.S. 259, 264 (1990) (Fifth Amendment violation, unlike Fourth Amendment violation, does not occur until evidence is used at trial).

115. *Cf.* Neil v. Biggers, 409 U.S. 188, 198 (1972) ("Suggestive confrontations are disapproved because they increase the likelihood of misidentification, and unnecessarily suggestive ones are condemned for the further reason that the increased chance of misidentification is gratuitous.").

116. At one point in the long legal process in the well-known case of Brewer v. Williams, 430 U.S. 387 (1977), lawyers for the defendant claimed that although their client had hidden the murdered girl's body, he was not the murderer. *See* Johnson, *The Return of the "Christian Burial Speech" Case,* 32 EMORY L.J. 351, 357–60 (1983).

117. *Cf.* McCormick, *Some Problems and Developments in the Admissibility of Confessions,* 24 TEX. L. REV. 239, 253 (1946) (citing a Texas statute that rendered otherwise inadmissible confessions admissible if they were corroborated, this at a time when Texas possibly had the most detailed legislative controls over police interrogation); *see also* Cross, *Confessions and Cognate Matters: An English View,* 66 COLUM. L. REV. 79, 86 (1966) (suggesting that some English cases had suggested the admissibility of corroborated and otherwise inadmissible statements).

Chapter 2

1. Friendly, *The Fifth Amendment Tomorrow: The Case for Constitutional Change,* 37 CINN. L. REV. 671, 672 (1968).

2. Dolinko, *Is There a Rationale for the Privilege against Self-Incrimination?,* 33 UCLA L. REV. 1063, 1147 (1986); *see also* Stuntz, *Self-Incrimination and Excuse,* 88 COLUM. L. REV. 1227 (1988).

3. 378 U.S. 478 (1964).

4. Crooker v. California, 357 U.S. 433 (1958); Cicenia v. LaGay, 357 U.S. 504 (1958). That these cases, which were consistent with precedent, were overruled just six years later demonstrates the revolutionary impact of the Warren Court. *See generally* Grano, *Introduction—The Changed and Changing World of Constitutional*

Criminal Procedure: The Contribution of the Department of Justice's Office of Legal Policy, 22 U. Mich. J.L. Ref. 395 (1989).

5. The precise scope of *Escobedo's* holding was not clear at the time. See Enker & Elsen, *Counsel for the Suspect:* Massiah v. United States *and* Escobedo v. Illinois, 49 Minn. L. Rev. 47 (1964); Robinson, Massiah, Escobedo, *and Rationales for the Exclusion of Confessions,* 56 J. Crim. L. Criminology & Police Sci. 412 (1965).

6. 378 U.S. at 486.

7. *Id.* at 485.

8. *Id.* at 486.

9. *Id.* at 487–88; *see also* Miranda v. Arizona, 384 U.S. 436, 466 (1966) (without protections in police station, safeguards at trial would be empty formalities because "the most compelling possible evidence of guilt, a confession, would have already been obtained at the unsupervised pleasure of the police").

10. 378 U.S. at 488.

11. White, *Police Trickery in Inducing Confessions,* 127 U. Pa. L. Rev. 581, 593, 604 (1979).

12. Dix, *Mistake, Ignorance, Expectation of Benefit, and the Modern Law of Confessions,* 1975 Wash. U.L.Q. 275, 330.

13. Arenella, *Rethinking the Functions of Criminal Procedure: The Warren and Burger Courts' Competing Ideologies,* 72 Geo. L.J. 185, 232–33 (1983).

14. Rosenberg & Rosenberg, *In the Beginning: The Talmudic Rule against Self-Incrimination,* 63 N.Y.U. L. Rev. 955, 1031 (1988). It is doubtful that the Talmudic rule influenced the development of the privilege at common law. *See* L. Levy, Origins of the Fifth Amendment 441 (1968).

15. Rosenberg & Rosenberg, *supra* note 14, at 956.

16. 5 J. Bentham, Rationale of Judicial Evidence, bk. 9, pt. 4., ch. 3, at 238 (1827).

17. *Id.* at 238–39 (emphasis in original).

18. *Id.* at 239; *see also* Stuntz, *supra* note 2, at 1234 n.22. Bentham's disdain for lawyers is apparent in his remarks.

19. Gifford, *Meaningful Reform of Plea Bargaining: The Control of Prosecutorial Discretion,* 1983 U. Ill. L. Rev. 37, 37; *see also* Alschuler, *Implementing the Criminal Defendant's Right to Trial: Alternatives to the Plea Bargaining System,* 50 U. Chi. L. Rev. 931 (1983).

20. Bordenkircher v. Hayes, 434 U.S. 357 (1978) (prosecutor offered five-year sentence if defendant pleaded guilty but threatened habitual offender prosecution, carrying mandatory life sentence, if defendant contested guilt; defendant refused offer; life sentence upheld).

21. *Id.* at 363–64; Santobello v. New York, 404 U.S. 257, 260 (1971) (if every case went to trial, states would have to increase many times their commitment of resources to criminal justice). Chief Justice Burger, who authored *Santobello,* made the same point in a published speech. Burger, *The State of the Judiciary—1970,* 56 A.B.A. J. 929, 931 (1970).

22. Arenella, *Reforming the Federal Grand Jury and the State Preliminary Hearing*

to Prevent Conviction without Adjudication, 78 MICH. L. REV. 463, 468–70, 523–24 (1980).

23. See, e.g., NATIONAL ADVISORY COMMISSION ON CRIMINAL JUSTICE STANDARDS AND GOALS, COURTS 47 (1973); Alschuler, supra note 19, at 943–44.

24. Cf. Damaska, Comparative Reflections on Reading the Amended Yugoslav Code: Interrogation of Defendants in Yugoslav Criminal Procedure, 61 J. CRIM. L. CRIMINOLOGY & POLICE SCI. 168, 170–71 (1970) (American system has built-in pressures to seek confessions; guilty plea system, unknown on the Continent, is a major factor).

25. See supra text accompanying note 9.

26. See supra text accompanying note 10.

27. See Frey, Modern Police Interrogation Law: The Wrong Road Taken, 42 U. PITT. L. REV. 731, 733–34 (1981) (that defendant, because of reliable confession, has no chance of acquittal is "wholly desirable"). Despite the statement in the text, legal arguments often reflect a sporting theory of justice. See Pound, The Causes of Popular Dissatisfaction with the Administration of Justice, 40 AM. L. REV. 729, 738–39 (1906) (lamenting that the sporting theory of justice "is so rooted in the profession in America that most of us take it for a fundamental legal tenet"). In another article, Pound traced the sporting theory to "the Anglo-Saxon bent for contentious procedure and love of a fair fight, and the desire of the pioneer American to see a forensic game of skill in backwoods court houses." Pound, The Canons of Procedural Reform, 12 A.B.A. J. 541, 543 (1926).

28. See, e.g., Donagan, The Right Not to Incriminate Oneself, 1 SOC. PHIL. & POL'Y 137, 143 (1984); Greenawalt, Silence As a Moral and Constitutional Right, 23 WM. & MARY L. REV. 15, 46 (1981) (not referring to the argument by name); Lewis, Bentham's View of the Right to Silence, 43 CURRENT LEGAL PROB. 135, 149 (1990); O'Brien, The Fifth Amendment: Fox Hunters, Old Women, Hermits, and the Burger Court, 54 NOTRE DAME LAW. 26, 35–40, 54 (1978).

29. 435 U.S. 957 (1978).

30. Id. at 959 (Marshall & Brennan, JJ., dissenting).

31. Gallegos v. Colorado, 370 U.S. 49, 54 (1962) (defendant not equal to police in knowledge and understanding); Haley v. Ohio, 332 U.S. 596, 599–600 (1948).

32. 378 U.S. at 488.

33. 384 U.S. 436, 460 (1966).

34. White, supra note 11, at 604.

35. Rosenberg & Rosenberg, A Modest Proposal for the Abolition of Custodial Confessions, 68 N.C. L. REV. 69, 75 (1989). Before Justice Fortas was elevated to the bench, he made much the same point. See Fortas, The Fifth Amendment: Nemo Tenetur Prodere Seipsum, 25 CLEV. B.A. J. 91, 98 (1954) ("equals, meeting in battle," under no obligation to furnish ammunition to each other); O'Brien, supra note 28, at 36–37; see also In re Gault, 387 U.S. 1, 47 (1967) (Fortas, J.) (Fifth Amendment "reflects the limits of the individual's attornment to the state" and "insists upon the equality of the individual and the state").

36. Rosenberg & Rosenberg, supra note 35, at 110.

37. Arenella, supra note 13, at 231 n.252, relying on Note, Interrogations in New Haven: The Impact of Miranda, 76 YALE L.J. 1519, 1614–15 (1967).

38. Friendly, *supra* note 1, at 693.

39. Enker & Elsen, *supra* note 5, at 65; *see also* Dolinko, *supra* note 2, at 1076–77 & n.74.

40. A strategy for successful police interrogation is necessary precisely because most wrongdoers are not inclined to offer spontaneous confessions or to find lectures about their moral obligations persuasive. F. INBAU, J. REID, & J. BUCKLEY, CRIMINAL INTERROGATION AND CONFESSIONS xvi–xvii (3d ed. 1986) [hereinafter F. INBAU]; Inbau, *Police Interrogation—A Practical Necessity*, 52 J. CRIM. L. CRIMINOLOGY & POLICE SCI. 16 (1961).

41. Enker & Elsen, *supra* note 5, at 66; Robinson, *supra* note 5, at 422; *see also* F. INBAU, *supra* note 40, at 79–81 (summarizing the interrogation process for converting a suspect's false denial into a truthful admission).

42. In Haley v. Ohio, 332 U.S. 596, 599–600 (1948), for example, the Court spoke of the dangers that the police tactics may have overwhelmed or crushed the fifteen-year-old defendant and made him a "victim first of fear, then of panic." It was in this context that the Court spoke of the defendant being no "match for the police in such a contest."

43. *Id.; cf.* Ellis, *Vox Populi v. Suprema Lex: A Comment on the Testimonial Privilege of the Fifth Amendment*, 55 IOWA L. REV. 829, 846 (1970) (defending Fifth Amendment's protection at trial by noting that innocent defendant may be no match for prosecutor); Lewis, *supra* note 28, at 149–51 (concern about reliability only reason favoring right of silence; concern has more force than Bentham realized).

44. *See* Caplan, *Questioning* Miranda, 38 VAND. L. REV. 1417, 1441–43 (1985); *cf.* Dolinko, *supra* note 2, at 1076 (no reason to want half of guilty defendants acquitted).

45. Greenawalt, *supra* note 28, at 46; *see also* Caplan, *supra* note 44, at 1436 (traditional inquiry was whether statement was voluntary, not whether police had upper hand).

46. Greenawalt, *supra* note 28, at 41.

47. Letter from Judge David L. Bazelon to Attorney General Nicholas Katzenbach (June 16, 1965), *reprinted in Equal Treatment in the Enforcement of the Criminal Law: The Bazelon-Katzenbach Letters*, 56 J. CRIM. L. CRIMINOLOGY & POLICE SCI. 498, 498 (1965) [hereinafter *Equal Treatment*] *and in* Kamisar, *Has the Court Left the Attorney General Behind?—The Bazelon-Katzenbach Letters on Poverty, Equality and the Administration of Criminal Justice*, 54 KY. L.J. 464, 486 (1966).

48. Ellis, *supra* note 43, at 848 (quoting PRESIDENT'S COMM'N ON LAW ENFORCEMENT AND ADMINISTRATION OF JUSTICE, THE CHALLENGE OF CRIME IN A FREE SOCIETY 44 (1967)).

49. Ellis, *supra* note 43, at 849.

50. Rosenberg & Rosenberg, *supra* note 14, at 960; *see also id.* at 1032 (Talmudic rule against self-incrimination "guaranteed that every accused, rich or poor, naive or sophisticated, would be accorded the same judicial process").

51. 378 U.S. at 482, 486, 490 n.13.

52. 384 U.S. at 470 (quoting Brief for the National District Attorney's Association at 14).

53. *Id.* at 472. Others have noted the influence of egalitarian concerns in *Miranda. See, e.g.,* Caplan, *supra* note 44, at 1456–57, 1469–71; Inbau & Manak, Miranda v. Arizona—*Is It Worth the Cost? (A Sample Survey, with Commentary, of the Expenditure of Court Time and Effort)*, 24 CAL. W. L. REV. 185, 185 (1987–88). Judge Friendly referred to the equal protection argument as "a ground bass that resounds throughout the *Miranda* opinion." Friendly, *supra* note 1, at 711.

54. A. BEISEL, CONTROL OVER ILLEGAL ENFORCEMENT OF THE CRIMINAL LAW: ROLE OF THE SUPREME COURT 105–6 (1955).

55. Letter from Attorney General Nicholas Katzenbach to Judge David Bazelon (June 24, 1965), *reprinted in Equal Treatment, supra* note 47, at 502, *and in* Kamisar, *supra* note 47, at 494.

56. Robinson, *supra* note 5, at 421 (citations omitted); *see also* Katzenbach letter in *Equal Treatment, supra* note 47, at 501, and in Kamisar, *supra* note 47, at 493 ("Acquittal of the guilty does not promote social justice."); Enker & Elsen, *supra* note 5, at 65 (to same effect).

57. Miranda himself confessed to the woman with whom he lived, and she testified against him at his second trial. State v. Miranda, 104 Ariz. 174, 450 P.2d 364 (1969); Kamisar, Miranda: *The Case, the Man, and the Players,* 82 MICH. L. REV. 1074, 1081 (1984) (*reviewing* L. BAKER, MIRANDA: CRIME, LAW AND POLITICS (1983)).

58. Katzenbach letter in *Equal Treatment, supra* note 47, at 501, and in Kamisar, *supra* note 47, at 493; *see also* Caplan, *supra* note 44, at 1456–58.

59. Kamisar, *supra* note 47, at 472 (emphasis in original).

60. *Id.* at 476 (emphasis in original). Former Attorney General Katzenbach had used the phrase "beat the rap" in his response to Judge Bazelon. *See supra* notes 47 and 55.

61. See *supra* note 55 and accompanying text.

62. Professor Kamisar recognized this, for he perceptively observed that Attorney General Katzenbach's argument against permitting indigent defendants to have appointed counsel in the police station was more persuasive as an argument against permitting any defendant, rich or poor, to have counsel's assistance in that forum. Kamisar, *supra* note 47, at 476–77, 481.

63. *Cf.* Bonventre, *An Alternative to the Constitutional Privilege against Self-Incrimination,* 49 BROOKLYN L. REV. 31, 63 (1982) (because equality can be assured by abolishing privilege against self-incrimination, reasons for guaranteeing privilege rather than abolishing it are not to be found in the equality argument).

64. Andresen v. Maryland, 427 U.S. 463, 476 (1976); Murphy v. Waterfront Comm'n, 378 U.S. 52, 55 (1964); Dolinko, *supra* note 2, at 1093; Westen & Mandell, *To Talk, to Balk, or to Lie: The Emerging Fifth Amendment Doctrine of the "Preferred Response,"* 19 AM. CRIM. L. REV. 521, 527 (1982). The trilemma may have been more difficult in a day when lying under oath was considered a sin against God. L. LEVY, *supra* note 14, at 24.

65. Bonventre, *supra* note 63, at 54.

66. Dolinko, *supra* note 2, at 1092–1107 & n.156; *see also* Dripps, *Foreword:*

Against Police Interrogation—And the Privilege against Self-Incrimination, 78 J. CRIM. L. & CRIMINOLOGY 699, 712 (1988).

67. Dolinko, *supra* note 2, at 1094. Relying not on a normative cruelty argument but rather on a substantive excuse theory premised on the difficulty of complying with legal requirements, Professor William Stuntz has argued that the Fifth Amendment functions to avoid the need to punish various kinds of excusable false statements. Stuntz, *supra* note 2, at 1239, 1295–96. Stuntz has also argued that his excuse theory explains why individuals are protected from being required to incriminate themselves but not from testifying against others. *Id.* at 1259–61. Even if this is so, Professor Stuntz has recognized that his excuse theory cannot really explain the Fifth Amendment's application in the police station. *Id.* at 1296.

68. L. LEVY, *supra* note 14, at 24; Donagan, *supra* note 28, at 145.

69. O'Brien, *supra* note 28, at 41; Bonventre, *supra* note 63, at 55; *see also* Thomas & Bilder, *Aristotle's Paradox and the Self-Incrimination Puzzle,* 82 J. CRIM. L. & CRIMINOLOGY 243, 257, 269–74 (1991) (self-incrimination principle embodies an ideology in which autonomy and choice are paramount values).

70. Y. KAMISAR, POLICE INTERROGATION AND CONFESSIONS 37 (1980) (emphasis in original).

71. Westen & Mandell, *supra* note 64, at 528.

72. In Pennsylvania v. Muniz, 496 U.S. 582 (1990), the Court, in an opinion written by Justice Brennan, acknowledged that the police cannot impose direct sanctions for false answers. Still, the Court insisted that "false testimony might itself prove incriminating, either because it links (albeit falsely) the suspect to the crime or because the prosecution might later prove at trial that the suspect lied to the police, giving rise to an inference of guilty conscience." *Id.* at 596 n.10. The inherent risk of discovery in falsehood, however, hardly seems adequate to create the truth-falsity-silence trilemma that supposedly underlies the protection against compulsory self-incrimination. *Id.* at 608 (concurring and dissenting opinion). Indeed, the majority could ultimately do no better than to fall back on the "intimate connection between the privilege against self-incrimination and police custodial questioning." *Id.* at 596 n.10 (quoting Miranda v. Arizona, 384 U.S. 436, 458 (1966)).

73. J. BENTHAM, *supra* note 16, at 230.

74. *Id.* at 231.

75. For Bentham's full argument, see *id.* at 230–38. *See also* Dripps, *supra* note 66, at 711–12.

76. Brown v. Walker, 161 U.S. 591, 637 (1896) (Field, J., dissenting); *see also* Ellis, *supra* note 43, at 838 (we "feel" the cruelty even though we cannot demonstrate it); Greenawalt, *supra* note 28, at 39 (intuition supports principle that it is cruel to force people to harm themselves even when infliction of same harm by others is warranted); *cf.* Thomas & Bilder, *supra* note 69, at 251 (discussing the connection between natural law basis and Hobbes's self-preservation principle).

77. *See, e.g.,* L. MAYERS, SHALL WE AMEND THE FIFTH AMENDMENT? 168–69 (1959); Dolinko, *supra* note 2, at 1090–1107; Friendly, *supra* note 1, at 683–84; Lewis, *supra* note 28, at 149; *see also* Seidman, *Rubashov's Question: Self-Incrimina-*

tion and the Problem of Coerced Preferences, 2 YALE J.L. & HUMANITIES 149, 149–51 (1990) (observing that these widely divergent views make the Fifth Amendment a "puzzle"; offering a consequentialist defense of the privilege). Bentham addressed the argument that no argument was needed to defend the protection against compulsory self-incrimination. J. BENTHAM, *supra* note 16, at 229–30 (assuming truth of proposition, proponent claims universal assent and suggests unreasonableness of dissent).

78. J. BENTHAM, *supra* note 16, at 232–33; *see also* Greenawalt, *supra* note 28, at 23–24. In Andresen v. Maryland, 427 U.S. 463 (1976), the Court, distinguishing a search for incriminating documents from a subpoena requiring the recipient to turn over the documents, upheld a search of a lawyer's offices.

79. Miranda v. Arizona, 384 U.S. 436, 460 (1966).

80. Donagan, *supra* note 28, at 140–41; *see also* O'Brien, *supra* note 28, at 44 (privilege against self-incrimination morally unacceptable as a governing principle in human affairs); Friendly, *supra* note 1, at 680 (to same effect).

81. Greenawalt, *supra* note 28, at 42. Judge Friendly defended a broader obligation: "Every hour of the day people are being asked to explain their conduct to parents, employers, and teachers. Those who are questioned consider themselves to be morally bound to respond, and the questioners believe it proper to take action if they do not." Friendly, *supra* note 1, at 680. Given what he described as "the universal belief in a duty to answer" in these private contexts, Friendly questioned why the same duty should not apply in state-individual relationships. *Id.* at n.48.

82. Donagan, *supra* note 28, at 139–40; *see also* Greenawalt, *supra* note 28, at 21 & n.12 (admitting, however, that claim that person is not morally obligated to confess is debatable). *But see* Bonventre, *supra* note 63, at 45 (Fifth Amendment privilege "offends our standards of civic decency"); Friendly, *supra* note 1, at 680.

83. Fortas, *supra* note 35, at 98–99.

84. *See* Dolinko, *supra* note 2, at 1089 (denying "unimpaired" right of self-defense); Dripps, *Self-Incrimination and Self-Preservation: A Skeptical View,* 1991 U. ILL. L. REV. 329, 330–37, 340–41, 346–48.

85. Donagan, *supra* note 28, at 140.

86. This conclusion is contestable. *See* Greenawalt, *supra* note 28, at 21 n.12.

87. Donagan, *supra* note 28, at 147. Professor Stuntz has argued that the Fifth Amendment basically applies when many individuals would find it difficult to comply with a requirement to tell the truth. Instead of the law recognizing an excuse defense for perjury in such circumstances, the Fifth Amendment, in his view, provides a less costly alternative. Stuntz, *supra* note 2, at 1229 (summarizing his thesis). From the perspective of this theory, of course, the Fifth Amendment "protects a category of *wrongful* conduct." *Id.* at 1293 (emphasis in original). For criticism of Professor Stuntz's theory, see Dripps, *supra* note 84, at 330–41; Schulhofer, *Some Kind Words for the Privilege against Self-Incrimination,* 26 VAL. U.L. REV. 311, 322–23 (1991).

88. Dolinko, *supra* note 2, at 1095–1101 & nn.172 & 175–76. For an elaboration of the limits on the defenses of duress and self-defense, see J. DRESSLER, UNDERSTANDING CRIMINAL LAW 191–96, 264–66 (1987). *See also supra* note 84.

Elaborating a distinction Professor Harry Frankfurt made between second-order volition and first-order desire, Thomas and Bilder have argued that "the state is forbidden from doing anything that causes S to make a statement when her second-order volition is to want her will to be not to want to answer questions." Thomas & Bilder, *supra* note 69, at 271 (building on H. FRANKFURT, THE IMPORTANCE OF WHAT WE CARE ABOUT 47–57 (1988)). By their own admission, however, the authors did not attempt "to justify, in normative terms," this principle. *Id.* at 257. Hence, they did not explain why autonomy should be protected in the self-incrimination context when the state is permitted to force choices on individuals in other contexts. For more detailed criticism of the Thomas-Bilder thesis, see Dripps, *supra* note 84, at 341–50.

89. Dolinko, *supra* note 2, at 1105–7; *see also* Dripps, *supra* note 84, at 347, 350 (examples of cruelty involve sadistic motives and gratuitous pain); Stuntz, *supra* note 2, at 1237–39 (rejecting cruelty argument).

90. Greenawalt, *supra* note 28, at 20–32.

91. *Id.* at 24. *See also supra* text accompanying note 78.

92. Dolinko, *supra* note 2, at 1069–70 (making both points). As Professor Schulhofer has stated, "Greenawalt's approach suggests that the government, having probably [*sic*] cause, *is* entitled to a response." Schulhofer, *supra* note 87, at 322 (emphasis in original).

93. Greenawalt, *supra* note 28, at 25. This point is further discussed in chapter 5.

94. Greenawalt, *supra* note 28, at 50 (no cause for dismay that individuals indirectly encouraged to cooperate); *see also* Bator & Vorenberg, *Arrest, Detention, Interrogation and the Right to Counsel: Basic Problems and Possible Legislative Solutions,* 66 COLUM. L. REV. 62, 70 (1966); Bonventre, *supra* note 63, at 50. That police in general "may take full advantage of a suspect's mistaken view that confession at the station is in his best interest" is consistent with Professor Stuntz's excuse theory of the Fifth Amendment. Stuntz, *supra* note 2, at 1264–68. For a contrary view, see Rosenberg & Rosenberg, *Miranda, Minnick, and the Morality of Confessions,* 19 AM. J. CRIM. L. 1 (1991).

95. Pieck, *The Accused's Privilege against Self-Incrimination in the Civil Law,* 11 AM. J. COMP. L. 585, 597 (1962). *See also,* P. DEVLIN, THE CRIMINAL PROSECUTION IN ENGLAND 50 (1960) ("[W]hile the English system undoubtedly does give the accused man the right to say nothing, it does nothing to urge him to take advantage of his right or even to make that course invariably the attractive one . . . ").

96. *Cf.* Schulhofer, *Confessions and the Court,* 79 MICH. L. REV. 865, 872 (1981) ("[T]he point was simply that we do (and should) find it unseemly for government officials systematically to seek out and take advantage of the psychological vulnerabilities of a citizen."); *see also,* Rosenberg & Rosenberg, *supra* note 94, at 29–31. *But see* Schulhofer, *supra* note 87, at 316–20 (rejecting traditional defenses of the privilege).

97. *Cf.* Dolinko, *supra* note 2, at 1106–7: "What these points do establish, I contend, is that the cruelty theorist owes us an explanation which, so far as I know,

has never been provided and which I, at least, cannot see how to construct." In short, it will not suffice simply to assert that "ethical and philosophical beliefs concerning the sanctity and value of human life" justify hostility to even voluntary confessions. *But see* Rosenberg & Rosenberg, *supra* note 94, at 30 (making such an assertion).

98. United States v. Washington, 431 U.S. 181, 187–88 (1977) (citations omitted) (words in brackets substituted for Court's references to the Constitution and the Fifth Amendment).

99. *See, e.g.,* Miller v. Fenton, 474 U.S. 104, 109–10 (1985); Tehan v. United States *ex rel.* Shott, 382 U.S. 406, 414 (1966); Murphy v. Waterfront Comm'n, 378 U.S. 52, 55 (1964); Malloy v. Hogan, 378 U.S. 1, 7 (1964); Culombe v. Connecticut, 367 U.S. 568, 582–83 (1961); Rogers v. Richmond, 365 U.S. 534, 540–41 (1961); Watts v. Indiana, 338 U.S. 49, 54 (1949).

100. *See, e.g.,* Doe v. United States, 487 U.S. 201, 212–13 & n.11 (1988) (compelling a grand jury target to authorize foreign banks to disclose his bank records does not violate Fifth Amendment, which reflects preference for accusatorial system); Allen v. Illinois, 478 U.S. 364, 375 (1986) (Fifth Amendment reflects that ours is an accusatorial not an inquisitorial system; nevertheless, civil proceedings under state's Sexually Dangerous Persons Act do not come under the Fifth Amendment); Andresen v. Maryland, 427 U.S. 463, 476 (1976) (admitting records into evidence that had been seized in search of lawyer's office did "not convert our accusatorial system of justice into an inquisitorial one"); Couch v. United States, 409 U.S. 322, 329 (1973) (summons on taxpayer's accountant did not involve "inquisitorial pressure" on taxpayer); California v. Byers, 402 U.S. 424, 450–57 (1971) (Harlan, J., concurring) ("hit and run" statute, unlike other reporting statutes, did not reduce the accusatorial system to a meaningless ritual).

101. Colorado v. Connelly, 479 U.S. 157, 181 (1986) (Brennan & Marshall, JJ., dissenting) (Court's holding ignores that accusatorial system, unlike inquisitorial counterpart, prefers not to rely on confessions); Smith v. Murray, 477 U.S. 527, 544–45 (1986) (Stevens, Marshall, Blackmun, & Brennan, JJ., dissenting) (majority's restrictions on habeas corpus review insufficiently sensitive to choice to have accusatorial rather than inquisitorial system); *see also* Degraffenreid v. McKellar, 494 U.S. 1071, 1071 (1990) (Marshall & Brennan, JJ., dissenting from denial of certiorari) (lower court failed to examine whether confession was obtained by inquisitorial means).

102. 475 U.S. 412 (1986).

103. *Id.* at 434, 468 (Stevens, Brennan, & Marshall, JJ., dissenting) (quoting Miller v. Fenton, 474 U.S. 104, 110 (1975)).

104. *Id.* at 457–58.

105. *Id.* at 459.

106. *Id.* at 468.

107. *Id.* at 460.

108. M. Damaska, The Faces of Justice and State Authority 88 & n.28 (1986); Damaska, *Evidentiary Barriers to Conviction and Two Models of Criminal Procedure: A Comparative Study,* 121 U. Pa. L. Rev. 506, 557–58 (1973); Friendly,

supra note 1, at 683. *But see* Brouwer, *Inquisitorial and Adversary Procedures—A Comparative Analysis,* 55 AUSTRALIAN L.J. 207, 208 (1981) (denying that term conjures up such images but conceding that it "is still viewed with suspicion by many common lawyers").

109. Damaska, *Adversary System,* in 1 ENCYCLOPEDIA OF CRIME AND JUSTICE 24, 26 (1983).

110. W. SCHAEFER, THE SUSPECT AND SOCIETY 70 (1967).

111. *Id; see also* Dripps, *supra* note 66, at 717 & n.78.

112. Robinson, *supra* note 5, at 422.

113. Damaska, *supra* note 109, at 24. In Colorado v. Connelly, 479 U.S. 157, 181–82 (1986) (Brennan & Marshall, JJ., dissenting), Justice Brennan both contrasted accusatorial and inquisitorial practices and claimed that our distrust of confessions stemmed, in part, from "their decisive impact upon the adversarial process."

114. Arenella, *supra* note 22, at 466 n.10 (emphasis in original). Professor Arenella was responding to Grano, Rhode Island v. Innis: *A Need to Reconsider the Constitutional Premises Underlying the Law of Confessions,* 17 AM. CRIM. L. REV. 1, 27 (1979). Because of his well-taken criticism that I used the terms at issue interchangeably, I have tried to be more careful here.

115. Arenella, *supra* note 22, at 465 n.5; *accord* Damaska, *supra* note 109, at 29 (accusatorial system encompasses adversary method); Goldstein, *Reflections on Two Models: Inquisitorial Themes in American Criminal Procedure,* 26 STAN. L. REV. 1009, 1016–18 (1974).

116. M. DAMASKA, *supra* note 108, at 3.

117. Arenella, *supra* note 22, at 465 n.5; Goldstein, *supra* note 115, at 1017.

118. Damaska, *supra* note 108, at 569.

119. M. DAMASKA, *supra* note 108, at 3–4.

120. J. LANGBEIN, PROSECUTING CRIME IN THE RENAISSANCE 130–32 (1974). *Cf.* Pizzi & Marafioti, *The New Italian Code of Criminal Procedure: The Difficulties of Building an Adversarial Trial System on a Civil Law Foundation,* 17 YALE J. INT'L L. 1, 7–10 (1992) (describing the "civil law paradigm").

121. Damaska, *supra* note 108, at 558; Jackson, *Theories of Truth Finding in Criminal Procedure: An Evolutionary Approach,* 10 CARDOZO L. REV. 475, 482 & n.33 (1988).

122. 475 U.S. at 434–35 n.1 (Stevens, Brennan, & Marshall, JJ., dissenting) (quoting Watts v. Indiana, 338 U.S. 49, 54 (1949)); *see also* Andresen v. Maryland, 427 U.S. 463, 476 (1976) (finding none of these attributes endangered by the introduction into evidence of documents seized during a search).

123. *See, e.g.,* Brouwer, *supra* note 108, at 210–11 (describing the functions of the *juge d'instruction* and the *chambre d'accusation* in France); Jescheck, *Principles of German Criminal Procedure in Comparison with American Law,* 56 VA. L. REV. 239, 245 (1970) (describing the initiating of charges in Germany).

124. Damaska, *supra* note 108, at 541.

125. Brouwer, *supra* note 108, at 208 (presumption recognized in France but operates differently); Damaska, *supra* note 108, at 541 and n.78; Jescheck, *supra* note 123, at 241 (Germany).

126. Damaska, *supra* note 108, at 546 (also observing that the difference between the two systems may be less significant in reality). Continental systems also make less use of affirmative defenses. *Id.* at 548–50.

127. *See* W. BEANEY, THE RIGHT TO COUNSEL IN AMERICAN COURTS 12 (1955) (right not established in England until 1903). The constitutional right to appointed trial counsel in the United States was not recognized in federal trials until 1938 and in state trials until 1963. Gideon v. Wainwright, 372 U.S. 335 (1963); Johnson v. Zerbst, 304 U.S. 458 (1938).

128. Brouwer, *supra* note 108, at 214 (France); Damaska, *supra* note 24, at 175 (Yugoslavia); Pizzi & Marafioti, *supra* note 120, at 11; Jescheck, *supra* note 123, at 246, 248; Note, *The Italian Penal Procedure Code: An Adversarial System of Criminal Procedure in Continental Europe*, 29 COLUM. J. TRANSNAT'L L. 245, 254, 274–75 (1991).

129. Damaska, *supra* note 24, at 171 & n.21; Damaska, *supra* note 108, at 527.

130. Brouwer, *supra* note 108, at 222; Damaska, *supra* note 24, at 170–71; *cf.* Note, *supra* note 128, at 274–75 (Italian code gives greater protection to suspect than American law).

131. Damaska, *supra* note 108, at 527 & n.41, 559; *see also* Brouwer, *supra* note 108, at 214; Dripps, *supra* note 66, at 713 & n.60; Pieck, *supra* note 95, at 589.

132. Watts v. Indiana, 338 U.S. 49, 55 (1949).

133. Cicenia v. La Gay, 357 U.S. 504 (1958).

134. Culombe v. Connecticut, 367 U.S. 568, 601–2 (1961).

135. Blair v. United States, 250 U.S. 273, 282 (1919). *See generally* Dession & Cohen, *The Inquisitorial Functions of Grand Juries*, 41 YALE L.J. 687 (1932).

136. By comparison, some continental countries may put more restrictions on the power to search and seize, at least in the initial stages of the investigation. Brouwer, *supra* note 108, at 212–13 (distinguishing police investigative powers and the broader powers accorded the examining magistrate in France). *But see* Damaska, *supra* note 108, at 522–23 & n.28 (indicating that continental countries are less restrictive but do employ safeguards against abuse).

137. Damaska, *supra* note 108, at 515–16 & n.13, 527–28.

138. Alschuler, *supra* note 19, at 1006.

139. Alschuler, *Plea Bargaining and Its History*, 79 COLUM. L. REV. 1, 42 (1979); *see also* Arenella, *supra* note 22, at 522.

140. Minnesota v. Murphy, 465 U.S. 420 (1984).

141. *Id.* at 451 (Marshall & Stevens, JJ., dissenting).

142. The Court has frequently ascribed such a burden to the government. *See, e.g.,* Miranda v. Arizona, 384 U.S. 436, 460 (1966); Murphy v. Waterfront Comm'n, 378 U.S. 52, 55 (1964).

143. Schmerber v. California, 384 U.S. 757 (1966), held that the Fifth Amendment protects only testimonial or communicative evidence. On the specifics, see Fisher v. United States, 425 U.S. 391, 405–14 (1976) (documents); United States v. Dionisio, 410 U.S. 1, 5–7 (1973) (voice); United States v. Mara, 410 U.S. 19 (1973) (handwriting); United States v. Wade, 388 U.S. 218, 222–23 (1967) (lineup);

Gilbert v. California, 388 U.S. 263, 265–67 (1967) (handwriting); Schmerber, *supra,* 761–64 (blood; dictum on fingerprints).

144. Doe v. United States, 487 U.S. 201 (1988).

145. *Id.* at 213 n.11. Justice Stevens argued that the court order crossed the line that separates "the kind of inquisition conducted by the Star Chamber and what we proudly describe as our accusatorial system of justice." *Id.* at 220 (Stevens, J., dissenting).

146. McKay, *Self-Incrimination and the New Privacy,* 1967 Sup. Ct. Rev. 193, 209; *see also* Bonventre, *supra* note 63, at 60; Dolinko, *supra* note 2, at 1067 n.24; Ellis, *supra* note 43, at 839; Friendly, *supra* note 1, at 686. With both friend and foe of the privilege in agreement regarding the circularity of the accusatorial system argument, one must marvel at the argument's persistence.

147. Arenella, *supra* note 22, at 466 n.10.

148. Greenawalt, *supra* note 28, at 46; *see also supra* note 45 and accompanying text.

149. *See, e.g.,* Bonventre, *supra* note 63, at 56–59; McKay, *supra* note 146, at 210–14; O'Brien, *supra* note 28, at 51–53; *see also* Gerstein, *Privacy and Self-Incrimination,* 80 Ethics 87 (1970).

150. Kastigar v. United States, 406 U.S. 441 (1972); *see also* Friendly, *supra* note 1, at 688–90; Stuntz, *supra* note 2, at 1234.

151. *See* Dolinko, *supra* note 2, at 1108–19; Stuntz, *supra* note 2, at 1232–33.

152. Dolinko, *supra* note 2, at 1118–19; Stuntz, *supra* note 2, at 1233; *see also* H. Friendly, Benchmarks 276 (1967) (taking blood from individual, which Court upheld shortly after *Miranda,* is more intrusive on privacy than police interrogation).

153. H. Friendly, *supra* note 152, at 277; *see also* Schulhofer, *supra* note 87, at 319–20 (rejecting privacy argument).

154. *Cf.* Dolinko, *supra* note 2, at 1077–80 (pointing to the due process clause); *see also* Dripps, *supra* note 66, at 713–15.

155. Rosenberg & Rosenberg, *supra* note 94, at 24 (emphasis in original).

156. *Id.* at 27.

157. Schulhofer, *supra* note 87, at 327.

158. *See generally* F. Inbau, *supra* note 40.

159. Schulhofer, *supra* note 87, at 327.

160. McCormick, *Some Problems and Developments in the Admissibility of Confessions,* 24 Tex. L. Rev. 239, 239–41 (1946); Rosenberg & Rosenberg, *supra* note 14, at 1033.

161. McCormick, *supra* note 160, at 240–41.

162. Robinson, *supra* note 5, at 415.

163. McKay, *supra* note 146, at 208; *see also* Dripps, *supra* note 66, at 715–16.

164. Schulhofer, *supra* note 87, at 332 (making this argument with respect to the application of the privilege at trial but referring to police interrogation as well).

165. *Id.*

166. Miranda v. Arizona, 384 U.S. 436, 460 (1966).

Chapter 3

1. J. Strong et al., McCormick on Evidence § 146 (4th ed. 1992); Dix, *Mistake, Ignorance, Expectation of Benefit, and the Modern Law of Confessions,* 1975 Wash. U. L.Q. 275, 279–83.

2. 110 U.S. 574 (1884).

3. Berger, *Legislating Confession Law in Great Britain: A Statutory Approach to Police Interrogations,* 24 U. Mich. J.L. Ref. 1, 8 (1990); Dix, *Federal Constitutional Confession Law: The 1986 and 1987 Supreme Court Terms,* 67 Tex. L. Rev. 231, 256–57 (1988); Dix, *supra* note 1, at 280.

4. 110 U.S. at 585. Following *Hopt,* the Supreme Court decided three more cases under common-law evidentiary standards: Sparf & Hansen v. United States, 156 U.S. 51 (1895); Pierce v. United States, 160 U.S. 355 (1896); Wilson v. United States, 162 U.S. 613 (1896).

5. In 1897, the Court first indicated that the Fifth Amendment's self-incrimination clause was a "crystallization" of the common-law voluntariness doctrine. Bram v. United States, 168 U.S. 532, 543 (1897). Professor Wigmore contended that no assertion "could be more unfounded." 3 J. Wigmore, A Treatise on the Anglo-American System of Evidence in Trials at Common Law § 823, at 250 n.5 (3d ed. 1940). *But see* Y. Kamisar, Police Interrogation and Confessions 35–36 (1980) (criticizing Wigmore's historical perspective; insisting that while history does not dictate application of the Fifth Amendment to police interrogation, it permits such application). The issue is discussed in chapter 5.

6. Brown v. Mississippi, 297 U.S. 278 (1936).

7. *See, e.g.,* Rogers v. Richmond, 365 U.S. 534, 544 (1961).

8. *See* Kamisar, *What Is an "Involuntary" Confession? Some Comments on Inbau and Reid's* Criminal Interrogation and Confessions, 17 Rutgers L. Rev. 728 (1963).

9. Culombe v. Connecticut, 367 U.S. 568, 602 (1961) (Frankfurter & Stewart, JJ.).

10. In *Culombe* itself, only Justice Stewart joined Justice Frankfurter's sixty-seven page opinion. Four justices, who concurred in the result, agreed only in part with Frankfurter's voluntariness analysis. Three justices expressed agreement with most of Frankfurter's analysis but disagreed with his application of the voluntariness doctrine to the facts of the case.

11. I have previously argued that both the substantive criminal law and the law of confessions require that we accept either the belief that free will exists or the soft determinist's or compatibilist's view that blame and responsibility are possible in a deterministic world. Grano, *Voluntariness, Free Will, and the Law of Confessions,* 65 Va. L. Rev. 859, 868–80 (1979); *see also* Dressler, *Exegesis of the Law of Duress: Justifying the Excuse and Searching for Its Proper Limits,* 62 S. Cal. L. Rev. 1331, 1357 n.156 (1989); Moore, *Causation and the Excuses,* 73 Cal. L. Rev. 1091, 1132–48 (1985). Although I believe that this argument is correct, there is no need to repeat it here.

12. 297 U.S. 278 (1936). The facts of this case were used for the hypothetical in chapter 1.

13. *See generally* Dressler, *supra* note 11; Newman & Weitzer, *Duress, Free Will and the Criminal Law*, 30 S. Cal. L. Rev. 313 (1957).

Throughout this chapter, the concepts of coercion and involuntariness are used interchangeably to discuss the impairment of volitional freedom. Depending upon one's initial definitions, however, it might be possible to say that a person acted voluntarily even though the person was coerced or that the person acted involuntarily even though the person was not coerced. The analysis that follows in the text makes such distinctions unwarranted. For general consideration of the connection between claims of coercion and claims of involuntariness, see A. Wertheimer, Coercion 287–306 (1987).

14. *See, e.g.,* Aristotle, Nichomachean Ethics bk. 3, 1110b15– 20; *see infra* notes 145–59 and accompanying text.

15. Aristotle, *supra* note 14, at 1109b30–1111b3.

16. *Id.* at 1110a1–5.

17. *Id.* at 1110a1–20.

18. *Id.*

19. Webster's Third New International Dictionary of the English Language 2564 (1971) uses *voluntary* to describe conduct "proceeding from the will" or produced "by an act of choice." This is consistent with Aristotle's usage. The dictionary then adds, however, that *voluntary* "implies freedom from any compulsion that could constrain one's choice." Rather than being inconsistent, these definitions reflect different usages of the same concept.

While *voluntary* and *involuntary* are often treated as opposites, Austin suggested this treatment was incorrect: "The 'opposite,' or rather 'opposites,' of 'voluntarily' might be 'under constraint' of some sort, duress or obligation or influence: the opposite of 'involuntarily' might be 'deliberately' or 'on purpose' or the like. Such divergences in opposites indicate that 'voluntarily' and 'involuntarily,' in spite of their apparent connection, are fish from very different kettles." Austin, *A Plea for Excuses,* in 57 Aristotelian Society Proceedings (1956–57) (footnotes omitted), *reprinted in* Freedom and Responsibility 6, 13 (H. Morris ed. 1961).

20. Most jurisdictions still refuse to recognize duress as a defense to murder. Dressler, *supra* note 11, at 1370–74. *But see* Model Penal Code § 2.09 (1985) (eliminating this limitation).

21. Aristotle, *supra* note 14, at 1110a25–30. I have substituted the term *excuse* for the term *forgive* in Aristotle's text because of the argument that forgiveness requires responsibility.

22. Frankfurt, *Coercion and Moral Responsibility,* in Essays on Freedom of Action 65, 77 (T. Honderick ed. 1973). The suggestion in these passages is that at some point coercion of the will becomes equivalent to physical coercion of the body, the precise point depending on an empirical inquiry into whether the person's volitional capacity was destroyed. *Id.* at 66. For a more recent and different account by Professor Frankfurt of what it means to be compelled, see H. Frankfurt, The Importance of What We Care About (1988).

23. 373 U.S. 503 (1963).

244 · Notes to Pages 62–63

244 · Notes to Pages 62–63

24. Philips, *Are Coerced Agreements Involuntary?*, 3 Law & Phil. 133, 137 (1984).

25. *Id.* Philips did not oppose the Court's holding that the confession was inadmissible. He objected only to the Court's conclusion that the confession was involuntary because the police had induced it by legally improper compulsion.

> In short, the court had two grounds for ruling Haynes confession inadmissible: (1) that it was entered involuntarily (his will was overborne), and (2) that it was induced by legally improper compulsion, i.e., legally improper means. It obscures both reasons, however, by offering the second as an explanation of the first.

Id. Philips is right if one accepts the definitions of voluntary and involuntary provided by Aristotle; his subsequent and seemingly contradictory conclusion that the defendant's will in *Haynes* might have been overborne under these definitions is incomprehensible.

26. *See, e.g.,* Dressler, *supra* note 11, at 1370–74 (arguing, contrary to his earlier thinking, that duress should be recognized as an excuse to murder); *see also* Model Penal Code § 2.09 (1985).

27. The thesis that coercion is a "moralized" concept is elaborated in A. Wertheimer, *supra* note 13. *See also* Dressler, *supra* note 11, at 1334 ("duress is a normative defense").

28. Professor Wertheimer, who has done the most thorough comparison of the law in these various areas, persuasively supports this thesis. See A. Wertheimer, *supra* note 13, at 3–175.

29. Fingarette, *Victimization: A Legalist Analysis of Coercion, Deception, Undue Influence, and Excusable Prison Escape*, 42 Wash. & Lee L. Rev. 65, 82 (1985).

30. A. Wertheimer, *supra* note 13, at 29 (emphasis in original).

31. Haley v. Ohio, 332 U.S. 596, 606 (1948) (Frankfurter, J., concurring).

32. Westen, *"Freedom" and "Coercion"—Virtue Words and Vice Words*, 1985 Duke L.J. 541, 565.

33. *See* A. Wertheimer, *supra* note 13, at 170–75 (summarizing his examination of several areas of the law); Thomas & Bilder, *Aristotle's Paradox and the Self-Incrimination Puzzle*, 82 J. Crim. L. & Criminology 243, 247–49, 262–65 (1991).

34. *But see* Schulhofer, *Reconsidering* Miranda 54 U. Chi. L. Rev. 435, 442–43 (1987) suggesting that the voluntariness language about "breaking the will" in the due process confession cases should be taken literally. For criticism of Schulhofer on this point, see Grano, Miranda's *Constitutional Difficulties: A Reply to Professor Schulhofer*, 55 U. Chi. L. Rev. 174, 182 (1988).

35. Bator & Vorenberg, *Arrest, Detention, Interrogation and the Right to Counsel: Basic Problems and Legislative Solutions*, 66 Colum. L. Rev. 62, 72–73 (1966); *see also* Kamisar, *supra* note 8, at 747.

36. For accounts of interrogation techniques that some might say drove their subjects to the breaking point, see R. Lifton, Thought Reform and the Psychology of Totalism (1961); A. Solzhenitsyn, The Gulag Archipelago pt. 1, ch. 4 (1973). *See also* Murphy, *Consent, Coercion, and Hard Choices*, 67 Va. L.

Rev. 79, 86 (1981) (suggesting that some cases, though few in number, involve situations where the individual has no capacity for control). We are familiar, however, with cases in which martyrs chose further pain and even death in preference to yielding. It seems equally accurate to say that those who did not resist chose not to be martyrs. In any event, we have no way of telling whether they could have resisted any longer. As Frankfurt has observed, "[t]here may be no way of discovering whether he [a person being severely tortured] spoke the word in submission to the threat of further pain, or whether—his will having been overcome by the agony he had already suffered—the word passed involuntarily through his lips." Frankfurt, *supra* note 22, at 65–66.

37. Fingarette, *supra* note 29, at 77. Because "it will be unclear whether the man dropped the knife because his fingers were forced open or because he wished to avoid a continuation of the pressure on his wrist," Frankfurt, *supra* note 22, at 65, we cannot be certain whether choice was exercised even when physical force is used to move another individual.

38. See *supra* text accompanying note 12.

39. G. FLETCHER, RETHINKING THE CRIMINAL LAW § 10.4.2 at 831 (1978).

40. Fingarette, *supra* note 29, at 72.

41. Westen, *supra* note 32, at 591–592.

42. *Id.* at 593.

43. *Cf.* A. WERTHEIMER, *supra* note 13, at 289–90:

If we say (narrowly) that B acts involuntarily only when his will is literally overborne, we give up the chance to say that constrained-volition coercion undermines voluntariness. If we say (broadly) that B acts involuntarily whenever he stands to suffer for his choice or whenever he acts under great psychic strain, then the involuntariness of B's act will be stripped of its moral force.

44. Miranda v. Arizona, 384 U.S. 436, 507 (1966) (Harlan, Stewart, & White, JJ., dissenting) (emphasis in original); *see also Developments in the Law—Confessions,* 79 HARV. L. REV. 935, 974 (1966) (issue is whether the pressures exerted by the police presented too great an obstacle to the free exercise of the defendant's judgment).

45. 384 U.S. at 515 (Harlan, J., dissenting) (law must "sift out *undue* pressure").

46. *Cf.* J. GLOVER, RESPONSIBILITY 11–13, 61, 78–81 (1970) (making the same point in discussing when coercion excuses individuals from responsibility for their actions).

47. Dix, *supra* note 1, at 335.

48. *Id.* at 336.

49. *See, e.g., id.* at 293; Kamisar, *A Dissent from the* Miranda *Dissents: Some Comments on the "New" Fifth Amendment and the Old "Voluntariness" Test,* 65 MICH. L. REV. 59, 94–104 (1966); Way, *The Supreme Court and State Coerced Confessions,* 12 J. PUB. L. 53, 65–66 (1963).

50. Kamisar, *supra* note 8, at 742.

51. Paulsen, *The Fourteenth Amendment and the Third Degree*, 6 STAN. L. REV. 411, 430 (1954).

52. Kamisar, *supra* note 8, at 759.

53. A. BEISEL, CONTROL OVER ILLEGAL ENFORCEMENT OF THE CRIMINAL LAW: ROLE OF THE SUPREME COURT 48 (1955).

54. Kamisar, *supra* note 8, at 759; *see also* Kamisar, *Police Interrogation and Confessions*, Remarks at U.S. Law Week's Constitutional Law Conference 12–16 (Sept. 12, 1987) (on file with author and at the University of Michigan Law School with Professor Kamisar).

55. Kamisar, *supra* note 8, at 745–46.

56. A. WERTHEIMER, *supra* note 13, at 38–46; 172; 267–68. *But see* Thomas & Bilder, *supra* note 33, at 268–69 (trying to avoid a normative inquiry).

57. A. WERTHEIMER, *supra* note 13, at 120.

58. Fingarette, *supra* note 29, at 81. To treat voluntariness simply as a shorthand for unfairness "is linguistically odd . . . it is, more importantly, a tacit shift of the logical center of interest of the inquiry." *Id.*

59. A. WERTHEIMER, *supra* note 13, at 121.

60. *Id.* at 179–91.

61. Frankfurt, *supra* note 22, at 65.

62. *Cf.* A. WERTHEIMER, *supra* note 13, at 180–81, 252–53, 307–8 (making the same point with regard to the issue of responsibility).

63. *Cf.* Haksar, *Coercive Proposals*, 4 POL. THEORY 65, 70–71 (1976) (discussing the nature of a coercion claim).

64. Murphy, *supra* note 36, at 84–85 (emphasis in original). Professor Westen stated the point a little differently:

> Instead of remembering that prescriptive coercion is bad because it is defined to be bad, and that descriptive coercion itself is neither good nor bad, we carelessly assume that all coercion is presumptively bad. Rather than demand . . . moral argument against particular kinds of coercion, we come to believe that . . . coercion itself [is] something to oppose.

Westen, *supra* note 32, at 592 (citations omitted).

65. The Model Penal Code defines duress in terms of wrongful threats that "a person of reasonable firmness in [the actor's] situation would have been unable to resist." MODEL PENAL CODE § 2.09(1) (1985). While the law of duress in contracts once employed a similar "person of ordinary firmness" test, today the standard is more commonly stated in terms of the actor not having a "reasonable alternative." E.A. FARNSWORTH, CONTRACTS § 4.18, at 279, 282 (2d ed. 1990).

Professor Joshua Dressler disagrees somewhat with Professor Wertheimer's description of this prong. He contends that the appropriate question is not whether the threat left the actor with no reasonable choice but rather whether the actor's choice in response to the threat was reasonable. Dressler, *supra* note 11, at 1366 n.194. This may be a better statement of what is involved in the analysis.

66. A. WERTHEIMER, *supra* note 13, at 30, 35, 172–74, 192–221, 308. *But see* Thomas & Bilder, *supra* note 33, at 265–69 (criticizing normative approach). Wertheimer takes the position that the two prongs are both necessary and sufficient for a claim of coercion, but this account may give insufficient attention to the normative aspect of causation. *See infra* notes 129–43 and accompanying text. For a more elaborate exposition of the necessary conditions for a claim of coercion, see Nozick, *Coercion,* in PHILOSOPHY, SCIENCE AND METHOD: ESSAYS IN HONOR OF ERNEST NAGEL (S. Morgenbesser et al. eds. 1969).

67. MODEL PENAL CODE § 2.09(1) (1985); E.A. FARNSWORTH, *supra* note 65, §§ 4.16–4.18, at 272, 282.

68. Colorado v. Connelly, 479 U.S. 157 (1986), supports Professor Wertheimer on this point. In *Connelly,* the defendant claimed that his confession was involuntary because internal voices compelled him to confess. The Court held that police coercion was necessary to make out a claim of involuntariness. *But see* Benner, *Requiem for* Miranda: *The Rehnquist Court's Voluntariness Doctrine in Historical Perspective,* 67 WASH. U. L.Q. 59, 122–43 (1989) (criticizing *Connelly* for ignoring the value of self-determination).

69. To understand why coercion claims cannot be empirically determined, it is essential to see that the choice prong, not just what Wertheimer labels the proposal prong, requires normative judgments. *See* A. WERTHEIMER, *supra* note 13, at 267–86; Fingarette, *supra* note 29, at 77, 93–94; Haksar, *supra* note 63, at 68. *But see* Thomas & Bilder, *supra* note 33, at 269–74 (seeking to embrace an empirical view about "second-order volitions"; admitting that external observers have no measure of these; positing presumptions to overcome this difficulty). For criticism of this latter view, see Dripps, *Self-Incrimination and Self-Preservation: A Skeptical View,* 1991 U. ILL. L. REV. 329, 341–50.

Although in a somewhat convoluted way, Justice Frankfurter reflected an awareness of the need for normative judgment when he said in Culombe v. Connecticut, 367 U.S. 568, 603 (1961), that the voluntariness inquiry required the Court to apply standards of judgment to the psychological facts. As he recognized, "[t]he notion of voluntariness is itself an amphibian. It purports at once to describe an internal psychic state and to characterize that state for legal purposes." *Id.* at 604–5.

70. *Cf.* A. WERTHEIMER, *supra* note 13, at 218 (insisting that his approach to coercion is "fundamentally neutral").

71. Fingarette, *supra* note 29, at 95; Westen, *supra* note 32, at 547.

72. The hypothetical comes from Frankfurt, *supra* note 22, at 76.

73. While Professor Dressler believes that duress should be available as a defense to murder, *see supra* note 26, he also approvingly predicts that "juries will not excuse all coerced killers." Dressler, *supra* note 11, at 1373.

74. Professor Kamisar has observed that the Supreme Court virtually adopted a per se rule that physical violence by the police renders a confession involuntary. Kamisar, *supra* note 8, at 756–58; *see also* Ashcraft v. Tennessee, 322 U.S. 143, 160 (1944) (Jackson, J., dissenting) (courts not too exacting about proof of causal effect when police use violence during interrogation). *But see* Lisenba v. California, 314 U.S. 219, 239–41 (1941) (causal connection required; where defendant admitted

that he confessed because codefendant had confessed, confession voluntary even though police struck defendant). The causation requirement remains to be discussed.

75. *Accord* Fingarette, *supra* note 29, at 70–71.

76. United States v. Jorn, 400 U.S. 470, 484 n.11 (1971) (pressure that would make a plea coerced not sufficient to render coerced, for double jeopardy purposes, defendant's decision to abort first trial by pleading guilty); *see also* Application of Buccheri, 6 Ariz. App. 196, 204, 431 P.2d 91, 99 (1967) (voluntariness in guilty plea context cannot be equated with voluntariness in law of confessions).

77. A. WERTHEIMER, *supra* note 13, at 153–54.

78. Note, *Undue Influence—Judicial Implementation of Social Policy,* 1968 WIS. L. REV. 569, 571.

79. A. WERTHEIMER, *supra* note 13, at 75–77.

80. 385 U.S. 493 (1967).

81. 400 U.S. 25 (1970).

82. Philips, *supra* note 24, at 134–36. Understanding Philips's error makes it clear that the Court did not put the cart before the horse in saying that the "acceptance of the basic legitimacy of plea bargaining necessarily implies rejection of any notion that a guilty plea is involuntary in a constitutional sense simply because it is the end result of the bargaining process." Bordenkircher v. Hayes, 434 U.S. 357, 363 (1978).

83. Sutherland, *Crime and Confession,* 79 HARV. L. REV. 21, 37 (1965). "The answer to Sutherland's (rhetorical) question is obvious. Its import is not." A. WERTHEIMER, *supra* note 13, at 119.

84. 384 U.S. 436 (1966).

85. Schulhofer, *supra* note 34, at 453. One may object at this point that the concept of compulsion embodied in the Fifth Amendment has a technical meaning that makes it different than the concept of coercion and that, accordingly, the criticism of the commentators in the text is wide of the mark. This objection is discussed and rejected in chapter 5, *infra.* One may argue that the concept of coercion in the Fifth Amendment requires less pressure than the similar concept embodied in the due process voluntariness doctrine, but at least in the context of confessions, to compel under the Fifth Amendment means to coerce.

86. The Supreme Court sometimes makes the same error. *See, e.g.,* Schneckloth v. Bustamonte, 412 U.S. 218, 223–24 (1973) (turning, without explanation, to the voluntariness doctrine in the confession cases to justify its treatment of voluntariness in the law of consent searches). Justice Marshall in dissent noted the error: "[The Court] applies a standard of voluntariness that was developed in a very different context, where the standard was based on policies different from those involved in this case." *Id.* at 280. This is to say not that *Schneckloth* was wrongly decided but only that its reasoning was flawed.

87. A. WERTHEIMER, *supra* note 13, at 202–21; 229–33.

88. Nozick, *supra* note 66, at 452–53.

89. *See, e.g.,* Haksar, *supra* note 63, at 66–70; Held, *Coercion and Coercive Offers,* in COERCION: NOMOS XIV 49 (J. Pennock & J. Chapman eds. 1972).

90. Professor Wertheimer has argued that a moral baseline should be used, at least when we are discussing the moral or legal question of whether the person alleging coercion should be held accountable for his actions. A. Wertheimer, *supra* note 13, at 206–20. In Professor Nozick's view, "[i]t may be that when the normal and morally expected courses of events diverge, the one of these which is to be used in deciding whether [a proposal] constitutes a threat or an offer is the course of events that the recipient of the action prefers." Nozick, *supra* note 66, at 451. Professor Westen has argued that both an "expectation" and a "prescriptive" baseline must be used to encompass all cases of coercion. Westen, *supra* note 32, at 586–87. For an account that seems to employ a factual baseline, see Feinberg, *Noncoercive Exploitation,* in Paternalism 201, 208–9 (R. Sartorius ed. 1983).

91. For discussions of the drowning hypothetical, *see, e.g.,* A. Wertheimer, *supra* note 13, at 207; Haksar, *supra* note 63, at 69; Nozick, *supra* note 66, at 449–50. From a legal as opposed to a moral perspective, A's proposal would be a threat if A was legally required to rescue B. Voluntariness issues in the law, however, frequently arise in situations that do not confront the actor with an antecedent legal obligation.

92. Feinberg, *supra* note 90, at 208–9.

93. Feinberg, however, views the millionaire's proposal as a coercive offer. *Id.* Compare the authorities in note 89, *supra,* defending the notion of coercive offers. *But see* A. Wertheimer, *supra* note 13, at 229–33 (agreeing that the proposal is an offer and defending the view that it is not coercive).

94. Westen, *supra* note 32, at 571, 589. Professor Westen did not mean by this that the issue was meaningless or silly but rather that it depended on how one defined the relevant baseline.

95. *See* Dressler, *supra* note 11, at 1337–38 (observing that while the threat-offer distinction seems semantically questionable, it correctly expresses our intuitive sense about when the law of duress should excuse the actor from criminal responsibility).

96. The common-law rule, adopted in this country, was that confessions made in response to promises were inadmissible. Dix, *supra* note 1, at 279–80 & n.6. But in Stein v. New York, 346 U.S. 156 (1953), a divided Supreme Court upheld a finding that a confession to murder was voluntary even though the police, among other things, made commitments to release the defendant's father from custody and to refrain from prosecuting his brother for parole violations. The Court did not suggest, however, that the claim of involuntariness was out of bounds. Moreover, the Court found it important that the defendant, seemingly in full control, apparently dictated the terms on which he would confess. *Id.* at 186.

Nozick, *supra* note 66, at 452–53, offers the hypothetical of a defendant who, in return for a promise not to prosecute him on one crime, agrees to name the culprit in another. Viewing the police proposal as an offer, but recognizing that many would say the defendant had been coerced into supplying the information, Nozick leaves the issue unresolved. Nozick's hypothetical, which does not involve the question of using a defendant's statement as evidence against him, demonstrates once again the importance of knowing why we are asking the coercion question. For purposes of the law of confessions, it helps little to know that the defendant in Nozick's hypothetical may have been coerced in some linguistic sense.

97. 372 U.S. 528 (1963).

98. *Id.* at 533.

99. The defendant, however, did receive a sentence of ten to eleven years' imprisonment. *Id.* at 529. Because the precise promises the police made cannot be ascertained from the Court's opinion, it is possible that suspicion about a broken promise may really explain the decision. For further discussion of the possibility that *Lynumn,* despite its words, may reflect a concern with something other than the impairment of volitional freedom, see *infra* notes 104–5 and accompanying text.

100. 372 U.S. at 534.

101. *Cf.* Westen, *supra* note 32, at 584 (emphasis in original): "A proponent 'threatens' for purposes of coercion when he conditionally promises to leave a recipient in a position in which it would be *wrong* by the society's standards for the proponent to leave him for refusing to do the proponent's bidding."

102. *See* A. WERTHEIMER, *supra* note 13, at 103 (claiming that such a theory has not been developed). Something like the suggested approach is needed to deal with the case of blackmail. If a blackmailer has a right to release the information to the public, a proposal not to do so, for a payment, really is an offer (i.e., a proposal to improve the recipient's situation) under the two baseline approaches earlier considered in the text. On the other hand, if the wrongfulness of the proposal (i.e., "I will not do what I have a right to do") stems from the proposal being conditioned on the payment of money, blackmail can be viewed as coercive. For a treatment of the blackmail problem, *see, e.g., id.* at 219–20 (suggesting, in this context, that we need a theory on the morality of proposals); Nozick, *supra* note 66, at 452 (not resolving the blackmail issue); Westen, *supra* note 32, at 584 & n.130 (suggesting that blackmail involves a threat because the blackmailer is obligated "to refrain from conditioning the transmission of information to the police on the recipient's not paying him blackmail"). Of course, the possibility exists that blackmail should not be treated as coercive. *See* Epstein, *Blackmail, Inc.,* 50 U. CHI. L. REV. 553, 566 (1983).

Something like the approach suggested in the text also helps to explain the view in contracts law that the defense of duress will obtain if a contract is induced by a proposal not to file criminal charges that would otherwise be justifiable. *See* E.A. FARNSWORTH, *supra* note 65, § 4.17, at 275. A proposal not to do what one has a right to do cannot be viewed as wrongful; linking the proposal to the recipient's agreement to contract may be so viewed. *See* A. WERTHEIMER, *supra* note 13, at 43–44, 101–2.

103. See *supra* note 102 for a similar discussion of blackmail.

104. The possibility cannot be discounted that *Lynumn,* despite its emphasis on coercion, was more concerned about cognitive exploitation than volitional impairment. *See also supra* note 99. That is, the police in *Lynumn* were informing the defendant about legal consequences relating to her most important personal interests. Perhaps it was unfair to have her evaluate these possible consequences unaided by anyone who could provide her a neutral evaluation. Stated differently, whether or not coercion is involved, police exploitation of parental instincts to keep one's children may be as improper as the exploitation of one's desire to come clean to a

member of the clergy. It also is possible that *Lynumn* really reflects a concern about the trustworthiness of confessions made under such circumstances.

105. *See supra* note 104. Interestingly, Professor Wertheimer seemingly argues against applying even the exploitation concept in the millionaire hypothetical. See A. WERTHEIMER, *supra* note 13, at 236–37. *But see id.* at 238–41 (arguing, by analogy to usury laws, that some noncoercive agreements might be overridden by considerations of exploitation).

106. As previously indicated, the Supreme Court suggested in its first confessions case that a confession induced by a promise was invalid. *See supra* text accompanying note 4. *See also* Dix, *supra* note 1, at 279–85 & n.6.

107. Bram v. United States, 168 U.S. 532, 557–58 (1897).

108. Rogers v. Richmond, 365 U.S. 534, 544 (1961).

109. Townsend v. Sain, 372 U.S. 293, 307 (1963).

110. Malloy v. Hogan, 378 U.S. 1, 7 (1964).

111. 367 U.S. 568 (1961). *See supra* text accompanying note 9.

112. *Id.* at 602.

113. *See* Ducasse, *Critique of Hume's Conception of Causality,* in PHILOSOPHICAL PROBLEMS OF CAUSATION 6 (T. Beauchamp ed. 1974) [hereinafter CAUSATION]. This is not to say that the concepts are interchangeable. Compulsion, for example, refers to a particular kind of causation. *See* Moore, *supra* note 11, at 1129–32 (arguing that causation does not imply compulsion). As discussed in the text, some may even question whether the term *causation* is an appropriate substitute for these other terms.

114. See also the discussion of Colorado v. Connelly, 479 U.S. 157 (1986), in note 68, *supra. But see* Benner, *supra* note 68, at 128–29 (arguing that, for due process purposes, the evidentiary use of an involuntary statement against a defendant is unfair regardless of whether the state's agents caused the defendant to make the statement).

115. *See* H.L.A. HART & T. HONORÉ, CAUSATION IN THE LAW 51–57 (2d ed. 1985) [hereinafter HART & HONORÉ]; Kadish, *Complicity, Cause and Blame: A Study in the Interpretation of Doctrine,* 73 CAL. L. REV. 324, 327–36 (1985).

116. HART & HONORÉ, *supra* note 115, at 51 (emphasis in original).

117. Kadish, *supra* note 115, at 360–61.

118. *Id.* at 360.

119. It is not contradictory to say that a person's choice may be caused. To say that *A* caused *B* to act does not imply that *B* did not exercise will or that *B*'s will was overborne. *See* Moore, *supra* note 11, at 1129–32. As Professor Moore has said,

Behavior may be an action even if caused by mental states, physiological events, or environmental stimuli. To explain an act, a choice, or a willing, in terms of its causal antecedents, is not to explain it out of existence. Suppose we were to discover the physiological determinants of willing the motions of our bodies. That knowledge would not show us that we did not will motions; rather, it would show us more about what those willings were.

Id. at 1133.

120. Kadish, *supra* note 115, at 330–31.

121. *See* Moore, *supra* note 11, at 1112–37.

122. Kadish, *supra* note 115, at 334.

123. Dressler, *Reassessing the Theoretical Underpinnings of Accomplice Liability: New Solutions to an Old Problem,* 37 HASTINGS L.J. 91, 126–27 (1985).

124. See *supra* text accompanying notes 28–35.

125. While trying to avoid the concept of causation, Professor Kadish acknowledged that accomplice liability requires some notion of a "but-for condition." Kadish, *supra* note 115, at 361.

126. *Cf.* Frisbie v. Collins, 342 U.S. 519 (1952) (illegal arrest does not bar prosecution).

127. Y. KAMISAR, *supra* note 5, at 17 n.21. The independent source doctrine in "fruit of the poisonous tree" analysis demonstrates the need for a causal connection between the police misconduct and the evidence to be excluded. *See* Silverthorne Lumber Co. v. United States, 251 U.S. 385 (1920); *cf.* Nix v. Williams, 467 U.S. 431 (1984) (adopting inevitable discovery doctrine). *See also infra* note 128.

128. In the absence of a causal connection to police impropriety, the Supreme Court has refused to suppress the evidence the police were seeking to obtain. *See* Lisenba v. California, 314 U.S. 219, 239–41 (1941) (discussed in note 74, *supra); see also* Ashdown v. Utah, 357 U.S. 426, 431 (1958) (defendant's emotional distress attributable to personal remorse rather than to police conduct); Thomas v. Arizona, 356 U.S. 390, 400 (1958) (that members of arresting posse twice lassoed defendant around the neck deplorable; however, confession not a product of fear engendered by these actions).

129. A. WERTHEIMER, *supra* note 13, at 74 (emphasis in original).

130. *Id.* at 267 n.1.

131. *Id.*

132. Professor Frankfurt presented a similar example of a person who, having decided to give his money to the first person he will meet on the street, immediately confronts an armed robber. According to Frankfurt, the person is coerced into surrendering his money only if he acts out of fear but not if he acts pursuant to his original intention. "Evidently a threat is only coercive when it causes its victim to perform, from a motive by which he would prefer not to be moved, an action which *complies* with the threat." Frankfurt, *supra* note 22, at 81–82 (emphasis in original).

133. Even if we did not excuse the actor, we would probably still want to hold the coercer guilty as an accomplice. *Cf.* G. WILLIAMS, CRIMINAL LAW, THE GENERAL PART 359 (2d ed. 1961) (person who merely facilitates crime is responsible as accomplice even if actor would have committed crime anyway). That the issue of causation on the same set of facts may produce one result under the law of duress and another under the law of accomplice liability is not troubling once it is recognized that the issue requires a normative judgment that may differ depending on the legal context.

134. The quotation marks are needed because, as already discussed, the concept of overpowering cannot be taken literally.

135. *But see* Westen, *supra* note 32, at 569 & n.95 (disagreeing with this assertion).

136. Frankfurt, *supra* note 22, at 79–81.

137. Fingarette, *supra* note 29, at 111.

138. Murphy, *supra* note 36, at 81.

139. Nozick, *supra* note 66, at 464.

140. *Cf.* Fingarette, *supra* note 29, at 99–102 (suggesting that the law of confessions in fact requires minimal causation).

141. Even outside the context of moral or legal responsibility, the cause selected as *the* cause, or the primary, paramount, or crucial cause, of an event will depend on our purpose in asking the causal question. For example, those seeking merely an explanation of an event may focus on a different cause than those seeking to influence or control future events. Genetic endowment may provide a better explanation of lung cancer, but cigarette smoking will be a more significant cause for those seeking to eradicate this disease. Professor Collingwood stated the point well:

> [A] car skids while cornering at a certain point, strikes the kerb, and turns turtle. From the car driver's point of view the cause of the accident was cornering too fast, and the lesson is that one must drive more carefully. From the county surveyor's point of view the cause was a defect in the surface or camber of the road, and that lesson is that greater care must be taken to make roads skid-proof. From the manufacturer's point of view the cause was defective design in the car, and the lesson is that one must place the center of gravity lower.

Collingwood, *Three Senses of the Word "Cause,"* in CAUSATION, *supra* note 113, at 122. For a slightly different but in some respects similar account, see HART & HONORÉ, *supra* note 115, at 32–41.

142. *See* A. AYER, THE FOUNDATIONS OF EMPIRICAL KNOWLEDGE 191 (1940); Gorovitz, *Causal Judgments and Causal Explanations,* in CAUSATION, *supra* note 113, at 235.

143. Because the facts rarely, if ever, will be as easy as in illustration (4), it is possible that difficulties of proof will support a but-for approach. This too, however, is a normative argument.

144. In Blackburn v. Alabama, 361 U.S. 199, 207 (1960), the Court explicitly stated that the preservation of the individual's freedom of will was not the sole constitutional interest at stake. *See also* A. WERTHEIMER, *supra* note 13, at 120.

145. Lisenba v. California, 314 U.S. 219, 236 (1941).

146. Rochin v. California, 342 U.S. 165, 173 (1952). *Rochin,* however, did not involve an issue of police interrogation.

147. 360 U.S. 315, 323 (1959). The Court also referred to the defendant's emotional instability, a fact not necessarily related to the impairment of volitional freedom. *Id.* at 322.

148. 361 U.S. 199, 207 (1960). Colorado v. Connelly, 479 U.S. 157, 164–65 (1986), distinguished but did not overrule *Blackburn.*

149. Because *exploitation* does not always have a pejorative meaning, the term *improper exploitation* is not redundant. A pitcher, for example, may be commended for exploiting a batter's weakness for high fast balls. Of course, one can posit in a given discussion that exploitation is being used in its negative sense, but speaking explicitly of improper exploitation is more likely to avoid confusion.

Because of its voluntariness terminology and fact situations that virtually always involved some element of duress, the Court never clearly isolated an unfair advantage or improper exploitation component of the due process law of confessions. Nevertheless, such a concern seems clear in cases that refer to such things as the defendant's intelligence and education, which seem to have little bearing on the issue of volitional freedom. *See, e.g.,* Davis v. North Carolina, 384 U.S. 737, 742 (1966) (describing defendant as an impoverished black with fourth-grade education); Culombe v. Connecticut, 367 U.S. 568, 609, 620, 628 (1966) (describing defendant as an illiterate whose intelligence quotient was 64); Reck v. Pate, 367 U.S. 433, 441–42 (1961) (emphasizing, among other factors, that nineteen-year-old defendant had subnormal intelligence and no prior experience dealing with police); Payne v. Arkansas, 356 U.S. 560 (1958) (referring to facts that nineteen-year-old defendant was mentally dull and had only a fifth-grade education); Fikes v. Alabama, 352 U.S. 191, 193, 196–97 (1957) (including defendant's third-grade education and history of mental illness in totality of relevant circumstances).

150. 361 U.S. at 207.

151. *Compare* Kamisar, *supra* note 8, at 747 ("Ridding one's soul of a sense of guilt is no less a rare, pure instance of a 'voluntary' confession when, unbeknown to the confessor, a lawman sits in the confessional.") *with* A. WERTHEIMER, *supra* note 13, at 111 ("A confession to a policeman posing as a priest . . . would not be coerced, but is arguably less than fully voluntary."). Professor Kamisar was suggesting not that courts would or should allow such a confession into evidence but only that it is not accurate to describe the confession as "involuntary." Kamisar's point is valid if one thinks of the voluntariness concept as applying only to volitional impairment—to duress or coercion.

152. ARISTOTLE, *supra* note 14, at 1110b15–20.

153. See *supra* note 149.

154. *See* E.A. FARNSWORTH, *supra* note 65, § 4.20, at 283–86; § 4.28.

155. *See* B. BARRY, POLITICAL ARGUMENT 97 (1965).

156. *See generally id.* at 97–102.

157. *See* chapter 1.

158. Kauper, *Judicial Examination of the Accused—A Remedy for the Third Degree,* 30 MICH. L. REV. 1224, 1246 (1932).

159. White, *Police Trickery in Inducing Confessions,* 127 U. PA. L. REV. 581 (1979).

Chapter 4

1. Rosenberg & Rosenberg, *A Modest Proposal for the Abolition of Custodial Confessions,* 68 N. CAR. L. REV. 69, 112–13 (1989).

2. For a collection of authors urging the Court to go beyond *Miranda,* see Caplan, *Questioning* Miranda, 38 Vand. L. Rev. 1417, 1425 n.47 (1985).

3. *Compare* Y. Kamisar, Police Interrogation and Confessions 155 n.20 (1980) (zero pressure impossible) *with id.* at 160 (compulsion exists whenever police conduct is likely to exert a tug on suspect to speak) (borrowing phrase from Miranda v. Arizona, 384 U.S. 436, 515 (1966) (Harlan, Stewart & White, JJ., dissenting). For present purposes, it is irrelevant that Professor Kamisar relied on the Fifth Amendment self-incrimination clause rather than the due process clause for his antitug thesis. The point in the text is only that we have good policy reasons for *not* equating every "tug" with compulsion. That the Fifth Amendment does not mandate such unsound policy is the subject of the next chapter.

4. *See generally* Grano, *Voluntariness, Free Will, and the Law of Confessions,* 65 Va. L. Rev. 859, 864–65 n.33 (1979); Schulhofer, *Confessions and the Court,* 79 Mich. L. Rev. 865, 877 (1981).

5. *Miranda* does not apply unless the suspect is in custody. Oregon v. Mathiason, 429 U.S. 492 (1977); Beckwith v. United States, 425 U.S. 341 (1976). On the application of the voluntariness doctrine to *Miranda* waivers, see Colorado v. Connelly, 479 U.S. 157 (1986).

6. Mincey v. Arizona, 437 U.S. 385 (1978); Harris v. New York, 401 U.S. 222 (1971).

7. Oregon v. Elstad, 470 U.S. 298 (1985).

8. New York v. Quarles, 467 U.S. 649, 655 n.5 (1984). The scope of the *Quarles* rationale remains to be seen. Because the Court recently held, in a break with the past, that the harmless error doctrine applies to voluntariness challenges on appeal, see Arizona v. Fulminante, 111 S. Ct. 1246 (1991), the potential for disparate treatment of *Miranda* and voluntariness violations for harmless error purposes no longer exists.

9. U.S. Const. amends. V & XIV. For a fresh historical analysis of the Fourteenth Amendment in its entirety, see W. Nelson, The Fourteenth Amendment: From Political Principle to Judicial Doctrine (1988).

10. Magna Charta ch. 39 (1215), *reprinted in* A. Howard, Magna Carta, Text and Commentary (1964). Differences in translation exist; some translations, for example, use "or" rather than "and" in the words the text quotes. Magna Charta was reissued by John's son, Henry III, the third time in 1225, with chapter 39 appearing as chapter 29.

11. 28 Edw. III, ch. 3 (1354); *see also* A. Howard, *supra* note 10, at 13; Amar, *The Bill of Rights and the Fourteenth Amendment,* 101 Yale L.J. 1193, 1248–49 (1992).

12. *See, e.g.,* Davidson v. New Orleans, 96 U.S. 97, 101–2 (1878) (due process lacks precision of definition); *see also* Corwin, *The Doctrine of Due Process of Law before the Civil War,* 24 Harv. L. Rev. 366, 460 (1911) [hereinafter Corwin, *The Doctrine*]; Corwin, *The Supreme Court and the Fourteenth Amendment,* 7 Mich. L. Rev. 643 (1909); Sutherland, *Privacy in Connecticut,* 64 Mich. L. Rev. 283, 286 (1965).

13. *See generally,* R. BERGER, GOVERNMENT BY JUDICIARY 193–200 (1977); Corwin, *The Doctrine, supra* note 12, at 370–71; Corwin, *The "Higher Law" Background of American Constitutional Law* (pts. 1 & 2), 42 HARV. L. REV. 149, 175–85 (1928), 42 HARV. L. REV. 365, 367–80 (1929); Jurow, *Untimely Thoughts: A Reconsideration of the Origins of Due Process of Law,* 19 AM. J. LEGAL HIST. 265 (1975).

14. 59 U.S. (18 How.) 272 (1856).

15. *Id.* at 276; *see also* Davidson v. New Orleans, 96 U.S. 97, 101–2 (1878) (reaching the same conclusion with respect to the states under the Fourteenth Amendment). In *Davidson,* as in *Murray,* the Court offered little historical support for this conclusion. The Court's argument seemed to rest entirely on the assumption that the due process protection would be hollow if the legislature could define the process that was due.

16. See Jurow, *supra* note 13, at 266–79.

17. Professor Akhil Amar claims that the Court, in effect, concluded that the Fifth Amendment due process requirement "incorporated" all the other procedural requirements in the Bill of Rights. This conclusion, to Amar, provides critical support for the Fourteenth Amendment incorporation doctrine. Because the framers could not have intended Fourteenth Amendment due process to differ in meaning from Fifth Amendment due process, the Fourteenth Amendment, he insists, must bind the states to the same Bill of Rights requirements that bind the national government. Amar, *supra* note 11, at 1249–50. This argument is clever, indeed a bit too clever. *Murray* can be understood more plausibly as reiterating that the "law of the land" in federal cases includes those constitutional provisions that bind Congress. One cannot similarly assume that the "law of the land" in state cases includes laws that bind only the national government. The requisite symmetry in the meaning of the two due process clauses is achieved by noting that they require their respective governments to adhere to their respective laws.

18. 59 U.S. (18 How.) at 276–77.

19. Some scholarship has questioned both that "due process" at common law meant the same thing as Magna Charta's "law of the land" and that it imposed restraints on the legislature. *See* Jurow, *supra* note 13, at 271, 279. For an earlier questioning of the first proposition, *see* Corwin, *The Doctrine, supra* note 12, at 368.

20. Just one year after *Murray,* the Supreme Court decided Dred Scott v. Sanford, 60 U.S. (19 How.) 393 (1857). Chief Justice Taney's opinion, joined at this point by only two other justices, suggested, among other things, that the Missouri Compromise was unconstitutional because a law depriving a citizen of property (a slave) merely because he entered a certain state "could hardly be dignified with the name of due process of law." *Id.* at 450. Thus, the Taney opinion applied the due process clause to invalidate an act of Congress, for the first time read the due process clause as imposing substantive rather than procedural restraints, and necessarily turned to a source outside the text to discover the applicable limitation. *See* R. BORK, THE TEMPTING OF AMERICA 28–34 (1990); J. ELY, DEMOCRACY AND DISTRUST 15–16 (1980); Corwin, *The Doctrine, supra* note 12, at 475–77. For an earlier case using similar reasoning in dicta, see Bloomer v. McQuewan, 55 U.S. (14 How.) 539, 553 (1852). *But see* Davidson v. New Orleans, 96 U.S. 97, 104–5 (1878)

(although suggesting that due process would be violated by a law that, without more, transferred title from *A* to *B,* also indicating that due process required only a fair trial according to applicable modes of procedure).

21. Hurtado v. California, 110 U.S. 516, 521, 528 (1884).

22. *Id.* at 528–29; *see also* Walker v. Sauvinet, 92 U.S. 90 (1878) (due process does not require states to provide civil jury trial). For support of *Hurtado*'s use of history in interpreting due process, see Pacific Mutual Life Ins. Co. v. Haslip, 111 S. Ct. 1032, 1048–54 (1991) (Scalia, J., concurring). A majority of the present Court nevertheless seems disinclined to say for all cases that historical usage proves compliance with due process.

23. *Hurtado,* 110 U.S. at 530–31, 535.

24. *Id.* at 535–36. The suggestion had been made before. *See, e.g,* Munn v. Illinois, 94 U.S. 113 (1876) (upholding state regulation of rates charged by grain elevators); Loan Ass'n v. Topeka, 87 U.S. (20 Wall.) 655 (1875) (invalidating a statute without actually invoking the Constitution's text). *See also supra* note 20.

25. Allgeyer v. Louisiana, 165 U.S. 578, 591 (1897). The Court did not protect the right to pursue "unlawful" callings. Bartemeyer v. Iowa, 85 U.S. (18 Wall.) 129, 136–37 (1884). The Court apparently felt that it, rather than the legislature, enjoyed the prerogative to declare what was "lawful" and "unlawful."

26. 198 U.S. 45 (1905).

27. Corwin, *The Doctrine, supra* note 12, at 467–68. Whether *Lochner* could be justified on the basis of the Fourteenth Amendment's privileges or immunities clause is a different question. *Cf.* W. NELSON, *supra* note 9, at 148–200 (Fourteenth Amendment intended to give some protection to rights of property and contract; *Lochner* wrong in failing to give adequate weight to framers' intentions not to alter radically the structure of federalism); Amar, *supra* note 11, at 1231 (suggesting, without resolving, the possibility of finding "unspecified" rights under the privileges or immunities clause).

28. 211 U.S. 78 (1908).

29. *Id.* at 113. In Allgeyer v. Louisiana, 165 U.S. 578, 589 (1897), the first substantive due process holding under the Fourteenth Amendment, the Court spoke of the "inalienable right" to pursue the occupation of one's choice. In Holden v. Hardy, 169 U.S. 366, 387, 389–90 (1898), a case rejecting a substantive due process challenge to a law limiting the hours miners could work, the Court spoke of immutable principles of justice inhering in the very idea of free government. For the view that *Twining* intended to apply the concept of fundamental justice only when a state disregarded an ancient procedure, see Pacific Mutual Life Ins. Co. v. Haslip, 111 S. Ct. 1032, 1050 (1991) (Scalia, J., concurring).

30. 287 U.S. 45, 68, 71–72 (1932).

31. *See* Mooney v. Holohan, 294 U.S. 103, 112 (1935) (due process violated by prosecutor knowingly using perjured testimony to convict defendant); Moore v. Dempsey, 261 U.S. 86, 91 (1923) (due process violated by verdict produced by mob domination).

32. *But cf.* Siegan, *Rehabilitating* Lochner, 22 SAN DIEGO L. REV. 453 (1985) (defending *Lochner* and economic substantive due process); *see also* S. MACEDO, THE

New Right v. The Constitution (1987); B. Siegen, Economic Liberties and the Constitution (1980).

33. Otis v. Parker, 187 U.S. 606, 608–9 (1903). Justice Stevens, like others, has observed that Justice Holmes did not reject substantive due process altogether. *See* Stevens, *Judicial Restraint*, 22 San Diego L. Rev. 437, 450 (1985).

34. Lochner v. New York, 198 U.S. 45, 56–57 (1905). When the Court revived substantive due process in Roe v. Wade, 410 U.S. 113, 116–17 (1973), it made the same disclaimer.

35. Snyder v. Massachusetts, 291 U.S. 97, 105 (1934).

36. *Id.* Justice Scalia has criticized this language for suggesting a "fundamental justice" inquiry even in cases not involving departures from historical procedures. *See* Pacific Mutual Life Ins. Co. v. Haslip, 111 S. Ct. 1032, 1051 (1991) (Scalia, J., concurring).

37. 297 U.S. 278 (1936).

38. *Id.* at 285–86.

39. *Id.* at 281, 283; *see also* Paulsen, *The Fourteenth Amendment and the Third Degree*, 6 Stan. L. Rev. 411, 415 (1954).

40. Olsen v. Nebraska, 313 U.S. 236 (1941). The writing had been on the wall since the mid-1930s. *See, e.g.,* West Coast Hotel v. Parrish, 300 U.S. 379 (1937); Nebbia v. New York, 291 U.S. 502 (1934). That the second era of substantive due process, see note 34, *supra*, is not yet moribund was made apparent in Planned Parenthood of Southeastern Pa. v. Casey, 112 S. Ct. 2791, 2804–8 (1992) (O'Connor, Kennedy, & Souter, JJ.); *id.* at 2843–47 (Blackmun, J.); *id.* at 2838–39 (Stevens, J.).

41. 309 U.S. 227 (1940).

42. *Id.* at 239–40.

43. *See, e.g.,* Lisenba v. California, 314 U.S. 219, 237–41 (1941); Ward v. Texas, 316 U.S. 547, 555 (1941); Ashcraft v. Tennessee, 322 U.S. 143, 153–54 & n.9 (1944); *id.* at 157–62, 170–71 (Jackson, J., dissenting); Lyons v. Oklahoma, 322 U.S. 596, 602 (1944); Malinski v. New York, 324 U.S. 401, 404 (1945); *id.* at 428–29 (Rutledge, J., dissenting in part). *See also* text accompanying note 9 in chapter 3.

44. In Brown v. Mississippi, 297 U.S. 278, 285–86 (1936), for example, the Court recognized that states were constitutionally free to dispense with the protection against judicially compelled self-incrimination and the right to trial by jury. Because of the due process clause, however, they could not embrace trial by ordeal or compulsion by torture. For a historical study supporting the view that the framers of the Fourteenth Amendment intended to protect individual rights without drastically altering the existing view of federalism, see W. Nelson, *supra* note 9.

45. Snyder v. Massachusetts, 291 U.S. 97, 114 (1934).

46. Lisenba v. California, 314 U.S. 219, 236–37 (1941). See also the discussion at the beginning of chapter 3.

47. *Id.* at 236; *see also* Ward v. Texas, 316 U.S. 547, 550 (1942) ("Each State has the right to prescribe tests governing the admissibility of a confession. In various States there may be various tests.").

48. *Lisenba*, 314 U.S. at 239. *But see* Dix, *Mistake, Ignorance, Expectation of Benefit, and the Modern Law of Confessions*, 1975 WASH. U. L.Q. 275, 291–92 (Supreme Court and lower courts failed to distinguish how criteria of common law and constitutional rules differed in substance).

49. Ashcraft v. Tennessee, 322 U.S. 143, 174 (1944) (Jackson, J., dissenting). *See also supra* note 44.

50. The Court's five-to-four decision in Haynes v. Washington, 373 U.S. 503 (1963), perhaps was unique in justifying the complaint that the finding of involuntariness went beyond anything that the Court's due process precedent could justify. *Id.* at 525 (Clark, Harlan, Stewart, & White, JJ., dissenting). For a discussion of earlier Supreme Court cases that protected the accused from relatively mild pressures and minor deprivations, see Gorecki, *Miranda and Beyond—The Fifth Amendment Reconsidered*, 1975 U. ILL. L.F. 295, 305–8; Paulsen, *supra* note 39, at 417–23. *Cf.* Benner, *Requiem for* Miranda: *The Rehnquist Court's Voluntariness Doctrine in Historical Perspective*, 67 WASH. U. L.Q. 59, 114 (1989) (approvingly asserting that "the Court progressively civilized the meaning of due process").

51. Moran v. Burbine, 475 U.S. 412, 424, 432–34 (1986). *But see* Benner, *supra* note 50, at 131–54 (1989) (criticizing *Burbine* as well as other cases).

52. Disagreement exists over the terminology that most accurately describes the two predominant schools of thought and the differences within these schools regarding interpretational methodology in constitutional law. *See, e.g.,* Grey, *Do We Have an Unwritten Constitution?*, 27 STAN. L. REV. 703 (1975) (using the terms *interpretivism* and *noninterpretivism*); Grey, *The Constitution as Scripture*, 37 STAN. L. REV. 1 (1984) (substituting *textualist* for *interpretivist*); Bennett, *Objectivity in Constitutional Law*, 132 U. PA. L. REV. 445 (1984) (using the terms *originalism* and *nonoriginalism*); *see also* R. BORK, *supra* note 20, at 143–60 (using the term *original understanding*). The terms *textualism* and *originalism* are used loosely in this chapter to suggest an interpretational approach that limits itself to enforcing norms that the Constitution's text explicitly or implicitly protects. The opposite terms suggest an approach that permits judges to make normative judgments that cannot be derived from the text. *Cf.* J. ELY, *supra* note 20, at 1 (using similar descriptions to contrast *interpretivism* and *noninterpretivism*). For purposes of this chapter, more precise definition is unnecessary.

53. This is a fundamental problem for scholarship in constitutional law. *See, e.g.,* R. BERGER, *supra* note 13, at 412–13 ("utterly unrealistic and probably impossible" to undo past Fourteenth Amendment mistakes); R. BORK, *supra* note 20, at 155–59 (too late to correct decisional mistakes that have become embedded in the nation's life).

54. *Cf.* Planned Parenthood of Southeastern Pa. v. Casey, 112 S. Ct. 2791, 2808–16 (1992) (O'Connor, Kennedy, Souter, JJ.) (giving extreme weight to stare decisis); *see also* Monaghan, *Stare Decisis and Constitutional Adjudication*, 88 COLUM. L. REV. 723 (1988); Powell, *Stare Decisis and Judicial Restraint*, 47 WASH. & LEE L. REV. 281 (1990); Sherry, *The Eleventh Amendment and Stare Decisis: Overruling* Hans v. Louisiana, 57 U. CHI. L. REV. 1260 (1990).

55. *See Planned Parenthood of Southeastern Pa. See also supra* note 52.

56. See Nomination of Robert H. Bork to Be an Associate Justice of the United States Supreme Court, 100TH CONG., 1ST SESS., Report of the Committee on the Judiciary, U.S. Senate (1987).

57. J. ELY, *supra* note 20, at 45.

58. *Id.* at 44. Even commentators who essentially view constitutional interpretation as involving choices among competing values generally endorse the view that judges should not simply rely on their own values. *See, e.g.,* A. BICKEL, THE LEAST DANGEROUS BRANCH 235–43 (1962); Tribe & Dorf, *Levels of Generality in the Definition of Rights,* 57 U. CHI. L. REV. 1057, 1095–96 (1990) (vital that judges make serious effort to control their own biases); *cf.* Benner, *supra* note 50, at 149 (criticizing approach to coercion that permits judges to rely on personal values). *But cf.* M. PERRY, THE CONSTITUTION, THE COURTS, AND HUMAN RIGHTS 123 (1982) (while judges must rely on personal values, "[s]urely there are *practical* limits to what a judge should say is constitutionally required or forbidden, his own values notwithstanding") (emphasis in original).

59. *Cf.* J. ELY, *supra* note 20, at 58 ("'We like Rawls, you like Nozick. We win, 6-3.'").

60. Such a due process approach is broader than the one recently advocated by Justice Scalia, *see supra* note 22, but it is easier to square with existing voluntariness precedent.

61. J. ELY, *supra* note 20, at 44, 48–54, 60–63.

62. Adamson v. California, 332 U.S. 46, 92 (1947) (Black, J., dissenting). On the procedural side, Professor Ely conceded that judgment necessarily is "somewhat untethered." J. ELY, *supra* note 20, at 20–21.

63. *See, e.g.,* Ely, *The Wages of Crying Wolf: A Comment on* Roe v. Wade, 82 YALE L.J. 920 (1973).

64. Adamson v. California, 332 U.S. 46, 68 (1947) (Frankfurter, J., concurring).

65. Rochin v. California, 342 U.S. 165, 170 (1952).

66. *Id.* at 171–72.

67. Poe v. Ullman, 367 U.S. 497, 542 (1961) (Harlan, J., dissenting).

68. Griswold v. Connecticut, 381 U.S. 479, 501 (1965) (Harlan, J., concurring); *cf.* Planned Parenthood of Southeastern Pa. v. Casey, 112 S. Ct. 2791, 2805–6 (1992) (O'Connor, Kennedy, & Souter, JJ.) (relying on both Frankfurter and Harlan). On the importance of taking federalism into account, see note 44, *supra.*

By citing Justice Harlan, I do not intend to indicate approval of substantive due process. Nevertheless, a textualist might concede that substantive due process would be far less threatening to representative government in the hands of judges like Justice Harlan. The Court's recent opinion in *Casey,* however, suggests that judges really like Harlan are a rare commodity.

69. Poe v. Ullman, 367 U.S. 497, 539–40 (1961) (Harlan, J., dissenting).

70. For a collection of essays discussing the meaning of the Ninth Amendment in this regard, see THE RIGHTS RETAINED BY THE PEOPLE (R. Barnett ed. 1989).

71. *See* Nomination of Robert H. Bork, *supra* note 56.

72. *See, e.g., Casey;* Pacific Mutual Life Ins. Co. v. Haslip, 111 S. Ct. 1032 (1991); Cruzan v. Director, Missouri Dept. of Health, 497 U.S. 261 (1990) (assuming that the due process clause encompasses a protected liberty interest in refusing unwanted medical treatment). *See also supra* note 22.

73. *But cf.* Graglia, *Judicial Review on the Basis of "Regime Principles": A Prescription for Government by Judges,* 26 S. TEX. L.J. 435, 441 (1985) (constitutional law "has nothing to do with the Constitution"). Differences between Frankfurter's and Harlan's philosophies need not be explored here.

74. *Compare* Moore v. East Cleveland, 431 U.S. 494, 502–3 & n.12 (1977) (opinion by Powell, J.) (relying on "the teachings of history" and on the traditions and "basic values" that underlie our society) *with id.* at 549–51 (White, J., dissenting) (criticizing Powell's approach as conveying too much discretion to the Court and arguing for an "implicit in ordered liberty" approach). *See also* Duncan v. Louisiana, 391 U.S. 145, 148–49 & n.14 (1968) (referring to "fundamental principles of liberty and justice which lie at the base of all our [i.e., Anglo-American or just American] civil and political institutions").

I have previously criticized these approaches as hopelessly subjective. *See* Grano, *Judicial Review and a Written Constitution in a Democratic Society,* 28 WAYNE L. REV. 1, 8–11, 25–27 (1981). I again emphasize that I am talking now about second best interpretational strategies.

75. For Justice Scalia's attempts to cabin the Court's reliance on history, see *Pacific Mutual Life Ins. Co.,* 111 S. Ct. 1032, 1048–54 (1991) (Scalia, J., concurring). *See also* Michael H. v. Gerald D., 491 U.S. 110, 127 n.6 (1989) (plurality opinion) ("We refer to the most specific level at which a relevant tradition protecting, or denying protection to, the asserted right can be identified."). Justices O'Connor and Kennedy refused to join this footnote. *Id.* at 132 (O'Connor & Kennedy, JJ., concurring in part). For a criticism of Scalia's approach, see Tribe & Dorf, *supra* note 58. The Court has elsewhere noted the difficulty of relying on history. *See, e.g.,* Garcia v. San Antonio, 469 U.S. 528, 544–45 (1985) (because American history represents a "continuum from before the Revolution to the present," courts can decide only by fiat when a practice is sufficiently longstanding to be rooted in history).

76. See *supra* notes 34 and 66 and accompanying text.

77. Rochin v. California, 342 U.S. 165, 172 (1952). Though the state courts had not reversed the defendant's conviction, Justice Frankfurter observed that all the state judges who expressed themselves on the matter condemned the police conduct at issue in the strongest language. *Id.* at 174. See also Justice Cardozo's words for the Court in Snyder v. Massachusetts, 291 U.S. 97, 127 (1934): "In whatsoever proceeding . . . the Fourteenth Amendment commands the observance of that standard of common fairness, the failure to observe which would offend men's sense of the decencies and proprieties of civilized life."

78. Benner, *supra* note 50, at 131; *see also* Rochin v. California, 342 U.S. 165, 175–76 (1952) (Black, J., concurring) (objecting to the nebulous standards used by the majority).

79. *See supra* note 50.

80. *Rochin,* 342 U.S. at 168.

81. *Id.* (quoting Justice Cardozo's opinions in Snyder v. Massachusetts, 291 U.S. 97, 105 (1934), and in Palko v. Connecticut, 302 U.S. 319, 325 (1937)). The Court has recently reiterated that the category of infractions that violate "fundamental fairness" is defined "very narrowly." Beyond the limitations in the Bill of Rights, "the Due Process Clause has limited operation." Estelle v. McGuire, 112 S. Ct. 475, 482 (1991); Dowling v. United States, 493 U.S. 342, 352 (1990).

82. *See supra* notes 65–66 and accompanying text.

83. *Cf.* Paulsen, *supra* note 39, at 429–32 (arguing for an "outrageousness" standard in the law of confessions).

84. Poe v. Ullman, 367 U.S. 497, 541–43 (1961) (Harlan, J., dissenting).

85. Tribe & Dorf, *supra* note 58, at 1105 ("Had *Griswold* involved the right to abortion, it might have come out differently, but if it had involved the right to drive without a seatbelt it would not even have been *Griswold.*"). Even better, contrast a mandatory seatbelt law with a law that takes A, the husband of B, and makes him the husband of C. Loan Association v. Topeka, 87 U.S. (20 Wall.) 655, 663 (1875) (giving this as example of a law the judiciary in a free society would declare void). That such a law would not be enacted does not defeat the point that the seatbelt law is fundamentally different. Likewise, the use of torture to procure a confession is fundamentally different from the use of trickery.

86. Rochin v. California, 342 U.S. 165, 172 (1952). Frankfurter added that this did "not make due process of law a matter of judicial caprice." *Id.*

87. *See* chapter 3, notes 46–48 and accompanying text.

88. *See supra* note 81 and accompanying text.

89. *Cf.* Kahn, *Confessions to Police,* 52 J. CRIM. L. 96, 96 (1988) (voluntariness as a condition of admissibility now a "well established principle of civilised laws"); *see also,* Benner, *supra* note 50, at 92–101 (tracing the early development of the voluntariness requirement); Johnson, *Confessions, Criminals, and Community,* 26 HARV. C.R.-C.L. L. REV. 327 (1991) (providing an elaborate explanation of why the voluntariness requirement is important).

90. 297 U.S. 278 (1936).

91. 384 U.S. 436 (1966).

92. Perhaps it can also be said that these principles are among the few that can plausibly be described as implicit in the concept of ordered liberty. See *supra* note 81 and accompanying text for a discussion of these concepts.

93. *See* J. LANGBEIN, TORTURE AND THE LAW OF PROOF 3–16 (1977).

94. *Id. But see* Damaska, Book Review, 87 YALE L.J. 860 (1978) (giving more credit to Enlightenment criticisms of torture).

95. International agreements have condemned the use of torture. *See, e.g.,* [European] Convention for the Protection of Human Rights and Fundamental Freedoms, Nov. 4, 1950, art. 3, 213 U.N.T.S. 221 (agreement by twenty-three European nations prohibiting torture and degrading treatment or punishment); Universal Declaration of Human Rights, 1948, G.A. Res. 217A (III), U.N. Doc. A/810, at 71 (1948) (same prohibition); Convention against Torture and Other Cruel, Inhu-

man or Degrading Treatment or Punishment, Dec. 17, 1984, G.A. Res. 39/46, 39 U.N. GAOR Supp. (No. 51) 197, U.N. Doc. A/39/51 (1984) (obligating party states to take legal measures to prevent torture; torture defined, in part, as infliction of severe pain or suffering, physical or mental, for the purpose of obtaining a confession). Citing these sources is not meant to suggest that international agreements automatically define what is fundamental for due process purposes; rather, these sources merely provide evidentiary support for the statement in the text that freedom from torture, whatever the original motives of the abolitionists, is now broadly considered a basic human right.

This is not to suggest that torture has disappeared from the world scene. The almost universal condemnation of torture is apparent, however, in what seems to be the widely perceived need to deny that torture was employed.

96. J. LANGBEIN, *supra* note 93, at 73–93, 129–39 (discussing torture in English practice). For a more detailed study of torture in England, see J. HEATH, TORTURE AND ENGLISH LAW (1982).

97. J. LANGBEIN, *supra* note 93, at 134–39.

98. *See* Benner, *supra* note 50, at 95–99; Berger, *Legislating Confession Law in Great Britain: A Statutory Approach to Police Interrogations,* 24 U. MICH. J.L. REF. 1, 8 (1990); Dix, *supra note 48,* at 279–85. English statutory law makes inadmissible confessions obtained by "oppression," defined, in accordance with the European Convention on Human Rights, *supra* note 95, as including "torture, inhuman or degrading treatment, and the use or threat of violence." *See* Police and Criminal Evidence Act, 1984, ch. 60, §§ 76(2), 76(8).

99. See sources cited *supra* note 95.

100. *See* Grano, *supra* note 4, at 868–80 (stressing the importance of the free will postulate in both substantive and procedural law); Pillsbury, *The Meaning of Deserved Punishment: An Essay on Choice, Character, and Responsibility,* 67 IND. L.J. 719 (1992); *see also* Pea v. United States, 397 F.2d 627, 634 (D.C. Cir.) (discussing the free will postulate), *aff'd en banc,* 397 F.2d 637 (D.C. Cir. 1967).

101. McCormick, *Some Problems and Developments in the Admissibility of Confessions,* 24 TEX. L. REV. 239, 241 (1946).

102. J. LANGBEIN, *supra* note 93, at 12–16.

103. *See* Langbein, *Torture and Plea Bargaining,* 46 U. CHI. L. REV. 3, 4–8 (1978) (safeguards in the law of torture never overcame the flaw that innocent persons were made to confess).

104. *Brown,* 297 U.S. at 285.

105. *Id.* at 285, 286. Were it possible to write on a clean slate, it might be worthwhile to explore whether freedom from torture should be regarded as one of the Fourteenth Amendment's "privileges or immunities of citizens of the United States." *See generally* W. NELSON, *supra* note 9; Amar, *supra* note 11.

106. 297 U.S. at 285–86.

107. *Miranda,* 384 U.S. at 457, 491–92, 518.

108. *Id.* at 457.

109. *Id.* at 518, 519 (Harlan, Stewart, & White, JJ., dissenting).

110. Blackburn v. Alabama, 361 U.S. 199, 206 (1960); *see also* Watts v. Indiana, 338 U.S. 49, 52 (1949); Chambers v. Florida, 309 U.S. 227, 237 (1940) (speaking of both physical and mental torture).

111. 324 U.S. 401 (1945).

112. *Id.* at 407.

113. It should be recalled that some disagreement exists over whether the defendant's capitulation must be the only reasonable choice or simply a reasonable choice. *See* chapter 3, note 65. While the limited nature of a due process inquiry may make the first choice more attractive, the case law seems more consistent with a standard somewhere between the first and second.

114. 309 U.S. 227 (1940). For other cases involving lengthy incarceration, see Davis v. North Carolina, 384 U.S. 737 (1966) (more than two weeks); Harris v. South Carolina, 338 U.S. 68 (1949) (several days); *Watts* (several days).

115. 309 U.S. at 239–40.

116. *Id.* at 236–37. *Cf.* County of Riverside v. McLaughlin, 111 S. Ct. 1661 (1991) (as a general matter, Constitution requires person to receive a judicial determination of probable cause within forty-eight hours of arrest).

117. 322 U.S. 143 (1944).

118. *Id.* at 154.

119. *Id.* at 157 (Jackson, J., dissenting) (emphasis in original).

120. According to Professor Paulsen, *Ashcraft* is the case in which the Court shifted its due process analysis from a concern about reliability to one about standards of decency. Paulsen, *supra* note 39, at 417.

121. *See* chapter 3, text accompanying notes 65–70. *See also supra* note 113.

122. *Cf.* Dressler, *New Thoughts about the Concept of Justification in the Criminal Law: A Critique of Fletcher's Thinking and* Rethinking, 32 UCLA L. Rev. 61 (1984) (distinguishing justification and excuse).

123. *See* Ritz, *Twenty-five Years of State Criminal Confession Cases in the U.S. Supreme Court,* 19 Wash. & Lee L. Rev. 35, 46 (1962) (making this claim); Comment, *The Decade of Change Since the Ashcraft Case,* 32 Tex. L. Rev. 429, 430 (1954) (Court paid no regard to how Ashcraft responded to police). What the Court disregarded is whether Ashcraft *could have* resisted, a pointless question as this chapter and the preceding one have tried to make clear.

124. 372 U.S. 528 (1963). *See* chapter 3, text accompanying notes 97–104.

125. For other cases involving possibly analogous facts, compare Harris v. South Carolina, 338 U.S. 68, 70 (1949) (sheriff threatened to arrest defendant's mother; defendant responded he would tell truth if sheriff did not get mother "mixed up in it"; Court, relying on other factors, finds confession involuntary) with Stein v. New York, 346 U.S. 156 (1953) (defendant confessed after negotiating commitments relating to father and brother; Court upheld use of confession relying on defendant's ability to dictate terms of confession).

126. For the irrelevance of the offer-threat distinction to the voluntariness issue in the law of confessions, see chapter 3.

127. *Ashcraft,* 322 U.S. at 162 (Jackson, J., dissenting). Race was obviously relevant in cases coming from the South in the 1930s and 1940s.

128. 332 U.S. 596 (1948).

129. *Id.* at 599.

130. *Id.* at 599–600.

131. *Id.* at 606–7 (Frankfurter, J., concurring).

132. *Id.* at 602–4, 607.

133. *Id.* at 606.

134. *Id.* at 606–7.

135. *Id.* at 620 (Burton, J., dissenting). Disputed facts about police violence had been resolved against the defendant at the trial level.

136. For cases more indicative of a due process violation and in which the defendant's age played a role in the Court's analysis, see Reck v. Pate, 367 U.S. 433 (1961) (nineteen-year-old defendant, with subnormal intelligence, held eight days; defendant inadequately fed and twice taken to hospital for illness); Payne v. Arkansas, 356 U.S. 560 (1958) (nineteen-year-old defendant held in custody over forty hours; officer indicated he could probably protect defendant from outside mob if defendant would tell the truth).

137. *See, e.g.,* Rogers v. Richmond, 365 U.S. 534, 543–44 (1961); Lisenba v. California, 314 U.S. 219, 236 (1941).

138. *See* Inbau, *Police Interrogation—A Practical Necessity,* 52 J. Crim. L. Criminology & Police Sci. 16 (1961).

139. F. Inbau, J. Reid, & J. Buckley, Criminal Interrogation and Confessions 216–17 (3d ed. 1986) [hereinafter F. Inbau]. The hypothetical facts were originally suggested in Rothman v. Regina, 1 S.C.R. 640, 697 (1981) (Lamer, J., concurring); *see also* Bator & Vorenberg, *Arrest, Detention, Interrogation and the Right to Counsel: Basic Problems and Possible Legislative Solutions,* 66 Colum. L. Rev. 62, 74 (1966) (law should not treat all deception the same).

140. J. Strong et al., McCormick on Evidence §§ 76.2, 87 (4th ed. 1992).

141. *Developments in the Law—Privileged Communications,* 98 Harv. L. Rev. 1450, 1555–56 (1985).

142. *Id.* at 1501. The clergy-communicant privilege has few detractors. *Id.* at 1556.

143. 347 U.S. 556 (1954).

144. McCormick, *supra* note 140, at § 98 & n.1 (citing The Duchess of Kingston's Trial, 20 How. St. Trials 573 (1776)).

145. *Id.* at §§ 76.2, 98.

146. *Developments in the Law, supra* note 141, at 1539.

147. *Id.* at 1546–47 & nn.116–19 (citing the AMA's Principles of Medical Ethics and the Hippocratic Oath).

148. *Id.* at 1545–48; *see also* McCormick, *supra* note 140, at § 98.

149. *Cf.* Dix, *Undercover Investigations and Police Rulemaking,* 53 Tex. L. Rev. 203, 221–24 (1975) (proposing a rule that would protect all professional relationships). That such a broad rule could be required by due process may be doubted.

150. Illinois v. Perkins, 496 U.S. 292, 297 (1990) (speaking in a Fifth Amendment context).

151. *Id.*

152. F. INBAU, *supra* note 139, at 96–125.

153. *Id.* at 68–74. For other surveys of the various techniques of deception, see Leo, *From Coercion to Deception: The Changing Nature of Police Interrogation in America,* 18 CRIME, L. & SOC. CHANGE 35, 43–47 (1992); Comment, *Police Use of Trickery As an Interrogation Technique,* 32 VAND. L. REV. 1167 (1979).

154. F. INBAU, *supra* note 139, at 133.

155. Weisberg, *Police Interrogation of Arrested Persons: A Skeptical View,* 52 J. CRIM. L. CRIMINOLOGY & POLICE SCI. 21, 32 (1961).

156. White, *Police Trickery in Inducing Confessions,* 127 U. PA. L. REV. 581, 627–28 (1979).

157. Greenawalt, *Silence as a Moral and Constitutional Right,* 23 WM. & MARY L. REV. 15, 40–41 (1981).

158. Dix, *supra* note 48, at 347. Dix would apply his approach even to statements volunteered without interrogation. *Id.* at 358. For other approaches to trickery, see Comment, *Guarding the Guardians: Police Trickery and Confessions,* 40 STAN. L. REV. 1544, 1609–11 (1988) (police trickery unfair; unsatisfactory to have one side "win . . . by not playing by the rules"); Comment, *supra* note 153, at 1190–1202 (substantive due process should prohibit confronting suspect with proof that does not exist).

159. Uviller, *Tricky Business: Under Cover with Gary Marx,* 14 LAW & SOC. INQUIRY 361, 369 (1989) (reviewing G. MARX, UNDERCOVER: POLICE SURVEILLANCE IN AMERICA (1988)).

160. *Id.* at 375; *cf.* Leo, *supra* note 153, at 54 ("As with covert means, deceptive interrogation techniques may be a necessary evil in modern society.").

161. Gorecki, *supra* note 50, at 306; *see also* Leo, *supra* note 153, at 54 ("While physical violence during police questioning is repugnant to modern sensibilities, there is little shared consensus about where to draw the line between permissible and impermissible deceptive police tactics, for the use of deception raises more subtle, complex, and morally vexing issues than physical coercion.").

162. State v. McKnight, 52 N.J. 35, 53, 243 A.2d 240, 250–51 (1968), *quoted in* Gorecki, *supra* note 50, at 307.

163. For a consideration of the competing arguments about lying, see S. BOK, LYING: MORAL CHOICE IN PUBLIC AND PRIVATE LIFE (1978); C. FRIED, RIGHT AND WRONG 54–78 (1978). The most we can say from the standpoint of society's judgment is that "deceptive interrogation practices are fraught with moral ambiguity." Leo, *supra* note 153, at 36, 54.

164. F. INBAU, *supra* note 139, at 319. The "movement from coercion to deception" may even be viewed as "a triumph in the rule of law." Leo, *supra* note 153, at 54.

165. Uviller, *supra* note 159, at 364.

166. Dix, *supra* note 48, at 284.

167. *Cf.* White, *supra* note 156, at 608–11. *See also* Bator & Vorenberg, *supra* note 139, at 74 ("Some forms of deception, such as deceiving a man as to his rights or having someone pose as his counsel, must clearly be prohibited.").

168. White, *supra* note 156, at 609 & n.150; *cf.* Doyle v. Ohio, 426 U.S. 610, 618 (1976) (violation of due process to tell defendant he has a right of silence and then to use silence against him); Santobello v. New York, 404 U.S. 257 (1971) (violation of due process to break promise in plea bargain).

169. Y. KAMISAR, *supra* note 3, at 11; Dix, *supra* note 48.

170. *Cf.* Neil v. Biggers, 409 U.S. 188, 198 (1972) (finding a due process violation in police use of a suggestive identification procedure).

171. *See* chapter 2, text accompanying note 148.

172. The approach advocated here is both different from and narrower than the approach I advocated in 1979. *See* Grano, *supra* note 4.

173. Y. KAMISAR, *supra* note 3, at 14 (reprinting a 1963 article).

174. Schulhofer, *supra* note 4, at 869–73.

175. *Id.* at 872. In reality, police interrogators today are less likely to resort to coercion than their predecessors. It has been suggested that *Brown v. Mississippi* more than *Miranda* helped to bring about this change. Leo, *supra* note 153, at 52, 54.

176. Schulhofer, *supra* note 4, at 872.

177. *Cf.* Moran v. Burbine, 475 U.S. 412, 425 (1986) ("Nothing in the Constitution vests in us the authority to mandate a code of behavior for state officials wholly unconnected to any federal right or privilege.").

178. Schulhofer, *supra* note 4, at 870.

179. Caplan, *supra* note 2, at 1432–34; Gorecki, *supra* note 50, at 310–11.

180. Berger, *supra* note 98, at 3.

181. *Id.* at 5. Pursuant to and supplementing statutory law, the British Home Office has also promulgated an extremely detailed Code entitled *Code of Practice for the Detention, Treatment and Questioning of Persons by Police Officers* (1985). For reviews of this code and its recent revisions, see both Berger, *supra,* and Wolchover & Heaton-Armstrong, *The Questioning Code Revamped,* 1991 CRIM. L. REV. 232.

182. Berger, *supra* note 98, at 64. *See also* Bator & Vorenberg, *supra* note 139, at 63 ("A legislature may also frankly engage in a process of line-drawing which in a court decision must seem arbitrary."). One should not assume that the local failure to address police interrogation before *Miranda* would persist if *Miranda* was removed from the books in the far different world of the 1990s.

Chapter 5

1. Grano, *Introduction—The Changed and Changing World of Constitutional Criminal Procedure: The Contribution of the Department of Justice's Office of Legal Policy,* 22 U. MICH. J.L. REF. 395, 395–402 (1989). *Contra* Arenella, *Rethinking the Functions of Criminal Procedure: The Warren and Burger Courts' Competing Ideologies,* 72 GEO. L.J. 185 (1983). For other essays on this topic, see THE BURGER COURT: THE COUNTER-REVOLUTION THAT WASN'T (V. Blasi ed. 1983); THE BURGER YEARS: RIGHTS AND WRONGS IN THE SUPREME COURT 1969–1986 (H. Schwartz ed. 1987); Saltzburg, *Foreword: The Flow and Ebb of Constitutional Criminal Procedure in the Warren and Burger Courts,* 69 GEO. L.J. 151 (1980); Seidman, *Factual*

Guilt and the Burger Court: An Examination of Continuity and Change in Criminal Procedure, 80 COLUM. L. REV. 436 (1980).

2. Crooker v. California, 357 U.S. 433 (1958); Cicenia v. LaGay, 357 U.S. 504 (1958).

3. Escobedo v. Illinois, 378 U.S. 478 (1964); Massiah v. United States, 377 U.S. 201 (1964).

4. 384 U.S. 436 (1966).

5. *Id.* at 460.

6. U.S. CONST. amend. V.

7. *Miranda*, 384 U.S. at 510 (Harlan, Stewart, White, JJ., dissenting).

8. Malloy v. Hogan, 378 U.S. 1 (1964).

9. *See, e.g.,* Barron v. Mayor and City Council, 32 U.S. (7 Pet.) 243 (1833). For analysis and support of *Barron,* see Amar, *The Bill of Rights and the Fourteenth Amendment,* 101 YALE L.J. 1193, 1198–1212 (1992).

10. Whitney v. California, 274 U.S. 357, 371 (1927); *id.* at 373 (Brandeis & Holmes, JJ., concurring); Gitlow v. New York, 268 U.S. 652, 666 (1925); *id.* at 672 (Holmes & Brandeis, JJ., dissenting); *cf.* Chicago, B. & Q.R. Co. v. Chicago, 166 U.S. 226 (1897) (due process requires just compensation when city takes property).

11. Justice Black, an opponent of substantive due process and "fundamental fairness" due process jurisprudence, tried to avoid the interpretational difficulty by insisting that the framers and ratifiers of the Fourteenth Amendment intended to apply *all* of the Bill of Rights to the states. *See* Duncan v. Louisiana, 391 U.S. 145, 162–71 (1968) (Black, J., concurring); Adamson v. California, 332 U.S. 46, 68–92 (1947) (Black, J., dissenting). For a more recent effort to defend Black's position by relying on the privileges or immunities clause, see J. ELY, DEMOCRACY AND DISTRUST 24–28 (1980). Ely is criticized on this point in Grano, *Ely's Theory of Judicial Review: Preserving the Significance of the Political Process,* 42 OHIO ST. L.J. 167, 171–73 (1981). For other defenses of incorporation relying on the privileges or immunities clause, see M. CURTIS, NO STATE SHALL ABRIDGE: THE FOURTEENTH AMENDMENT AND THE BILL OF RIGHTS (1986); Amar, *supra* note 9 (relying on the privileges or immunities clause but rejecting total incorporation). *See also infra* note 34.

12. In Cantwell v. Connecticut, 310 U.S. 296 (1940), the Court applied the First Amendment's free exercise clause to the states and in Everson v. Board of Educ., 330 U.S. 1 (1947), it applied the First Amendment's establishment clause to the states. For a review of the incorporation that occurred in the 1960s, see Duncan v. Louisiana, 391 U.S. 145 (1968).

13. 211 U.S. 78 (1908).

14. *Id.* at 110.

15. *Id.* at 113; *see also* Palko v. Connecticut, 302 U.S. 319, 324 (1937) (dictum that states may dispense with the privilege).

16. 332 U.S. 46 (1947).

17. *Id.* at 54–55; *see also* Dripps, *Foreword: Against Police Interrogation—And the Privilege against Self-Incrimination,* 78 J. CRIM. L. & CRIMINOLOGY 699, 718 (1988) ("There is a difference between compelled testimony and a coerced confession.").

18. 332 U.S. at 59 (Frankfurter, J., concurring). *But see* Levy, *The Right against Self-Incrimination: History and Judicial History,* 84 Pol. Sci. Q. 1, 2–8 (1969) (criticizing *Twining*'s use of history).

19. 378 U.S. 1 (1964).

20. Y. Kamisar, Police Interrogation and Confessions 79 (1980) (quoting Herman, *The Supreme Court and Restrictions on Police Interrogation,* 25 Ohio St. L.J. 449, 465 (1964)). Kamisar also faulted the *Malloy* opinion's use of history. Y. Kamisar, *supra,* at 45.

21. 378 U.S. at 6–8. As discussed later in this chapter, the Fifth Amendment has different meanings in different contexts. To the extent that the Court saw a similarity between Fifth and Fourteenth Amendment voluntariness doctrine, see the text *infra* at notes 135–37, it was on solid ground. This similarity, however, would not justify application to the states of Fifth Amendment requirements going beyond voluntariness.

22. 367 U.S. 643 (1961).

23. 378 U.S. at 8.

24. *Id.* at 7–9.

25. *See* Dripps, *supra* note 17, at 718 n.80, 729 (citing, among other cases, Malinski v. New York, 324 U.S. 401, 416 (1945), and Brown v. Mississippi, 297 U.S. 278, 285 (1936)). *See also supra* note 21 and *infra* text accompanying notes 135–37.

26. Dripps, *supra* note 17, at 729.

27. Andresen v. Maryland, 427 U.S. 463 (1976) (Fifth Amendment does not protect evidence seized in search); Schmerber v. California, 384 U.S. 757 (1966) (Fifth Amendment does not protect physical evidence).

28. *Mapp* overruled Wolf v. Colorado, 338 U.S. 25 (1949). *Wolf* merely affirmed what had been the law since Weeks v. United States, 232 U.S. 383 (1914), created a federal exclusionary rule.

29. 378 U.S. at 7.

30. Much of the discussion in chapter 2 negates the argument that the Fifth Amendment privilege reflects a fundamental principle of justice. *See also* Foote, *Confessions and the Right of Silence in Japan,* 21 Ga. J. Int'l & Comp. L. 415 (1991) (documenting dim view Japanese take regarding restrictions on police interrogation); Thomas, *The So-Called Right to Silence,* 14 N.Z.U. L. Rev. 299 (1991) (urging repeal of the "so-called" right).

31. Dripps, *supra* note 17, at 729. One might claim, however, that the protection against compulsory self-incrimination is rooted in *American* history and tradition. *Cf.* Levy, *supra* note 18, at 2–8 (criticizing *Twining*'s review of history). Although Justice Harlan was prepared to concede that protection from imprisonment for failure to answer questions was so rooted, he correctly noted that not all aspects of the Fifth Amendment's protection similarly are fundamental. *Malloy,* 378 U.S. at 15–17 & n.1, 24–30 (Harlan, J., dissenting). *See also infra* notes 32–34 and accompanying text.

32. *See, e.g., Malloy,* 378 U.S. at 24–27 (Harlan, J., dissenting). For Holmes's suggestion, see Gitlow v. New York, 268 U.S. 652, 672 (1925) (Holmes & Brandeis,

JJ., dissenting) (states may have more leeway in regulating speech than Congress). *See also supra* text accompanying note 10.

33. *See supra* note 11.

34. *Malloy,* 378 U.S. at 10–11 (majority opinion). Justice Brennan's approach, which combined selective incorporation with a non-watered down application to the states of incorporated provisions, would be coherent under the incorporation analysis offered by Professor Amar. *See supra* note 11. Suffice it to observe, however, that the Court has not embraced anything resembling Professor Amar's approach. Nor is it likely to do so, for under his approach the Court would at least have to consider both incorporating the Fifth Amendment's indictment provision and the Seventh Amendment's civil jury trial provision and reversing its incorporation of the First Amendment's establishment clause. Amar, *supra* note 9, at 1248–50, 1264; *see also* Amar, *The Bill of Rights as a Constitution,* 100 YALE L.J. 1131, 1157–61, 1183–99 (1991). Aside from pragmatic considerations that make such changes unlikely, Professor Amar's views on incorporation are controversial on the merits. *See, e.g.,* W. NELSON, THE FOURTEENTH AMENDMENT: FROM POLITICAL PRINCIPLE TO JUDICIAL DOCTRINE 117–19 (1988) (incorporation puzzle solved by understanding Fourteenth Amendment as guaranteeing equal but not absolute protection of rights); Harrison, *Reconstructing the Privileges or Immunities Clause,* 101 YALE L.J. 1385, 1391–96, 1465–66 (1992) (similar).

35. See Johnson v. Louisiana, 406 U.S. 356, 371–77 (1972) (Powell, J., concurring) (adopting Harlan's view; casting fifth vote, first, with one set of four justices to read Sixth Amendment in federal cases as requiring unanimity, second, with remaining four justices to allow states to dispense with unanimous jury verdicts).

36. A defender of expansive readings of the Fifth Amendment, historian Leonard Levy has acknowledged that *Miranda* "expanded the right beyond all precedent." Claiming, however, that the "ghost of John Lilburne wrote that opinion," Levy has defended it as consistent with the right's "historical spirit and purpose." Levy, *supra* note 18, at 28. Even if Levy is correct about the Fifth Amendment's purpose and spirit, his concession regarding Fifth Amendment precedent is fatal to any claim that *Miranda's* controversial requirements are rooted in the traditions and conscience of our nation.

37. 168 U.S. 532 (1897), *cited and quoted in Miranda,* 384 U.S. at 461–62.

38. 168 U.S. at 542.

39. *Id.* at 543, 548.

40. 3 J. WIGMORE, A TREATISE ON THE ANGLO-AMERICAN SYSTEM OF EVIDENCE IN TRIALS AT COMMON LAW § 823, at 250 n.5 (3d ed. 1940).

41. *Id.* at 250 (emphasis in original). Wigmore asserted that the common-law confessions rule essentially asked whether an inducement created "any fair risk of a false confession." *Id.* § 824, at 252.

42. *Id.* n.5.

43. 8 *id.* § 2266, at 387 (emphasis in original).

44. *Id.* § 2250, at 298–301; *see also* M. BERGER, TAKING THE FIFTH 1–20 (1980) (summarizing the history); E. MORGAN, BASIC PROBLEMS OF EVIDENCE 127 (1954) (not clear how original protests against ex officio oaths grew into a right of a defen-

dant in a common-law court to refuse to answer questions). On the seventeenth-century ambivalence about the scope of the protection, see L. LEVY, ORIGINS OF THE FIFTH AMENDMENT 325–26 (1968) (judicial questioning of accused persisted in preliminary examinations into eighteenth century).

45. 8 J. WIGMORE, *supra* note 40, § 2266, at 387; *see also* 3 *id.* § 818–19, at 232–38.

46. 3 *id.* § 823, at 249. Actually, Wigmore denied that the *theories* of the two rules had any connection. In another sentence, he denied that the rules had "any historical connection." *Id.* at 250 n.5.

47. J. MAGUIRE, EVIDENCE OF GUILT 15–17 (1959); E. MORGAN, *supra* note 44, at 129–31.

48. Levy, *supra* note 18, at 26; *see also* L. LEVY, *supra* note 44, at 495 n.43; Urick, *The Right against Compulsory Self-Incrimination in Early American Law,* 20 COLUM. HUMAN RTS. L. REV. 107, 117 n.39 (1988). Even more recently, Professor Lawrence Herman has joined the list of Wigmore's critics. Herman, *The Unexplored Relationship between the Privilege against Self-Incrimination and the Involuntary Confession Rule* (pts. 1 & 2), 53 OHIO ST. L.J. 101, 170–95, 53 OHIO ST. L.J. 497, 529–50 (1992).

49. Benner, *Requiem for* Miranda: *The Rehnquist Court's Voluntariness Doctrine in Historical Perspective,* 67 WASH. U. L.Q. 59, 68 (1989).

50. E. MORGAN, *supra* note 44, at 129–30.

51. Given the historical development of the privilege beyond the mandatory oath requirement, it is no large step to say that the police, like others, may not assert a claim of right to an answer. Accordingly, there is no need to quarrel with Professor Herman's argument that the protection against compulsory self-incrimination applies to the police. Herman, *supra* note 48, pt. 2, at 529–50. *Bram,* however, had equated this protection and the common-law voluntariness rule. This equation was wrong.

It is common to refer to the "privilege" against self-incrimination. The danger is that this shorthand phrase can cause one to overlook that the Fifth Amendment condemns not self-incrimination as such but only government acts that *compel* individuals to become a witnesses against themselves. Professor Benner, who supports *Miranda,* has conceded the distinction: "It is important to note at the outset that this Article treats the 'privilege' against self-incrimination as an analytically distinct legal relation, separate and apart from the 'right' to freedom from compelled self-incrimination guaranteed by the Fifth and Fourteenth Amendments of the Constitution." Benner, *supra* note 49, at 61 n.2.

52. E. MORGAN, *supra* note 44, at 129–30.

53. *Id.* at 130.

54. *Id.* at 130 n.9. Kevin Urick does cite pre-*Bram* state cases that applied the privilege to the issue of coerced confessions, but his discussion fails to acknowledge the many cases that did not. Urick, *supra* note 48, at 116–23. Interestingly, when courts cited the privilege, they did so in support of a rule against extracting confessions by torture, violence, or threats of violence. *Id.* In other words, giving support to the position later argued in this chapter, these cases used the privilege to support a voluntariness requirement.

Although Professor Herman also criticizes Wigmore's history, he acknowledges that most of the English cases and treatises up to 1850 fail to note any relationship between the privilege and either the newly emerged voluntariness rule or police interrogation; likewise, he admits that the vast majority of American cases up to 1850 did not draw any connection between the two doctrines. Herman, *supra* note 48, pt. 1, at 147–70. Not to be deterred by such silence, however, Herman concludes that these authorities "settle nothing and leave the crucial issues open to speculation and debate." *Id.* at 170; *see also id.* at 195–209 (providing the rationale for this conclusion).

55. J. MAGUIRE, *supra* note 47, at 16 n.3.

56. Wigmore himself made this point:

The sole relationship is found in the general spirit of protection and caution which our legal system shows toward an accused. But this spirit is equally responsible for the rule about reasonable doubt, the rule about 'corpus delicti,' the rule about lists of witnesses, and several others peculiar to criminal cases; and there is no more reason for linking the privilege with the one than with the others . . . .

8 J. WIGMORE, *supra* note 40, § 2266, at 388.

57. J. MAGUIRE, *supra* note 47, at 16 n.3.

58. C. McCORMICK, HANDBOOK OF THE LAW OF EVIDENCE 155 (1954). For Levy's reliance on McCormick, see L. LEVY, *supra* note 44, at 495 n.43; Levy, *supra* note 18, at 26 n.102.

59. Levy, *supra* note 18, at 26 n.102; *see also* Herman, *supra* note 48, pt. 1, at 177–80, pt. 2, at 546.

60. Of course, it might be a fair characterization to say that the oath requirement, because of the "cruel trilemma" that it imposed, could have subjected devoutly religious persons, such as the Puritans, to mental torture. Benner, *supra* note 49, at 69 n.32, 75. This would provide little support, however, for those who would extend the privilege beyond the oath requirement.

61. L. LEVY, *supra* note 44, at 32–36, 326. For a stronger denial of any connection between the privilege and the abolition of torture, see J. LANGBEIN, TORTURE AND THE LAW OF PROOF 134–37 (1977); Dolinko, *Is There a Rationale for the Privilege against Self-Incrimination?*, 33 UCLA L. REV. 1063, 1078 (1986) (view of privilege as safeguard against torture "belied by history, by constitutional doctrine, and by common sense").

62. Levy, *supra* note 18, at 26 n.102.

63. *Id.*

64. Recent scholarship has also cast doubt on Levy's effort to root the privilege in a struggle between the common law and ecclesiastical law and practice. Helmholz, *Origins of the Privilege against Self-Incrimination: The Role of the European Ius Commune*, 65 N.Y.U. L. REV. 962 (1990).

65. Benner, *supra* note 49, at 68.

66. *Id.* at 68–69.

67. *Id.* at 100.

68. *Id.* at 101.
69. *Id.* at 109.
70. *Id.*
71. *Id.* at 65.
72. *Id.* at 157.
73. *Id.* at 62–63 & n.7, 157. *See also supra* note 51.
74. Benner, *supra* note 49, at 64.
75. *Id.* at 89.
76. *Id.* (quoting L. Levy, *supra* note 44, at 430). Levy's views on textualism and original meaning jurisprudence are amplified in his more recent work:

> In the glorious act of framing a social compact expressive of the supreme law, Americans tended simply to draw up a random catalogue of rights that seemed to satisfy their urge for a statement of first principles—or for some of them. That task was executed in a disordered fashion that verged on ineptness. Original intent as the basis of constitutional jurisprudence seems, therefore, equally disordered or irrational, for its premises are based on illusions.

L. Levy, Original Intent and the Framers' Constitution 252–53 (1988); *cf.* M. Berger, *supra* note 44, at 2 (historical evidence concerning privilege should be considered relevant but not controlling).
77. L. Levy, *supra* note 44, at 422–25.
78. Benner, *supra* note 49, at 64, 83–84, 92, 158–59.
79. *Id.* at 65, 102–6, 159.
80. *Id.* at 160.
81. *Id.* at 160–61.
82. *Id.* at 70–75. The literature favoring a broad reading of the privilege has a tendency to rely on arguments that individuals asserted, whether or not those individuals prevailed. *See, e.g.,* Herman, *supra* note 48, pt. 2, at 538–44.
83. Benner, *supra* note 49, at 75–76.
84. *Id.* at 77.
85. Helmholz, *supra* note 64, at 972–74, 990 n.136.
86. *Id.* at 972, 974–89.
87. 1 & 2 Phil. & M. ch. 13 (1554); 2 & 3 Phil. & M. ch. 10 (1555). Kevin Urick has acknowledged that most American states had similar statutes. Urick, *supra* note 48, at 121 n.55.
88. Benner, *supra* note 49, at 80; *see also* Y. Kamisar, *supra* note 20, at 51–53; Schulhofer, *Reconsidering* Miranda, 54 U. Chi. L. Rev. 435, 438 (1987). The practice of conducting such examinations may have preceded the sixteenth-century statutes. *See* Wolchover, *Validating the Accused's Confession,* 47 Mod. L. Rev. 535, 542 (1984).
89. Benner, *supra* note 49, at 81–82.
90. *Id.* at 83; L. Levy, *supra* note 44, at 329; Urick, *supra* note 48, at 121 n.55.
91. In a highly publicized report in 1986, the Justice Department's Office of Legal Policy criticized *Miranda* as having no basis in history or precedent. Office of

LEGAL POLICY, U.S. DEP'T OF JUSTICE, "TRUTH IN CRIMINAL JUSTICE" Series, Report No. 1, *The Law of Pre-trial Interrogation* 118 (1986), *reprinted in* 22 U. MICH. J.L. REF. 437 (1989). Referring to this as the Meese Report, Benner described this conclusion as "either a product of unbelievable ignorance or the result of a 'willful disregard' of the English heritage from which our accusatory system of criminal justice arose." Benner, *supra* note 49, at 83. It was neither, unless one contends that our system arose from English events that postdated its development.

92. L. MAYERS, SHALL WE AMEND THE FIFTH AMENDMENT? 15–16, 101, 175–76, 310–11 (1959). People v. McHahon, 15 N.Y. 384 (1857), illustrates the narrow scope given the self-incrimination protection in midcentury. Arrested for the murder of his wife, the defendant was brought before a coroner's inquest, put under oath, and examined. His testimony was used at his trial. The court of appeals reversed the conviction but explicitly disclaimed reliance on the privilege:

> [W]hen the law rejects a disclosure made under oath by a person charged with crime, it does so, not because any right or privilege of the prisoner has been violated, but because it is deemed unsafe to rely upon it as evidence of guilt. This is strongly to be inferred from that class of cases in which it has been held that, although a confession has been obtained by stratagem, by fraud, by violation of confidence or even of an oath, still, if reliable, the law will avail itself of it.

Id. at 390. The statements about the voluntariness doctrine are also revealing. That the court reversed the conviction, however, suggests a broad view of what might affect reliability.

93. L. MAYERS, *supra* note 92, at 176; *cf.* Berger, *Rethinking Self-Incrimination in Great Britain,* 61 DEN. L.J. 507, 510 (1984) (procedure changed as justices of the peace assumed a more judicial role).

94. HOME OFFICE, REPORT OF THE WORKING GROUP ON THE RIGHT OF SILENCE 8 (1989) (typed document); *see also* Barrett, *Police Practices and the Law—From Arrest to Release or Charge,* 50 CALIF. L. REV. 11, 16–21 (1962); Markman, *Miranda v. Arizona: A Historical Perspective,* 24 AM. CRIM. L. REV. 193, 198 (1987); Note, *An Historical Argument for the Right to Counsel during Police Interrogation,* 73 YALE L.J. 1000, 1039–40 (1964).

95. L. LEVY, *supra* note 44, at 375; *see also* Urick, *supra* note 48, at 125 (privilege was not self-executing at common law or in nineteenth-century America).

96. Benner, *supra* note 49, at 159.

97. *Id.* at 104.

98. Berger, *supra* note 93, at 510.

99. Berger, *Legislating Confession Law in Great Britain: A Statutory Approach to Police Interrogations,* 24 U. MICH. J.L. REF. 1, 10 n.34 (1990).

100. Dix, *Mistake, Ignorance, Expectation of Benefit, and the Modern Law of Confessions,* 1975 WASH. U. L.Q 275, 281–84; *see also* Urick, *supra* note 48, at 116–18 (citing English authorities applying a voluntariness test). *See also supra* note 92.

101. *Miranda,* 384 U.S. 436, 458 (1966).

102. *Id.* at 461.

103. Kamisar, *Equal Justice in the Gatehouses and Mansions of American Criminal Procedure,* in Criminal Justice in Our Time 1, 30 (A. Howard ed. 1965) [hereinafter Kamisar, *Equal Justice*] (internal citations omitted). For the cite to McCormick, *see supra* note 58. *See also* Herman, *supra* note 48, pt. 2, at 538; Kamisar, *A Dissent from the* Miranda *Dissents: Some Comments on the "New" Fifth Amendment and the Old "Voluntariness" Test,* 65 Mich. L. Rev. 59, 65–82 (1966) [hereinafter Kamisar, *A Dissent*].

104. *See, e.g.,* O. Stephens, The Supreme Court and Confessions of Guilt 205 (1973) (only ban on questioning would remove coercion that concerned *Miranda*); Driver, *Confessions and the Social Psychology of Coercion,* 82 Harv. L. Rev. 42, 60–61 (1968) (abolition of police interrogation may be necessary to eliminate coercion); Weisberg, *Police Interrogation of Arrested Persons: A Skeptical View,* 52 J. Crim. L. Criminology & Police Sci. 21, 46 (1961) (any pre-judicial interrogation "irreconcilable with the privilege"); *cf.* Rosenberg & Rosenberg, *A Modest Proposal for the Abolition of Custodial Confessions,* 68 N.C. L. Rev. 69, 111–13 (1989) (even volunteered custodial statements should be excluded).

105. The origins of the rule protecting the defendant from having to assert the privilege at trial are obscure. J. Strong et al., McCormick on Evidence § 114 (4th ed. 1992); 8 J. Wigmore, *supra* note 40, § 2268.

106. Weisberg, *supra* note 104, at 21; *cf.* Way, *The Supreme Court and State Coerced Confessions,* 12 J. Pub. L. 53, 66 (1963) ("Is it not strange to realize that what happened in most of these cases would never be sanctioned as procedure inside a courtroom?").

107. Y. Kamisar, *supra* note 20, at xi–xii; Kamisar, *Equal Justice, supra* note 103, at 11–25.

108. *See supra* note 99 and accompanying text. *See also* A. Beisel, Control Over Illegal Enforcement of the Criminal Law: Role of the Supreme Court 104 (1955) (police interrogation performs seventeenth-century function of judicial questioning that privilege abolished).

109. For a review of the debate and developments in England, see Berger, *supra* note 93; Berger, *supra* note 99.

110. Damaska, *Comparative Reflections on Reading the Amended Yugoslav Code: Interrogation of Defendants in Yugoslav Criminal Procedure,* 61 J. Crim. L. Criminology & Police Sci. 168, 169 (1970). The Japanese, in particular, have been wary of restraints on effective police interrogation. Foote, *supra* note 30.

111. Damaska, *supra* note 110, at 177; *see also* M. Damaska, The Faces of Justice and State Authority 192 (1986).

112. Brouwer, *Inquisitorial and Adversary Procedures—A Comparative Analysis,* 55 Australian L.J. 207, 207, 221 (1981).

113. This insight is not new. *See, e.g.,* R. Pound, Criminal Justice in America 88 (1929). Professor Kamisar sees the privilege as having played more of a role than separation of powers in ending judicial examination of the accused. Kamisar, *A Dissent, supra* note 103, at 72–76.

114. From both separation-of-powers and fairness perspectives, Michigan's now infrequently used one-person grand jury procedure, in which a judge conducts a criminal investigation, is an anomaly. M.C.L.A. § 767.3.

115. *Cf.* Barrett, *supra* note 94, at 18; Dession & Cohen, *The Inquisitorial Functions of Grand Juries,* 41 YALE L.J. 687, 691 (1932) (making these points about the investigative grand jury). On the need for the interrogation of suspects, see Inbau, *Police Interrogation—A Practical Necessity,* 52 J. CRIM. L. CRIMINOLOGY & POLICE SCI. 16 (1961). Inbau's argument remains unrebutted. *Cf.* Markman, *supra* note 94, at 224–26 (*Miranda* has damaged law enforcement).

116. *See, e.g.,* NATIONAL COMMISSION ON LAW OBSERVANCE AND ENFORCEMENT, Report No. 11, *Lawlessness in Law Enforcement* 5 (1931); W. SCHAEFER, THE SUSPECT AND SOCIETY 76–81 (1967); L. WEINREB, DENIAL OF JUSTICE 129–34, 147–64 (1977); Bonventre, *An Alternative to the Constitutional Privilege against Self-Incrimination,* 49 BROOKLYN L. REV. 31, 64–76 (1982); Greenawalt, *Silence as a Moral and Constitutional Right,* 23 WM. & MARY L. REV. 15, 51–52 (1981); Kauper, *Judicial Examination of the Accused—A Remedy for the Third Degree,* 30 MICH. L. REV. 1224 (1932), *reprinted in* 73 MICH. L. REV. 39 (1974); McCormick, *Some Problems and Developments in the Admissibility of Confessions,* 24 TEX. L. REV. 239, 277 (1946); Pound, *Legal Interrogation of Persons Accused or Suspected of Crime,* 24 J. CRIM. L. CRIMINOLOGY & POLICE SCI. 1014, 1017 (1934).

117. Y. KAMISAR, *supra* note 20, at 81; Kamisar, *Equal Justice, supra* note 103, at 22. Not everyone concurs in this judgment. *See, e.g.,* L. WEINREB, *supra* note 116; McCormick, *supra* note 116.

118. *See, e.g.,* Kamisar, A *Dissent, supra* note 103, at 82–85.

119. L. MAYERS, *supra* note 92, at 1; G. WILLIAMS, PROOF OF GUILT 38 (2d ed. 1958).

120. 8 J. WIGMORE, *supra* note 40, § 2268, at 388 (emphasis in original); *accord* J. DRESSLER, UNDERSTANDING CRIMINAL PROCEDURE 340 (1991); McCORMICK, *supra* note 105, at 334. For both early and more recent case support, see United States v. Burr, 25 Fed. Cas. 38 (C.C. Va. 1807) (opinion of Marshall, C.J.); Garner v. United States, 424 U.S. 648 (1976).

121. Garner v. United States, 424 U.S. 648 (1976).

122. United States v. Kordel, 397 U.S. 1 (1970); *see also* M. BERGER, *supra* note 44, at 74.

123. *Garner,* 424 U.S. at 654; United States v. Monia, 317 U.S. 424, 427 (1943).

124. United States v. Wong, 431 U.S. 174, 179 n.8 (1977); United States v. Washington, 431 U.S. 181, 186–90 (1977); United States v. Mandujano, 425 U.S. 564, 580–81 (1976) (plurality opinion); United States v. Dionisio, 410 U.S. 1, 10 n.8 (1973); *see also* M. BERGER, *supra* note 44, at 75–76.

125. Oregon v. Mathiason, 429 U.S. 492 (1977); Beckwith v. United States, 425 U.S. 341 (1976).

126. The reasons for the special rule at trial are uncertain, various, and not all based on concerns going to the heart of the privilege. M. BERGER, *supra* note 44, at 74–75; 8 J. WIGMORE, *supra* note 40, § 2268, at 392–96.

127. L. Levy, *supra* note 44, at 326–27, 344–47, 354–55, 430; L. Mayers, *supra* note 92, at 221.

128. Rosenberg & Rosenberg, *supra* note 104, at 108–9.

129. Kamisar, *A Dissent, supra* note 103, at 92 (criticizing the government's argument in Anderson v. United States, 318 U.S. 350 (D.C. Cir. 1943)); *see also* Schulhofer, *supra* note 88, at 442–43 & n.17.

130. *Miranda*, 384 U.S. at 461, 467, 477–78.

131. *Id.* at 457; *see also* Herman, *supra* note 48, pt. 2, at 524–27 (Fifth Amendment voluntariness requirement more protective than due process voluntariness requirement).

132. *Bram*, 168 U.S. at 558.

133. *See* Ziang Sung Wan v. United States, 266 U.S. 1, 14 (1924) (dictum); Wilson v. United States, 162 U.S. 613, 623–24 (1896) (lack of warnings and lack of counsel did not render statement involuntary); Sparf v. United States, 156 U.S. 51, 55 (1895). The pre-*Bram* cases are relevant because *Bram* purported to equate the Fifth Amendment and the voluntariness requirement.

134. Powers v. United States, 223 U.S. 303 (1912) (cross-examination of defendant); Wilson v. United States, 162 U.S. 613, 622–24 (1896) (questioning done by United States Commissioner).

135. 322 U.S. 143 (1944).

136. *Id.* at 154 n.9. The previous due process case was Lisenba v. California, 314 U.S. 219 (1941).

137. *See also supra* note 21.

138. 371 U.S. 341 (1963).

139. *Id.* at 347–50. The due process case was Rogers v. Richmond, 365 U.S. 534 (1961).

140. 371 U.S. at 378–79 & n.19 (Black, Warren, Douglas, JJ., dissenting).

141. *See, e.g.,* Frazier v. Cupp, 394 U.S. 731 (1969); Greenwald v. Wisconsin, 390 U.S. 519 (1968) (per curiam). The voluntariness approach in these cases did not differ from that in Darwin v. Connecticut, 391 U.S. 346 (1968) (per curiam), a case that could not have been governed by Malloy v. Hogan's, 378 U.S. 1 (1964), application of the Fifth Amendment to the states because it was tried before the date of that decision. *Compare* Colorado v. Connelly, 479 U.S. 157, 163 (1986) (Court has retained due process focus even after applying the Fifth Amendment to the states) *with id.* at 169–70 (Fifth Amendment concern in *Miranda* context, like due process concern, is governmental coercion).

142. 425 U.S. 341 (1976).

143. *Id.* at 347–48; *see also* Arizona v. Fulminante, 111 S. Ct. 1246, 1251–53 (1991) (relying on due process voluntariness cases with regard to coerced confession issue state court had resolved under Fifth Amendment). The Court in *Fulminante* also indicated that the voluntariness standard articulated in *Bram* is not fully consistent with more recent precedent. *Id.* at 1251.

144. 431 U.S. 181 (1977).

145. *Id.* at 186–88.

146. Schulhofer, *supra* note 88, at 442–43. *See also* Herman, *supra* note 48, pt. 2, at 525 n.661 (discussing the conflicting positions that Schulhofer and I have taken).

147. Schulhofer, *supra* note 88, at 443.

148. 380 U.S. 609 (1965).

149. Schulhofer, *supra* note 88, at 453.

150. Baxter v. Palmigiano, 425 U.S. 308, 317–19 (1976).

151. *See* Tague, *The Fifth Amendment: If an Aid to the Guilty Defendant, an Impediment to the Innocent One*, 78 GEO. L.J. 1, 15–18 (1989). Because the defendant did not testify in *Griffin*, the Court was not confronted with a voluntariness issue. Its holding was that comment on the defendant's silence penalized the defendant for exercising his rights.

152. *Griffin* is strongly criticized in Greenawalt, *supra* note 116, at 57–59. For both an excellent review of the historical background and an argument that *Griffin* should be overruled or limited, see OFFICE OF LEGAL POLICY, U.S. DEP'T. OF JUSTICE, "TRUTH IN CRIMINAL JUSTICE" SERIES, Report No. 8, *Adverse Inferences from Silence* (1989), *reprinted in* 22 U. MICH. J.L. REF. 1005 (1989). *See also* Thomas, *supra* note 30, at 320–21.

153. OFFICE OF LEGAL POLICY, *supra* note 152, at 1112.

154. G. WILLIAMS, *supra* note 119, at 58–63; Berger, *supra* note 93, at 540 & nn.213–16. A statute in 1898 prohibited comment by the prosecutor.

155. Schulhofer, *supra* note 88, at 442.

156. *Miranda*, 384 U.S. at 533–34 (White, J., dissenting).

157. Stuntz, *Self-Incrimination and Excuse*, 88 COLUM. L. REV. 1227, 1231 n.7 (1988); *see also* Dolinko, *supra* note 61, at 1063–64 (privilege a "relic of particular practices and conflicts of pre-Revolutionary times").

158. *See* McNaughton, *The Privilege against Self-Incrimination: Its Constitutional Affectation, Raison d'Etre, and Miscellaneous Implications*, 51 J. CRIM. L. CRIMINOLOGY & POLICE SCI. 138 (1960); *cf.* W. SCHAEFER, *supra* note 116, at 61 (doctrine is "in search of a reason").

159. 8 J. WIGMORE, *supra* note 40, § 2251, at 304.

160. Y. KAMISAR, *supra* note 20, at 160.

161. *Id.* at 155 n.20.

162. United States v. Washington, 431 U.S. 181, 187–88 (1977). For the full quotation, see chapter 2 at note 98.

163. *Id.* at 187.

164. Schulhofer, *supra* note 88, at 445.

165. Y. KAMISAR, *supra* note 20, at 42 n.2.

166. *Miranda*, 384 U.S. at 467–68.

167. For articles building on the premise of such a right, see, for example, Greer, *The Right to Silence: A Review of the Current Debate*, 53 MOD. L. REV. 709 (1990); Schiller, *On the Jurisprudence of the Fifth Amendment Right to Silence*, 16 AM. CRIM. L. REV. 197 (1979).

168. *Cf.* Greenawalt, *supra* note 116, at 25 (making these points in the context of inquiring into the existence of a "moral right to silence"). Justice Thomas of New

Zealand overstated this point in claiming that "the right is no more than a residual capacity not to do something which the community otherwise enjoins." Thomas, *supra* note 30, at 320.

169. H. FRIENDLY, BENCHMARKS 271 (1967).

170. *Id.* at 250 n.72 (emphasis in original); *cf.* Westen & Mandell, *To Talk, to Balk, or to Lie: The Emerging Fifth Amendment Doctrine of the "Preferred Response,"* 19 AM. CRIM. L. REV. 521, 533 (1982) (Fifth Amendment does not create right to remain silent "as opposed to a right to avoid compulsory self-incrimination in other ways").

171. Schneckloth v. Bustamonte, 412 U.S. 218, 280–81 (1973) (Marshall, J., dissenting).

172. *Id.* at 281.

173. *Miranda*, 384 U.S. at 478 (denying that police have such an obligation).

174. Benner, *supra* note 49, at 63.

175. Fletcher v. Weir, 455 U.S. 603 (1982); Jenkins v. Anderson, 447 U.S. 231 (1980).

Chapter 6

1. *Cf.* McNeil v. Wisconsin, 111 S. Ct. 2204, 2207–10 (1991) (contrasting Fifth and Sixth Amendment rights to counsel). The Sixth Amendment's text explicitly speaks of counsel's role in providing assistance: "In all criminal prosecutions, the accused shall enjoy the right . . . to have the Assistance of Counsel for his defence." U.S. CONST. amend. VI.

2. The discussion in chapter 5, at notes 31–36, recognized that it may be too late in the day to challenge incorporation as such.

3. This would not be true under Professor Amar's approach to incorporation. Amar, *The Bill of Rights and the Fourteenth Amendment,* 101 YALE L.J. 1193 (1992). As indicated in chapter 5, however, the Court is not likely to embrace Professor Amar's controversial theory.

4. 287 U.S. 45 (1932).

5. *Id.* at 69.

6. *Id.* at 68.

7. *Id.* (quoting Holden v. Hardy, 169 U.S. 366, 389 (1898)).

8. 372 U.S. 335, 344–45 (1963) (applying the Sixth Amendment right to counsel to the states).

9. 287 U.S. at 68–69. Of course, *Powell* itself limited the right to counsel to the special circumstances of that case. In his concurring opinion in *Gideon*, however, Justice Harlan relied on procedural due process rather than the Sixth Amendment for a per se right to counsel in felony cases. *Gideon*, 372 U.S. at 349–52 (Harlan, J., concurring).

10. Concurring in *Gideon's* holding, which applied the right to counsel to state felony trials, Justice Harlan stated that he did not read the Court's cases "to suggest that by so holding, we automatically carry over an entire body of federal law and apply it in full sweep to the states." *Id.* at 352 (Harlan, J., concurring).

11. 304 U.S. 458 (1938).

12. W. BEANEY, THE RIGHT TO COUNSEL IN AMERICAN COURTS 27–36 (1955).

13. Cf. Foote, *Confessions and the Right to Silence in Japan,* 21 GA. J. INT'L & COMP. L. 414, 432–34 (1991) (right to counsel during interrogation does not include right to appointed counsel).

14. The facts are taken from Cicenia v. LaGay, 357 U.S. 504, 505–6 (1958). The Supreme Court essentially adopted the lower court's statement of the facts. *See* Application of Cicenia, 148 F. Supp. 98, 99–100 (D.N.J. 1956), *aff'd,* 240 F.2d 844 (3d Cir. 1957) (per curiam).

15. 357 U.S. at 509. See also Justice Jackson's well-known statement in Watts v. Indiana, 338 U.S. 49, 58–59 (1949). The Court did not observe, as it well might have, that *Cicenia* itself was such a case, the murder having remained unsolved for more than two years and the statements of the accomplice's wife not being admissible in court.

16. Crooker v. California, 357 U.S. 433, 441 (1958) (emphasis in original). Justice Brennan, who did not participate in *Cicenia,* joined the dissent in *Crooker,* thereby rendering *Crooker* a five-to-four decision.

17. *Cicenia,* 357 U.S. at 510.

18. For cases upholding the confession, *see, e.g.,* Stroble v. California, 343 U.S. 181, 198 (1952) (lawyer denied permission to see defendant); Gallegos v. Nebraska, 342 U.S. 55, 64–67 (1951). For cases finding the confession involuntary, *see, e.g.,* Haley v. Ohio, 332 U.S. 596, 597–600, 604 (1948); Malinski v. New York, 324 U.S. 401, 405 (1945).

19. 162 U.S. 613 (1896).

20. *Id.* at 623–24.

21. 168 U.S. 532 (1897).

22. 322 U.S. 143, 154 n.9 (1944).

23. Culombe v. Connecticut, 367 U.S. 568, 601 (1961) (Frankfurter & Stewart, JJ.).

24. 357 U.S. at 510 (quoting Hoag v. New Jersey, 356 U.S. 464, 468 (1958)).

25. All three federal courts in *Cicenia* expressed disapproval of the police conduct regarding counsel. 357 U.S. at 508–9; 240 F.2d at 844; 148 F. Supp. at 104.

26. State v. Grillo, 11 N.J. 173, 93 A.2d 328 (1952).

27. People v. Crooker, 47 Cal. 2d 348, 303 P.2d 753 (1956).

28. Annotation, *Effect of, and remedy for, infringement of right of accused to communicate with his attorney,* 23 A.L.R. 1382, 1387–90 (1923); *see also* W. BEANEY, *supra* note 12, at 127.

29. 4 N.Y.2d 256, 264–68, 150 N.E.2d 226, 231–32, 173 N.Y.S.2d 793, 800–2 (1958) (Desmond, J., dissenting), *rev'd on other grounds,* 360 U.S. 315 (1959).

30. People v. Di Biasi, 7 N.Y.2d 544, 166 N.E.2d 825, 200 N.Y.S.2d 21 (1960).

31. Annotation, *Admissibility of confession, admission, or incriminatory statement of accused as affected by fact that it was made after indictment and in the absence of counsel,* 90 A.L.R.2d 732, 740–42 (1963).

32. Spano v. New York, 360 U.S. 315 (1959). In Crooker v. California, 357 U.S. 433 (1958), the companion case to *Cicenia,* there were four dissenting votes.

See supra note 16. With Justice Stewart, the dissenters seemingly had become a majority. *See* Y. Kamisar, Police Interrogation and Confessions 169–70 (1980); Tomkovicz, *An Adversary System Defense of the Right to Counsel against Informants: Truth, Fair Play, and the* Massiah *Doctrine,* 22 U.C. Davis L. Rev. 1, 12 (1988).

33. 360 U.S. at 327 (Stewart, Douglas, & Brennan, JJ., concurring).

34. *Id.* Justice Stewart thus completely embraced the position of the dissenting judges on the New York Court of Appeals. *See supra* note 29 and accompanying text.

35. 377 U.S. 201 (1964).

36. Kamisar, Brewer v. Williams, Massiah, *and* Miranda: *What Is "Interrogation"? When Does It Matter?,* 67 Geo. L.J. 1, 34 (1978).

37. 377 U.S. at 204 (quoting from Justice Stewart's concurring opinion in *Spano*).

38. *Id.* at 205 & n.5; *see, e.g.,* People v. Waterman, 9 N.Y.2d 561, 175 N.E.2d 445, 216 N.Y.S.2d 70 (1961). *See also supra* note 30 and accompanying text.

39. *But see* Enker & Elsen, *Counsel for the Suspect:* Massiah v. United States *and* Escobedo v. Illinois, 49 Minn. L. Rev. 47, 131 (1964) ("real issue" in *Massiah* involved scope of Fifth Amendment); Note, *The Pretrial Right to Counsel,* 26 Stan. L. Rev. 399, 403–4 & n.27 (1974) (*Massiah* has Fifth Amendment overtones). *Contra* Kamisar, *supra* note 36, at 37–39. Professor Kamisar has proved to be correct. *See* Illinois v. Perkins, 496 U.S. 292 (1990) (*Miranda* does not apply to use of jail plants).

40. 378 U.S. 478 (1964).

41. The Court had applied the self-incrimination clause to the states just one week before. Malloy v. Hogan, 378 U.S. 1 (1964).

42. 378 U.S. at 479, 484, 492.

43. *Id.* at 486.

44. See chapter 2, notes 3–10 and accompanying text.

45. 378 U.S. at 486.

46. *Id.* at 487.

47. *Id.* at 485–86, 488–91.

48. *Id.* at 493–94 (Stewart, J, dissenting).

49. *Id.*

50. *Escobedo* both framed the issue and stated its holding in terms of the Sixth Amendment right to counsel. 378 U.S. at 479, 491 (majority opinion).

51. *Id.* at 494 (Stewart, J., dissenting).

52. *Id.* at 484 (majority opinion).

53. Of course, Justice Stewart's *Spano* concurrence in 1959 was based on the Fourteenth Amendment's due process clause, not on the Sixth Amendment's right to counsel clause. Justice Stewart never explained his apparent belief that these two clauses provided identical protection in this area.

54. *See* Enker & Elsen, *supra* note 39, at 58–84.

55. 384 U.S. 436 (1966).

56. *Id.* at 441 (emphasis added).

57. *Id.* at 442.

58. *Id.* at 465–66. In his dissenting opinion, Justice Harlan correctly observed, albeit with some overstatement, that *Escobedo* "contains no reasoning or even general conclusions addressed to the Fifth Amendment and indeed its citation in this regard seems surprising in view of [its] primary reliance on the Sixth Amendment." *Id.* at 512 n.9 (Harlan, Stewart, & White, JJ., dissenting).

59. Under the narrowest reading of *Escobedo,* taken from a paragraph that starts with the words "we hold," a Sixth Amendment violation occurred only when the investigation focused on the suspect, the suspect was in custody, the police denied the suspect's request for a lawyer, the police did not warn the suspect of the right to remain silent, and the police engaged in a process of interrogation designed to elicit incriminating statements. 378 U.S. at 490–91. For perhaps a broader statement of the holding, see *id.* at 492. The conflicting views about *Escobedo*'s scope are reviewed in Kamisar, *supra* note 36, at 25 n.145.

60. Kamisar, *supra* note 36, at 24.

61. Hoffa v. United States, 385 U.S. 293, 309–10 (1966), decided only six months after *Miranda,* made it clear that the Court would not extend the Sixth Amendment's application to the prearrest use of informants. *Hoffa* is discussed *infra* at notes 153–57.

62. Astute commentators, however, were cognizant of the issues. *See, e.g.,* Enker & Elsen, *supra* note 39, at 80–83 (discussing *Massiah*'s and *Escobedo*'s possible application to the precharge use of informants and to on-the-street questioning).

63. 388 U.S. 218 (1967).

64. Kirby v. Illinois, 406 U.S. 682, 687 (1972).

65. *Id.* at 689.

66. 384 U.S. 719, 729 (1966).

67. Indeed, *Johnson* cited *Miranda* in support of this proposition. *Id.* at 729; *see also* Uviller, *Evidence from the Mind of the Criminal Suspect: A Reconsideration of the Current Rules of Access and Restraint,* 87 COLUM. L. REV. 1137, 1155–56 & n.64 (1987).

68. 430 U.S. 387 (1977).

69. 475 U.S. 412 (1986); *see also* Maine v. Moulton, 474 U.S. 159 (1985) (right to counsel attaches to postcharge use of informant but not to use of informant to uncover other crimes); United States v. Gouveia, 467 U.S. 180 (1984) (no right to counsel in precharge interrogation of inmates in administrative detention).

70. 475 U.S. at 428–29.

71. *Id.* at 430.

72. *Id.* at 432; *see also* Uviller, *supra* note 67, at 1158.

73. Kamisar, *supra* note 36, at 95–96.

74. *See, e.g.,* Moran v. Burbine, 475 U.S. 412, 429–32 (1986); United States v. Gouveia, 467 U.S. 180, 187–89 (1984).

75. For example, as if still responding to *Escobedo*'s claim that the adversary judicial proceeding line exalted form over substance, Justice Stewart's *Kirby* plurality insisted that this line was "far from a mere formalism." 406 U.S. at 689.

76. The Court found a valid waiver of *Miranda* rights in *Burbine*. 475 U.S. at 420–28.

77. *Escobedo*, 378 U.S. at 486.

78. This description of the *Massiah* right occurred in Maine v. Moulton, 474 U.S. 159, 176 (1985).

79. *See supra* note 1.

80. *Escobedo*, 378 U.S. at 485, 486.

81. *But see* H. FRIENDLY, BENCHMARKS 254 (1967) (recognition of right to counsel at police station requires "radical textual surgery").

82. W. BEANEY, *supra* note 12, at 8–11, 24; F. HELLER, THE SIXTH AMENDMENT TO THE CONSTITUTION OF THE UNITED STATES 109 (1969); Post, *The Admissibility of Defence Counsel in English Criminal Procedure*, 5 J. LEGAL HIST. 23 (1984). The practice in England may not have been as stringent as the law. Note, *An Historical Argument for the Right to Counsel during Police Interrogation*, 73 YALE L.J. 1000, 1018–30 (1964). (The Note's author was Charles Donahue, now a law professor at Harvard.)

83. W. BEANEY, *supra* note 12, at 12, 14–22, 25; F. HELLER, *supra* note 82, at 109–10; Note, *supra* note 82, at 1030–31.

84. W. BEANEY, *supra* note 12, at 22–24, 28–30, 32–33; F. HELLER, *supra* note 82, at 110; Note, *supra* note 82, at 1031, 1033.

85. W. BEANEY, *supra* note 12, at 32–33.

86. *See supra* text accompanying notes 11–13.

87. *Cf.* Note, *supra* note 82, at 1032–34 (demonstrating this concern).

88. Johnson v. Zerbst, 304 U.S. 458, 462–63 (1938); Powell v. Alabama, 287 U.S. 45, 69 (1932). *But see* H. FRIENDLY, *supra* note 81, at 253 (criticizing *Johnson* as without basis in the Sixth Amendment's language or history).

89. 368 U.S. 52 (1961).

90. *See* Enker & Elsen, *supra* note 39, at 50.

91. 399 U.S. 1 (1970).

92. United States v. Ash, 413 U.S. 300, 310 (1973).

93. State v. Murphy, 87 N.J.L. 515, 530, 94 A. 640, 646 (1915). For the description of the claim as novel, see *id.* at 529, 94 A. at 646. The force of the court's statement is not reduced by its references to other areas, such as the taking of guilty pleas, to which the right to counsel did not then apply but to which it would appropriately apply today. Defendants should learn of possible defenses before submitting to conviction; they need to know whether their actions really violated the law. Enker & Elsen, *supra* note 39, at 66. Revealing one's knowledge about an event and submitting to conviction, however, are two quite different things. A guilty plea, unlike a confession, is not "a thing entirely apart from defense upon a trial."

94. Note, *supra* note 82, at 1034.

95. *Id.* at 1041.

96. *Id.* at 1042.

97. *Id.* at 1034.

98. *Id.* at 1048.

99. *Id.* at 1049.

100. H. FRIENDLY, *supra* note 81, at 254; Enker & Elsen, *supra* note 39, at 65–66.

101. Enker & Elsen, *supra* note 39, at 66.

102. H. FRIENDLY, *supra* note 81, at 254.

103. *Id.* at 256.

104. Tomkovicz, *supra* note 32, at 10–11, 22.

105. *Id.* at 33 n.163 (quoting W. BEANEY, *supra* note 12, at 44); *id.* at 2 (describing the Court as legal teacher). One may appropriately ask whose visions and aspirations Professor Tomkovicz had in mind.

106. *Id.* at 34 n.164.

107. *Id.* at 34 n.163. One may appropriately ask whose evolving attitudes Professor Tomkovicz had in mind.

108. In another passage of his article, Professor Tomkovicz seemed to recognize that the reasons a Court gives for expanding a constitutional protection should be "rooted in constitutional text, history, or objectives." *Id.* at 30.

109. *Id.* at 40.

110. *Id.*

111. *Id.* at 41–42.

112. Uviller, *supra* note 67, at 1176.

113. *See also id.* at 1177.

114. This is the advice that a lawyer would give in the vast majority of cases. Watts v. Indiana, 338 U.S. 49, 59 (1949) (Jackson, J., concurring); *see also* Uviller, *supra* note 67, at 1161 & n.90.

115. W. SCHAEFER, THE SUSPECT AND SOCIETY 53 (1967).

116. Tomkovicz, *supra* note 32, at 65.

117. *Id.* at 70–71.

118. *Id.* at 49–50.

119. Cluchey, Maine v. Moulton: *The Sixth Amendment and "Deliberate Elicitation": The Defendant's Position,* 23 AM. CRIM. L. REV. 43, 54 (1985).

120. H. FRIENDLY, *supra* note 81, at 277. *But see* Tomkovicz, *supra* note 32, at 60 n.246 (advocating a change in the law to make counsel available when physical evidence is taken from the accused).

121. Cluchey, *supra* note 119, at 58; Tomkovicz, *supra* note 32, at 49, 51, 55.

122. By defining the notion of sport to connote a system dedicated to play in accordance with the rules, Professor Tomkovicz tried to defend a modified sporting theory of justice. Tomkovicz, *supra* note 32, at 47–49. Regarding police interrogation, however, the appropriate rules are the matter in issue.

123. Uviller, *supra* note 67, at 1175 (citations omitted).

124. *See, e.g.,* ABA MODEL RULES OF PROFESSIONAL CONDUCT, Rule 4.2 (1983):

In representing a client, a lawyer shall not communicate about the subject of the representation with a party the lawyer knows to be represented by another lawyer in the matter, unless the lawyer has the consent of the other lawyer or is authorized by law to do so.

For the view that bar associations often take an insider's position in formulating ethics rules, one that may ignore the public interest and other applicable legal requirements, see Cramton & Udell, *State Ethics Rules and Federal Prosecutors: The Controversies over the Anti-Contact and Subpoena Rules,* 53 U. PITT. L. REV. 291, 306–15 (1992).

125. Uviller, *supra* note 67, at 1179. To the extent that the ethics rule is intended to protect the client's legal interests, not just the attorney-client relationship, Uviller's argument may be overstated. *See* Cramton & Udell, *supra* note 124, at 324–27. *But see id.* at 327–28 (also noting—with approval, *id.* at 331–that most courts interpret the anticontact rule in criminal cases as not exceeding existing constitutional limitations).

126. Cramton & Udell, *supra* note 124, at 332–33.

127. Uviller, *supra* note 67, at 1179. For the ABA version of the rule, see *supra* note 124.

128. Cramton & Udell, *supra* note 124, at 335.

129. *Cf. id.* at 344–46 (arguing for a narrow view of the alter ego theory).

130. Uviller, *supra* note 67, at 1180; *see also* Cramton & Udell, *supra* note 124, at 319–24, 346–49, 358–59 (noting the controversy on this point and agreeing that the exception may be interpreted as applicable to criminal cases).

131. Uviller, *supra* note 67, at 1180; *cf.* Cramton & Udell, *supra* note 124, at 359 (recommending that the disciplinary rule apply only after Sixth Amendment rights have attached).

132. Uviller, *supra* note 67, at 1180–81.

133. *Id.* at 1182.

134. Spano v. New York, 360 U.S. 315, 327 (1959) (Stewart, Douglas, & Brennan, JJ., concurring).

135. 287 U.S. 45 (1932).

136. Massiah v. United States, 377 U.S. 201, 205 (1964) (quoting *Powell,* 287 U.S. at 57). The trial judge in *Powell* had appointed the entire bar—meaning no one lawyer in particular—to represent several illiterate black men who were charged in capital cases with raping two white girls. In finding a constitutional violation, the Court stressed that from arraignment until the beginning of trial, the defendants needed lawyers to engage in consultation, investigation, and preparation. *Powell* relied on two state cases that likewise were concerned with the need for defense counsel to have an opportunity to prepare a defense. Batchelor v. State, 189 Ind. 69, 125 N.E. 773 (1920); People *ex rel.* Burgess v. Risley, 66 How. Pr. (n.s.) 67 (N.Y. Sup. Ct. 1883). Indeed, the right to consult with counsel prior to trial was well recognized in state cases prior to *Powell,* a time when no court recognized a right to have counsel's assistance during police interrogation. *See* Annotation, *supra* note 28. In short, *Powell* provided no support for the right created in *Massiah. See also* Uviller, *supra* note 67, at 1159 & n.82.

137. Escobedo v. Illinois, 378 U.S. 478, 494 (1964) (Stewart J., dissenting).

138. *Id.* at 493–94.

139. *Id.* at 494.

140. *Id.*

141. *Id.*

142. While a grand jury may issue a subpoena to a targeted suspect, United States v. Washington, 431 U.S. 181 (1977); United States v. Dionisio, 410 U.S. 1, 10 n.8 (1973), its authority to issue a subpoena to an already charged individual has been questioned. United States v. Doe, 455 F.2d 1270, 1273 (1st Cir. 1972).

143. United States v. Henry, 447 U.S. 264, 295 (1980) (Rehnquist, J., dissenting).

144. *Id; see also* Uviller, *supra* note 67, at 1190.

145. Massiah v. United States, 377 U.S. 201, 210 n.1 (1964) (White, Clark, & Harlan, JJ., dissenting).

146. Kuhlman v. Wilson, 477 U.S. 436 (1986); *see also* Uviller, *supra* note 67, at 1172–73.

147. Uviller, *supra* note 67, at 1167.

148. 430 U.S. 387 (1977). *Williams* is meticulously analyzed in Kamisar, *supra* note 36, and in Kamisar, *Foreword: Brewer v. Williams—A Hard Look at a Discomfiting Record*, 66 GEO. L.J. 209 (1977).

149. 430 U.S. at 398 (quoting Kirby v. Illinois, 406 U.S. 682, 689 (1972)).

150. *Id.* at 399.

151. Kamisar, *supra* note 36, at 81 n.480.

152. *Id.* at 81.

153. 385 U.S. 293 (1966).

154. *Id.* at 310.

155. Kamisar, *supra* note 36, at 60.

156. Oregon v. Mathiason, 429 U.S. 492 (1977) (invitation to come to station); Beckwith v. United States, 425 U.S. 341 (1976) (friend's home).

157. *Cf.* Kamisar, *supra* note 36, at 86 n.503 (making a suggestion along these lines).

158. For the outline of a different argument than that presented in the text, see Dix, *Undercover Investigations and Police Rulemaking*, 53 TEX. L. REV. 203, 229 (1975).

159. Kirby v. Illinois, 406 U.S. 682, 689–90 (1972).

160. Uviller, *supra* note 67, at 1166.

161. F. MILLER, PROSECUTION: THE DECISION TO CHARGE A SUSPECT WITH A CRIME 9–19 (1970).

162. United States v. Marion, 404 U.S. 307, 320 (1971). Professor Uviller pointed to *Marion* as discrediting Stewart's argument. Uviller, *supra* note 67, at 1167.

163. State v. Murphy, 87 N.J.L. 515, 531, 94 A. 640, 646 (1915). For the previous quotation from this case, see *supra* text accompanying note 93.

164. 384 U.S. 436 (1966).

165. *Id.* at 469.

166. *Id.* at 537 (White, Harlan, & Stewart, JJ., dissenting).

167. *Id.* at 470.

168. *Cf.* McNeil v. Wisconsin, 111 S. Ct. 2204, 2207–10 (1991) (contrasting Fifth and Sixth Amendment rights to counsel); *see also* Kamisar, *supra* note 36, at 48, 50, 57 n.322, 63–69.

169. Kirby v. Illinois, 406 U.S. 682, 688 (1972) (emphasis in original).

170. Moran v. Burbine, 475 U.S. 412, 422–23 (1986) (emphasis added) (citations omitted).

171. 479 U.S. 523 (1987).

172. *Id.* at 530 (quoting Oregon v. Elstad, 470 U.S. 298, 316 (1985)).

173. 479 U.S. 564 (1987).

174. *Id.* at 577.

175. *Escobedo,* 378 U.S. at 486.

176. *Id.* at 486, 487–88.

177. *Id.*

178. 496 U.S. 292 (1990).

179. *Id.* at 297.

180. *Id.*

181. H. Friendly, *supra* note 81, at 271.

182. See *supra* note 16 and accompanying text.

Chapter 7

1. 384 U.S. 436 (1966).

2. *Id.* at 439.

3. *Id.* at 440–91.

4. *Id.* at 491.

5. *Id.* at 491–99.

6. *Id.* at 533 (White, Harlan, & Stewart, JJ., dissenting).

7. *Id.* at 444–45, 478–79 (majority opinion) (summarizing the new rules).

8. *Id.* at 467.

9. *Id.* at 505 (Harlan, Stewart, & White, JJ., dissenting).

10. *Id.* at 477 (majority opinion). Five years later, the Court disregarded this statement as dictum. Harris v. New York, 401 U.S. 222 (1971).

11. 384 U.S. at 475–76. The Court subsequently moderated the force of this discussion. North Carolina v. Butler, 441 U.S. 369 (1979).

12. 384 U.S. at 473–74. The Court subsequently interpreted this language to give the police some flexibility. Michigan v. Mosley, 423 U.S. 96 (1975).

13. 384 U.S. at 474–75. The Court subsequently interpreted this language as creating a rigid per se rule. Edwards v. Arizona, 451 U.S. 477 (1981).

14. 384 U.S. at 468 n.37. The Court subsequently held that silence can be used for impeachment purposes when no *Miranda* warnings are given. *See, e.g.,* Fletcher v. Weir, 455 U.S. 603 (1982).

15. 384 U.S. at 476 n.45.

16. *Id.* at 463 n.32.

17. *Id.* at 477–78. The Court subsequently affirmed this dictum in Berkermer v. McCarty, 468 U.S. 420 (1984).

18. *But see* Stone, *The* Miranda *Doctrine in the Burger Court,* 1977 Sup. Ct. Rev. 99, 107–8 (criticizing the Court for not adhering to *Miranda*'s dicta).

19. 417 U.S. 433, 439–47 (1974) (plurality opinion).

20. *Id.* at 439.

21. *Id.* at 444.

22. *Id.* at 445.

23. 440 U.S. 450 (1979).

24. *Id.* at 459. Voluntary statements taken in violation of the *Miranda* rules may be used for impeachment purposes. Oregon v. Hass, 420 U.S. 714 (1975); Harris v. New York, 401 U.S. 222 (1971).

25. 467 U.S. 649 (1984).

26. *Id.* at 654 (quoting *Tucker,* 417 U.S. at 444).

27. *Id.* at 655 n.5.

28. *Id.* at 684 n.7 (Marshall, Brennan, & Stevens, JJ., dissenting); *see also* Michigan v. Mosley, 423 U.S. 96, 113 (1975) (Brennan & Marshall, JJ., dissenting) ("[T]he cost of assuring voluntariness by procedural tests, independent of any actual inquiry into voluntariness, is that some voluntary statements will be excluded."). *But see* Oregon v. Elstad, 470 U.S. 298, 349 (1985) (Brennan & Marshall, JJ., dissenting) (in apparent contradiction of their statement in *Quarles,* stating that use of a statement in violation of *Miranda* is a "flat violation" of the Fifth Amendment).

29. 470 U.S. 298 (1985).

30. *Id.* at 306.

31. *Id.* at 307. The Court did say that *Miranda* created an irrebuttable presumption of compulsion, *id.,* and Justice Brennan applauded this statement as recognizing the "flaws in the logic of *Tucker* and *Quarles,*" *id.* at 349 (Brennan & Marshall, JJ., dissenting). As the quotations in the text indicate, the Court did no such thing. Indeed, it relied on the holdings of *Tucker* and *Quarles* to support the proposition that "a simple failure to administer *Miranda* warnings is not in itself a violation of the Fifth Amendment." *Id.* at 306 n.1 (majority opinion).

32. 479 U.S. 523 (1987).

33. Edwards v. Arizona, 451 U.S. 477, 484–85 (1981) (interpreting *Miranda*'s dictum to require a rigid per se rule); *Miranda,* 384 U.S. at 474. *See also supra* notes 12–13 and accompanying text.

34. 479 U.S. at 528.

35. 498 U.S. 146 (1990).

36. *Id.* at 151 (quoting Fare v. Michael C., 442 U.S. 707, 718 (1979)).

37. United States v. Henry, 447 U.S. 264, 289 (1980) (Rehnquist, J., dissenting).

38. Massiah v. United States, 377 U.S. 201, 205–6 (1964). In *Escobedo,* which, as discussed in chapter 6, the Court no longer views as a Sixth Amendment case, the Court explicitly said that the police conduct was "in violation" of the Sixth Amendment. Escobedo v. Illinois, 378 U.S. 478, 491 (1964).

39. 430 U.S. 387 (1977).

40. *Id.* at 397–98, 400.

41. 447 U.S. 264 (1980).

42. *Id.* at 274.

43. 474 U.S. 159 (1985).

44. *Id.* at 176; *see also id.* at 177, 180.

45. *Id.* at 180.

46. 475 U.S. 625 (1986).

47. *See supra* notes 33-35 and accompanying text.

48. 494 U.S. 344 (1990).

49. *Id.* at 345, 349–50.

50. *See supra* notes 10 and 24 and accompanying text.

51. 494 U.S. at 353–54.

52. Schulhofer, *Reconsidering* Miranda, 54 U. Chi. L. Rev. 435, 448 (1987).

53. *See also* Office of Legal Policy, U.S. Dep't of Justice, "Truth in Criminal Justice" Series, Report No. 3, *The Sixth Amendment Right to Counsel under the* Massiah *Line of Cases* 27 (1986), *reprinted in* 22 U. Mich. J.L. Ref. 661, 696 (1989). *But see id.* at 21–23, 22 U. Mich. J.L. Ref. at 691–93 (suggesting that *Massiah*'s exclusionary remedy as opposed to its right to counsel might appropriately be viewed as prophylactic).

54. Kamisar, *The "Police Practice" Phases of the Criminal Process and the Three Phases of the Burger Court,* in The Burger Years 143, 152–57 (H. Schwartz ed. 1987).

55. *Miranda,* 384 U.S. at 458.

56. *Id.* at 467. For other references to the "inherent" compulsion of custodial interrogation, see *id.* at 468, 478.

57. *Id.* at 490.

58. *Id.* at 491.

59. *Id.* at 467. For other references to this possibility, see *id.* at 444, 478–79, 490.

60. Despite a similar invitation to legislative bodies, the Court does not seem to view the right to counsel at lineups established by United States v. Wade, 388 U.S. 218 (1967), as prophylactic. *See* Grano, *Prophylactic Rules in Criminal Procedure: A Question of Article III Legitimacy,* 80 Nw. U.L. Rev. 100, 119–22 (1985).

61. 384 U.S. at 439.

62. *Id.* at 457.

63. *Id.*

64. *Id.* at 479.

65. *Id.* at 468–69, 471–72.

66. *Id.* at 447.

67. *Id.* at 492.

68. *Id.* at 494.

69. *Id.* at 496.

70. *Id.*

71. *Id.*

72. *Id.* at 497.

73. *Id.* at 498.

74. *Id.* at 499.

75. *Id.* at 503–4 (Clark, J., concurring and dissenting).

76. See chapter 5, note 156 and accompanying text (discussing Justice White's one-question hypothetical in *Miranda,* 384 U.S. at 533–34).

77. Schulhofer, *supra* note 52, at 448.

78. 384 U.S. at 535–36 (White, Harlan, & Stewart, JJ., dissenting).

79. *Id.* at 536.

80. For statements by Justices Brennan and Marshall, see *supra* note 28 and accompanying text.

81. Kamisar, *supra* note 54, at 155.

82. *Id.* at 157 (emphasis added).

83. *See supra* notes 10, 24, and 50 and accompanying text.

84. Schulhofer, *supra* note 52, at 450; *see also* Loewy, *Police-Obtained Evidence and the Constitution: Distinguishing Unconstitutionally Obtained Evidence from Unconstitutionally Used Evidence,* 87 MICH. L. REV. 907, 925–26 (1989).

85. Schulhofer, *supra* note 52, at 453.

86. 5 U.S. (1 Cranch) 137 (1803).

87. *Id.* at 177.

88. "We are not final because we are infallible, but we are infallible only because we are final." Brown v. Allen, 344 U.S. 443, 550 (1953) (Jackson, J., concurring).

89. Chapter 6 discussed the Court's rejection of *Escobedo* as a Sixth Amendment case.

90. 14 U.S. (1 Wheat.) 304 (1816).

91. 19 U.S. (6 Wheat.) 264 (1821).

92. 14 U.S. (1 Wheat.) at 347–48.

93. *Id.* at 345.

94. *Cf.* Murdock v. Memphis, 87 U.S. (20 Wall.) 590 (1874) (in reviewing state cases, Supreme Court may decide only federal questions). Whether *Murdock* reflects underlying constitutional limits is discussed in Field, *Sources of Law: The Scope of Federal Common Law,* 99 HARV. L. REV. 881, 920–23 (1986). *See also* Hart, *The Relations between State and Federal Law,* 54 COLUM. L. REV. 489, 501–4 (1954).

Under the doctrines of pendent and ancillary jurisdiction, federal courts may decide questions of state law. They may not, however, override state court determinations of state law. *See generally* M. REDISH, FEDERAL JURISDICTION: TENSIONS IN THE ALLOCATION OF JUDICIAL POWER 59–63, 74 & n.140 (1980).

95. 304 U.S. 64 (1938).

96. *Id.* at 78–79 (quoting Baltimore & O.R.R. v. Baugh, 149 U.S. 368, 401 (1892)).

97. Monaghan, *The Supreme Court, 1974 Term—Foreword: Constitutional Common Law,* 89 HARV. L. REV. 1, 2–3, 20–23 (1975).

98. 304 U.S. 64 (1938).

99. *Id.* at 78.

100. Monaghan, *supra* note 97, at 10, 13–17. Monaghan attributed the term "specialized" common law to Friendly, *In Praise of* Erie—*and of the New Federal Common Law,* 39 N.Y.U. L. Rev. 383, 405 (1964).

101. Monaghan, *supra* note 97, at 18.

102. Grano, *supra* note 60, at 130–31; Schrock & Welsh, *Reconsidering the Constitutional Common Law,* 91 Harv. L. Rev. 1117, 1139–40 (1978).

103. Friendly, *supra* note 100, at 408 n.119; *see also* Field, *supra* note 94, at 891.

104. Hart, *supra* note 94, at 531. For criticism of the assumption of broad common-law authority in admiralty and maritime cases, see M. Redish, *supra* note 94, at 81–82, 97–100. *Cf.* Field, *supra* note 94, at 917–18 (disputing that case for common law in admiralty cases is stronger than in diversity cases).

105. *Cf.* Merrill, *The Common Law Powers of Federal Courts,* 52 U. Chi. L. Rev. 1, 30 (1985) (such an interpretation, even if questionable, resolves the legitimacy issue).

106. Federal Judiciary Act of 1789, ch. 20, § 34, 1 Stat. 73. The statute required federal courts in "trials at common law" to regard "the laws of the several states" as "rules of decision," except as otherwise provided by the Constitution, treaty, or statute. The current version, which extends this requirement to "civil actions," can be found at 28 U.S.C. § 1652 (1982).

107. *See, e.g.,* Westen & Lehman, *Is There Life for* Erie *after the Death of Diversity?,* 78 Mich. L. Rev. 311, 336–39 (1980); *see also* Ely, *The Irrepressible Myth of* Erie, 87 Harv. L. Rev. 693 (1974); *cf.* Redish, *Federal Common Law, Political Legitimacy, and the Interpretive Process: An "Institutionalist" Perspective,* 83 Nw. U.L. Rev. 761, 766 n.19 (1989) (given recent developments, it could be argued that "*Erie's* constitutional component is no longer good law").

108. 41 U.S. (16 Pet.) 1 (1842).

109. 304 U.S. at 77.

110. *Id.* at 77–78; *see also* Friendly, *supra* note 100; Gelfand & Abrams, *Putting* Erie *on the Right Track,* 49 U. Pitt. L. Rev. 937, 946–52 (1988); Hill, *The* Erie *Doctrine and the Constitution* (pts. 1 & 2), 53 Nw. U.L. Rev. 427, 541 (1958); Mishkin, *Some Further Last Words on* Erie—*The Thread,* 87 Harv. L. Rev. 1682 (1974).

111. 304 U.S. at 79–80.

112. Field, *supra* note 94, at 920.

113. *Id.* at 922. Actually, Field was talking about both *Erie* and Murdock v. Memphis, 87 U.S. (20 Wall.) 590 (1874). *See supra* note 94 and accompanying text.

114. Field, *supra* note 94, at 928; *see also id.* at 896.

115. *Id.* at 929.

116. *Id.*

117. *Id.* at 950–51.

118. *Id.* at 942.

119. *Cf.* Redish, *supra* note 107, at 768–83 (discussing various broad models of statutory interpretation).

120. Field, *supra* note 94, at 942.

121. Textile Workers Union v. Lincoln Mills, 353 U.S. 448 (1957) (grant of jurisdiction in labor statute implicitly provided courts with lawmaking authority). The commentator whose work Field analyzed was Friendly, *supra* note 100.

122. Field, *supra* note 94, at 942.

123. Redish, *supra* note 107, at 794 (emphasis in original).

124. *Id.* at 793.

125. Monaghan, *supra* note 97, at 43.

126. Contrast the statement from *Erie supra* at note 96.

127. 469 U.S. 528 (1985).

128. *See, e.g.,* Van Alstyne, *The Second Death of Federalism,* 83 MICH. L. REV. 1709 (1985). The first death occurred in the post-1936 cases.

129. Mishkin, *supra* note 110, at 1683–85.

130. *Id.* at 1683–86. The Tenth Amendment reserves to the states those powers not delegated by the Constitution to the United States. U.S. CONST. amend X.

131. Redish, *supra* note 107, at 791–92; *see also* Merrill, *supra* note 105, at 15–19; *cf.* Field, *supra* note 94, at 924 (after asking why it matters which branch of the federal government acts, recognizing that it could matter to the states). *But see* Westen & Lehman, *supra* note 107, at 340–41.

132. New York v. United States, 112 S. Ct. 2408 (1992) (Congress may regulate interstate commerce but may not compel states to do so).

133. Beale, *Reconsidering Supervisory Power in Criminal Cases: Constitutional and Statutory Limits on the Authority of the Federal Courts,* 84 COLUM. L. REV. 1433 (1984).

134. 455 U.S. 209 (1982).

135. *Id.* at 221; *see also* Mu'Min v. Virginia, 111 S. Ct. 1899, 1903 (1991); Chandler v. Florida, 449 U.S. 560, 582–83 (1981); Cupp v. Naughten, 414 U.S. 141, 146 (1973); Cicenia v. LaGay, 357 U.S. 504, 508–9 (1958).

136. 318 U.S. 332 (1943).

137. 354 U.S. 449 (1957).

138. Hogan & Snee, *The* McNabb-Mallory *Rule: Its Rise, Rationale and Rescue,* 47 GEO. L.J. 1, 26–28 (1958); McCormick, *Some Problems and Developments in the Admissibility of Confessions,* 24 TEX. L. REV. 239, 270–75 (1946).

139. Strauss, *The Ubiquity of Prophylactic Rules,* 55 U. CHI. L. REV. 190 (1988); *see also* Schulhofer, *supra* note 52, at 448.

140. Monaghan, *supra* note 97, at 26.

141. 372 U.S. 335 (1963).

142. 303 U.S. 444 (1938).

143. Strauss, *supra* note 139, at 196–97.

144. 303 U.S. at 451.

145. Although such rules are not pervasive, others undoubtedly can be identified. *See, e.g.,* Grano, *supra* note 60, at 111–15.

146. United States v. United States District Court, 407 U.S. 297 (1972). The presidential practice is discussed in *id.* at 310–11 & n.10.

147. *Cf.* Mishkin, *The Vagueness of "Federal Law": Competence and Discretion in the Choice of National and State Rules for Decision,* 105 U. PA. L. REV. 797, 800 (1957) ("entirely unreal" to view statutory enactment as "totally self-sufficient and exclusive legislative process"); *see also* Hill, *The Bill of Rights and the Supervisory Power,* 69 COLUM. L. REV. 181, 181 (1969).

148. *See, e.g.,* Johnson v. Zerbst, 304 U.S. 458, 464–65 (1938) (waiver standards for Sixth Amendment right to counsel).

149. Professor Field's definition of common law is sufficiently broad to include rulings on what the Constitution mandates when the ruling is "not clearly suggested" by the text. Field, *supra* note 94, at 890–96. Such a definition blurs the line between the law making and the interpretive processes. *See also infra* note 151.

150. Redish, *supra* note 107, at 785 (discussing statutory interpretation).

151. *Id.* at 790 n.115. It has been argued that the difference between interpretation and the promulgation of common law rules is one of emphasis or degree rather than kind. Westen & Lehman, *supra* note 107, at 331–36. This view is simply wrong. Redish, *supra* note 107, at 788 (creating common law and statutory interpretation qualitatively distinct both conceptually and politically); Redish, *Continuing the* Erie *Debate: A Response to Westen and Lehman,* 78 MICH. L. REV. 959, 963–64 (1980) (federal statute is an act of Congress; federal common law is not). *See also supra* note 149.

152. 386 U.S. 18 (1967).

153. *Id.* at 21–23.

154. *Id.* at 46–47 (Harlan, J., dissenting).

155. L. TRIBE, AMERICAN CONSTITUTIONAL LAW 167–68 (2d ed. 1988).

156. *See* Kelman, *Federal Habeas Corpus as a Source of New Constitutional Requirements for State Criminal Procedure,* 28 OHIO ST. L.J. 46, 59 (1967) (supporting federal court rejection of state procedural rules blocking consideration of federal rights even though state rules do not violate Constitution); Mause, *Harmless Constitutional Error: The Implications of* Chapman v. California, 53 MINN. L. REV. 519, 520 (1969).

157. *See, e.g.,* Henry v. Mississippi, 379 U.S. 443 (1965); *see also* M. REDISH, *supra* note 94, at 216–21, 226–29; Field, *supra* note 94, at 964–67.

158. 253 U.S. 17 (1920).

159. *Id.* at 24.

160. M. REDISH, *supra* note 94, at 222. For a somewhat different reading of *Ward,* see Monaghan, *Third Party Standing,* 84 COLUM. L. REV. 277, 294 n.97, 296 n.111 (1984). *See also* Field, *supra* note 94, at 972–73 & n.394.

161. "This Constitution, and the Laws of the United States which shall be made in Pursuance thereof . . . shall be the supreme Law of the Land; . . . any Thing in the Constitution or Laws of any State to the Contrary notwithstanding." U.S. CONST. art. VI, cl. 2.

162. M. REDISH, *supra* note 94, at 221. *See also supra* note 155 and accompanying text.

163. Redish, *supra* note 107, at 790 n.115.

164. L. TRIBE, *supra* note 155, at 167.

165. *Id.*

166. 470 U.S. 298 (1985).

167. *Id.* at 307.

168. *Id.* at 349 (Brennan & Marshall, JJ., dissenting). *See also supra* note 31.

169. Schulhofer, *supra* note 52, at 448.

170. *See* Lego v. Twomey, 404 U.S. 477 (1972) (prosecution has burden of proving voluntariness by a preponderance of the evidence); *see also* Colorado v. Connelly, 479 U.S. 157 (1986).

171. U.S. CONST. art. I, § 8, cl. 18 gives Congress the power "[t]o make all Laws which shall be necessary and proper for carrying into Execution the foregoing Powers, and all other Powers vested by this Constitution in the Government of the United States, or in any Department or Officer thereof." The clause received an expansive reading in McCulloch v. Maryland, 17 U.S. (4 Wheat.) 316 (1819).

172. Van Alstyne, *The Role of Congress in Determining Incidental Powers of the President and of the Federal Courts: A Comment on the Horizontal Effect of the Sweeping Clause,* 40 LAW & CONTEMP. PROBS. 102, 107–29 (1976).

173. U.S. CONST. art. I, § 1 vests in Congress "[a]ll legislative [p]owers *herein granted*" while art. II, § 1 and art. III, § 1 respectively vest "the executive [p]ower" in the president and "the judicial [p]ower" in the courts (emphasis added).

174. Beale, *supra* note 133, at 1468–77.

175. *Cf.* Redish, *supra* note 107, at 795 ("key prerequisite" to legitimate gap filling in statutory interpretation is whether issue *must* be resolved before statute may be applied).

176. I now believe that I ceded too much constitutional ground in previously defending broader incidental federal judicial power in state cases. See Grano, *supra* note 60, at 143–47 (suggesting Court may have had authority to create rebuttable presumption in *Miranda*).

177. J. STRONG ET AL., MCCORMICK ON EVIDENCE § 342 (4th ed. 1992).

178. *Id.*

179. Faretta v. California, 422 U.S. 806 (1975).

180. Grano, Miranda's *Constitutional Difficulties: A Reply to Professor Schulhofer,* 55 U. CHI. L. REV. 174, 187 (1988).

181. The examples in the text make inexplicable Professor David Strauss's assertion that the alleged difference in kind rather than degree between rebuttable and conclusive presumptions "rings false" and "proves false." Strauss, *supra* note 139, at 192.

Chapter 8

1. 384 U.S. 436 (1966).

2. Kamisar, *A Dissent from the* Miranda *Dissents: Some Comments on the "New" Fifth Amendment and the Old "Voluntariness" Test,* 65 MICH. L. REV. 59, 59 (1966).

3. SPECIAL COMMITTEE ON CRIMINAL JUSTICE IN A FREE SOCIETY, AMERICAN BAR ASSOCIATION CRIMINAL JUSTICE SECTION, CRIMINAL JUSTICE IN CRISIS 9, 28

(1988) [hereinafter CRIMINAL JUSTICE IN CRISIS]. I have not sought to examine the validity of the survey techniques, and by citing the study I do not mean to endorse its conclusions. *Cf.* Letter from Fred E. Inbau, John Henry Wigmore Professor of Law Emeritus, Northwestern University, to George E. Bushnell, Jr., Chairman, A.B.A. House of Delegates (Jan. 10, 1989) (copy on file with author) (criticizing both the survey procedures and the committee for not considering opposing viewpoints).

4. CRIMINAL JUSTICE IN CRISIS, *supra* note 3, at 33.

5. Rhode Island v. Innis, 446 U.S. 291, 304 (1980) (Burger, C.J., concurring); *see also* New York v. Quarles, 467 U.S. 649, 660, 663 (1984) (O'Connor, J., concurring and dissenting).

6. Easterbrook, *Stability and Reliability in Judicial Decisions*, 73 CORNELL L. REV. 422, 431, 433 (1988).

7. *Id.* at 424 (emphasis added) (using these words to describe the judiciary's general approach to stare decisis).

8. Burnet v. Coronado Oil & Gas Co., 285 U.S. 393, 406–10 (1932) (Brandeis, J., dissenting). Going against the conventional wisdom, Judge Easterbrook has suggested that stare decisis should play *more* of a role in constitutional cases. Easterbrook, *supra* note 6, at 429–33. Without going as far as Judge Easterbrook, Professor Maltz has argued that Brandeis's argument for less commitment to constitutional as opposed to nonconstitutional precedent is "at best overstated." Maltz, *Some Thoughts on the Death of Stare Decisis in Constitutional Law*, 1980 WIS. L. REV. 467, 468–72; *see also* Monaghan, *Stare Decisis and Constitutional Adjudication*, 88 COLUM. L. REV. 723, 742 (1988). *But see* Note, *The Power That Shall Be Vested in a Precedent: Stare Decisis, the Constitution and the Supreme Court*, 66 B.U. L. REV. 345, 364–75 (1986) (arguing for relaxation or even abandonment of stare decisis in constitutional adjudication).

9. *See* Cooper, *Stare Decisis: Precedent and Principle in Constitutional Adjudication*, 73 CORNELL L. REV. 401, 408–10 (1988); Note, *supra* note 8, at 350–53, 364–71. *But see* Note, *Constitutional Stare Decisis*, 103 HARV. L. REV. 1344, 1355–59 (1990) (relying on Article V's amendment provision to support a strong doctrine of stare decisis in constitutional cases).

10. Easterbrook, *supra* note 6, at 422.

11. Monaghan, *supra* note 8, at 752–53; Note, *supra* note 9, at 1349–50.

12. Monaghan, *supra* note 8, at 749.

13. *Cf.* Planned Parenthood of Southeastern Pa. v. Casey, 112 S. Ct. 2791, 2808–16 (1992) (O'Connor, Kennedy, & Souter, JJ.) (relying on stare decisis in refusing to reconsider Roe v. Wade, 410 U.S. 113 (1973)).

14. Monaghan, *supra* note 8, at 743; *see also* Note, *supra* note 8, at 358–64; Note, *supra* note 9, at 1345–47.

15. Planned Parenthood of Southeastern Pa. v. Casey, 112 S. Ct. 2791, 2808 (1992) (O'Connor, Kennedy, & Souter, JJ.).

16. Israel, *Gideon v. Wainwright: The "Art" of Overruling*, 1963 SUP. CT. REV. 211, 219–29.

17. *Planned Parenthood,* 112 S. Ct. at 2808–9 (O'Connor, Kennedy, & Souter, JJ.).

18. Note, *supra* note 9, at 1346–47.

19. *Id.* at 1346.

20. OFFICE OF LEGAL POLICY, U.S. DEP'T OF JUSTICE, "TRUTH IN CRIMINAL JUSTICE" SERIES, Report No. 1, *The Law of Pre-trial Interrogation* 62–64, 122–27 (1986) [hereinafter OLP REPORT], *reprinted in* 22 U. MICH. J.L. REF. 437, 510–12, 568–572 (1989); *see also* Markman, *The Fifth Amendment and Custodial Questioning: A Response to "Reconsidering* Miranda," 54 U. CHI. L. REV. 938, 945–48 (1987) [hereinafter Markman, *The Fifth Amendment*]; Markman, Miranda v. Arizona: A *Historical Perspective,* 24 AM. CRIM. L. REV. 193, 224–26 (1987).

21. Schulhofer, *Reconsidering* Miranda, 54 U. CHI. L. REV. 435, 455–60 (1987); *see also* CRIMINAL JUSTICE IN CRISIS, *supra* note 3, at 33–34; Kamisar, *Remembering the "Old World" of Criminal Procedure: A Reply to Professor Grano,* 23 U. MICH. J.L. REF. 537, 684 & n.164 (1990) (denying a negative effect on law enforcement and citing other commentators who have reached the same conclusion).

22. Markman, *The Fifth Amendment, supra* note 20, at 947.

23. Inbau, *Over-Reaction—The Mischief of* Miranda v. Arizona, 73 J. CRIM. L. & CRIMINOLOGY 797 (1982).

24. Inbau & Manak, Miranda v. Arizona—*Is It Worth the Cost? (A Sample Survey, with Commentary, of the Expenditure of Court Time and Effort),* 24 CAL. W. L. REV. 185 (1988). *But see* Lippman, *A Commentary on Inbau and Manak's "*Miranda v. Arizona—*Is It Worth the Cost? (A Sample Survey, with Commentary, of the Expenditure of Court Time and Effort),"* 25 CAL. W. L. REV. 87 (1988).

25. 18 U.S.C. § 3501(a) (1985).

26. *Id.* § 3501(b).

27. *Id.*

28. Cooper v. Aaron, 358 U.S. 1 (1958). Arguably, *Cooper* marked an extension of the power of judicial review recognized in Marbury v. Madison, 5 U.S. (1 Cranch) 137 (1803). *See, e.g.,* Gunther, *The Subtle Vices of the "Passive Virtues"—A Comment on Principle and Expediency in Judicial Review,* 64 COLUM. L. REV. 1, 25 (1964).

29. *See, e.g.,* Cox, *The Role of Congress in Constitutional Determinations,* 40 U. CINN. L. REV. 199, 247–61 (1971). As Professor Cox recognized, it may not be correct to characterize the inherent compulsion conclusion as factual. *Id.* at 250; *cf.* Miller v. Fenton, 474 U.S. 104 (1985) (voluntariness a legal rather than a factual issue).

30. *See, e.g.,* Burt, *Miranda and Title II: A Morganatic Marriage,* 1969 SUP. CT. REV. 81. U.S. CONST. amend XIV, § 5 gives Congress power "to enforce" the amendment's provisions. Professor Burt's article, as well as Professor Cox's, *supra* note 29, reflected ambiguities in Katzenbach v. Morgan, 384 U.S. 641 (1966) (giving expansive reading to § 5 power in a voting rights case).

31. Gandara, *Admissibility of Confessions in Federal Prosecutions: Implementation of Section 3501 by Law Enforcement Officials and the Courts,* 63 GEO. L.J. 305 (1974); OLP REPORT, *supra* note 20, at 72–74, 22 U. MICH. J.L. REF. at 519–21.

32. Funk v. United States, 290 U.S. 371, 382 (1933); Livingston v. Story, 34 U.S. (9 Pet.) 632 (1835); Wayman v. Southard, 23 U.S. (10 Wheat.) 1 (1825). *See generally,* Beale, *Reconsidering Supervisory Power in Criminal Cases: Constitutional and Statutory Limits on the Authority of the Federal Courts,* 84 COLUM. L. REV. 1433, 1435–41 (1984).

33. See chapter 7.

34. OLP REPORT, *supra* note 20, at 80, 103, 22 U. MICH. J.L. REF. at 527, 549–50. Even before the Court began to describe *Miranda* as prophylactic, Professor Archibald Cox saw the potential in this argument. Cox, *supra* note 29, at 250–53; *see also* Monaghan, *The Supreme Court, 1974 Term—Foreword: Constitutional Common Law,* 89 HARV. L. REV. 1, 26–30 (1975) (Congress may modify "constitutional common law").

35. OLP REPORT, *supra* note 20, at 104, 22 U. MICH. J.L. REF. at 550–51.

36. Actually, such an interpretation of the Fifth Amendment would be so mistaken and so unwise that the case for overruling would still be strong.

37. Williams v. Florida, 399 U.S. 78, 118 (1969) (Harlan, J., concurring and dissenting) (referring to incorporation of Sixth Amendment right to trial by jury). Harlan was prepared to overrule even well-known cases that he thought "responsible for bringing about serious distortions and incongruities in . . . constitutional law." Coolidge v. New Hampshire, 403 U.S. 443, 490 (1971) (Harlan, J., concurring) (arguing that Mapp v. Ohio, 367 U.S. 643 (1961), should be overruled).

38. In contrast, the Court took great pains to justify its claim of authority both to review the constitutionality of federal statutes and to review state court decisions interpreting federal law. Marbury v. Madison, 5 U.S. (1 Cranch) 137 (1803); Martin v. Hunter's Lessee, 14 U.S. (1 Wheat.) 304 (1816).

39. Monaghan, *supra* note 34, at 43.

40. *See* cases cited in chapter 7 at notes 134–35.

41. *See generally* chapter 7.

42. *See, e.g.,* Oregon v. Elstad, 470 U.S. 298 (1985) ("fruit of the poisonous tree" doctrine); New York v. Quarles, 467 U.S. 649 (1984) (public safety exception).

43. 168 U.S. 532 (1897).

44. *Id.* at 558.

45. New Jersey v. Portash, 440 U.S. 450 (1979); Oregon v. Hass, 420 U.S. 714 (1975); Harris v. New York, 401 U.S. 222 (1971).

46. *Quarles,* 467 U.S. at 655 n.5.

47. Israel, *supra* note 16, at 225.

48. *Id.*

49. *Quarles,* 467 U.S. at 664 (O'Connor, J., concurring and dissenting).

50. *Id.* at 679 (Marshall, Brennan, & Stevens, JJ., dissenting).

51. Harryman v. Estelle, 616 F.2d 870, 873–74 (5th Cir. 1980) (en banc).

52. C. WHITEBREAD & C. SLOBOGIN, CRIMINAL PROCEDURE 382 (3d ed. 1992).

53. 1 W. LAFAVE & J. ISRAEL, CRIMINAL PROCEDURE 485 (1984); White, *Defending* Miranda: *A Reply to Professor Caplan,* 39 VAND. L. REV. 1, 7–9 (1986).

54. Caplan, *Questioning* Miranda, 38 Vand. L. Rev. 1417, 1433–34 (1985).

55. F. Inbau & J. Reid, Criminal Interrogation and Confessions 1 (2d ed. 1967). *But see* White, *Police Trickery in Inducing Confessions*, 127 U. Pa. L. Rev. 581 (1979) (criticizing many of the recommended tactics).

56. *See also* Grano, *Selling the Idea to Tell the Truth: The Professional Interrogator and Modern Confessions Law*, 84 Mich. L. Rev. 662 (1986) (reviewing F. Inbau, J. Reid, & J. Buckley, Criminal Interrogation and Confessions (3d ed. 1986)).

57. *Miranda*, 384 U.S. at 545 (White, Harlan, & Stewart, JJ., dissenting).

58. For more elaborate discussion, see Grano, Miranda v. Arizona *and the Legal Mind: Formalism's Triumph over Substance and Reason*, 24 Am. Crim. L. Rev. 243 (1986).

59. 391 U.S. 1 (1968).

60. *Id.* at 7–8 (White, Harlan, & Stewart, JJ., dissenting).

61. *See also* Orozco v. Texas, 394 U.S. 324, 326 (1969) (*Miranda* applies to all questioning of persons in custody).

62. 429 U.S. 492 (1977) (per curiam).

63. *Id.* at 495.

64. *Id.* (emphasis in original).

65. *Id.* at 496.

66. *Id.* at 496–97 (Marshall, J., dissenting).

67. *Id.* at 496 n.1. Marshall cited LaFave, *"Street Encounters" and the Constitution:* Terry, Sibron, Peters, *and Beyond*, 67 Mich. L. Rev. 39, 105 (1969). The relevance of even the subjective test for custody to the issue of actual compulsion to speak is far from clear.

68. *See* United States v. Hall, 421 F.2d 540, 544 (2d Cir. 1969) (criticizing subjective tests for custody), *cert. denied*, 397 U.S. 990 (1970); *see also* Smith, *The Threshold Question in Applying* Miranda: *What Constitutes Custodial Interrogation?*, 25 S.C. L. Rev. 699, 713 (1974).

69. Berkemer v. McCarty, 468 U.S. 420, 442 (1984).

70. 446 U.S. 291 (1980).

71. *Id.* at 301.

72. *Id.* at 302 n.7. If intended to state a factual presumption, this double negative is "extremely dubious." *Id.* at 311 n.8 (Stevens, J., dissenting).

73. *See* Kamisar, Brewer v. Williams, Massiah, *and* Miranda: *What Is "Interrogation"? When Does It Matter?*, 67 Geo. L.J. 1, 22 (1978) (interrogation need not exist for Fifth Amendment compulsion to be present).

74. 446 U.S. at 303. For criticism of *Innis*, see White, *Interrogation without Questions:* Rhode Island v. Innis *and* United States v. Henry, 78 Mich. L. Rev. 1209 (1980).

75. 446 U.S. at 305 (Marshall & Brennan, JJ., dissenting).

76. 496 U.S. 582 (1990) (plurality opinion).

77. *Id.* at 601 (quoting the amicus brief of the United States, which in turn quoted United States v. Horton, 873 F.2d 180, 181 n.2 (8th Cir. 1989)). *Innis* had suggested that such questions might not be deemed "interrogation," *see* the text *supra* at note 71, but the plurality preferred to view the questions as interrogation

exempted from *Miranda*'s holding. Concluding that the defendant's responses to all eight questions were not testimonial, four justices found it unnecessary to address the booking question issue. 496 U.S. at 606–8 (Rehnquist, C.J., White, Blackmun, & Stevens, JJ.).

78. 496 U.S. at 601–2 & n.14.

79. *Id.* at 600. The plurality relied on the lower court's conclusion, uncontested by the state, that this question constituted custodial interrogation. The plurality rejected the state's argument that the defendant's response was nontestimonial. Justice Marshall, who dissented from the creation of a booking question exception, joined the plurality in reversing the conviction. *Id.* at 608–16 (Marshall, J., concurring and dissenting). *See also supra* note 77.

80. 496 U.S. 292 (1990).

81. Indeed, some courts had found *Miranda* applicable to the jail plant situation. *See, e.g.*, Holyfield v. State, 101 Nev. 793, 711 P.2d 834 (1985).

82. 496 U.S. at 296–99. The Court relied in part on Kamisar, *supra* note 73, at 63, 67.

83. In Berkemer v. McCarty, 468 U.S. 420, 435–42 (1984), the Court relied on the reduced potential for compulsion in exempting questioning during ordinary, temporary street stops from *Miranda*'s requirements. In the same opinion, however, the Court adhered to the rigid, black-letter approach that *Miranda* becomes applicable the moment the officer makes a formal arrest. *Id.* at 434–35, 442–43.

84. 779 F.2d 970 (4th Cir. 1985).

85. *Mathis* is discussed *supra* at notes 59–61.

86. 779 F.2d at 973.

87. *Id.* at 974.

88. 63 N.Y.2d 316, 472 N.E.2d 13, 482 N.Y.S.2d 237 (1984).

89. *Id.* at 326, 472 N.E.2d at 18, 482 N.Y.S.2d at 242 (Jason, J., dissenting).

90. 638 F.2d 582 (3d Cir. 1980).

91. *Id.* at 582–89; *id.* at 589 (interrogation issue difficult).

92. *Id.* at 589–91 (Adams, J., concurring); *id.* at 590 (custody issue difficult).

93. *Id.*

94. *Id.* at 591–97 (Weiner, J., dissenting).

95. *Id.* at 595.

96. *Id.*

97. *Id.* at 590 (Adams, J., concurring).

98. *Id.* at 597 (Weiner, J., dissenting).

99. *Id.*

100. To his credit, however, Chief Judge Seitz discussed the custody issue in terms of *Miranda*'s underlying rationale. *Id.* at 584–89.

101. *Id.* at 597–98 (Gibbons, J., dissenting from denial of petition for rehearing en banc).

102. *Id.* at 598.

103. See *supra* text accompanying note 51.

104. 442 U.S. 707 (1979).

105. *Id.* at 719.

106. Edwards v. Arizona, 451 U.S. 477, 484–85 (1981).

107. Oregon v. Bradshaw, 462 U.S. 1039, 1045 (1983) (defendant initiated conversation about investigation by asking what was going to happen to him).

108. *Id.* at 1051 (Powell, J., concurring).

109. Michigan v. Mosley, 423 U.S. 96, 104 (1975).

110. *See* Kamisar, *The* Edwards *and* Bradshaw *Cases: The Court Giveth and the Court Taketh Away,* in 5 J. Choper, Y. Kamisar & L. Tribe, The Supreme Court: Trends and Developments, 1982–1983, 153, 157 (1984).

111. *Miranda,* 384 U.S. at 475 (emphasis added).

112. 441 U.S. 369 (1979).

113. *Id.* at 373 (emphasis added).

114. *Id.* at 377–78 (Brennan, Marshall, & Stevens, JJ., dissenting).

115. 453 U.S. 355 (1981) (per curiam).

116. *Id.* at 364 (Stevens, Brennan, & Marshall, JJ., dissenting).

117. *Id.*

118. Kamisar, *Police Interrogation and Confessions: Will* California v. Prysock *Prove to Be a Substantial Setback for* Miranda?, in 3 J. Choper, Y. Kamisar, & L. Tribe, The Supreme Court: Trends and Developments, 1980–1981, 137, 145 (1982).

119. *Id.* at 146. Duckworth v. Eagan, 492 U.S. 195 (1989), subsequently upheld *Miranda* warnings that included a statement that the police had no way of giving the suspect a lawyer but that one would be appointed, if the suspect so wished, if and when he went to court. Again, Professor Kamisar was critical. Kamisar, Duckworth v. Eagan: *A Little-Noticed* Miranda *Case That May Cause Much Mischief,* 25 Crim. L. Bull. 550 (1989). Distinguishing *Prysock,* which "presented a much closer question," Kamisar insisted that the *Eagan* warnings failed to convey the substance of the *Miranda* right to appointed counsel prior to any questioning. *Id.* at 551–53 & n. 12.

If the issue is whether the police substantially or adequately complied with *Miranda*'s dictates, Professor Kamisar is correct in viewing *Eagan* as more troublesome than *Prysock.* Even on these terms, however, one cannot dismiss as implausible the Court's conclusion that the *Eagan* warnings in their entirety satisfied *Miranda.* To debate the issue on these terms, however, is to miss the point of the text. Whether the police fully conveyed, adequately conveyed, or inadequately conveyed the substance of the four *Miranda* warnings has little to do with whether the suspect was compelled to become a witness against himself.

Professor Kamisar did not claim that Eagan was actually compelled to incriminate himself. Nor did he even address the issue of actual compulsion other than to ask how the *Eagan* warning could have advanced the "goal" of dispelling the compulsion inherent in custodial interrogation. *Id.* at 554.

120. 678 F.2d 1331 (9th Cir. 1982).

121. Y. Kamisar, J. Israel, & W. Lafave, Modern Criminal Procedure 598 (6th ed. 1986) (citations omitted).

122. Israel, *supra* note 16, at 222 (listing such experience as a typically expressed justification for overruling a decision).

123. *See* Planned Parenthood of Southeastern Pa. v. Casey, 112 S. Ct. 2791, 2808 (1992) (O'Connor, Kennedy, & Souter, JJ.) (listing this as a justification for overruling).

124. When Garcia v. San Antonio Metro. Transit Auth., 469 U.S. 528 (1985), overruled National League of Cities v. Usery, 426 U.S. 833 (1976), the Court found unworkable the rule of the latter case, which had immunized certain state governmental activities from federal control. The Court did not say that it was impossible to apply the *Usery* rule but rather that the distinctions the rule required courts to make were "elusive at best." 469 U.S. at 539. The Court also said that the *Usery* rule bred inconsistencies because it was divorced from principles of self-government. *Id.* at 547. *Miranda* likewise breeds inconsistency and formalism because its black letter rules are divorced from Fifth Amendment principles.

125. Escobedo v. Illinois, 378 U.S. 478, 486–89 (1964). Professor Kamisar disagrees that *Miranda* and *Escobedo* are cut from the same philosophical cloth. Kamisar, *supra* note 21, at 575–84. True enough, as he asserts, *Miranda* "compromised" by not adopting the broadest possible reading of *Escobedo*. Nevertheless, *Miranda* extended *Escobedo,* for *Escobedo*'s holding did not require warnings and waivers from all custodial suspects. More importantly, *Miranda* shared *Escobedo*'s concern that custodial suspects are no match for their interrogators.

To deny that the two cases are compatible philosophically, to deny that they reflect essentially the same world view, is to blink at reality. As Justice White remarked in his *Miranda* dissent, "the not so subtle overtone" of the Court's opinion was "that it is inherently wrong for the police to gather evidence from the accused himself." *Miranda,* 384 U.S. at 538 (White, Harlan, & Stewart, JJ., dissenting). Justice White also fairly read the *Miranda* Court as expecting that few suspects would waive the newly created *Miranda* rights. *Id.* at 536.

126. Miranda v. Arizona, 384 U.S. 436, 481 (1966) (emphasis added).

127. *Id.*

128. Crooker v. California, 357 U.S. 433, 441 (1958); Cicenia v. LaGay, 357 U.S. 504, 509 (1958); Watts v. Indiana, 338 U.S. 49, 58–59 (1949) (Jackson, J., concurring).

129. *Miranda,* 384 U.S. at 480.

130. *Id.* at 455.

131. *Id.* at 470–71.

132. *See* Stuntz, *Self-Incrimination and Excuse,* 88 Colum. L. Rev. 1227, 1287–88 (1988).

133. 475 U.S. 412 (1986).

134. *Id.* at 422. The Court, more accurately, might have said, "never, except in *Escobedo* and *Miranda*."

135. Colorado v. Spring, 479 U.S. 564, 576–77 (1987).

136. Connecticut v. Barrett, 479 U.S. 523, 530 (1987).

137. 475 U.S. at 426.

138. *Id.* (citations omitted).

139. *Id.* at 427.

140. Y. Kamisar, Police Interrogation and Confessions 87–89 (1980); Kamisar, *supra* note 21, at 579–84; Schulhofer, *supra* note 21, at 460–61.

141. Moran v. Burbine, 475 U.S. 412, 426 (1986).

142. Uviller, *Evidence from the Mind of the Criminal Suspect: A Reconsideration of the Current Rules of Access and Restraint,* 87 Colum. L. Rev. 1137, 1168 (1987).

143. Y. Kamisar, *supra* note 140, at 47 n.11, 222–23; Ogletree, *Are Confessions Really Good for the Soul?: A Proposal to Mirandize Miranda,* 100 Harv. L. Rev. 1826 (1987); Schulhofer, *supra* note 21, at 461; *see also* Caplan, *supra* note 54, at 1425 n.47 (citing authorities).

144. Kuh, *Interrogation of Criminal Defendants: Some Views on Miranda v. Arizona,* 35 Fordham L. Rev. 169, 233–35 (1966).

145. Grano, *Police Interrogation and the Constitution: Doctrinal Tension and an Uncertain Future,* 25 Crim. L. Bull. 5, 23 (1989).

146. *See, e,g.,* Minnick v. Mississippi, 498 U.S. 146 (1990).

147. Ingber, *Procedure, Ceremony and Rhetoric: The Minimization of Ideological Conflict in Deviance Control,* 56 B.U. L. Rev. 266, 294 (1976).

148. *Id.* at 294 & n.168.

149. *Id.* at 294.

150. Caplan, *supra* note 54, at 1471.

151. *Id.*

152. *Id.* at 1471–72.

153. *Id.* at 1472.

154. *Id.*

155. *Id.* at 1469.

156. *Cf.* Bumper v. North Carolina, 391 U.S. 543 (1968) (consent to search not voluntary when it amounts to acquiescence to claim of lawful authority).

157. Herman, *The Unexplored Relationship between the Privilege against Self-Incrimination and the Involuntary Confession Rule* (pt. 2), 53 Ohio St. L.J. 497, 525 n.661 (1992).

158. *See* OLP Report, *supra* note 20, at 113–14, 22 U. Mich. J.L. Ref. at 560.

159. See *supra* text accompanying notes 25–27.

160. *See* OLP Report, *supra* note 20, at 105, 22 U. Mich. J.L. Ref. at 551–52. *See also* Y. Kamisar, *supra* note 140, at 132–37; Berger, *Legislating Confession Law in Great Britain: A Statutory Approach to Police Interrogations,* 24 U. Mich. J.L. Ref. 1, 54–57 (1990) (British requirement limited to interviews at police station).

161. Caplan, *supra* note 54, at 1475.

162. *Cf.* Kamisar, *Edward L. Barrett, Jr.: The Critic with "That Quality of Judiciousness Demanded of the Court Itself,"* 20 U.C. Davis L. Rev. 211–12 (1987) (suggesting that *Miranda* was on the brink of such a requirement; speculating that such a requirement would have added fuel to the charge the Court was legislating).

163. *See* Berger, *supra* note 160, at 54–57 (discussing these issues); *see also id.* at 3 (constitutional law focus of American law deters legislative reforms).

164. *See* chapter 2, note 15 and accompanying text.

165. *Miranda,* 384 U.S. at 517 (Harlan, Stewart, & White, JJ., dissenting); *see also* Caplan, *supra* note 54, at 1475–76.

Table of Authorities

References in this table are to the chapter and endnote number in which each authority is cited. (Ch. 1: n. **80**, for example, indicates that the authority is cited in chapter 1, endnote 80.) Bold type indicates that the authority is explicitly mentioned in the text of the book.

Articles and Books

C. ALLEN, LEGAL DUTIES (1931): Ch. 1: n. **80**

Alschuler, *Implementing the Criminal Defendant's Right to Trial: Alternatives to the Plea Bargaining System,* 50 U. CHI. L. REV. 931 (1983): Ch. 1: nn. 16, **20,** 28; Ch. 2: nn. 19, 138

Alschuler, *Plea Bargaining and Its History,* 79 COLUM. L. REV. 1 (1979): Ch. 2: n. 139

Amar, *The Bill of Rights and the Fourteenth Amendment,* 101 YALE L.J. 1193 (1992): Ch. 4: nn. 11, 17, 27, 105; Ch. 5: nn. 9, 34; Ch. 6: n. 3

Amar, *The Bill of Rights as a Constitution,* 100 YALE L.J. 1131 (1991): Ch. 5: n. 34

Annotation, *Admissibility of confession, admission, or incriminatory statement of accused as affected by fact that it was made after indictment and in the absence of counsel,* 90 A.L.R.2d 732 (1963): Ch. 6: n. 31

Annotation, *Effect of, and remedy for, infringement of right of accused to communicate with his attorney,* 23 A.L.R. 1382 (1923): Ch. 6: nn. 28, 136

Arenella, *Reforming the Federal Grand Jury and the State Preliminary Hearing to Prevent Conviction without Adjudication,* 78 MICH. L. REV. 463 (1980): Ch. 1: nn. 7, 52, **96;** Ch. 2: nn. **22, 114–17,** 139, **147**

Arenella, *Rethinking the Functions of Criminal Procedure: The Warren and Burger Courts' Competing Ideologies,* 72 GEO. L.J. 185 (1983): Ch. 1: nn. 8, 18, 52, **89, 92–95, 101–4, 1089;** Ch. 2: nn. **13, 37;** Ch. 5: n. 1

ARISTOTLE, NICHOMACHEAN ETHICS: Ch. 3: nn. 14, **15–18,** 21, 152

Austin, *A Plea for Excuses,* 57 ARISTOTELIAN SOCIETY PROCEEDINGS (1956–57), reprinted in FREEDOM AND RESPONSIBILITY (H. Morris ed. 1961): Ch. 3: n. 19

A. AYER, THE FOUNDATIONS OF EMPIRICAL KNOWLEDGE (1940): Ch. 3: n. 142

L. Baker, Miranda: Crime, Law and Politics (1983): Ch. 2: n. 57

Barrett, *Police Practices and the Law—From Arrest to Release or Charge,* 50 CALIF. L. REV. 11 (1962): Ch. 5: nn. 94, 115

B. BARRY, POLITICAL ARGUMENT (1965): Ch. 3: n. 155

305

Caplan, *Questioning* Miranda, 38 VAND. L. REV. 1417 (1985): Ch. 2: nn. 44, 45, 53, 58; Ch. 4: nn. 2, 3, 179; Ch. 8: nn. 54, 143, **150–53, 161,** 165

Cluchey, Maine v. Moulton: *The Sixth Amendment and "Deliberate Elicitation": The Defendant's Position,* 23 AM. CRIM. L. REV. 43 (1985): Ch. 6: n. 119

Collingwood, *Three Senses of the Word "Cause,"* in PHILOSOPHICAL PROBLEMS OF CAUSATION (T. Beauchamp ed. 1974): Ch. 3: n. 141

Comment, *The Decade of Change Since the Ashcraft Case,* 32 TEX. L. REV. 429 (1954): Ch. 4: n. 123

Comment, *Guarding the Guardians: Police Trickery and Confessions,* 40 STAN. L. REV. 1544 (1988): Ch. 4: n. 158

Comment, *Police Use of Trickery As an Interrogation Technique,* 32 VAND. L. REV. 1167 (1979): Ch. 4: nn. 153, 158

Cooper, *Stare Decisis: Precedent and Principle in Constitutional Adjudication,* 73 CORNELL L. REV. 401 (1988): Ch. 8: n. 9

Corwin, *The Doctrine of Due Process of Law before the Civil War,* 24 HARV. L. REV. 366 (1911): Ch. 4: nn. 12, 19, **27**

Corwin, *The "Higher Law" Background of American Constitutional Law* (pts. 1 & 2), 42 HARV. L. REV. 149 (1928), 42 HARV. L. REV. 365 (1929): Ch. 4: n. 13

Corwin, *The Supreme Court and the Fourteenth Amendment,* 7 MICH. L. REV. 643 (1909): Ch. 4: n. 12

Cox, *The Role of Congress in Constitutional Determinations,* 40 U. CINN. L. REV. 199 (1971): Ch. 8: nn. 29, 34

Cramton & Udell, *State Ethics Rules and Federal Prosecutors: The Controversies over the Anti-Contact and Subpoena Rules,* 53 U. PITT. L. REV. 291 (1992): Ch. 6: nn. 124, **126,** 128–31

Cross, *Confessions and Cognate Matters: An English View,* 66 COLUM. L. REV. 79 (1966): Ch. 1: n. 117

M. CURTIS, NO STATE SHALL ABRIDGE: THE FOURTEENTH AMENDMENT AND THE BILL OF RIGHTS (1986): Ch. 5: n. 11

Damaska, *Adversary System,* in 1 ENCYCLOPEDIA OF CRIME AND JUSTICE 24 (1983): Ch. 2: nn. 109, 113, 115

Damaska, *Book Review,* 87 YALE L.J. 860 (1978): Ch. 4: n. 94

Damaska, *Comparative Reflections on Reading the Amended Yugoslav Code: Interrogation of Defendants in Yugoslav Criminal Procedure,* 61 J. CRIM. L. CRIMINOLOGY & POLICE SCI. 168 (1970): Ch. 2: nn. 24, 128; Ch. 5: n. 110

Damaska, *Evidentiary Barriers to Conviction and Two Models of Criminal Procedure: A Comparative Study,* 121 U. PA. L. REV. 506 (1973): Ch. 1: nn. **15,** 27, 73, **81, 87–88,** 99; Ch. 2: n. 108

M. DAMASKA, THE FACES OF JUSTICE AND STATE AUTHORITY (1986): Ch. 1: nn. 16, **29–39,** 42, 72; Ch. 2: nn. 108, 116, 124, 129, 136; Ch. 5: n. 111

Damaska, *Presentation of Evidence and Factfinding Precision,* 123 U. PA. L. REV. 1083 (1975): Ch. 1: nn. 54, 64, **65**

Dession & Cohen, *The Inquisitorial Functions of Grand Juries,* 41 YALE

Dession & Cohen (*continued*)
L.J. 687 (1932): Ch. 2: n. 135; Ch.
5: n. 115
Developments in the Law—Confessions,
79 HARV. L. REV. 935 (1966): Ch.
3: n. 44
*Developments in the Law—Privileged
Communications,* 98 HARV. L.
REV. 1450 (1985): Ch. 4: nn. 141,
146
P. DEVLIN, THE CRIMINAL PROSECU-
TION IN ENGLAND (1960): Ch. 2:
n. 95
Dix, *Federal Constitutional Confession
Law: The 1986 and 1987 Supreme
Court Terms,* 67 TEX. L. REV. 231
(1988): Ch. 3: n. 3
Dix, *Mistake, Ignorance, Expectation of
Benefit, and the Modern Law of Con-
fessions,* 1975 WASH. U. L.Q. 275:
Ch. 2: n. **12;** Ch. 3: nn. 1, **47,** 96,
106; Ch. 4: nn. 48, **87,** 98, **158,
166;** Ch. 5: n. **100**
Dix, *Undercover Investigations and Police
Rulemaking,* 53 TEX. L. REV. 203
(1975): Ch. 4: n. 149; Ch. 6: n. 158
Dolinko, *Is There a Rationale for the
Privilege against Self-Incrimination?,*
33 UCLA L. REV. 1063 (1986):
Ch. 2: nn. **2,** 39, 44, 64, 77, 84,
89, 97, 146, 151; Ch. 5: nn. 61,
157
Donagan, *The Right Not to Incriminate
Oneself,* 1 SOC. PHIL. & POL'Y 137
(1984): Ch. 2: nn. 28, **82–85**
Dressler, *Exegesis of the Law of Duress:
Justifying the Excuse and Searching
for Its Proper Limits,* 62 S. CAL. L.
REV. 1331 (1989): Ch. 3: nn. 11,
20, 26, 65, 73, 95
Dressler, *New Thoughts about the Con-
cept of Justification in the Criminal
Law: A Critique of Fletcher's Think-
ing and* Rethinking, 32 UCLA L.
REV. 61 (1984): Ch. 4: n. 122

Dressler, *Reassessing the Theoretical Un-
derpinnings of Accomplice Liability:
New Solutions to an Old Problem,*
37 HASTINGS L.J. 91 (1985): Ch.
3: n. **123**
J. DRESSLER, UNDERSTANDING CRIMI-
NAL LAW (1987): Ch. 1: nn. 17, 55,
63; Ch. 2: n. 88
J. DRESSLER, UNDERSTANDING CRIMI-
NAL PROCEDURE (1991): Ch. 5: n.
120
Dripps, *Foreword: Against Police Interro-
gation—And the Privilege against
Self-Incrimination,* 78 J. CRIM. L.
& CRIMINOLOGY 699 (1988): Ch. 2:
nn. 66, 75, 111, 131, 154, 163; Ch.
5: nn. 17, 25, **31**
Dripps, *Self-Incrimination and Self-Pres-
ervation: A Skeptical View,* 1991 U.
ILL. L. REV. 329: Ch. 2: nn. 84,
87, 89; Ch. 3: n. 69
Driver, *Confessions and the Social Psy-
chology of Coercion,* 82 HARV. L.
REV. 42 (1968): Ch. 5: n. 104
Ducasse, *Critique of Hume's Conception
of Causality,* in PHILOSOPHICAL
PROBLEMS OF CAUSATION (T.
Beauchamp ed. 1974): Ch. 3: n.
113

Easterbrook, *Stability and Reliability in
Judicial Decisions,* 73 CORNELL L.
REV. 422 (1988): Ch. 8: nn. **6–7,**
8, **10**
Ellis, *Vox Populi v. Suprema Lex: A
Comment on the Testimonial Privi-
lege of the Fifth Amendment,* 55
IOWA L. REV. 829 (1970): Ch. 2:
nn. 43, **48–49,** 76, 146
J. ELY, DEMOCRACY AND DISTRUST
(1980): Ch. 4: nn. 20, 52, **57–59,
61;** Ch. 5: n. 11
Ely, *The Irrepressible Myth of* Erie, 87
HARV. L. REV. 693 (1974): Ch. 7:
n. 107

Statutes, Reports, and Proposed Standards

Table of Cases

References in this table are to the chapter and endnote number in which each case is cited. (Ch. 5: n. **16**, for example, indicates that the case is cited in chapter 5, endnote 16.) Bold type indicates that the case is explicitly mentioned in the text of the book.

Roe v. Wade, 410 U.S. 113 (1973): Ch. 4: n. 34; Ch. 8: n. 13

Rogers v. Richmond, 365 U.S. 534 (1961): Ch. 2: n. 99; Ch. 3: nn. 7, 108; Ch. 4: n. 137; Ch. 5: n. 139

Rothman v. Regina, 1 S.C.R. 640 (1981): Ch. 4: n. 139

Santobello v. New York, 404 U.S. 257 (1971): Ch. 2: n. 21; Ch. 4: n. 168

Schmerber v. California, 384 U.S. 757 (1966): Ch. 2: n. 143; Ch. 5: n. 27

Schneckloth v. Bustamonte, 412 U.S. 218 (1973): Ch. 3: n. 86; Ch. 5: n. 171

(Dred) Scott v. Sanford, 60 U.S. (19 How.) 393 (1857): Ch. 4: n. 20

Shotwell Manufacturing Co. v. United States, 371 U.S. 341 (1963): Ch. 5: nn. **138–40**

Silverthorne Lumber Co. v. United States, 251 U.S. 385 (1920): Ch. 3: n. 127

Smith v. Phillips, 455 U.S. 209 (1982): Ch. 7: nn. **134–35**

Smith v. Murray, 477 U.S. 527 (1986): Ch. 2: n. 101

Snyder v. Massachusetts, 291 U.S. 97 (1934): Ch. 4: nn. 35, 45, 77

Spano, People v., 4 N.Y.2d 256, 150 N.E.2d 226, 173 N.Y.S.2d 793 (1958): Ch. 6: n. **29**

Spano v. New York, 360 U.S. 315 (1959): Ch. 3: n. **147**; Ch. 6: nn. **32– 34**, **134**

Sparf & Hansen v. United States, 156 U.S. 51 (1895): Ch. 3: n. 4; Ch. 5: n. 133

Spring, Colorado v., 479 U.S. 564 (1987): Ch. 6: nn. **173–74**; Ch. 8: n. 135

Stein v. New York, 346 U.S. 156 (1953): Ch. 3: n. 96; Ch. 4: n. 125

Stewart, People v., 62 Cal. 2d 571, 400

P.2d 97, 43 Cal. Rptr. 201 (1975): Ch. 1: n. 59

Stroble v. California, 343 U.S. 181 (1952): Ch. 6: n. 18

Swift v. Tyson, 41 U.S. (16 Pet.) 1 (1842): Ch. 7: n. **108**

Tehan v. United States *ex rel.* Shott, 382 U.S. 406 (1966): Ch. 2: n. 99

Textile Workers Union v. Lincoln Mills, 353 U.S. 448 (1957): Ch. 7: n. 121

Thierman, United States v., 678 F.2d 1331 (9th Cir. 1982): Ch. 8: n. **120**

Thomas v. Arizona, 356 U.S. 390 (1958): Ch. 3: n. 128

Townsend v. Sain, 372 U.S. 293 (1963): Ch. 3: 109

Tucker, Michigan v., 417 U.S. 433 (1974): Ch. 7: nn. **19, 20–22**, 26

Twining v. New Jersey, 211 U.S. 78 (1908): Ch. 4: nn. **28–29**; Ch. 5: nn. **13–15**

United States v. United States District Court, 407 U.S. 297 (1972): Ch. 7: n. 146

Verdugo-Urquidez, United States v., 494 U.S. 259 (1990): Ch. 1: nn. 111, 114

Wade, United States v., 388 U.S. 218 (1967): Ch. 2: n. 143; Ch. 6: n. **63**; Ch. 7: n. 60

Walker v. Sauvinet, 92 U.S. 90 (1878): Ch. 4: n. 22

Ward v. Board of County Commissioners, 253 U.S. 17 (1920): Ch. 7: nn. **158–59**

Ward v. Texas, 316 U.S. 547 (1941): Ch. 4: nn. 43, 47

Washington, United States v., 431 U.S. 181 (1977): Ch. 2: n. 98; Ch. 5: nn. 124, **144**, 162; Ch. 6: n. 142

328 · Table of Cases

Index

invocation of, 177
Justice Stewart's position regarding,
  150–54, 164–66
need for legal help and, 145, 151,
  158, 165–71, 216
police interrogation and, 155–64
policy reasons for, 28, 156–58, 161,
  216
preliminary arraignment as trigger
  for, 166
preliminary examination and, 156
rejection of, 119, 148–49, 153, 164,
  217
retained counsel's effect on, 154, 166
Sixth Amendment rationale for, 145,
  151, 155–64, 171
at trial, 155, 158, 190
unwise self-incrimination and, 145,
  158–63, 169–71, 216–17
use of informants and, 150–52, 166–
  67, 177
wrongful conviction and, 156–58
Rules of Decision Act, 186

Sixth Amendment. *See also* Right to
  counsel
as great generality, 159
nonprophylactic application of, 176–
  77
prophylactic application of, 177–78
rights included in, 169
Sporting code. *See* Fox-hunter's argument
Star Chamber, 46–47, 124, 129, 139
Stare decisis
in common law cases, 199
in constitutional law, 94, 199
effect of formalism on, 215
effect of illegitimacy on, 204
factors in applying, 200–202
inconsistency in cases and, 216
pragmatic considerations in applying,
  200
random application of, 200
stability concern and, 200

State sovereignty, 184–85, 189
Supervisory power
over state courts, 189–93, 204–5, 221
prophylactic rules and, 185–91, 204
Supremacy of federal law, 184, 193–94,
  202
Supreme Court. *See also* Judicial review
authority to review federal questions
  in state cases, 184
authority to state law, 185
fallibility of, 184, 204
as legal educator, 159

Tenth Amendment. *See* Federalism
Threats. *See* Offers
Torture. *See also* Protection against
  compulsory self-incrimination
condemnation of, 100–102, 126
psychological, 103
Trickery. *See* Cruelty argument;
  Miranda requirements; Right to
  counsel; Voluntariness
Truth
epistemological objection to, 12
ideological constraints on, 5–10
importance of confessions to, 31,
  140–41, 217
mens rea and, 13
metaphysical objection to, 12
other systems and, 16
as procedural objective, 5–8, 16, 82
protection of the innocent and, 17–
  18, 55, 158
relative primacy of, 10–16
values that compete with, 17–24, 109,
  158, 219

Video recording, 116, 221
Volitional impairment. *See also* Causation; Overborne will
Voluntariness
causation and, 73–75, 99, 105
choice prong of, 67, 99, 104–5
codefendant hypothetical and, 112
and cognitive impairment, 60, 79, 109